W. Schertler, B. Schmid, A M. Tjoa,
and H. Werthner (eds.)

Information and Communications Technologies in Tourism

Proceedings of the International Conference
in Innsbruck, Austria, 1994

Springer-Verlag Wien New York

Univ.-Prof. Dr. Walter Schertler
Strategisches Tourismusmanagement
Universität Trier, Trier, Federal Republic of Germany

Univ.-Prof. Dr. Beat Schmid
Institut für Wirtschaftsinformatik
Hochschule St. Gallen, St. Gallen, Switzerland

Univ.-Prof. Dipl.-Ing. Dr. A Min Tjoa
Institut für Angewandte Informatik und Informationssysteme

Univ.-Ass. Dipl.-Ing. Dr. Hannes Werthner
Institut für Statistik, Operations Research und Computerverfahren
Universität Wien, Vienna, Austria

Printed on acid-free and chlorine-free bleached paper

With 116 Figures

ISBN-13: 978-3-211-82543-3 e-ISBN-13: 978-3-7091-9343-3
DOI: 10.1007/978-3-7091-9343-3

PREFACE

The conference **ENTER - International Conference on Information and Communications Technologies in Tourism** represents a first attempt

- to provide an international forum for the discussion of the role of telecommunication and information systems in tourism,
- to inform potential users and people concerned with the importance of such technologies and to explain their functioning
- to give an opportunity to the research community, nowadays scattered into different areas of research, to discuss their results on a common platform, and, finally,
- to intensify the contact and the communication between researchers, system developers and users.

The tourism and the leisure industry are among the most prospering sectors in industry, although they also have economic problems at the moment - similar to all other sectors. In Austria, for example, tourism is of central importance, in 1990 the tourist industry made 133.7 billions of Austrian Shillings (≈ 11 billions US$) of income in foreign currencies and 70% of the Austrian deficit in the trade balance is covered by that sum. In the province of the Tyrol approx. 42 millions of overnights and 7.4 millions of arrivals were counted in 1990, responsible for about 25% - 35% of the regional gross domestic product.

In addition, this sector experiences a fast technological development. Although a time delay to other sectors can be observed, numerous applications of computer technology already exist: backoffice solutions in hotels, travel agencies and tourist boards; information systems enabling direct access for tourists via multi media; use of network and telecommunication facilities on a regional, national and international level. It can be estimated that these networks will reach the home consumer market in a not too far away future, enabling direct access to several information sources from the living room. This will open new opportunities but also new competitors to the suppliers of tourist products.

However, the tourist market has several specific characteristics with regard to the use of technological infrastructure:

- On the demand side computerized reservation and general distribution systems (CRS and GDS), managed by big airlines, are well organized and technological pioneers. In the past they typically focused on the business traveller, nowadays they also try to cover the vacation sector. These systems work on a world-wide level and are highly sophisticated. However, it should be added that the information provided is rather poor and also selective, which may restrict its usefulness for the promotion of an entire tourist region.
- Similar to CRS/GDS several tour operators have begun to develop their own systems, although with varying success.
- The supplier´s side of this market can be characterized as a small or medium industry (very often family enterprises); developments towards regionally, nationally or internationally working information systems are rather rare or not existing at all. This circumstance shows - besides several other reasons - the disadvantage of a limited access to the market in both directions, which may become even worse.
- One organizational instrument to deal with this limitation may be constituted by public tourist boards. These public organizations promote the product without selling it. The tourist boards can thus be seen as a non-computerized information system, gathering information about the local, regional or national tourist product and distributing this information. On the other hand, they also have to deliver information back to the local suppliers, informing them about current trends, the general market situation and national as well as international competition.

It can be concluded that the different participants in this market are very differently prepared to meet the technological challenge. In addition, a changing behaviour of tourists can be observed: they tend to more and shorter vacations, often based on ad hoc decisions; they ask for precise and fast information; and generally, they ask for a better service. Thus, to gain a competitive advantage, it is crucial to provide easy access to information, to structure this information with respect to different needs and views and to fill systems with a sufficient amount of information without overloading them. We live in a society characterized by an overabundance of information, so it is necessary to personalize information.

This is the background to the discussion about telecommunication and information systems in the field of tourism with its main topic of electronic markets. Several questions can be stated as done in the following, yet not exhaustive, list:

- How can an equal and fruitful cooperation for all participants take place?
- At what time should one participate in this development and enter the electronic market, what are the dangers of entering too early or too late?
- How will the coordination mechanisms change, what are the consequences to the different participants in the market?
- How will the daily work change and which new things will we have to learn?
- How should such systems be built or changed, how should they be constructed not to prevent organizational or social changes?
- How should one enter, either participate in existing systems or build a new system from scratch?
- How can it be guaranteed that all these different systems can communicate with each other, does there exist a well defined semantics of touristic terms?
- Is the environment prepared, are both the infrastructure and the know-how sufficiently available?
- What can we learn from other sectors, how are information systems used for example in the transport industry?
- How can tourist information systems cooperate with or enforce electronic systems and initiatives in other areas related to tourism, e.g. in agriculture?
- May the investment in technological infrastructure of a small and medium industry enable or favour a development similar to that discussed in the theory of industrial districts?

These and other questions will be treated in this volume, we cannot expect them all to be answered. However, the volume shows that we are approaching the target to enter the information age well-informed and to participate in an active manner in this process.

We want to add a final comment: as researchers in this huge field we have up to now been forced to present our research results at different conferences or to publish them in different journals, either of computer science, information systems, business administration and so on. This is also why we wanted to provide a common platform, bringing together in an interdisciplinary way different research fields but all dealing with the same subject. We think that we were successful with this approach: as a result of our Call for Papers we accepted papers from over 17 countries all over the world dealing with issues such as economics, organization, software engineering, modeling, distribution, information systems and data bases. They are all published in this volume.

A further emphasis is laid on invited lectures on selected topics such as electronic markets and tourism, the strategic dimension of information systems, changes in the activity of marketing due to new technologies, the Tyrolean information system TIS, the behavior of and the facilities for the tourist in the year 2000, the future role of public tourist boards, changes in the management of a hotel, the policy of the EC with regard to small and medium industries, telecommunication initiatives in rural areas, destination marketing systems, non-European initiatives, the problem of standards and the specific role of such systems for tourist boards. These presentations are directed towards both touristic practitioners and researchers, due to the importance of these topics they are also included in this volume.

We think that these proceedings as well as the conference ENTER - planned as a permanent forum repeated every two years - show that we chose a proper approach, it reflects in a good way the topical discussion on a common platform and may provide the basis for further work and research.

Finally, we want to thank the organizers of ENTER: the Congress Center Innsbruck and the Tirol Werbung (Tyrolean tourist board), especially their managing directors Georg Lamp and Andreas Braun. Without their support and cooperation these proceedings as well as the conference could not have been done. Furthermore, Arno Ebner, Renate Danler, Mechthild Ellmerer, Kathrin Schöpf and Michael Spechtenhauser stimulated the development of the conference programme and contributed essentially to the organization. We also want to mention the reviewers, who not only refereed the papers but also improved them by providing numerous comments. Silvia Schilgerius, at Springer Verlag Wien, moved the editing process along with steady persistence. To all of them our special thanks.

Walter Schertler Trier
Beat Schmid St. Gallen
A Min Tjoa Wien
Hannes Werthner Wien

CONTENTS

INDEX OF AUTHORS

ELECTRONIC MARKETS IN TOURISM

B. Schmid

Institute for Information Management,
University of St. Gallen

Abstract

Following a short introduction outlining the concept of electronic markets and the structure of the tourism industry respectively, we will briefly portray the status quo of electronic markets in this sector. In conjunction to this, the forseen technological developments, as well as possible architectures for the future tourism market and moreover their effect on the tourist industry will be discussed.

Electronic Markets

Prior to formulating a working definition of an electronic market (EM), let us consider the functions of markets in our economic system. According to traditional market theory, markets are defined as economic places of exchange where - ceteris paribus - aggregate demand meets aggregate supply. Markets serve to allocate resources, skills and products by way of coordinating economic activities through competition:- the key factor in optimizing such allocation, in the quest to yield maximum economic welfare. Pertinent information is contained in the prices quoted for the products or services generated. Traditional market theory however, tends to over-simplify matters: Its assumptions include perfect market transparency, complete information and perfect competition - conditions that are unanimously regarded as being unrealistic. We can identify two further applicable coordination mechanisms: corporations (hierarchies) and co-operation.

The relevance of hierarchies and co-operations is contained in their corresponding transaction costs - that is to say - the costs accruing from information gathering, negotiation and actual settlement of market transactions [3].

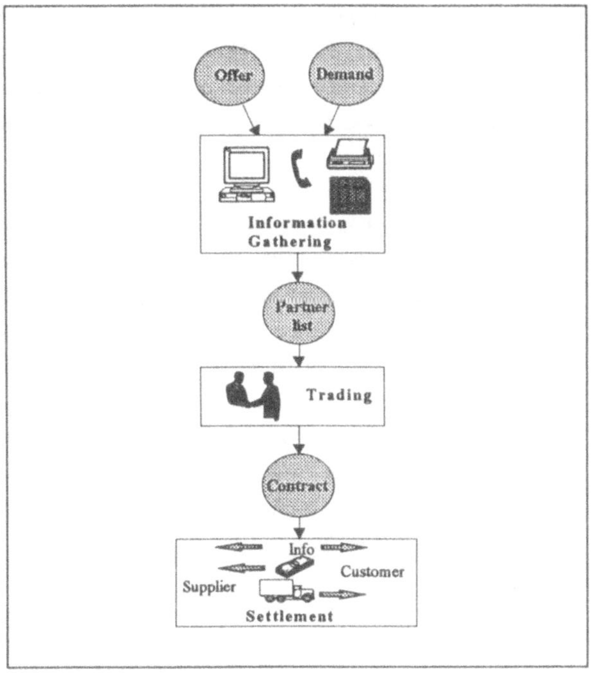

Figure 1: Three-Phase-Model

Each transaction is thus comprised of three phases:

- *Phase 1: Information gathering.* On the input side, information pertaining to available products and/or services, their specifications, suppliers and delivery terms is required. On the output side, potential end-consumers must necessarily be identified. In addition, general information reflecting current market conditions, branch and/or technological trends - will prove most expediant. This phase thus determines potential market partners and their respective offers and/or demand.
- *Phase 2: Negotiation.* As soon as all pertinent information has been evaluated, we may proceed to contact potential transaction partners. Terms and conditions (ie. of payment

and delivery, warranties, additional services etc.) must now be agreed upon. The legal basis for further transactions is thereby established. A contract results.

- *Phase 3: Settlement.* In this latter phase, the concrete transactions are dispatched. It may consist of various sub-transactions depending on the goods or services in question. Physical goods - for example - require transactions relevant to packaging, storage, shipping, insurance, customs clearance and so forth. Derived transactions, such as purchasing, forwarding services or insurance, are also initiated. The physical exchange of goods is accompanied by financial transaction - as well as - information flows. All three phases are integral to the coordination process.

The following definition is based on the above mentioned concepts of coordination and - the phase model [10]: *EMs in the narrow sense may be defined as market places put into action by means of telematics. They support all phases of market inter-transaction, including the formulation of prices for goods and services.* They consequently contribute to the realization of the ideal market as an abstract place of exchange with complete information - whereby transaction costs do not apply. In reality, electronic markets have the faculty to reduce transaction costs ostensibly.

Since present day EMs are not as yet actual markets offering all-encompassing functionality, we ought to apply a more liberal definition: *EMs in a broader sense may be understood as information systems supporting one or more phase and/or function of coordination within market systems.* This definition includes coordination systems beyond company boundries, in so far as they are used by a multitude of partners with equal participation rights on both the demand and supply sides.

EMs are characterized by the following features:

- *Ubiquity*: EMs are open 24 hrs - every day - for any user, anywhere, having access to the telecommunication network.
- *Easy access to information*:- although information assymetries cannot be avoided completely.
- *Low transaction*:- throughout.

2. Tourism Industry

Tourism may be understood as the consumption, production and distribution of services for travellers who dwell in some place other then their domiciles or workplace for at least 24 hours. Shorter sojourns are regarded as mere excursions [5]. This lucid definition stems from the United Nations Conference on International Travel and Tourism.

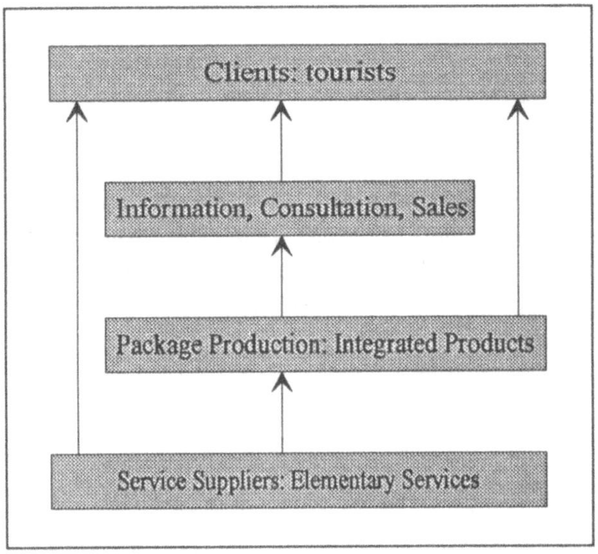

Figure 2: Tourism Industry - Functional View

The tourism industry is comprised as follows:

- Production of the elementary services by the industrys *primary players*: air, rail and sea travel; hotel and related bed arrangements; car rental; entertainment, leisure time and basic services such as travel insurance.
- The *end-consumer* of these services: single, family and group travellers.
- *Intermediaries*: producers of packages comprising the elementary services which are then either sold directly or indirectly (ie. tour operators); Sales offices - selling elementary services and packages alike (ie. travel agencies); regional and sundry organisations that either sell, or mediate specialized products and services (ie. tourism associations, cooperative societies and so on).

The assembly of packages - or - the consolidation of several elementary services to form a package offer, is inherently a production process, resulting in products such as:- City destination flights with hotel, including sight-seeing excursions; escorted travel; fixed package tours with full board and lodging and specialized (eg. sport related) programs. This activity is to be distinguished from the provision of tourist *information*, *consultation* activities - and the *sale* of tourism related services. These latter activities are primarily catered for by travel agencies in so far as they are trans-regional. Regional needs (excluding sale) on the other hand, are wholly or partially covered by regional tourism associations or boards. Trans-regional package products are chiefly generated by tour operators, the local spectrum once again being attended to by the various tourism associations, yet also by primary players such as hotels, or transportation concerns. Figure 3 broadly outlines the industrys institutional structure [9].

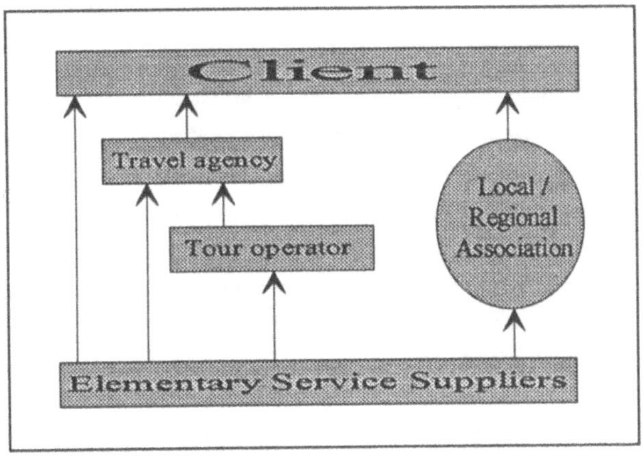

Figure 3: Tourism Industry - Institutional Structure

3. EM in Tourism

The tourist industry deals in non-stockable goods. An unsold seat on a given flight at check-in time cannot be recuperated and must duly be written off. Time is thus a critical factor. The industry is furthermore highly information-intensive and is characterized by zealous competition and shrinking margins. These conditions were and are, prime movers for launching and developing computer supported coordination systems. It is no surprise that numerous such systems have already taken root and are consistantly being extended in terms of functionality.

Reservation Systems

Reservation systems are amoungst the first electronic system applications to be implemented in the tourism industry and may be seen as a given component of the electronic tourism market. They were initially employed for the sole use of a few primary players - namely - airline carriers as well as large hotel chains and car rental companies. Only gradually did such proprietors make their terminals - initially intended for internal use only - available to partners and travel agencies alike. These terminal services naturally tended to favour the originators products which resulted in information biases and distortions. Small airliners in particular were at a grave disadvantage in early flight-reservation systems, resulting in their enforced opening in the USA. Similar developments took place in europe where terminals were made available to travelburos, yet in terms of the Multi-Access Concept [4]. Each airline was connected independantly - even though over a single interface - an arrangement that ensured against competitive disadvantages for any one of the participating members. The users however had to do without jointly administered booking directories accommodating all airline carriers. Moreover, the particulars of each given system had to be known and applied. The predecessors to British Airways - BEA and BOAC - together with other european airliners and a software concern, subsequently founded TRAVICOM, in order to develop a more comprehensive booking system. From a technical point of view, the establishment of a common system language is of central importance here. The system however only caters for business-orietated air travel. The leisure industry was rendered to videotext.

This concept was adapted and implemented by other national markets - in Germany - with START [4]. Travel agencies came to be the primary users, whereby their expanding needs, due to the increase in international travel, led to demands for greater system functionality including direct access to other national booking directories and support during the actual settlements phase for activities pertaining to billing, travel costs control, and so on. This gave rise to the CRS or GDS - that is - Computer Reservation and Global Distribution Systems respectively. Following a spate of fusions and takeovers, there remain three worldwide CRS consortiums:

- GALILEO International, resulting from the fusion between COVIA, brainchild of United Airlines and its various european partners - and - its european counterpart, GALILEO.

- SABRE, a system developed by AMR - parent company of American Airlines.
- WORLDSPAN, owned by Delta Airlines and TWA.

Since 1987, Lufthansa has - together with three other leading european airliners - developed and implemented AMADEUS which is by and large geared towards its european clientele. These systems commonly not only allow for the booking of flights, but moreover, permit direct access to systems administered by car rental companies, sea carrier consortiums, hotel chains and others. The payment of services rendered by way of credit card - for example, is also possible, as is the generation and printing of tickets [1].

In this way a large bag of services is made available to the travel agencies - or indirectly - the client. One can therefore secure personal "turn-key" travel arrangements (incl. concert hall bookings) in a single visit to a travel buro, and emerge with ticket in hand. The sheer scope of these services has resulted in increased marketing efforts on the leisure-time front, as opposed to business travel.

System-users are moreover limiting themselves to the use of one system only, due to the escalating complexity involoved. This trend has forced system builders to intergrate their respective systems by permiting direct access from one GDS to another by way of ones own user-interface and communication network [4]. The user of one GDS therefore, has potential access to all others. Competition subsequently takes place in terms of user-interfaces (user-friendliness, functionality etc.), and in accordance with the number of system-clients that may be boasted.

There remains no reason for corporate clients, as well as private people, to be denied access to these systems. Corresponding products are presently being developed and introduced.

National Sales and Distribution Systems

The tourism branch of the various national markets have largely been determined historically and generally reflect differing needs, as is demonstrated by the multitude of national computer support systems: Germany and SWIFT, France and ESTEREL, Britains TRAVICOM, Austrias TRAVIAUSTRIA, TRAVISWISS and so forth - examples to be found in the european market. These branch solutions mostly include an office-automation module. They furthermore allow for the direct access to diverse reservation systems and those systems of the major tour operators. This latter module is of great relevance to the electronic tourism markets. Many systems are presently being made available - in suitable form - to smaller, as well as private customers (eg. SWISSLINE and START/Btx). Besides PC and videotext access, the successful implementation of ATMs (Automated Teller Machines) is also being investigated (joint venture projects:- START; DB; TUI and Lufthansa).

Another direct-sale possibilty lies in selling via telephone (STARTs Audiotext), or fax (a SABRE variant). With the continuing integration of the PC, fax and telephone technologies, further offerings are to be expected.

National systems gain validity due to their ability to pool local offers into a coherent whole. The inclusion of regional systems (see below) is not only conceivable, but also of logical merit. The systems supply the participating travel agencies with a platform for inter-buro communication. Large travel concerns are able to communicate with their various branch offices; non-IATA-licence holders may communicate with their licensed counterparts in order to confer print orders for flight tickets [11].

Tour operators, as previously mentioned, either sell their products via their own sales offices or indirectly through independent travel agencies. They are increasingly operating via computer supported distribution systems - often by way of videotext. A worthy example of this is a system owned by the british travel agency, Thomson Holidays -christened TOPS - which has been successfully implemented since 1986 [2]. Printed travel catalogues however, continue to hold the upper hand. The EUROTOP project, with its aim to produce an electronic catalogue, represents an interesting alternative [8]. The paper medium is to be replaced by an electronic, distributed information carrier. Since pictorial representations are of major signifigance in this industry, EUROTOP has been designed to allow for the input, digitalization, storage and output of pictures. The foremost advantage of such a system lies in the swift brochure modifications possible, in reaction to changes. This corresponds to a substantial need that cannot be covered by the traditional print media. Further advantages are the supply of up-to-date information and databases with potent search functionality. The incorporation of visual aids began at various stages and by way of differing media: CD-Roms and distributed networks. The EC RACE-Project - ESSAI - plans to exploit optic-fibre technology to the fullest. Multimedia is bound to take the spot light.

Regional-Association Systems

Regional tourism associations increasingly realise, that offers which are not made available electronically, are bound to fall short of the global tourism market and will merely retain local impetus. In order to compete with the larger hotel chains, it is necessary to make the selection of accommodation possibilties, that family businesses and other non-hotel chain concerns supply - as well as additional regional tourism services, directly available over globally accessible reservation systems. Many such regional systems have been, or are in the course of being founded and may either apply to very small regions (such as Multimedia Graubünden, or in Germany - SI-Tour for the region Siegen-Wittenstein), or larger regions as in the case of TIS (Tirol-Informationssystem) [12] and the planned austrian system - MEHR. Many of these systems also allow for the *sale* of regional services, whereas others amount to sheer - often multimedia orientated - information systems. The offers are supposedly made available to international reservation systems. Several are pure multimedia information systems. Some are closed systems, others are open to all.

It should be noted that the majority of these systems - national and regional have only been introduced quite recently. The development of tourism EMs may be in its infancy, but growing at an accelerated pace.

4. Technological Developments

Each exchange of information pre-requires compatible information instances. The most important information carriers are people themselves, who, until very recently comprised the sole *active* instances as such: a person is able to respond to questions and solve problems by appling known information. The remaining information carriers such as paper, remain passive - able to hold information, but not apply it independantly.

Information technology has - for the first time - allowed for the technical construction of an active information carrier: a computerized information object can accept commands, relay information on its state at a given point in time, complete related tasks and solve defined problems. The functionality of this technology may be appropriately demonstrated in terms of word processing. A given text appearing on the monitor "understands" a large number of operations previously only comprehended by a secretary perhaps: besides the supplementation, correction and obliteration of the text displayed, it can moreover reformat itself, appear in different type formats, realize a page break, print itself and so forth. Just in terms of this example, we have in recent years experienced the tranfer of knowledge from specialized workers to word processing systems, and thereby to information objects of the type:- text. This process is still in its beginning stages and remains far from completion. We are to experience continued innovation pertaining to active information objects over the next few years, whereby "Know-How" will be increasingly integrated.

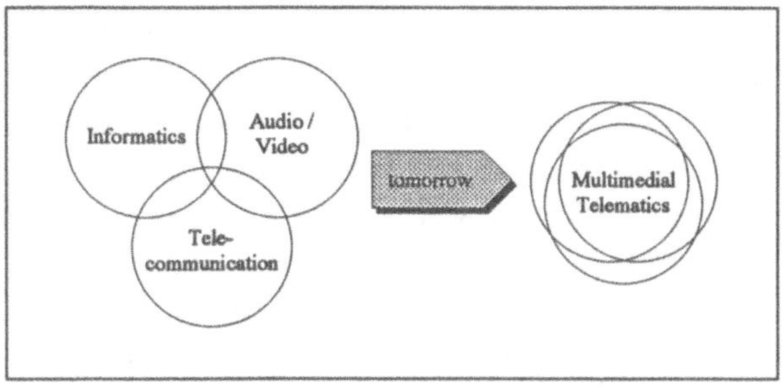

Figure 4: The development of multimedial telematics

We are presently at the threshold of a new and sweeping wave of technology. This is characterized by the mergence of information technology - responsible for the founding of active information carriers - on the one hand and telecommunication processes, as well as audio-video technology on the other. The digitalization of sound and video is one aspect. This development is in full throttle and is responsible for realizing digitalized sound-carriers, leading to the cornering of an ample niche in the consumer electronics market. Computer graphics is in its primary stages and is bound to bring us digitalized television within the next decade. The media is presently swamped with articles and documentaries alike, informing on the related possibilities and consequences. Even more noteworthy is the integration of these technologies with information technology itself. This is reflected in the realms of computer graphics and animation, that allow for photo-realistic depictions of mathematically calculated objects - right up to virtual reality. The multimedia PC could dominate the field by the mid-1990's, paving the way for important new applications.

The fusion between telecommunication and audio-video technology is embodied by the radio and television - technologies with which we are well acquainted. At present, digitalization merely serves to augment quality. If we however take the concept of *interactivity* into consideration, a new dimension springs to the fore. The union of information technology and telecommunication has been underway for several years. Electronics Markets are one of its fruits.

Telematics enables us to free the active information objects from particular platforms and to convey them to the global telecommunications media. They thus become *ubiquitous, active* information objects, exhibiting the characteristics of virtual machines. An electrical postbox, is an example of such an object: one may, if one has access to the telecommunication medium, at any given time or place make use of its functionality to send and receive electronic mail. An analogy is to be found in electronic travel catalogues with ordering facilities, as well as reservation systems. The previously mentioned text objects as encountered in word-processors, are also to be rendered placeless within the next few years and may likewise be understood as virtual machines. All this will finally be fully realized when there has been a global standardization of text-based documentation in terms of the ODA/ODIFF protocols. Every text, not only on ones own PC, but also those at hand on an accessible network server may then be opened and modified as seen fit. An analogue process - ie.- the standardization of tourism information remains unattained.

The newly found technology allows for a totally novel approach to organising work processes. At least three views may be distinguished:

- **View 1:** In terms of the individual *workers and consumers* a entirely new enviroment is created, whereby a spate of information objects that are in part produced and maintained in geographically displaced areas - are made available:- objects that were previously not accessible. The electronic mailboxes and flight reservation systems already referred to, serve as solid illustrations.
- **View 2:** In terms of the *objects* (or applications) themselves, the possibility of geographically distributed instances such as people or computer programmes accessing and processing these objects simultaneously, holds true.
- **View 3:** Up until now, it had only been possible for *groups* to work in a given place, whether under normal office conditions or at meetings to which they had to commute. Telecommunications have made the synchronized communication between displaced workgroup members possible. Following teleconferencing, videoconferencing amounts to one of the primary realizations of this work mode. Such *virtual rooms*, in which one may work together, will be implemented more and more - if not take centre stage - in the not to distant future.

In the tourism industry, two such virtual work-and-communication areas awake particular interest: EMs and the virtual office.

The virtual, ubiquitous office, that is realised with the technology outlined above, will permit radical new forms office interaction. This development began in the wake of increased office automization whereby more and more documents were being made available on servers within a communications network, which could then be accessed and processed from the individual workstations. This technology permits one to work from home or from ones holiday resort, in so far as a communication link can be established to the required office server. The distinction between work and leisure time are being newly defined - with consequences for tourism.

The consequences of EMs on a macro as well as micro level are bound to be far reaching. With the exception of regional markets, tourism information that has not been made available to the EMs will not come to light. Suppliers of tourism services are required to establish the pre-requisites for their beneficial presence in these electronic markets. EMs allow for - and enforce - the purchase of goods and services, there, where they are optimally priced - globally.

5. Prospective Tourism Market Architectures

As expounded upon above, the tourism market will comprise a global, integrated market as is already the case in many areas already today. There have already been substantial steps made in its direction. From a technical point of view however, several crucial elements are still lacking [10]. In order to attain a fully open EM, several aspects are to be realized.

1. Tourism services, especially the elemetary services such as flights and hotel accommodation, must necessarily be offered in *standardized* form. Alpha-numerical information, could and ought to be presented in terms of UN/EDIFACT; viable protocols for multimedial coverage are currently in the making. Services are to be made available on accessible *servers* which constitute a vital component of open systems.
2. The standardized, elementary services are to be put up on offer in *electronic markets* that should allow for stock-exchange-similar price determination. This ensures that last minute offers are competitively priced and that the prices may be seen as valuable information carriers - a reflection of complete information.
3. *Package production* (ie. by tour operators) will in future also be carried out in EMs. These packages will in turn be offered to the different tourism segments in standardized form. Besides fixed package arrangements, individual ad hoc compilations should be made possible (reverse marketing).
4. The EMs catering to particular tourism segments should not only be able to make their offers available, but also be in the position to accept customer queries, so that potential suppliers are able to make their services known to these clients and even adapt them where necessary.
5. Clients are to have *direct access* to the EMs.

Figure 6 broadly illustrates this ideal EM environment. The package assembly process may potentially take place in a multi-level manner.

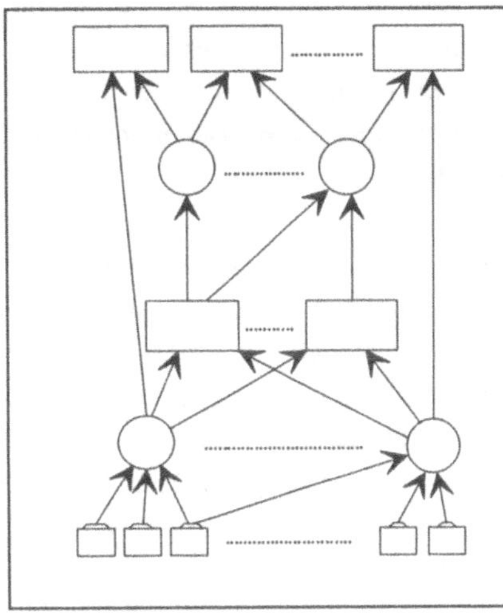

Figure 5: EM Architecture

The electronic markets will naturally be hybrid systems: besides the fully computerized markets, there will always be those where personal consultation, decision support and so on will continue to play a crucial role.

The described developments are evidently propelled by economic necessity, especially where the technology allows for such architectures.

An open, global electronic tourism market has consequences to bear [6]. The economical pressure to move in its direction stems from its faculty to squeeze transaction costs to a minimum - in this information intensive industry. Should these transaction costs once again be augmented by multimedial product presentations, then only in so far as increased financial yields may be realized. In summary, a selection of the seemingly most probable and important aspects - in the writer's opinion - below:

- The tourism service suppliers must make their standardized, interactive offers available in an appropriate server environment. The quality of *access possibilities* and *product presentation* are as important as the actual product quality itself. Regional systems, like flight reservation systems, will have to be made accessible worldwide.

- The producers of integrated packages will have to strive for the necessary flexibility to enable *individually tailored arrangements* - based on the principle of reverse marketing. The Know-How of these package producers may remain specialized. The generated products must on the one hand be competitively priced - and on the other - presented electronically.

- Information evaluation for clients and customer-related consultation, as well as the *design* of tailored solutions (ie. individual packages), should be organisationally distinguished from actual *production* due to the divergent Know-How required. This does not mean ofcourse, that the same organistion may not carry out both types of activities. The gathering of relevent information, as well as the ordering of products, shall take place electronically. (This facit of the value chain is already highly computerized.)

- The *direct sale* of services to *end-consumers* must increasingly be realized via the electronic media [7]. The PC, or its off-spring products serve as important terminal access points. Public terminal points may prove just as central to ensuring a satisfying solution.

- The necessary *systems* for tour operators and sales offices alike, should be *developed jointly* or left to specialists. The tourism industry must not practice competition by centering on its systems, but rather through its generated products.

These requirements are directed at a tourism industry bearing the profile currently evidenced. As soon as fibre-optic technology (IBC, or Information Highway concepts) has been concretely established - and high quality multimedial productions have come to be expected - (incl. virtual reality), new product design and innovative production - as well as - distribution systems will be called for. For the time being, it is essential to master the basics.

References

1. Bodendorf, F., Schulz, A.: Computergestützte Reisevertriebssysteme und ihre überbetrieblichen Auswirkungen. In: Newsletter des Kompetenzzentrums Elekfronische Märkte Nr. 3, Hochschule St. Gallen, 1992.
2. Bruce, M.: Technological change and competitive marketing strategies. In: Witt, Stephen F.; Moutinho, L.: Tourism Marketing and Management Handbook, New York usw. Prentice Hall, pp. 455-458, 1989.
3. Coase, R.H.: The nature of the firm, in: Economica, 4, pp. 386-405, 1937.
4. Ellis, M. A.: Elektronische Reservationssysteme. In: Newsletter des Kompetenzzentrums Elektronische Märkte, Nr. 3, Hochschule St. Gallen, 1992.
5. Kirstges, T.: Expansionsstrategien im Tourismus. Wiesbaden, Gabler Verlag, 1992.
6. Kropp, W.: Elektronische Reisevertriebssysteme: Von der Strichliste zum Global Ring. In: Roth, P., Schrand, A. (Hsg.): Touristic-Marketing. Das Marketing der Tourismus-Organisation, Verkehrsträger, Reiseveranstalter und Reisebüros, München, Verlag Franz Vahlen, 1992.
7. Lenner, K.C.: Ohne Direktverkauf können wir nicht überleben. In: Unabhängige Zeitschrift für Touristik und Geschäftsverkehr, Hannover, Nr. 5, pp. 133-135, 1993.
8. Lüttich, K.H.: EUROTOP - ein europäisches Projekt zur Entwicklung und Erprobung des elektronischen Reisekatalogs. Newsletter des CC EM, Nr. 3, Hochschule St. Gallen, pp. 4-5, 1992.
9. Ritz, D.: Elektronische Märkte verändern die Tourismusbranche. In: io Management Zeitschrift 61, Nr. 1, Verlag Industrielle Organisation BWI ETH Zürich, 1992.
10. Schmid, B.: Elektronische Märkte - Electronic Markets. In: Wirtschaftsinformatik, Vol. 35, No. 5, pp. 465-480, 1993.
11. Stohler, H.: TRAVISWISS - Neue Wege in Verkauf und Distribution. In: Newsletter des Kompetenzzentrums Elektronische Märkte, Nr. 3, Hochschule St. Gallen. 1992.
12. Werthner, H: TIS-Tiroler Informations System. In: Wirtschaftsinformatik, Nr. 35, pp. 43-50, 1993.

STRATEGY AND INFORMATION TECHNOLOGY IN THE TOURIST INDUSTRY

Prof.dr. Pieter M. Ribbers

Tilburg University (The Netherlands) Department of Information Systems And Accountancy

0. Abstract

The market of the tourist industry is changing. Customized combinations of different services are requiring timely, and cost effective combined services from the different parties in the tourist industry. Strategic changes are supported or even triggered by advanced information technology. The paper treats the changing role of information technology in general and for the tourist industry in particular. The discussion ends with some critical success factors for realizing the "strategic" applications of IT.

1. Introduction

In the january 1992 issue of a Dutch journal on Information Systems, a leading article was published entitled: "Manager underestimates possibilities IT". The article reported on a survey, conducted by Nolan, Norton & Co in co-operation with the Society on Strategic Planning (VSB), among 58 managers from large Dutch companies. All of them considered data processing and thus information systems, as a liability. The majority of the respondents claimed efficiency improvement and making the accounting operations better, to be the major objective of applying information technology. Strategic motives to invest in IT were largely ignored. Two third of Dutch enterprises could dramatically improve their competitive position by better utilizing the potentials of information technology, was the general conclusion of the study.

The reference to the article indicates the general theme which is addressed in this paper: how can information technology add value to the business, and in particular to the businesses in the tourist industry?

Information technology has the potential to contribute to the overall profitability of the company. However, applications of information technology do represent important commitments of resources. From an economic point of view these commitments have to be justified such as any other investment.

In this article we will argue that due to changes in market conditions and in information technology itself the role of IT in business is changing. At first IT was employed as a technology to reduce cost; nowadays IT has the potential to change the business conditions. This change in perspective affects also the problem of identifying and justifying interesting applications of IT.

2. Traditional views

The traditional ideas in the literature on planning of information systems are based on concepts developed by Anthony. In his book "Planning and Control systems: a framework for analysis, published in 1965, he introduces the thought that an organization should be managed through a hierarchy of plans. Well known became the distinction between strategic planning, management control, and operational control. With this distinction it became possible to discern various organizational applications of computerized information systems. Concepts like "management information systems", "decision support systems", "structured decision systems", and "executive information systems" were used to indicate various applications of IT to support management on various levels.

Anthony's framework was also the starting point for those authors who made an inventory of information systems organizations need to have. A clear example of this is Nolan's normative application portfolio, published in the seventies.

He distinguished applications for respectively top management, middle management and operational management.

A primary characteristic of this traditional approach, is the view that information systems are tactically and internally oriented. They contribute to the realization of the existing strategic plans, mainly by improving efficiency of the existing operations. From a capital budgeting point of view, investments in information technology are considered as replacement investments.

3. Changes in the competitive agenda.

In the past decade the competitive agenda of most industries has changed. First, efficiency was the dominant business driver; during the seventies quality of products and services became an differentiating performance measure in the competitive strategy. At present it becomes clear that meeting high levels of quality requirements is a necessary, but not a sufficient condition to remain in business. Business conditions are more dynamic and unpredictable than they ever have been. The cutting edge for the business of the near future will be time. The ability to compress time required for product design, production, delivery and service will be the strategic differentiator, given the required performance on quality and, also, on efficiency. Due to international competition, improvements in efficiency will be necessary to maintain or increase market share.

Also the travel industry has become a capricious market, which is changing continuously and sometimes abrupltly. In a recent study published by Moret, Ernst & Young Management Consultants, the following developments were reported. Rivalry between competitors is considered high. Products and services are undergoing rapid changes.

Consumers have become more individualistic and have changing expectations with regard to their leisure time. To an increasing extent they want a package of customized combined services, in which e.g. different transport modes are combined for short stays at different destinations. Also the importance of business trips is increasing; often they are combined with short private holidays. Generally speaking there is a trend towards more frequent but shorter stays abroad.

The implementation of new business strategies obviously benefits from advanced information and telecommunications technologies. Sharper competition in a turbulent environment affects the need for information, and triggers the application of advanced IT. Moreover, the development of information technology itself has accelerated the pace of change in the business environment. These technologies, like basic computers, software, telecommunications are not totally new; however, the revolutionary improvement in their technical and economic performance forms a huge technology push. In addition, formerly stand-alone information technology equipment is increasingly interconnected through telecommunication facilities, enabling new forms of cooperation between organizations.

4. A strategic perspective on Information Management

The traditional views with regard to information systems are unable to handle the information problems related to this new business environment. As information technology is apparantly affecting a company's position in the industry, the traditional views have to be extended with strategic considerations. As Wiseman says: " The application just described is an instance of a "strategic information system" (SIS), a use of information technology intended to support or change the competitive strategy of the enterprise. SIS represent a new information system variety, radically different from those countenanced by the conventional prespective" (Wiseman, 1988).

Strategic information systems are not primarily oriented towards improved efficiency. The primary motive to invest in those systems is to gain a better competitive position or to defend ones competitive position. Compared to the traditional applications, these systems are:

- strategically oriented (as opposed to tactically oriented),
- primarily focused on the company's environment,
- intended to affect primarily revenue, instead of cost,
- affecting the company's general policy.

The dynamics between business- and information technology developments have been described in Parker and Benson's EWIM model. Information Technology is in two ways related to the changing business environment. First, it is clear that dynamic business conditions have an effect on information needs and trigger the application of IT. In the EWIM model, this is called "alignment": the support of actual business strategy by IT. On the other hand IT itself is a cause of change of the business environment by enabling new products, creating new markets and changig the way business is done. In the EWIM model this is called "impact": the enabling of new business strategies by IT.

Almost every organization is affected by these developments; however the degree of influence may differ. There will be differences per industry and per individual company in a industry. One may e.g. compare the "information intensity" of an insurance company to a cement producer. Cash, McFarlan and McKenney developed a strategic grid, which classifies organizations dependent on the strategic importance of their existing applications on one side, and the strategic importance of future applications on the other side. By combining both criteria, one gets a well known Boston two by two matrix. The reasoning is obvious. If information management is critical for a company's market position, so will be tuning of information management to general business management.

As reported in the Moret, Ernst & Young study, within the tourist industry there are big differences between individual organizations, concerning the extent to which IT is applied. Some (big) company's are advanced, others are at the beginning. Nevertheless it may be stated that IT has been important for company's in the travel industry to gain competitive advantages. The situation will however soon exist that IT has become a competitive necessity. Those touroperators who started with reservation systems not only have improved their own business operations, but also created a barrier for potential new entrants to the industry.
Moreover, at present the business of an important tour operator could not be run without IT anymore. The tourist industry has become very "information intense". It would be impossible to handle all the data processing and communication involved in making large amounts of customized, combined trips supplemented with different service packages, without the support of IT.

5. Strategic analysis as a starting point.

Information Management concerns the question what information systems the organization should have. In the past decades various methods were developed to analyze information needs and business processes. Examples of these methods are ISAC and BSP. As said before the primary intention of them is improving the existing organization, focussing on internal (accounting) processes. In this way potential IS projects could be detected. As those investments were regarded as replacement investments, for deciding whether or not to invest in those projects, traditional capital budgeting criteria could be used, like net present value and internal rate of return. These aproaches were in line with the tactical use of IT.

The question is on what basis IS decisions should be made, when strategic motives are becoming important. Under these circumstances the traditional approaches fail. As they leave the environment out of the scope of the study, important applications, from a strategic perspective, are overlooked. Using capital budgeting approaches is also problematic, as the benefits of strategic systems are hard to quantify. Recent literature in the field builds upon the ideas of Michael Porter. His frameworks of competitive analysis and "value-chain"- versus "value system" analysis are used as instruments to improve the competitive position with information technology.

Porter has advocated that realizing a competitive advantage, is a core concern of strategic planning. This advantage is grounded on the value products and services represent for the customer. A company should try to satisfy customer demand in a better way than its competitors. Driving forces in this process, are performance measures dictated by the market. To survive in the competitive struggle, a company's primary concern should be how to improve its performance in order to enhance customer satisfaction. For this purpose, performance measures have to be identified, operationalized, and translated into specific measures for each individual business activity.

A first area of concern, is the company's competitive position in the industry. The competitive position is the combined result of five forces: (1) the bargaining position of suppliers, (2) bargaining position of customers, (3) the threat of new entrants, (4) the rise of new products and substitutes, and (5) the existing rivalry in the industry.

At first Porter did not include the effects of information technology in his analysis. Nevertheless his framework has proved to be very helpful in assessing the effects of IT on an industry. Also seen on a company level, it is possible for the individual organization to protect or to enhance its competitive position by purposefulle applying information technology. This subject is extensively discussed in literature; I will suffice with giving some examples.

Interorganizational systems can influence the power relations between suppliers and customers. Use of telecommunication in order to exchange order- and product data reduces the flexibility to change business partners. Information technology has the potential to significantly raise entrance barriers to the industry. Required investments as well required know how may prevent potential competitors to enter the market. Through information technology products may disappear or new products may come to existence. An example is the threatening of the market of encyclopedias and professional journals by database technology and imaging technology.

Given its competitive position a company has to choose for a competitive strategy. In Porter's framework a company may choose either for a cost strategy, or for a quality strategy.

For each strategy the performance measures are different. The cost strategy requires efficiency, standardization, economies of scale etc; the differentiation strategy requires everything needed to meet high and perhaps changing quality standards. I do not want to discuss here the question whether the choice is really "either..or". The main point which is of relevance, is the fact that strategy is related to operational performance measures dictated by the market.

The relation with information management becomes then obvious. Strategy determines required performance, performance may be supported and/or improved by information systems. Even the strategy may be enabled by IT. Deciding which systems are needed is thus clearly a business responsibility. Those who are in responsible for the business results, bear the responsibility of choosing, prioritizing required IS applications.

6 Some conclusions for the tourist industry

The tourist industry comprises touroperators and travel agencies. Touroperators make up travel-arrangements based on transport (plane, bus, train, own transport, and cruises), accomodation (hotels, boarding-houses, bungalows), and specific services. The providers of transport, accomodation and services, are the "suppliers" to the industry. Travel agencies form a link between touroperators and customers. Often a tour-operator controls a network of travel-agents, thus controlling the entire process of service delivery to the customer. From the tour operator's point of view, as well the travel agencies as the final consumer are considered "customers". Most travel agents sell services of various tour operators. As said before, the rivalry in the industry is strong. Also market developments were discussed earlier: there is a trend towards customization of services, shorter and combined trips, more uncertainty in the market. Adequate and timely service at a reasonable price have become the performance measures for the modern touroperator.

Looking at the "value system" of the tourist industry, the changes in the tourist market demand affect the services offered by the various suppliers, like airlines, and hotels. Charter company's offer schedules with higher frequencies, or offer regular airline services possibly in combination with other transport modes; touroperators are making reservations in regular airline services, thus reducing their dependency on charter companies; combinations of reservatons of airline seats and hotelrooms are realized.

The industry is reacting by vertical integration of different service providers. All parties may benefit from creating adequate win win situations: touroperators sell more travel arrangements, airlines sell more seats, hotels more beds etc. Examples of vertical integration are:

- big touroperators buying chains of travel agencies;
- big touroperators having fixed agreements with with airline companies and hotel chains; through their revenue they have built up a bargaining power. The competitive position of the smaller touroperators is threatened.

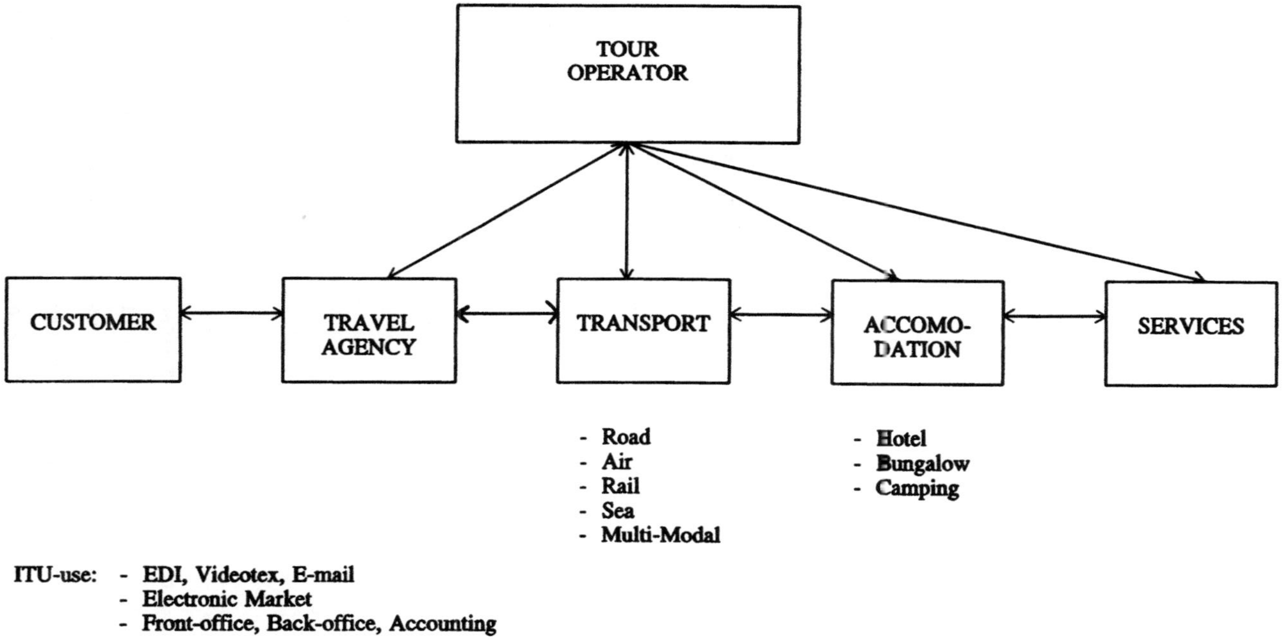

Exhibit 1: The value system in the tourist industry

It is clear that information technology is playing an important role in these developments. Integration in the value (travel) system is supported by interorganizational systems. Adequate use of IT thus enables the touroperator to be responsive to the customer, and at the same time to keep operating costs within reasonable limits. I mention a few examples:

- Electronic data interchange, videotex applications, electronic mail enable timely information between the partners in the value system (compare Travelnet in the Dutch Tourist industry).
- Electronic markets may confront supply and demand of resp. for empty beds, empty seats per transport mode for the various destinations (compare Teleroute in road freight transport, connecting 20,000 users all over Europe).
- Adequate integration of front office (e.g.reservation) and back office systems (planning, management information) of touroperators and travel agencies.

Based the experience with other industries some critical success factors may be distinguished:

- Strong business support: buiness managers in the tourist industry have to understand the relevance of IT for their business.
- Economic benefit for each partner: sometimes innovative win/win situations have to be created.
- Willingness to cooperate: strong industry rivalry counteracts the realization of interorganizational systems.
- Government support for infrastuctural investments.

References

Benjamin, R., Rockart, J., Morton, M., Information Technology: a strategic opportunity. Sloan Management Review, Spring 1984.

Parker, M.M., Benson, R.J., Trainor, H.E., Information Economics; Linking Business Performance to Information Technology. Prentice Hall 1988.

Farell, C., Song, J., Strategic uses of IT. SAM Advanced MAnagement Journal, Winter 1988.

Johnston, H., Vitale, M., Creating competitive advantage with interorganizational information systems. MIS quarterly, june 1988.

MacFarlan,F., Information Technology changes the way you compete. Harvard Business Review, july/august 1984.

Porter, M.E., Millar, V., How information gives you competitive advantage. Harvard Business Review, july/august 1985.

Rockart, J.F., Short, J.E. (1989), IT in the nineties: Managing Organizationial Interdependence. Sloan Management Review, Winter 1989.

Westrenen, C., van, De toepassing van informatie-technologie in de bedrijfsvoering. Raad van de Centrale Ondernemings- organisaties; Moret, Ernst & Young, Management Consultants, Utrecht 1992.

Wiseman, C., Strategic Information Systems, Homewood Illinois, Irwin, 1988.

"TOURIST & GUEST 2000"

WILHELM DANTINE

DR. FESSEL + GFK - INSTITUT

2000 b.c.: **ÖTZI**
2000 ago: **APOSTLES, OVID**
2000 a.c.: **?**

The tourist 2000 before Christ: The man of the Hauslabjoch "Ötzi", wasn't he a tourist? 2000 years ago, there where the apostles. Where they tourists either? But also Ovid, he was not a tourist in our sense, but was his exile on the black sea so far away from some of our touristic destinations? The tourist 2000, will he be much different, going to some exile ghetto, more voluntarily, but does he?

GENERAL CHANGES

And will there be much change in the upcoming seven years, pardon, six years and one month until 2000? Are there really different attitudes in tourism consumption within the first world? How will this develop in the second, former communist world? Are there changes only in quantitative and not in qualitative aspects, and what kind of? This six to seven years seem to be too short to report great changes in motives, attitudes and needs.

In an Europe-wide survey, that GFK-EUROBUS conducted on tourism in 18 European countries in spring 1993, "warm climate" and "nature" were still the leading motives respectively factors of choosing a holiday country. But "cultural sights" are as "value for money" not so far away from top.

In 1990, 35% of all European holidays taken abroad, were "sun and beach" holidays; 25% were recreational holidays, 17% were city holidays and 10% were round trips, also leading to some cities. So there are three segments, which were not so much different in 1990. Of course, long holidays are more focused on "sun and beach" holidays as "city holidays" are more focused on short holidays. "Recreational holidays" are short as well as long holidays. These figures are based on data of the European Travel monitor 1990.

Region per region, country per country, the preferences are different and this will influence the development in the next decade. Beside of "nature", the "gentle tourism" becomes more and more important, especially in markets with increasing tourism rate in the future. Besides of the economical problems at the moment, the South-European countries are expected to show a dynamic development in outgoing tourism, as perhaps at the end of this millenium, the Eastern European countries will do, too. They do not have too much in mind with gentle tourism, but they are very much interested in cultural sights and good value for money. Of course, in "warm climate", too.

As far as we can see now, the changes in destinations are not that dramatic, for example: When in 1989 the algue-problem at the Adriatic coast in Italy got obvious, there was a decrease in visitors coming from some important markets, but more important was, that people went to the same destination, but changed their behaviour. Italian trips are becoming more and more important on cultural purposes. The market share was not much lower than it was in the years before, but people stayed for less time and other purposes.

Nevertheless, in Europe a slight decrease in the "sun and beach" segment can be predicted. If you take in account the destinations outside Europe as well, this decrease will be a significant one. The environmental factor "ozone" can also lead to a stronger loss within this "sun and beach" segment.

Besides of the influences of the actual economical situation in Europe, the megatrends show more and shorter holidays, as well as more different holidays including trends for more recreation, relaxation, fitness, but also sports, shopping, adventure, amusement and so on. The most increasing segment should be the cultural orientated holiday, not only in form of city-trips. Business trips, incentive tourism and so on are not included in this performance.

It is obvious, that tourist destinations, which can offer some of this factors, are better prepared to the future than others, especially considering the environmental aspect or a fair relation between value and money. At least it is very important, how the guests will be treated by the local people, which is not only meaning profit in tourism. Even here in the Tyrol and especially in Innsbruck, where, more than in other parts of Austria, mass-tourism show some negative aspects - traffic, noise and uproar - the chances for Austria seem to be quite good looking to the future.

NEW TOURISM?

Motives are influencing the choice of destinations. Experience with destination is still the most important factor for loyalty or influences the choice of a new destination recommended by friends and relatives. This will still be very important also in the future. But if tourism is in transition, as Ms. Poon says in her new book: "Tourism, Technology and Competitive Strategies", which short-time influences will these "new tourism" have on organisation and technical equipment? 1)

Ms. Poon shows a very outpointed comparison between old and new tourists (new consumers). 1)

Old and new tourists compared:

Old tourists	New tourists
Search for the sun	Experience something different
Follow the masses	Want to be in charge
Here today, gone tomorrow	See and enjoy but not destroy
Just to show that you had been	Just for the fun of it
Having	Being
Superiority	Understanding
Like attractions	Like sports
Precautious	Adventurous
Eat in hotel dining room	Try out local fare
Homogeneous	Hybrid

She also predicts, that approximately in the year round 2000 the decreasing development in old tourism will be at the same level as the increasing new tourism, but this will be just a picture. Rather important for the future development is that new life-styles develop faster as in the past, and will also have more short-time influence on tourism.

This new tourist will be:
- more experienced in travel
- better educated
- more sensitive to environment
- more flexible in free-time and appreciate the different
- more and more single household
- more flexibility in age (seniors)
- perhaps at least tourist as a profession?

Time is too short to bring it up to reality until the year 2000, but we are and tourism business is on that way, and the consequences on this developments will take place very soon. In developed markets there will be a decrease in package holidays, while in the low developed markets, like South-Europe and Eastern Europe an increase in package tourism is to be predicted in the next years.

FUTURE INFORMATION SOURCES

Our latest study in Austria will show this - the results are not ready yet in detail, but will be reported at the conference - showing the foreseen preferred information on destinations and tour-operators in the year 2000.

What is in the Austrians' view, a small, but prosperous market in outgoing tourism having not so much experience in package-tours, but an increasing development in this matter during the last three years, what will be their most popular sources of information?

It is not my task to show the reasons why the Austrians were going that late to the package-market, but the Austrians' attitudes and their thoughts about the future will be very interesting indeed. Perhaps Austria is a good indicator how things might develop in the eastern, but also in some southern countries of Europe.

The content of this survey are questions about the information which is in use right now for personal holiday-planning (1), what kind of information will be used by the other Austrian holiday-makers (2) and which will be used in the year 2000 by the respondent himself (3) and which will be used by the other tourists in the year 2000 (4). These items are: catalogues per season and destinations, video-tapes, travel-guides, books and tapes, TV-programmes, teletext-information, booking-possibilities on TV and booking and payment via TV.

INFORMATION SOURCES

	present		in 2000	
		only 1 answer		only 1 answer
	1	2	3	4
Catalogues with price-lists/ seasonal	50	51	20	15
Catalogues with price-lists/ destinations	35	28	14	8
Rented videotapes	4	2	9	9
Travelguides (books)	25	6	10	2
Info about destinations in TV programs	7	3	12	10
Teletext	3	1	16	16
Info & Booking	1	1	13	15
Info/booking & Paying	1	6	11	12

Results in percentages: FESSEL + GFK "Future Information Sources on Tourism", N = 1.000; representative for Austrians 14 years and above, November 1993.

The figures show that catalogues will lose their dominating position, on lower level the book-travelguides, too. Regarding electronical information systems, there is not much difference between personal usage and projections to the other tourists in 2000. But people have the feeling, they will stay more with traditional information than the others will do. There is no majority to one of the items.

An open ended question gives the opportunity to tell something more detailed about the ideal holiday-information-system in the year 2000 in the nowaday tourists' view. At last there are some items about the personal attitude to these information-systems, e. g. how many tourists cannot imagine travel-booking without personal advise at the travel agency or what kind of people prefer the convenience of booking from at home up to the influence of the choice of different catalogues and at least also the problem of the general "more tech - more touch" relation.

ATTITUDES TO FUTURE INFORMATION-SYSTEMS

These results show also some careful approach to the new techniques. So the convenience of home-booking will not be accepted directly (more agree partly), also the customers cannot imagine that much the lack of personal advise in the agency. "Paper wasting" seems to be a good argument while opinions are split in getting cheaper offers.

	agree	**disagree**	**partly agree**
no problem with no more checking the catalogues	50	16	29
personal advise in the travel agency is absolutely necessary	45	22	29
no more paper wasting with catalogues	42	18	35
videos and films are closer to the truth than catalogues	35	19	40
it is convenient to book from at home	34	18	43
travelling should be cheaper without catalogues and agencies	30	33	31
pleasure starts with choosing the most interesting offer in the agency	27	27	40

Results in percentages: FESSEL + GFK "Future Information Sources on Tourism", N = 1.000; representative for Austrians 14 years and above, November 1993.

AUSTRIA'S CHANCES

Regarding the specific situation in Austria's incoming tourism, we may ask about the effects on some typical segments that are important to a major destination like Austria, being also a country with one of the highest dependences on incoming tourism:

Austria seems to have good chances for:

- The natural ressources and its central location at the heart of Europe besides of regarding traffic, needs.
- The good environmental conditions which are accepted also in the opinion of guests and tourists.
- The latest trends working for Austria as a close, various destination for short time decisions.
- The multipurpose trips in connection with cultural events and experience.
- The renaissance of "Sommerfrische" and "Bergurlaub", as recreational antithesis against "sun and beach".
- Growing target groups, which were not present that much in Austria up to now, will gradually substitute, better supplement, the traditional guest of more or less "German character".
- The growing mutual effects regarding seasons, segmentation, e.g. city trips or mountain hiking, and destinations in general will also be useful.
- New markets in new regions (East-/Middle-Europe)

The tradtional markets, guests coming from Germany and Austria should be protected in their traditional attitudes by new accents like

- experience and adventure (young hedonists)
- more offers to kiddy-fitting holidays (young families)
- improvement in various offers to attract also pretentious tourists

This could, better should happen in connection with improving touristical supra- and infrastructure

leading to higher per capita revenues. The residents' (local people's) positive attitude cannot be stressed unlimited ("Tourismusgesinnung"). So one of the objectives will be shifting the growing demands in more and different seasons respectively new regions, eager in having more tourism.

Coming back to our main topic, together with a good value for money relation and excellent information systems, not only in a technical way, Austria' position will look very solid in the year 2000.

1) Poon, Auliana, 1993. "Tourism, Technology and Competitive Strategies", C.A.B. International, Wallingford

"TOURISM 2000 - AN INFORMATION BUSINESS"

Univ.-Prof. Dr. W. Schertler

Professor for "Organization and Strategic Management" and Director of the European Tourism Institute at the University of Trier, Germany

1. Tourism - the Next Hightech Industry

It is summer a few years`hence and you want to lay on an outdoor grill. You call up the American barbecue page on your computer screen and the system linking your home with the local restaurant or supermarket asks whether the meal will be for two or for a party, what sort of appetisers, main courses or desserts you want. All screen options are illustrated, some with videos. You tap in your preferences and recipes with ingredients. Brand names and prices can be called up and print out by your small, document proofed laser printer. You order the shop electronically with a simple barcode scanning device or direct from the screen. The goods are delivered through a secure entry point in your home. "It all sounds blissfully effortless, if somewhat soulless. However, a US study has shown that 64 % of people dislike going to the supermarket for their basic shopping... The figure is quoted by Andersen Consulting which has opened a $5m retail centre in the UK to demonstrate how technology can be applied to meet the pace of change in the industry."(Financial Times, p. 10)

This Financial Times report from November 1993 is only one of the several news which learn us what and how information technology will change our life within the next couples of years.

There is no evidence why this development shouldn`t be relevant for tourism as well as for the catering or retail industries: At the weekend you sit around the TV-Computer with your family, planning your short time holiday next week. You call the Holiday Express TV Channel calling up the Tourist Information Center of your preferred destination for specific information like snow conditions or special events for kids and you look the information video of several hotels you are interested to stay in. When you made your choice you will book the hotel rooms and all the necessary reservations directly. Your desktop laser printer will print all the information handouts, the tickets for the train and your seat reservation, the entrance tickets for the kid-show or for the ski school as well as the reservation slip for Peter, the family`s favorite ski instructor. On Monday your secretary will check your flight information, prices and special discounts of the week, then she will book your prefered seat in the Airbus A320 and will get your ticket just out of her printer - no waiting for your travel agent`s answer, no mailing time or time consuming detour to your travel agent`s office located in crowdy downtown to get your ticket. And it will be cheaper than years ago when tour operators and travel agencies asked for paying their information clearing services for your holiday or business trips. Also the hotel will offer you cheaper room rates because you booked directly.

Again, this is not a Jules Verne like vision of the future. The Financial Times article mentioned before already figured out that this is possible today and will be convenient for an increasing number of consumers in the near future. For example, Thomas Cook Travel Management has developed a new booking system called System Four which integrates not only all relevant information necessary for booking flights, hotels and car hires but offers also a profile of the customer`s preferencies like non-smoking room or business facilities. "Technology will be the key differential between travel management companies in the future."(Financial Times, p.IV)

Information technology is also becoming increasingly important in the internal management of hotel systems integrating check-in/check-out, telephone and electronic key, minibar control, customer correspondance and communications, yield management, financial reports, energy control etc.

These are only some examples how new technologies will transform the tourism industry by realising new organizational relations between principals, agents and consumers.

The industry shake-out in tourism will offer new opportunities but also new threats to all of the market participants. New strategies for survival and new structures of developing, producing, selling and distributing touristic "products" and services will be necessary. But the success of these new strategies in the tourism industry will correlate immediatly with our ability to cultivate the change process behind. Concerning tourism information and communication systems we have to consider that computer based information systems will penetrate other areas of consuming behaviour like tele-banking or tele-shopping. The "Nintendo kids" generation will deal new information technology in tourism completely different than their parents.

What we see now is not a further change like those in the past. It is a revolution which will change the tourism industry fundamentaly: consumer behaviour as well as the basics of competition.

a) Focus change in the development of tourism management

Looking at the development of the functional focus tourism management realized in the past fifty years you can identify five crucial phases:

Phase 1: **"Pioneering the industry"**

After World War II and the reconstruction period European tourism started as an economic phenomen on becoming more and more relevant in terms of turnover as well as of importance for the political integration within Europe. Tourist demand increased significantly from year to year, provocating and stimulating the entrepreneurial people allover Europe to invest in this growing industry.

Phase 2: **"Capacity Focus"**

Planning and building up the necessary capacities have had to follow the increasing demand for travel and tourism services: Tourism and travel infrastructure like airline or highway networks, restaurants, hotel accomodations, leasure parcs, sightseeing guides etc. were dominated by volume driven thinking in an extremly growing industry. Mass tourism began to evolve.

Phase 3: **"Advertising Focus"**

Once the capacities and the support of basic needs of customers are realized tourism mass markets can`t be dealt as uniform and monolithic unit. Tourism became more sophisticated and needed more differentiated marketing strategies. The need for offensive advertising campaigns or public relations and communications increased significantly. Specialization in the tour operating business (e.g. clubs, wilderness safaries) or in the travel agencies sector as well as in the hotel and restaurant business can document the growing necessity for segmenting the markets and business areas. In the worldwide airline or hotel business branding evolves as a crucial factor for success.

Phase 4: **"Administration Focus"**

Tourism has grown up to a major industry in countries like Austria, Spain, Italy or Greece and became more complex to manage. Tourism strategies tried to realize economies of scale by increasing the level of concentration, vertical integration and distribution. Tour operators know very well that their profits rely to a great extent on these strategic decisions. Yield management offers new methods for more profit in the tourism industry, which is a huge industry in terms of turnover or transported passengers, but quite often an unattractive industry in terms of profitability. That means tourism is still a low-margin business, fixed cost driven and, once the cumulated growth rate decreases, with poor attractiveness to get sustainable appreciation from the investors` point of view. Cost leadership is dealt as the most important strategy for success, not only for the private but also for the public sector. There tourism policy programs focus on more coordination on regional and state levels and on more efficient public tourism management in incoming institutions or public tourism organizations which provide international advertising or public relations and local tourist information.

Phase 5: **"Distribution Focus"**

In every shrinking demand situation marketing becomes the most important management function. And it will be of great importance for success in the tourism industry as well. But marketing decisions and objectives will focus much more on the distribution than on advertising function. The future profitability in tourism will depend more on the capability of market access, on the influence on global distribution channels and especially on the time to market.

The new technologies and the new information and communication systems in tourism are both: a dramatic strategic challenge for all tourism related businesses and markets as well as a significant cultural change in suppliers and customers behaviour.

b) Information based tourism business

If you look at tourism as a service industry you can understand that information is one of the most important quality parameters for servicing actions. The wrong departure time information or the fact that you didn`t know that all hotel rooms or cars are rented are influencing the consumer behaviour significantly because they determine the value of the service provided by tour operators, travel agencies, hotel room or car renting. In this sense you can say that suppliers in the tourism industry add value and get paid for it on three levels: the action, the information and the communication level. The lack of information and commuication influence the whole value chain dramatically.

All investments in high quality standards of hardware facilities, food and beverage, management systems, staff training and marketing don`t pay back if information is not accurately available or wrong. This is relevant for the private industry sector in tourism as well as for the public non profit organizations like federal advertising bureaus or local tourist offices.

c) Time based competition in tourism

"Today`s innovation is time-based competition. Demanding executives at aggressive companies are altering their measures of performance from competitive costs, quality, *and* responsiveness. ....Companies are obtaining remarkable results by focusing their organization on responsiveness." (Stalk/Hout, p. 1)

Indeed, traveling becomes more individualistic and more specialized, decisions for shorter holidays are taken much more spontaneously and the customers become much more experienced in appreciating added value in tourism.

That means on one hand that the demand for quicker, more flexible and multivarious offers will increase. On the other hand new networks of cooperation will evolve: Suppliers in tourism like hotels, airlines or buses will sell their services directly to the customers. Vice versa the tourists can communicate directly with them. Therefore all traditional agent functions in tourism industry must be revised completely. Travel agencies for example will have problems to get paid for their service. Customers neither see added value in analysing a catalogue nor do they want to wait for urgent needed information. They want direct dialogue and communication with their suppliers. Of course that doesn`t mean that all travel agents will disappear but each of them has to understand and to evaluate the new information technology trends for the relevance of future survival in the industry. Tourism will be the next Hightech industry. Therefore tourism information and communication systems, I use the idiom TICS, are crucial factors for strategic success in the industry.

2. Need for Strategic Management

The visions for survival in tourism are "speed" and "global distribution". Tourism management must realize that time based management as well as information and communication management will represent the core competences of every player in the tourism business: suppliers and agents. Today but of increasing importance in the future tourism will turn into a time and information driven business. Time and communication based competition will formulate the new "rules of the game" and change the whole structure of the industry.

Therefore we should orientate the further reasoning much more at the theory of industrial economics than at technical issues. The computer and telecommunication industry will deliver the hardware systems and software applications. Men in tourism must deliver orgware competence in using them correctly and sufficiently.

So I suggest to follow the theory of the Strategic Management Approach and to emphasize on the strategic thrill of time and communication based competition as well as on the change management problem of the introduction and acceptance of new information and communication systems in tourism industry.

a) The Industrial Economics Approach

The theory of industrial economics focus on the analysis of an industry. Central elements of this research model are market structure, market conduct and performance as well as the relations between these elements. "This hypotheses predict in general that the market structure of an industry determines or strongly influences the crucial aspects of its market conduct and thus indirectly determines certain strategic dimensions of its market performance" (Bain 1968, p. 430, Williamson 1986).

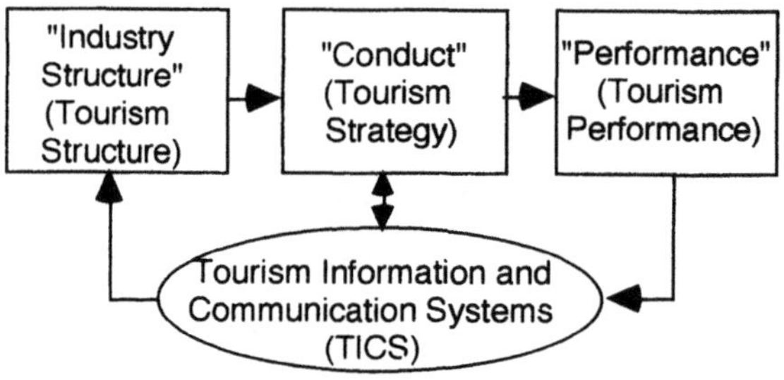

Figure 1: TICS and the market structure-conduct-performance model

As far as it concerns the tourism industry, we must ask the question: "How does new TICS change the structure of market participants and how do they have to change their competitive behaviour? How do they influence the progress and success of tourism industry?

b) The Strategic Management Approach

In general this approach offers a conceptual framework for longterm survival in an industry. Its specific elements like vision, strategy, organizational structure and corporate culture allow an objective-driven integration of several activities, budgets and programs as well as controlling activities.

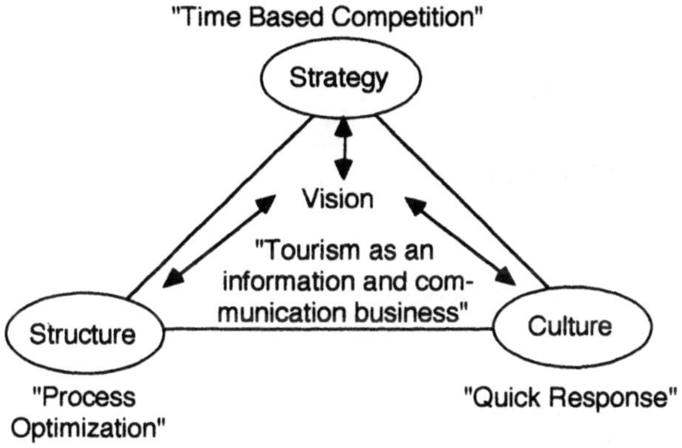

Figure 2: TICS and the Conceptual Framework of Strategic Management

Management attention is focused on "factors for success" like speed, information quality, access to distribution channels or the way the business unit managers communicate with the customers. Strategic management tries to understand the rules for the business` success in the future.

Strategies are driven by benchmarking activities which compare the own company or business unit with them of the competitors to get a better idea about the strengths and weaknesses in competition. The analysis of trends and their opportunities and threats for the future development in tourism are important information within the decisionmaking process. But strategic management asks for more than vision or strategies. It also asks to understand the necessity to change the organizational background for strategic success. If companies in tourism have to become faster it is necessary to increase the responsiveness of the organization by providing equivalent structures for "quick response". The traditionally thinking tourism industry will face fundamental change of attitudes concerning on-line customer communication, organizational redesign in logistics, optimization of destination-information or reservation and booking processes.

Those who are familiar with strategic management know that the best strategic concept can`t produce results without a firm understanding and support of the people working out the concept. Tourism management has to be very keen about leadership style, motivation and human resource management within the company. As part of the service industry tourism manager have to take into account that their employees spend much more time in direct contact to the customers than they do. Successful strategic management empowers people by flattening the hierarchy or providing intensive communication between management, staff and clients.

New strategies, new structures, but old culture don`t fit. The acceptance of new technologies like multimedia requires also hightech friendly attitudes and behaviour patterns of the people involved to develop a "winning culture" as time based competitor. His characteristic is to fulfill requirements of the customer faster than others do, to deliver products and services earlier and to offer quicker response to the customer.

To be faster in action and quicker in response is very hard to imitate by your competitor because so called organizational capabilities can be protected very well as a competitive advantage for very long time. Therefore all investments spent in the development of TICS are of high return on investment potential.

References

Bain, J.S.: Industrial Organization, 1968

Drucker, P., Managing the Non-profit Organzation, 1990

Fisher, A.: Tapping Into Convenience, in: Financial Times, November 11,1993

Porter, M.E.: The Contributions of Industrial Organization to Strategic Management, in: Academy of Management Review, Nr. 4 /1981, pp. 609 - 620

Porter, M.E.: Competitive Strategy, 1980

Stalk, G. jr., Hout, M. T.: Competing Against Time, 1990

Williamson, O.E.: Economic Organization, New York 1986

Taylor, P.: An Accommodating Computer Does the Booking, in: Financial Times, November 9, 1993

Witt, F. St., Moutinho, L.: Tourism Marketing and Management Handbook, 1989

Change demands on hotel management

Johann Ruisz

CONNECT Vermittlungs- und Serviceges.m.b.H.

In the following paper I wish to review in detail those areas of hotel management subject to change brought about by new data and communications technologies. The main point of emphasis is on innovations made in the sectors of purchasing and merchandise economy. It should be borne in mind that the majority of such innovations come from outside sources rather than within (either from data service providers or merchandise suppliers). The organisational side of most undertakings is not prepared for these innovations. For that reason the following report sets out to illustrate the demands made on the daily routine and the necessity for training in addition to possible alliances and trends.

Information and communication not only constitute the fundamentals of social co-existence, but also form the basis of each and every economic process. As competition becomes fiercer, not only does the quantity of information increase, but also the demand for processed and condensed information serving a useful end for decision-making purposes. The supply of this data comes in the form of purchase-information systems, mainly through the technical medium of the computer and telephone. In this context information is referred to as being data arriving at the hotel from outside sources as well as leaving the undertaking itself, all of which is then gathered, processed and subjected to evaluation.
The structural make-up of the hotel and restaurant catering business is characterised by a large number of undertakings (44,7 %) operating without employees. Chiefly of interest as far as this topic is concerned and thus the object of our study here, are those enterprises operating with a staff of more than five employees.

"Structural make-up of the hotel and restaurant catering trade in Austria"
(from: The Tourist Trade in Figures, 26th Edition published in April 1990 and issued by the Federal Department of Trade and Industry)

Number of workplaces	Number of employees
19,056	0
9,213	1
9,079	2-4
3,317	5-9
1,375	10-19
485	20-49
94	50-99
20	100-199
6	200-499
1	500-999
42,646	

Changes in management resulting from new information and communication technologies are described with regard to the effects they have - due to the higher information status - on the segments of purchasing and merchandise economy. The effects on other business segments are also illustrated.

The Basic Situation

The lion`s share of the turnover generated in the hotel and restaurant catering branch is earned by about 5,200 enterprises staffed by between 5 and 50 employees. The majority of these undertakings are private family-run establishments as distinct from the large - and for the most part international - chains.

On the one hand, organisation is adapted to the specialities, abilities and inclinations of the individual members making up a family-run enterprise. Another determining factor is that relating to whether the undertakings are kept open during the summer and/or winter seasons. "Purchasing" is one of the favourite occupations of many proprietors whose capacities in this respect are, however, limited to the time available prior to the commencement of the season. This is when they display a keen interest in price comparisons as well as in negotiating prices and terms with suppliers. It is also the time when in odd cases some preordering is carried out and when orders end up being placed, as a rule, with "regular"suppliers.

Information used to provide the basis for price comparisons resulting from order-sets (the miscellaneous ranges, above all those presented by the wholesale food trade), offers sent out in the form of circulars or personal encounters with suppliers` representatives. Such comparisons are mainly carried out by reviewing offers made by other competitors in the field and the proprietors` own records - mostly accounts rendered the previous season or the year before.
Less than one fifth of the enterprises are members of a purchasing organisation offering a complete range of services including purchase comparisons and recommendations. The advantage of such comparisons and recommendations for the enterprises concerned is the reliable basis of information they provide, frequently serving as a starting point for proprietors` own negotiations since decisions to effect purchases are left entirely to the discretion of the members themselves.

As far as I am able to assess, documentation recording the consumption of certain goods within defined periods of time exists in fewer than 500 enterprises included in the structural make-up previously described

Merchandise procurement during the season thus becomes the actual "purchasing" process owing to the absence of planned rules and binding instructions. For the most part, the task of purchasing and procuring merchandise as well as in-house merchandise control is carried out by a single person. It is only subject to multi-stage organisation in those areas affording greater ease of control, e.g. in the case of beverages. In merchandise sectors representing essentially higher cost factors but which are considerable more difficult to organise, as for example fresh meat supplies, all functions are under the control of the chef.

In the restaurant segment itself, the cost of amounts to between 30 % and 50 % of the turnover depending on the category of the selection offered. This broad margin comes about as a result of the wide range of different types extending from the fast-food restaurant through to the gourmet`s temple. It is also affected by the relevant proportion of alcoholic beverages which, due to their high taxation ratio, do not permit a sufficiently high calculation to be made. The quality of the figures appears extremely unsatisfactory to both the entrepreneur himself and to the outside observer and calls for extensive survey. The reason why these figures are subjected to such little investigation is mainly ascribed to the basic quality of the source material. I am not aware of any business in the operating structure previously described that operates a full-cost accounting system and I only know of few enterprises that employ merchandise costs based on any formula applied to preliminary costing. Most of them learn of their merchandise costs from a simple consumption calculation:
Initial stock based on before-season stocktaking
+ Incoming goods during the current season
- Final stock based on end-of-season stocktaking
= Consumption.
Consumption x 100: turnover = merchandise cost proportion. And the majority only become aware of this information during the next following season.

As regards the "holiday hotel" type, the main emphasis of the net product is on the proceeds obtained from rooms and beds where capacity utilisation demands cover, according to survey, merchandise costs by far. Here, the margin in even broader than is the case involving restaurants, namely between 9 % and 30 % and is explained by the considerable difference in the prices obtainable, substantiated by differing categories, the respective sites, regional infrastructure and the specific overall package offer.

Within the general spectrum relating to enterprise management, the purchasing side has meanwhile come to quality for a far lower ranking status than it assumed ten years ago. Although, on average, every third Schilling is expended on purchases, far greater priority is now accorded to such issues as personnel recruitment, business reconstruction or expansion, taxation, the five-day working week and a host of other topics. This is partly because a large number of undertakings are affiliated to purchasing organisations and the activities of these enterprises result in benefit while providing security to members and leaving them with more time to concentrate on other tasks. This tends to bring about a shift in priorities. The "side effects" caused by these organisations have led to a reduction of the overall pricing structure; the very demand for a "hogast price" made by non-members leads to subsequent improvements in what suppliers have to offer.

What should not be overlooked either, is the absence of serious requirements needed in order to master the demands brought about by forthcoming changes. When Austria becomes a member of the EC, competition amongst suppliers will undoubtedly be somewhat fiercer accompanied by lower purchase price standards.
Lack of planning capability and inadequate assessment of reliability and commitment is driving existing purchasing organisations to their limits. The relative increase in benefit, even if involving extra effort, is proceeding more and more on a reduced scale in the sense of "more of the same kind". The motto must surely read "Something different from what has gone before" and the experience of the trade organisations in their course of development over the past 15 years may very well serve as an example. For entrepreneurs not desirous of committing themselves to organisations, the alternative will be to accept traders` merchandise economy systems. Individual coupling up to modern electronic systems will presumably have to be ruled out due to cost and security reasons. What remains, apart from the purchase and trade organisations, is for data processing companies, now to be found offering software systems - primarily for the front office area - to set standards.

Why have these computer-aided merchandise economy systems so far failed to meet with success?

And let us face it, they have not (or not yet?) experienced any breakthrough!
The number of installed systems is marginal and where they do exist, only a fraction of them are operated successfully.
This may be attributed to the following causes:

- ➔ The variety of different products needed for running a restaurant its enormous. Consumer goods, goods subject to constant re-procurement in the food and non food merchandise segments may extend to ~ 2.000 different varieties. As far as the enterprise is concerned, this means maintaining vast quantities of data apart from the actual equipment.
  If items subject to periodical replenishment such as appointments, glasses, cutlery, chinaware etc. are to be recorded, the number of articles thus maintained may rise to ~ 5.000.
- ➔ The diversity of the range is just as extensive. If an entrepreneur wishes to compare the 2.000 items selected by him with those of other suppliers, he would need to have data available covering 10.000 products. Currently there is not a single supplier in the consumer goods business providing electronic data media information on products or prices.
- ➔ Incoming goods have to be recorded manually. Neither do suppliers provide any of these data on electronically readable media.
- ➔ Invoice checking is likewise a manual process for which no data media are available.
- ➔ In the majority of cases, in-house storage management is organised in such a way that merchandise distribution within the undertaking is effected without internal offsetting.
  Incoming goods = merchandise consumption. This also rules out the possibility of semi-automatic

ordering including automatic ordering suggestions. The introduction of a multi-stage storage organisation system is avoided for reasons pertaining to cost.

➔ The absence of an in-house storage management system obviously makes current stock checking impossible. Nevertheless, periodic stock-taking assessment is essentially facilitated if the system has access to updated prices.

➔ Recipe control is hampered by both rational and emotional obstacles. More often than not, recipes are not available or the chef is not prepared to compile them. The wide and individual range of dishes is laid down both by the chef and proprietor. And when the post of chef falls vacant again in the following season, everything undergoes change once more. A premium award system should be introduced for chefs for disclosing recipes of their creations.

➔ The systems are too complex, aggravated by over elaborate handling. In addition, evaluation proceeds on too large a scale with too many codes insufficiently condensed.

The experience gained by hoteliers in working with data processing systems, above all in the front office area, is reiterated in the sector of merchandise economy. Any system - regardless of whether it is based on good or bad criteria - is intended to make up for lack of organisation within the enterprise. A fatal error! Planned purchasing and optimum organisation are the prerequisites necessary for a merchandise economy system to function properly. Management skills are required!

In the purchasing department

In practice, frequent use is made of the term "purchasing" to denote the operative activity of the supply process. However, the main point of emphasis and attention should be placed on the strategic element-long-term, creative approach. The practice of thinking purely in terms of price must be allowed to give way to optimisation of the price:performance ratio. The following main tasks call for consideration:

- market research
- competent comparison of offered merchandise ranges
- order-placing negotiations.

As distinct from purchasing, the term "procurement" implies providing the enterprise with merchandise and supplies including own resources.

Development and formulation of the purchasing policy should be regarded as constituting an essential management function. And purchasing policy always forms part of the overall business policy, on the basis of which an enterprise defines its line of conduct in the market:

- What proportion is own-production output to assume?
- Should a dynamic course of development (frequent-change,constant introduction of new products) be aimed at?
- Is a high quality level to be attained/maintained?

As a result of entrepreneurial decision-making relating to "the proportion of own-production output being high" purchasing is restricted purely to basic products - thus eliminating convenience!"

The price policy adopted by an enterprise has an effect on purchase decisions:

- Is it worth having a large number of suppliers for the sake of price advantages?
- Is it desirable to limit the number of suppliers to a few and to build up permanent relations with these suppliers or it is desired to take every opportunity offered in the market and resort to price advantages by constantly changing suppliers?

Purchase policy is prevalent in all enterprises, sometimes without their actually being aware of it and without their having recorded it in writing. Despite this, it is of importance to be conscious of and lay down in writing the principles and objectives of purchasing policy as derived from business policy. Staff members must be familiar with the policy so as to be able to make the right decisions in cases where there is constant conflict of objectives.

An efficiently run purchasing department exercises an essential influence on the success of the enterprise:

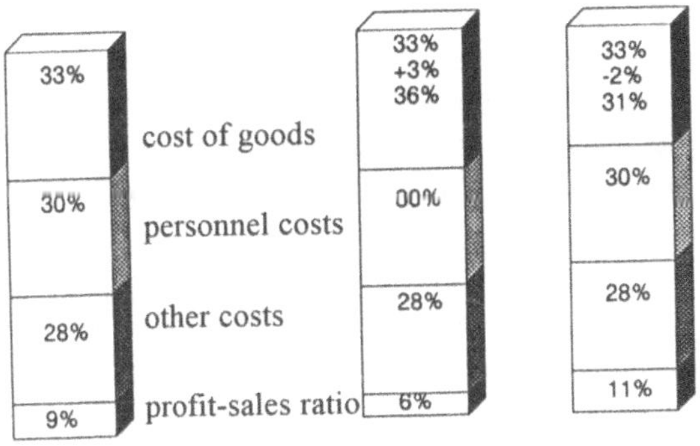

A) If the purchasing department fails to ward off price increases of +9%, the profit-sales ratio will fall by 1/3;

B) If, on the other hand, it succeeds in attaining price reductions by 6%, the profit-sales ratio will increase by 22%. This mains that if the cost structure cannot be changed, turnover extension of 22% is necessary in order to arrive at the same rate of return.

During the past number of years, considerable changes made to cost structure have led to a completely new form of cost structure emerging (but only when enterprises act accordingly). One example is meat, where merchandise expenditure rose from 39% to 45% as a result of purchasing pre-cut portions prepared ready for cooking. Counteracting his, it became possible to increase the previous net trading profit from 1.9%, due to the reduction of wage costs and other running expenses, to 6.7%.

Management skills are required!

In logistics

A survey carried out in spring 1993 and focusing on merchandise procurement at a 2-season holiday hotel was productive of the following results:

Breakdown of merchandise categories

	Purchase p.a.	Number of Deliveries	Ø Value of each Delivery
1. Meat, sausage	2.127.000	362	5.876
2. Milk, cheese	690.000	260	2.654
3. Fruit/veget.	577.000	430	1.342
4. Frozen foods	430.000	148	2.905
5. Breads/pastr.	210.000	245	857
6. Fish	684.000	246	2.780
7. Groceries	854.000	153	5.582
8. Wine, beverag	1.738.000	225	7.728
9. Non-food	387.000	55	7.036
TOTAL	7.697.000	2.124	3.624

- During the 1992 accounting year, the hotel effected purchase valued at AS 7,7 million.
- 58 suppliers are listed (points to heavy concentration).
- The food & beverage - and non-food - consumer goods section lists 1,400 items (likewise revealing heavy concentration).
- 262 opening days = 37 weeks, 12 weeks of which were in the peak season, leaving 25 weeks in the off-peak season.
- 2,124 deliveries over the year based on a 37-week opening period resulted in 57 arrivals from suppliers per week.
- The average merchandise value per delivery amounted to AS 3,623.-

(The lowest value in supplies effected by retail food trading companies amounts to five times as much).

The objective set was to define maximum possible concentration and to quantify the resulting advantages.

The food wholesaler is widening his assortment and adding to his range of services to cater for the specific requirements of hotels and restaurants (above all as regards fresh supplies). He is increasing the frequency of deliveries to 5 times per week during 12 weeks of the peak season and 3 times per week during the 24 weeks making up the off-peak season. By taking such action he is in a position to deliver 60% of the merchandise requirements.

	No. of Stops	Ø Value of Delivery
Previous:		
Total	2.124	3.624
Now:		
Wholesaler	135	22.000
Other Suppliers	1.050	4.500
Total	1.185	6.500

Economising potential as applied to in-house routine:

- Reduction from 2.214 to 1.185 stops = - 939
- Saving of time per merchandise take-over process: approx. 20 minutes = 313 hours
- Saving of time as applied to administration by reducing delivery notes and invoices: approx. 12 minutes = 188 hours
- Reduction in cost 500 hours Ø AS 180.- = AS 90.000.-

The economising potential arising as an outcome of concentrating on one single partner and commitment to accept deliveries for one year results in a reduction of merchandise costs by AS 465.000.- (-6%)

For those concerned - both the hotelier and food wholesaler, the realisation of this project is tantamount to a radical change in procedure and the previous cultural setting:

➔ Departure from standard level to professionalism.

➔ Departure from isolated combat to integrated partner (willingness and ability to co-operate is the new quality).

➔ Departure from individual solutions in favour of the system-approach.

This model brings us to the following conclusion:

The future will be decided by integrated data and communication systems as far as certain demands are met.

Data providers will come up with standard solutions applicable to the sector of merchandise economy or management, that is solutions not integrated in a tie-in system. (Refer to hogadata). This enables users to obtain important data for in-house service comparisons:
- Product/merchandise group analyses
- ABC-assessments
- marginal costing
- stock-taking differences
- inter company comparisons

Of importance to ensuring effective co-operation in EOP (exchange-of-experience) groups is not only willingness to exchange figures, bur also the quality and reproducibility of data.

Resistance applied to the sale and the introduction of individual installations will be encountered by:
- The entrepreneur himself. He is not likely to effect his decision until having realised the utility value of new data technologies. Hitherto, his priority has been centred on finding suitable measures to control merchandise flow. He needs to be convinced of the benefit to be obtained from informative data, having previously regarded himself capable of managing the undertaking without technical means of assistance.
- Members of staff. Frequent personnel changes necessitate continual training of new staff. The effect of personnel being familiar with standard systems, such as in the front office area, and being able to transfer this knowledge to the respective undertakings will only materialise on a long-term basis. A merchandise economy system will only become stabilised if a member of the entrepreneur`s family himself assumes the task of "coaching".
- Cost. It should be borne in mind that hardware costs will no longer continue to weigh heavily and that software, together with software maintenance prices, will be within the scope of the existing and familiar front office systems. Nevertheless, personnel costs will constitute the greatest factor by far. The circumstance that the entire flow of data is required to be processed manually and that this work needs to be relocated or sited not within the environment of the accounts department but rather the purchasing department makes it necessary to employ a member of staff for this purpose. Whether or not system providers will be required to provide support in this area remains to be seen.
- In-house organisation. The decision to introduce data processing technology in general is determined by its acceptance. This alone will serve to improve the organisation system. Realisation of the fact that the introduction of data processing systems calls for stable organisation structures has been an experience which many enterprises have come to learn fairly late and which has turned out all the more painful.

Personally speaking, I estimate the prospects relating to high installation density of isolated data systems to be negligible. Absence of the communications element - the tie-in dialogue - will prove an obstacle.

Only two groups fulfil the necessary prerequisites for the realisation of integrated systems:
Purchasing or co-operative societies and food wholesalers or a combination of the two.
The aims pursued by both groups are by and large identical even if the motives tend to differ. In providing an extensive palette of services, both succeed in attaining improved and powerful market positions.
The range of services will comprise:
- Servicing the information module. Hitherto, exchange of information between central divisions (dealers and co-operative organisations) and members / customers has continued to proceed by post. Order-sets, circulars, special offers, lists of suppliers and terms and conditions constitute primary sources of information. In future, these will be made available via electronic data media. To ensure efficiency in operating the system, it will be absolutely essential to clarify with the customer

all aspects concerning the handling as well as the content of the data provided. Not all data have to be made available, but only those relating to the enterprise concerned. Data maintenance, e.g. product master data, must only be effected in respect of those items or products purchased in the enterprise. Fully integrated systems used in the dialogue process serve to provide the customer with access to information not required by him permanently on his own system.

- Servicing of the incoming goods module. Recording of incoming merchandise precisely itemised is essentially facilitated by the automatic transfer of suppliers into the merchandise economy system, thus removing a considerable obstacle to the running of the enterprise.
- Servicing of the ordering module. The function of recording the ordered quantities is supported by information on consumption from previous periods. Recording is carried out by means of mobile units of data acquisition equipment, transfer of the order being effected to the dealer by telephone. Information on special offers, current daily prices or changes made to ranges and assortments can be conveyed more quickly, thus ensuring that the orderer is equipped with "real data".
- Servicing of the accounting module. The invoices are sent out by means of data media. Invoice checking and recording is carried out automatically.

The above description is but a preview as applied to the catering trade. Currently, there are no integrated merchandise economy systems yet to be found operating in Austria. Nevertheless, I am certain that within a few years from now, the trend already accomplished in the retail food trade will be realised in the catering branch as well.

The trend will emanate from those wholesale food dealers who are desirous of consolidating and enhancing their position as partners to the catering trade.
It is they who will offer bonds of alliance to those enterprises able and willing to concentrate up to 60 % of their purchase potential on one dealer. As regards a further 20 % of the requirements, they will offer to make arrangements with special suppliers to act as "forwarders" for them in assuming logistics. The resulting effects on cost reduction and increased earnings for the respective enterprises have already been described above in the example of a hotel undertaking. For ecologically sensitive locations this is a basic approach to bring about drastic reduction of delivery movements and the inevitable traffic load.
These wholesalers will likewise act as essential suppliers of information for the merchandise economy systems.
They will create compatibility between the customer`s and dealer`s data processing systems, thus facilitating linkage up to their merchandise economy systems. Employing electronic order-sets, they will provide ranges of merchandise adapted to the customer`s requirements. In order to attain a high degree of concentration, wholesalers will be required to co-ordinate their organisation systems more precisely to the specific requirements of the branch. The class of wholesaler likely to achieve success is he who is able to combine streamlined dealer organisation facilities with the degree of flexibility needed within the branch. Here again, this calls for management quality to be applied. As a result of the high quality of the decision-making data they provide, modern, efficient data and communication systems can prove a valuable aid to good management though incapable of replacing good business executives. On the contrary, these people are indispensable for their proper functioning.

TIS Tourism Information System for the Tyrol

Arno Ebner

TIS GmbH

ABSTRACT

TIS stands for "Tourism Information System" and is an information network which currently supports 100 decentralized users. It has been in operation since 1991. TIS is used solely for information purposes, and has no reservation functions. The author discusses the general touristic and political background leading to the creation of the system, and the various goals that the information system can serve.

1. Introduction

Modern information systems are one of the keys to corporate growth and to the further development of whole industries, all the more so as the two major trends on the marketplace today, namely *fragmentation* and *globalization,* both contribute to the growing complexity of business operations. National and international organizations have become increasingly dependent on powerful computer systems at all levels of operation, i.e. production, sales order processing, monitoring, documentation and communication.

The decision to implement such complex systems cannot be taken solely on the basis of "hard-cash" cost/benefit relationships, as it is rarely possible to quantify the costs, let alone the benefits, with any degree of accuracy. The arguments involved therefore relate more to qualitative factors and strategic considerations with regard to guaranteeing future options. [1]

Such systems have not been installed to date in the Austrian national incoming tourism industry, mainly due to the complex and small-scale structures of the supply side and the absence of an appropriate communications infrastructure. On the other hand, the airlines and tour operators act on a worldwide basis and with global infrastructures including computer-based information and reservation systems. Within a tourism industry, as it continues to grow in economic importance, there is therefore a discrepancy between the highly professional international operators and carriers with their sophisticated data processing and communications networks on the one hand, and a small-business local supplier community lacking in advanced support systems and often the relevant knowledge on the other.

This situation is clearly unsatisfactory for the healthy development of tourism at the regional level, and the solution adopted in the Tyrol, Austria's most advanced tourism region, with a wide choice of summer and winter vacation facilities, has been to develop what is now known as the Tourism Information System for the Tyrol, or TIS for short.

2. Tourism in Austria

Tourism is a key industry in Austria. Total annual turnover for the leisure industry as a whole comes to about AS 400 billion (approx. $ 35 billion). In 1990 Austria's foreign currency earnings from tourism came to AS 133.7 billion, which covers 70% of the country's trade deficit. [3] For its part, the Tyrol is the most important tourist region in Austria, and is responsible for almost 50% of the country's foreign currency earnings. In 1992 the Tyrol, with 46.3 million bednights, accounted for approximately 35% of the Austrian total. Within the Tyrol itself tourism is the source of 25-35% of gross regional product.

A typical feature of the Austrian tourist industry is the institution of the public tourist board, organized at the national, regional and local levels. These tourist boards have primarily marketing functions, and can be described in general as the marketing division of Austria's incoming tourism industry as a whole. This again is a result of the country's small-business supplier structure, with a preponderance of family businesses, which in themselves pay relatively little attention to public relations and marketing. This is left to the tourist boards, which are financed by the local tourist industry via mandatory contributions. And yet these bodies have only a supporting function. They promote the product, but they do not sell it. That is left to the individual supplier or to incoming agents operating mainly at the regional level. Basically, the function of the tourist boards is that of a non-computerized information system, gathering information about the local, regional or national tourist product and distributing the information to the relevant markets worldwide. At the same time, tourist boards provide local suppliers with the information they need on current trends, the general market situation, and the national and international competition. They also have certain overriding public, social, ecological and ethical functions. To that extent their task is twofold: to promote a product and inform the market, i.e. the clients, on the one hand, and to deliver information to the local suppliers, on the other.

Today there are 254 local tourist boards in the Tyrol. Along with the regional authorities and the Federation of Hoteliers, they are affiliated to the Tyrolean Tourist Board ("Tirol Werbung" in German). The task of "Tirol Werbung" is to promote the Tyrol as a tourist product at the regional level and to offer support to the local tourist boards. The various tourist boards thus form one large network, and the local boards all participate in the formulation of overall marketing strategies. Equally "Tirol Werbung", although effective in its supporting function, has no independent decision-making powers. This ensures that different interests and points of view within the industry are always respected.

The same structure and division of labour also applies at the level of the Austrian National Tourist Board ("Österreich Werbung"), which runs 24 Austrian National Tourist Offices in the fifteen countries of the world which provide Austria with most of her visitors.

3. The TIS system

TIS has been set up as an information-based system serving two goals and comprising two corresponding information modules: an information module designed to inform clients about the Tyrol as a tourism product, and a marketing/management information module designed to provide the relevant market data. The latter module is for the use of the local tourist boards and suppliers only.

The information module

The main subjects in the system's information module are listed below. The system employs a database manager that permits the links between the various information classes to be defined as required, with a database metastructure that keeps a check of the database relations.

Traffic and weather information

Snow conditions
Weather reports
Road and traffic conditions
Water temperatures for bathing
Glacier conditions

All entries are structured geographically (by resort or district).

Tourist products and services

Sports facilities (skilifts, tennis courts etc.)

Rentals
Courses
Sports events
Special offers and programmes

In addition to their geographical structure, these items are also listed by the activity involved (e.g. tennis, skiing, hobbies) and also by the equipment required. The database also links the supplier to a detailed description of the product or service. The link between an activity and the equipment required (e.g. skiing and skis) is defined in the metastructure to support efficient query procedures.

Events

Events are listed with the exact location, event type (sports, cultural) and the precise activity involved (e.g. downhill ski race - skiing, opera - music).

Restaurants and accommodation

Overnight facilities
Camping
Restaurants

This is perhaps the most important section of the tourist information provided, and the items are listed in full detail (see fig.1).

Family products and services

The family is currently one of the main focuses of tourism policy, and family products and services therefore represent a main information class in the database. The section contains a full description of facilities that specifically cater to families with children. In addition, the family facility attribute is part of the relational database structure and can be applied to any item where relevant.

Public transport and timetables

Timetables
Historical trains, boats, etc.
Specific tourist routes, e.g. toll roads in the mountains

The user can enter his/her place of departure and required destination, plus desired travel time and means of transport (e.g. plane, train), and the system generates an individual itinerary and schedule.

Local information

Resort services, e.g. post offices, travel agencies, tourist board, medical care, etc.
Routes to the resort
General information
Places of interest/sightseeing

The relation between locality and district is administered in this section as a resort may belong to more than one district.

User access is via an interface with a menu structure, with additional user convenience available in the form of abbreviated search inputs and direct switching between menu levels. In general, user-friendliness and fast learning were the main design principles.

Number of TIS system partners - annual overview

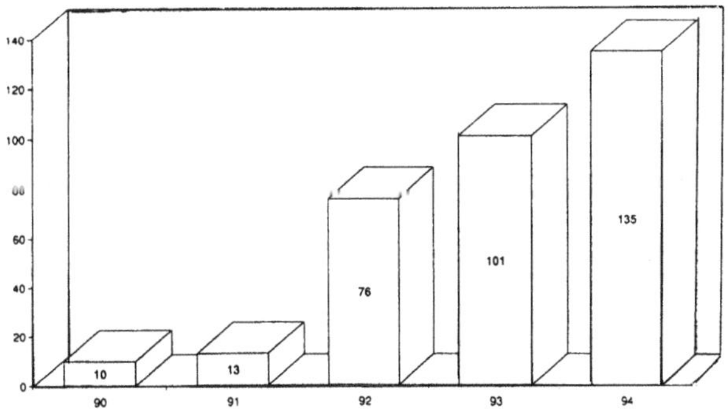

The management information module

This module is of central importance for the acceptance of the system by the local tourist boards. It also represents a milestone of a professionalization strategy for the boards, involving not only the provision of computer support but also the introduction of modern management know-how. The local boards normally employ a staff of between two and fifteen, who typically have had no contact with information technology in the past and no access to the type of data and tools listed below. The contents of the management information module were based on a questionnaire sent to all local boards.

Addresses
This is a central address pool comprising all addresses listed within the organization, i.e. tourist boards, tour operators, journalists, etc. as well as members of the public who have asked for information.

Organizational charts
This unit contains the Who's Who and the organizational structure of "Tirol Werbung" and related organizations including the Austrian National Tourist Board.

Subsidies
This section lists information on where and how suppliers can apply for financial support and what conditions have to be met.

Promotional materials
The material is classified by type (brochure, slide, video), motif, source and price.

Media data
The media data unit comprises a brief description of the media plus prices, publication schedules and advertising rates.

Promotion groups
Suppliers with similar products who have formed regional promotion groups are listed.

Press conferences
The information includes who is speaking where, when and about what.

Media advertising schedule
This unit shows who is advertising ("Tirol Werbung" or local board) when and in which media, including the theme, opportunities for participation and the price.

Trade fairs
The information includes name, date, venue, prices, organizer, and how to participate.

Marketing diagram
This is a list of special events, including aims, dates and a general description.

Statistics
The statistics listed relate to both the various source countries and competitor destinations, and include such items as bednights and arrivals for the various categories, periods and districts, plus statistics on the supplier industry and infrastructure.

Mail box
This offers an electronic mail facility.

Educational programmes and courses
All courses that are relevant for visitors are stored, including subject, location, date and name of teacher/trainer.

Literature
The unit lists relevant articles and books plus sources.

Dictionary
This is a glossary of common words in various languages.

Decision support tools
The tools offered include time series analyses, statistical tools and market portfolio calculations.

System architecture

One of the principal design goals was to strengthen the autonomy and flexibility of the local tourist boards. For that reason a centralized system was rejected in the initial planning phase and a distributed approach chosen. This permits data to be stored locally, where they are most frequently used, which thus reduces data transport costs. The central office operates as a communications server and is responsible for data distribution.

Like the central office, the remote users also have access to the entire database. Updates are distributed to every site daily so that data accessed from any point in the system is one day old at most, which is adequate for purely information purposes. The system also offers regional flexibility in that the local tourist boards can define their own data requirements. Although each tourist board is supplied with the complete infrastructure, it may fill out only the subjects which are relevant. Thus the local tourist boards are responsible for keeping their data up to date. Local data input requirements are defined on a geographical basis, while "Tirol Werbung" is responsible for all central information.

On the other hand, a *fully* distributed database approach was not selected for a number of reasons:

a) The telecommunications infrastructure available could not support such a service at a reasonable price.

b) The type of information usage does not explicitly call for such an approach (one-day updating is sufficient).

c) The users have to learn to manage their systems and ensure that they are always available. Above all, the hardware in use at the local boards would not be able to handle a fully distributed database system.

d) The system needs to be tested - and this is now being done - in terms of both the loads imposed on the lines of communication and local demand for non-local information. The results can then be used to assess the need for a distributed environment in a pure information system.

Updating itself is performed overnight in two cycles. First, central office calls up all local updates. The data are added to the central database and a consistency check is performed. Then the individual local data packages are prepared and distributed.

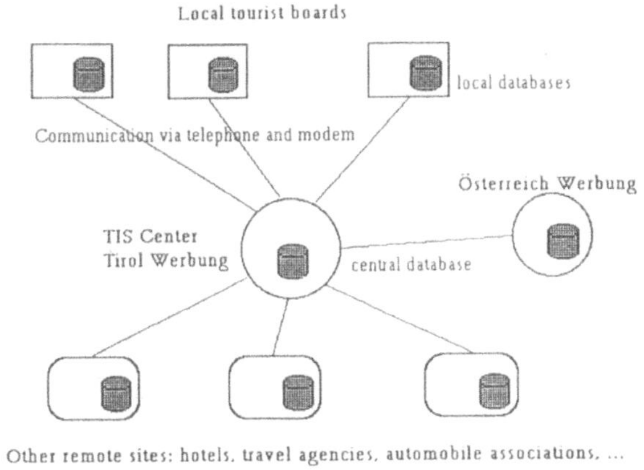

TIS network (in the form of a star)

An IBM RS 6000 is used as the host in the central office, and communications within the system are handled by modem and telephone lines. The communications and update software is modular in design, and the modules can be changed - to use a different protocol, for example - without having to modify the application. The system is written in a 4GL database language and is independent of the operating system. At present the various users work with MS-DOS, Unix, AIX, Novell Netware and OS/2, although IBM compatible PC's running under MS-DOS are the most common configuration.

4. Present status

TIS is now run by TIS GmbH, a company owned 100 % by "Tirol Werbung". This has advantages in terms of structural change and scope for future developments. Strategic planning and management are the responsibility of the operating company, while software development and implementation has been contracted out. The system is currently used by a hundred local tourist boards, Austrian National Tourist Offices (in Paris, Amsterdam and Vienna), the Austrian, Dutch and German automobile associations (ÖAMTC, ADAC, ANWB), Minitel, Telesystem Tiroler Kabel TV and START Amadeus.

Quality of Training

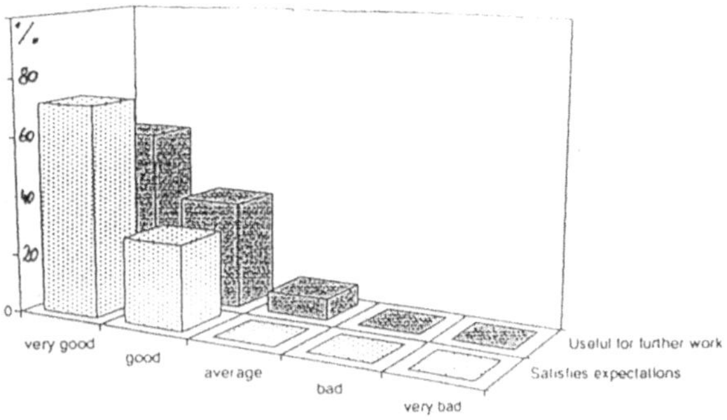

Quality of TIS Service

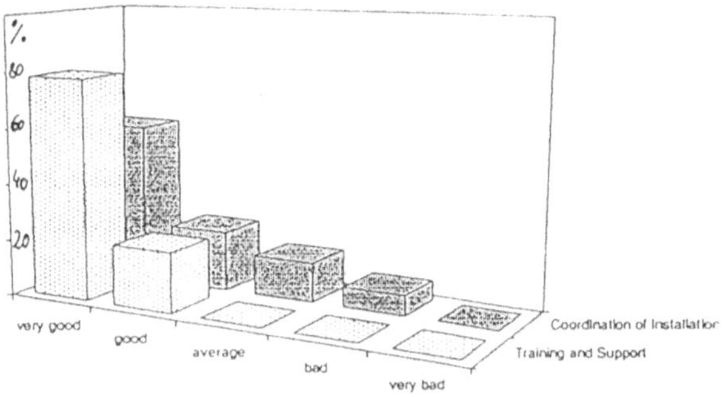

Quality of TIS Software

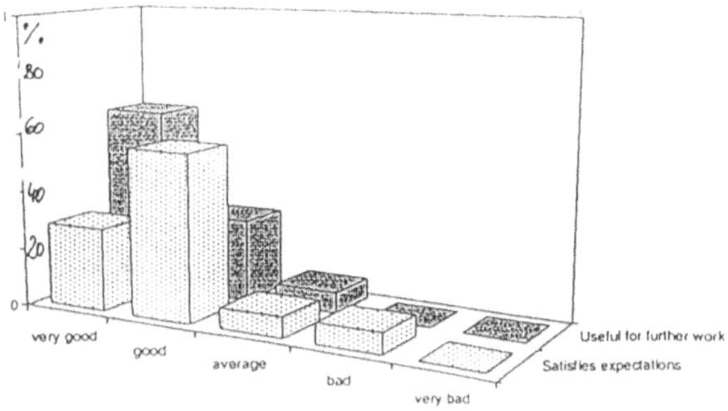

Results of questionnaire, submitted to the tourist boards

5. Long-term system capabilities

From experience with the system to date it is reasonable to assume that TIS is going to prove a useful tool - among others - in dealing with long-term problems within the tourist industry. The following table lists a number of relevant areas and the problem-solving potential of the information system implemented.

The supply industry

Lack of organization and communications
The improvement to communications available from TIS is obvious. Local operators and organizations can interact and upgrade their performance without detriment to others. The availability of information on the competition and market forces makes suppliers, including small businesses, more aware of the needs of the marketplace. This communication aspect benefits both the private and the public sector, including the Tyrolean Tourist Board itself, which automatically receives the information it needs for efficient working.

Overlapping competition from the small business structure
A knowledge of the various products and services available on the local market is a key to effective alliances and co-operative activities. TIS therefore increases contacts between businesses. This does not induce market concentration but collaboration. Small-size suppliers may also be made less vulnerable and more flexible in reacting to new market requirements. TIS provides access to the relevant information.

Excess capacities and the unbalanced utilization of tourist resources
Suppliers can structure their products with respect to capacity constraints and can gain better access to distribution facilities. The information available from TIS can be used for improving usage patterns along the time axis and in geographical distribution.

Low level of expertise

The level of knowledge and professionalism can be improved by installing the communications infrastructure, by offering related training facilities, and by providing permanent access to the information and tools available via the management information module.

The changing structure of demand

The emancipation of tourists makes them

more selective before their vacation

more active during their vacation

more critical in terms of product information

With the help of such a system tourists can be better informed before and during their vacation, i.e. at home and in the Tyrol. Furthermore, information makes for enhanced product transparency, and tourists who are well informed are also more critical, which in turn may lead to a better product.

More holidays, shorter stays

This tendency requires a faster information flow. That is what a system like TIS can provide in all the details, whereas GDS and tour operators have not been able to do so to date. To that extent, the system should also be useful for international tour operators and GDS.

More late bookings

This aspect again calls for better access to information, which may additionally support reservation systems, too.

Market globalization

In the face of international competition, such an information system enhances the position of the Tyrol as the first holiday region to offer such a service. With respect to other destinations, it constitutes a competitive advantage at the strategic level.

6. Conclusion

TIS is the first tourism information system in the strict sense of the term on the international market. It is performing well in the environment in which it has been installed, and there are strong indications that it could become a valuable strategic tool for the Tyrolean tourism industry.

With reference to the problem-solving potential of TIS as listed in Table 4, such an information system should also be considered in the context of the ongoing debate on flexible specialization and industrial districts. Although it would be beyond the scope of this brief paper to provide an in-depth discussion of the application of this theory to tourism and tourist areas, a number of key concepts and features such as regional integration, small business units and intercompany co-operation are also to be found in the TIS approach. On the other hand, whereas this theory analyzes industrial developments in specific regions like the "third Italy" and describes the preconditions to be met for such developments, TIS has been installed to induce a specific process or modification in a region that is already well developed. It is up to the local, regional and national authorities to create an environment in which the process can take place. In addition to general financial and legal measures, the creation of the necessary technological infrastructure, including such systems as TIS, must be one of the basic requirements. This does not mean substituting private enterprise and entrepreneurial spirit, but rather encouraging it. To that extent, TIS is more than a tourism information system; it is a significant political and economic measure in the overall development of the Tyrol.

For the future, a number of enhancements are planned for the TIS system with the aim of accessing additional channels of distribution.

a) Development work is now being carried out on a complex multimedia system based on touch-screen technology to communicate relevant information to the tourist or client directly.

b) TIS data are to be made available to international distribution systems. In this context, it is important to ensure that the product *Tyrol* is communicated in its entirety and not just parts of it. In addition, the information will also be supplied to home consumer networks such as Minitel in France.

c) TIS will most probably be developed into a nationwide system to be called TIS Austria.

The development and management of a system like TIS must be viewed as a continuous process and not just as a single project. TIS represents an organizational measure rather than a technological solution to improve the competitive posture of the Tyrolean tourism industry on an increasingly complex market.

7. Bibliography

1. Werthner H., Wirtschaftsinformatik, 35 (1993)

2. Pyke F., Becattini G., Sengenberger W. (eds.), Industrial districts and local economic regeneration. International Institute for Labour Studies, Geneva, 1990.

3. Tourism in Austria 1990 (in German: Der Fremdenverkehr in Österreich im Jahre 1990). Österreichisches Statistisches Zentralamt, Heft 1.011. Wien, 1991.

Telecommunication in Rural Areas

Sixtus Lanner

Arbeitsgemeinschaft Ländlicher Raum

According to opinion polls, the cultural landscape is of high importance for tourism. What the term "cultural landscape" actually denotes is hardly ever investigated. There is common agreement that a multitude of variables have to be combined in order to convey the notion of a "touristic cultural landscape". Agriculture is an essential factor within this concept.

"We have to convince as many farmers as possible to remain within their surroundings. There is no other way to preserve a a cultural landscape created in the course of milleniums", stresses the EC Commission.

According to a study carried out by the Fessel Institute in 1992, two third of the people questioned list rural agriculture in the first place (65%), six out of ten denote the support of trade and business within their region as the most important measures for the preservation of the rural area's characteristics and finally, less than one third consider the continued existence of the domestic tourist industry as top priority.

With the term **rural** urban people very often associate the romantic idea of a farm with happy hens, a number of cows, sheep or pigs, hardly any (noisy) machines, no plant-protective agents and no artificial fertilizers. Many farmers would prefer this kind of agriculture. To be internationally competitive, however, they have to choose a different economic strategy, yet not necessarily in favour of mass production. Many farmers in topographically difficult, yet touristically interesting regions decide on "regional specialties", others, in their turn, have to look for extra income. Nowadays, two out of three Austrian farmers are dependent on an additional job - with rising tendancy.There is much discussion going on about the position of sideline-agriculture. Some consider it a cumbersome competition, others - among them much to our regret the EC - regard sideline-agriculture only as a transitional stage on the way to migration or even complete surrender.
I have every reason to believe that the protection of the cultural landscape not only depends on the **cultivation** of the countryside but I consider settlement policies as equally relevant. We can only protect the social structure of this area by looking upon the rural area and its development as a whole, integrating all professional and population groups, the sideline-farmers being of special importance. I do not consider sideline-agriculture as a transitional stage but as a socio-politically important permanent state. This requires that we provide attractive jobs **within the region itself**, comprising for example the refinement of rural raw materials, the field of tourism, traditional craft and trade or even a completely new area, namely telecommunication.

Sliding from Time to Space

The industrial society was characterized by a trend towards centralization. In the information society, however, other tracks have become possible: efficient, decentralized structures, thus creating new prospects for the countryside. Thanks to better work sharing the urban areas would suffer far less from traffic and environmental problems. The advantages are self-evident:

- less commuting
- more leisure time
- less energy consumption
- protection of the environment
- reinforcement of the economic power of the region

The species of the "time-sliders" with their flexible working hours might be followed by the "space-sliders", the latter ones alternatively working in their office, at home or in a telehouse.

There may be townspeople who also own a house in the countryside and who will henceforth not only spend their leisure time there but who will probably also fulfill an ever-growing part of their professional duties from within the country. Above all it will be possible for the intellectual elite of rural areas to get a job in their home region more easily, thus restoring creative power and political influence.

The rural areas might be offered new opportunities and prospects via an interesting sideline. Experiences in our neighbouring countries have proved very promising:

The Swiss government, for example, set up a branch of the national post office in Schiers, a small mountain village in

Grisons, employing via telecommunication within the exchange service 111 a staff of about 50 people who therefore do not have to commute from other regions.

The Bavarian national government has dislocated the central penalty authority from Munich to Vietach near Straubing, making 160 employees benefit from this, something that could not have become possible without telecommunication.

Even more revolutionary seems the "space-sliding model" of the ministerial bureaucracy in The Hague/The Netherlands. Starting from the Ministry of Transport approximately 400 civil servants of the Ministry of Finance and the Ministry of Economics work about three days a week in their home region and only have to commute to the central authority the remaining two days.

These models display the manifold employment opportunities in rural areas offered by a new, ecologically beneficial technology which may give rise to completely new perspectives for the preservation of the cultural landscape.

The Telehouse - an Institutional Service for the Region

Of course the new technology affords financial means. There would be no sense in purchasing those expensive facilities and devices individually. Therefore, we have chosen in Austria an organizational model for **joint** use of technical facilities.

Lets recall the times when an individual telephone connection for each household was far from being a matter of course. In order to get into contact with the outside world, public telephones had to be consulted.
The telehouse on the whole works according to the same rules and principles. The fundamental idea in this case is also based on a common institution that can be used by everybody against payment. The three most important goals thereby are:

- Training and further education within the region
- Service for small and medium businesses, resulting in the reinforcement of the regional economic capacities
- the creation of new jobs via decentralized structures

By means of six pilot projects we want to test the advantages but also the drawbacks of this strategy.

First of all, telehouse proves to be an important trigger, offering in many cases a new feeling of uprise within the region itself.

Educational programmes within the region are fairly easy to organize. At the telehouse Michelbeuern/Salzburg for example, about 1.000 interested persons have been trained so far. In the course of the training cooperation proves successful as practiced for example between the telehouse Hartberg/Styria and the Institute for Economical Promotion.

The service for small and medium businesses is by far more difficult. The threshold fear of this new technology is an aspect not to be underestimated, often combined with a lack of ideas and of imagination as to what kind of support this new technology might offer. The head of the telehouse ought to be capable of offering made-to measure solutions to the plant managers, guaranteeing beforehand that certain working processes will thus become less expensive, of higher quality and of better performance.

The most difficult task is the creation of new jobs via decentralized structures. Obviously, it is hard to imagine that somebody can do a good job if they cannot be constantly supervised. Public institutions like the central post office (compare the example of Switzerland mentioned above), the ministries (see the example of the Netherlands) or the provincial governments (like in the example of Bavaria) have shown hardly any willingness so far to take that risk.

In the field of tourism there exist promising approaches. The telehouse Freiwald/Upper Austria for example is just setting up a cooperation between the Upper Muehlviertel, the South of Bohemia and the Bavarian Forest.

The telehouse Michelbeuern is also an example of establishing a platform for "European village renewal". Austria might achieve an anticipation position within Europe due to its rich experience in this area. At present, an already existing basic model cannot be further developed due to the lack of financial means.

Eschenau/Lower Austria has discovered an interesting gap in the market by administrating and caring for the so called eco-points-model for true to nature agriculture.
By the way, at the tollhouse Michelbeuern there developed as a by-product a platform for the exchange of used musical instruments which is also well received by Switzerland and Germany.

The telehouse in Zwettl/Lower Austria focuses on a collection of agricultural supplies and offers services within the region such as office work for small businesses. A branch office - the telehouse Litschau - as well as cooperations with partners in the Czech Republic and Upper Austria represent the beginning of supra-regional network connection.

The telehouse of St. Georgen in the Innviertel/Upper Austria is only in initial stage so far, its primary goal is to support farmers via the joint use of expensive feeding or fertilizing programmes for an optimum and hence low-cost application.

The development and ne work connection, respectively, of rural areas via telecommunication might also solve an unsatisfactory situation within scientific collaboration between agriculture and tourism. There is a high demand within the tourist and hotel industry for high-quality products from our farmers. There is often uncertainty as to where these goods can be purchased. In this case a useful network connection via telecommunication might provide valuable information exchange and coordination.

Following the Austrian example, Luxemburg established a telehouse in Arsdorf one year ago. The EC grants generous subsidies for it within the Leader-Programme

The idea of the telehouse originally comes from Scandinavia. There exist equally successful models in Germany, France and Switzerland.

The whole of Austria at local rates

One of the reasons why telecommunication meets with difficulties in rural areas is due to the high transmission charges of the post.
"No employer in his right senses is ready to finance a telecommunication job in the countryside as long as transmission costs for the same amount of data are up to 16 times higher than within a congested area with a digital automatic exchange", recently wrote me a young entrepreneur from the Waldviertel.
Uniform rates as with the letter-post should be aimed at in the long term. Only if the product "information" is available at an equal price for all consumers and can be distributed at the same cost, a central business structure will have a fair chance.

Today, it is generally understood that efficient motorways constitute an important prerequisite for regional development. The expenses for road construction are met by the community. "Tele-roads", however, should pay their way - according to common agreement. As long as this unequal handling of the costs of infra-structure is being carried out, remote areas will have little or no chance at all.

Finally, it is necessary to reconsider regional subsidies. Technological centres at the peripheries of congested areas are being generously supported. For decentralized use of the idea of telecommunication, however, there are hardly any means available.

"In the 90's the supply of telematic systems will grow rapidly within the cities ... yet, there will also be the need for appropriate telecommunication systems and services in rural areas in order to contribute substantially to the revival of the countryside. The courses for this must already be set today lest the prospects offered should not be lost", as stated in a declaration of principles of the EC Commission.

Impulses for the countryside

The countryside needs a perspective of hope. If we want young active people to decide in favour of this area, we have to emphasize more than ever the positive aspects of the rural area.
The countryside has a high value of living, leisure and recreation, an almost unaffected environment and clear structures, thus offering more prospects for participation and creation in public life and it might soon be particularly appreciated - due to its qualities of life - as a "productive factor of some higher system". Already today we are talking about the so-called K- (or C- in English) regions which are synonymous for know-how, competence, creativity, culture, craft and communication.

What is most important is to combine the positive aspects of the rural structures with the modern technological possibilities. Then we will no longer have to worry about the protection and existence of our rural cultural landscape.

Standard specifications as the basis for salesoriented tourism

Rainer Blencke

Institut für Freizeit- und Tourismusberatung

Particularly in context with the internationalization of its fields of activity the entire economy within the country and abroad is focusing on so-called standards.

The development in data processing, which is a relatively new branch in the field of operating systems, makes evident where a lack of standardization can lead to, as it faces a virtual flood of different technical and incompatible possibilities. Especially tourism in Germany has suffered from this situation for years. This may be a reason for the fact that up to now technical marketing structures have actually not been set up in Germany. In particular with applications software which is built up upon operating systems problems can suddenly occur if the module of choice is not compatible with the hardware available or one only just purchased.

So standards are of great significance in this field in order to counteract the problem mentioned above and other difficulties.

Basically standards are "the uniform establishing of terms, kinds, sizes, shapes, colours, measurements, labelings, types, materials, samples, recipees and suchlike that are acknowledged by those concerned. In contrast to historical standards (standards of taste, measurements like cubit, fathom, foot, meter etc.) modern standardization results from an effort to standardize in accordance with definite principles aiming at uniformization and consequently in order to create a basis for order and a run-up in performance within the fields of engineering, administration, economy and science hence as a means of rationalization."(Gablers Wirtschaftslexikon)

In his book "Communication with ISDN" Dr. Horst Edgar Martin defines the necessity for standardization and standard specification in communication thus in information exchange in touristic systems as follows:

Communication is built upon agreements which the communicating partners have developed for their co-operation or upon those given. For this reason each communicating activity, i.e. each information exchange, presupposes certain agreements between the sender, i.e. the source of information, and the recipient, i.e. the information seeker. In general these agreements should include as many partners as possible. Therefore a communication standard is the basis of our global communication-system for the transmission of voice, text, visual portrayal and data. Enginners had to create such standards anew for technical communication, whereas we automatically use such standards in linguistic communication. Information does not only have to be exchanged amongst people: There is a necessity for far more extensive agreements, than for example in linguistic communication, with equipment that is used for communication suchlike facsimile terminals, manufacturing control or data-processing institutions.

In this connection we talk of communication between the partners man and process. Communication in an area with only one language is called communication within a closed group. Only those who master the language code of this section of the population or who have learned it can exchange information unrestrictedly.

Yet the ideal communication would take place from anyone to anyone without converting nor barriers. This is how we have to look at communication between processes, too. In order to make life easier for themselves producers or users define certain characteristicts for a closed (probably only producer-specific) system and lay them down as specification, that is as the language of the system in a system specification.
Standards and standard specifications are not to be seen as static elements, but as a developing process, even though nowbody will be willing nor capable to question the DIN A4 format. Yet, were standards static, unleaded petrol wouldn´t exist today, since the DIN-standard for leaded petrol is a different one than that for unleaded petrol.

Also the institutions that introduce and fix these standards are not, as is often supposed, law-making bodies, but associations, organizations and suchlike, which are supported by a multitude of private-sector companies.

For the tourist industry (in particular in the field of incoming) and with view to our subject of today this means that we could compare the situation in this branch to that in Babylon after the disaster.

Quite a lot of marketers, contributors, tourist industry institutions etc. work on their target groups with their own phraseology and conditions.

The means and formulations with the help of which guests are presented offers is quite interesting. The guest is expected to speak or understand "all languages" that have developed in the length and breadth of the country. We expect our target group, our customers to kindly adapt to us, i.e. to the producer or marketer.

Be the guest so kind as to make the effort to recognize or read all our coinages. Do we want the guest to be able to read our accomodation indices at all?

I asked of myself what we ask of our guests by taking the trouble to rummage through about 50 accomodation indices. For everyone who does the same the discussion for or against standards and standard specifications is superfluous, I believe.

The initiative of the German tourist industry association (DFV, Deutscher Fremdenverkehrsverband), the German Association of Travel Agencies (DRV, Deutscher Reisebüroverband) and the German Association of the Hotel and Catering Industry (DEHOGA, Deutscher Hotel- und Gaststättenverband) which aims at the development of a standard in Germany has triggered off a lot of reaction.

This standard, TIN, is being introduced in Germany since the beginning of this year and it is applied in many informational meetings and seminars at the basis. One aim surely is to minimize the unvafourable conditions mentioned above.

So TIN in Germany is a beginning. Yet during the first seminars at the basis it already became evident that expecially the categorization/classification is facing some opposition. Especially the Bavarian model deviates from that of TIN (touristic information standard). This association takes on far more tasks - which it executes with the aid of a private limited liability company - than it was provided for in the beginning.

Yet the most important point is, that the Incoming-Organisations don`t become Supreme Judges but can refer to numerous committees for classification.

The fact, that individual activities in the single federal states can lead to deviations and therefore be obstructive to a transparent supply, however, is quite disadvantageous.

Another problem to be mentioned in this context is comparability and transparence on an international scale. A guest who knows the German system of stars as will expect these symbols to have a similar or the same meaning like in Germany.

Is it only a vision or will it be possible to have a uniform system of classification within a certain area (for example within the EC) or is such a situation desireable at all?

The realization of ideas and critique about the TIN, which is often uttered, partly with justification and partly without, livens up the structures.

What is the situation then within the entire German-speaking area? Shall we set up uniform standards here or not?

You may wonder why we should be calling for internationalization, if already within Germany we have several different regulations.

Seen from the angle of the guest and with view to the advantages wich he will experience it is surely useful to establish uniform regulations across the frontiers. In spite of the fact, however, that we ought to have a good look at this thought already now, we have to follow the rule "when building a house you need to start in the cellar".

These initial difficulties, however, must not hide the fact that many possibilities are already being taken.

Within EDIFACT for example one group of standards goes faces big trouble in comparing the German term "Reservierung" to the English "reservation". At the first sight both formulations have the same meaning. According to liguists, however, a closer look from the point of view of the respective language reveals considerable differences.

Similar problems occur in German liguistic usage with terms like "Reservierung"(reservation as to keep a seat etc. vacant for someone, yet almost booked), "Buchung"(booking as to register) and "Option"(option as to have the right to a seat f.ex.,

Even though in 1993 Germany had to post enormous losses in this sector, the question arises of in how far these - only German - efforts suffice against the background of an increasing internationalization of travelling.

International marketing is likely to take place almost only indirectly. For this reason rules are set up by START and Amadeus, so an interface to START is the regulating factor here.

As a consequence national markets set up their rules according to demand, product and linguistic usage, so that we are not in need of a European TIN. The transitions between the systems, however, must be realized by the CRS (computer reservation system). Yet, due to different languages, cultures etc. it is almost impossible to introduce this TIN.

So the task of the distribution systems is to adapt the processed, standardized data to the interests of the target markets.

TIN was realized in close cooperation with START, its codes and functions were set up following those of START. Where ever there is a lack of linking, connections are being introduced in the course of time. In addition to this with German/City-Soft START offers an access wich is in accordance with TIN.

This is only true for marketing via professional sales middlemen, but where else and who else will be in a position to sell our offers in international markets?

The guest is the centre of all endeavours. The guest wishes to be offered information and possibilities to book as quick, comfortable, sure and comprehensive as possible. (Dr. Fried und Partner)

These four priciples can only be met, if systems with data processing are available.

So, given that the structures of the interface towards outside respectively towards the travel agency go together or are set, the transposition of this standard at the basis is to be given top priority.

DESTINATION MARKETING SYSTEMS

Philip Haines

Infocentre Travel Systems Ltd.
Meon House, College St. Petersfield, Hampshire, ENGLAND GU32 3JN

This paper defines Destination Marketing Systems (DMS), with reference to systems currently in use by Tourist Boards. It explains the architecture of such systems with particular reference to the integration of information retrieval, reservations and marketing facilities. It explains how DMS technology can help a Tourist Board measure its effectiveness through the fulfilment mechanisms offered by such systems. It further details how this technology is important in enabling small tourism enterprises to compete with large suppliers, often based outside of the destination, and bring economic benefit to the destination.

Introduction

Mr Chairman, Ladies and Gentlemen, thank you for giving me the opportunity to speak to you today. I have noted over recent years a steadily growing interest in the topic I am about to address, with conferences being held in all parts of the world and many projects being contemplated or started. However it is arguably two years since we have had an international gathering in Europe and this event is therefore very timely. As a keen skier I am delighted to be in Austria, and particularly the Tyrol, at this time of the year!

I would like to start by giving you a brief overview of our company's activities in this arena. Infocentre first became involved in destination marketing systems in the late 1980's after winning a contract to develop an integrated information and reservation system for HiLine, a company established by the public sector in Scotland to create a central reservations facility for tourists wishing to visit Northern Scotland.

Up to that point we were a supplier of reservations systems to companies in the private sector of the leisure travel industry, particularly in North America and the UK, a continuing focus today. Following on from HiLine, in the public sector, we have been involved in projects in Switzerland, South Africa and numerous activities in Asia Pacific. As advisors to the Pacific Asia Tourist Authority (PATA) we helped to commission a paper, subsequently published by PATA and jointly authored by Gilbert Archdale, our next speaker, organised a conference successfully held last year in Singapore and will be following this with another conference, co-sponsored by PATA, the Pacific Telecommunications Council and Tourism Canada to be held in Vancouver next month.

Today our clients include destinations, hotel groups, rail companies, cruise companies, specialist tour operators and other companies involved in the leisure travel industry. However they all share one thing a common - a need to offer the best and most cost-effective method for marketing leisure travel.

This includes identification, contacting and converting the potential traveller into a revenue earning actual traveller to the benefit of their organisation and the destination they are visiting. Indeed it does not stop here, because an actual traveller is the best point to start in finding more potential travellers in the future, be it a repeat visit or a recommendation to family and friends. In short providing a reservation system in isolation is not acceptable anymore, it must be part of the complete marketing mix.

Today I will be talking about Destination Marketing Systems (DMS), what are they, what do they consist of and what value do they have? As I progress, I will highlight some examples from Europe and then Gilbert Archdale will look at some non-European initiatives.

Destination Marketing Systems - A definition

At this conference, and elsewhere, you will hear many similar terms and acronyms -

> Destination Databases (DDS), Destination Management Systems (DMS), Visitor Servicing Systems, Travel Information Systems (TIS), Destination Information Systems (DIS), Central Reservation and Information Systems (CRIS) and probably others.

I prefer to refer to them all as **Destination Marketing Systems (DMS)** for several reasons.

First, it places into focus the real reason for the technology - part of the total marketing plan for a destination.

Second, it does not emphasise **information** or **reservations** but, implicitly, draws the two together, underlining their interdependence.

Third, it allows for the term to cover a wide range of systems with different focuses.

Although these systems can exist at local or regional levels, for the purposes of international distribution we believe a national system is preferable, and I will therefore refer to DMS as if they are operating at a national level.

Most of my talk today will be about the newly developing DMS that fully integrate both the pre-trip and post-arrival information process with reservations capability. There are many, equally valid systems, which address different or singular aspects of the requirements, such as pre-trip information, post-arrival information, reservation systems with little or no information aspects, product databases for administrative purposes, etc. However today I will focus on, what has been called, fully structured destination marketing systems.

There is a need for these systems so that the many small suppliers, that make up the bulk of the tourism infrastructure in many countries, can compete with the large hotel, air and tour operators who have full access to sophisticated computer technology.

I would now like to move on to look in more detail at the constituent parts of a DMS. We see these as the following:

Product Database	-	containing accommodation, transportation, attractions and public facilities.
Client Database	-	containing profile detail (client history, contact information) of actual and potential travellers.

Marketing Facilities	-	comprehensive selection criteria and mail-merge facilities. Relational database capabilities, Summary information for marketing planning.
Information Retrieval	-	A fulfilment mechanism to easily seek out targeted information relevant to the enquirer.
Reservations	-	the ability to hold the information profile for a potential client and book a full range of tourism services - accommodation, transportation etc.
Distribution	-	the ability to offer the above via communications technology.

Product Databases

Product databases are in an evolving state - they have traditionally been used by tourist offices for administration purposes and may need substantial enhancement to function as an information database. However this transition is important because it is the first step towards moving away from having a cost overhead towards something that can be a revenue earner.

In order to be valuable it is important that product databases are comprehensive, this is usually achieved by making entry a no-charge item.

It is interesting, though, that such is the value of information an organisation such as Japan Travel Bureau, a major source of tourists to Europe, compiles and constantly updates their own information database (TiPs) on destinations their tourists will visit enabling JTB staff to handle information enquiries from potential travellers directly.

Information in Product Databases will come from both the public and private sectors. It will need to be kept up to date and different methods can be used for this depending on the frequency of updating. For example, ski resorts will need to update a DMS on a daily or even more frequent basis with weather, open lifts and runs etc.

Information concerning items that can subsequently be booked will require inventory and pricing to be held as well as description of facilities, location etc. These items could be accommodation, transportation, tours and the like.

Public sector information will cover items such as weather, travel conditions, details about parks, museums, galleries, travellers' advisories, etc.

Client Databases

The private sector has been steadily moving towards sophisticated database marketing techniques - note the use of customer loyalty programs in the travel industry such as frequent flyer and stayers. These prove the value of client databases and the value such databases have.

Some destinations have already realised the importance of targeted information to the private sector and are already supplying, or selling, information about potential travellers who wish to go white water rafting, for example, to organisers of those activities.

The major tenets of database marketing are:

> Past consumer behaviour is the best predictor of future behaviour.
>
> A purchase is simply one event. A customer's true worth is his lifetime value.
>
> Customers are more important than non-customers.
>
> Certain customers are more important than other customers.
>
> Customers are likely to share certain characteristics.

To make the database of value it needs to be targeted and response driven. It needs to be presented so that participants perceive a value, a sense of belonging and it must be affordable. Again witness the success of frequent flyer programs - according to a study in America, by the late eighties, because of frequent flyer programs a traveller's tolerance for delay had risen to 3.5 hours from 30 minutes, before changing airlines.

Destinations are in a good position to build visitor databases. They can gather information from visitors to information centres and publicly owned attractions and facilities. They can collect data from those who telephone or mail in. They can set up, with the private sector, special interest clubs eg Club France in North America.

Marketing Facilities

We have already started to identify marketing facilities when discussing client databases - the importance of loyalty programs, the selling of targeted information to the private sector etc.

The client database will be in constant need of marketing activity to improve its quality. But what of marketing directed towards actual purchase by clients?

I have already mentioned Club France in North America, operated by the French Government Tourist Office, to which members pay $65 per year for the privilege of belonging. This group is then targeted by the private sector, for example a recent joint promotion with the United Airlines frequent flyer program, and offered specific opportunities to purchase and visit France. Another similar example is the "Royal Britain welcomes Visa" cooperative program between Visa and the British Tourist Authority. Both are examples of relational database technology merging the client databases of two organisations to the benefit of both.

In other words these examples underline the necessity to be able to segment your client database to create most value from it. The easier you can make it to identify and reach - whether by mail or phone - your potential travellers, the better.

Summary information from client databases can also form an important element in the marketing planning process for a destination. DMS offers the destination the ability to measure its marketing effectiveness, something that is very difficult for traditionally operating tourist boards to do.

Information Retrieval

In a sophisticated DMS there will be a fulfilment mechanism by which the product database can be searched quickly and easily to locate information pertinent to the enquirer. The Tirol Information System (TIS), here in Austria is an example of a system specifically designed to supply tourist information to the marketplace and information on trends and markets to local suppliers. Those of you who attended the earlier presentation by Arno Ebner will have heard more about this system. DMSs being designed today allow for the information requested by a potential traveller to be stored as part of his client profile.

Reservations

The essence of a well-designed reservation system, as part of a DMS, is to take the client profile and offer the minimum number of qualifying products to close the sale. This might result in one night booked in a small guest house or an entire itinerary on a driving tour complete with ferries, theatre bookings, and the like.

The HiLine system in Scotland was designed to offer all these facilities and has the benefit of high quality customer documentation, designed to add to the overall level of customer satisfaction. In this instance information pertinent to the particular reservation is printed as part of the customer information pack, for example, details of a particular event being held at the time the traveller will be staying there.

Another example of a recently designed DMS in Europe is the Gulliver project in Ireland. You can hear more about this in session R14 from John Rafferty. Again a full range of accommodation is featured on the system from hotels to bed and breakfasts, youth hostels, self catering, cabin cruisers and the like.

Distribution

The complex actions of providing targeted information and reservations capabilities mean that, for the most part today, DMS rely on telesales rather than electronic distribution.

Purchase of leisure travel products today is through two main channels - direct to the consumer and through the travel industry via travel agents.

Travel agents are used to electronic product distribution through airline Global Distribution Systems (GDS) and through specifically designed systems for the purchase of leisure products, such as videotex in the UK. To extend DMS to this channel means working with at least these two technologies.

There are various methods of using the airline GDS but, in essence, the choice is between using software provided by the GDS (a host system) or using the GDS solely for connection to the travel agent (a gateway or pass through system).

Unfortunately there are not many suitable host systems for DMS. GDS hotel systems have a number of inherent disadvantages for DMS operators such as being dependant on airport codes, having limited pricing capabilities, and no focus on information. American Airlines SABRE is developing a destination based host system - CONCIERGE - which may help. There are two important advantages of host based systems though - consistent types of access by different providers and commitment to training travel agents by the GDS. These two areas are important because, unless it is easy to use a DMS it will not be used by the travel agent.

If a gateway system is used there may be no commonality between access to one DMS and another and the destination itself must take responsibility for training travel agents in usage - not a task to be underestimated. This could work if destinations worked together to ensure common forms of access to their DMS. PATA is involved in trying to promote destinations to work together and events such as this will also help.

With regard to electronic distribution directly to the traveller this will take somewhat longer. There are, and will continue to be, a growing number of experiments such as ATIS in the Netherlands, with CD-ROM technology, videos, diskettes, often incorporating multimedia technology and ISDN and ATM communications technology. Some particularly innovative ideas may appear as add-ons to in-room services in hotels, and home shopping services such as Prodigy in the US. My own view is that this will not make a quantum leap forward until interactive television arrives - now much closer since the recent announcements of a joint venture between Microsoft and Time-Warner.

Conclusion

In the two years since some of us were meeting in Perugia, Italy there have been many developments in this field. The tourism industry throughout Europe is characterised by a multitude of small business all needing to compete with large companies having sophisticated computer technology. There is a demand from travellers for more frequent holidays, more individual itineraries, more complex travel - DMS can enable the small suppliers to compete effectively to the economic benefit of all if the right financing can be found.

Acknowledgements

G. Archdale/R. Stanton
Destination Databases: Issues and Priorities. 1992.

C. Jones
Applications of Database Marketing in the Tourism Industry. 1993.

M. Owari
Travel Information Database in Japan. 1992.

Dr. P. Sheldon
Issues in the development of Destination Information Systems. 1992.

E.R.Wayne
HiLine - A Case Study. 1991.

NON-EUROPEAN INITIATIVES AND SYSTEMS

GILBERT ARCHDALE, M.A., F.T.S.
Director ASW Consulting
The Old School House, Enmore Green, Shaftesbury SP7 8LP, England
Tel. and Fax: +44 747 53459

ABSTRACT

"The factors that lie behind the emerging electronic markets in tourism; their exploitation, especially in the USA, by major vendors and travel agency chains; and lessons to be drawn from these developments by European tourism authorities."

Mr. Chairman, Ladies and Gentlemen. It is a privilege to address this distinguished gathering and to be in a country and a destination with such an extremely positive image, a result of the work of its highly profess-ional and effective national and regional tourism organisations. This conference is proof of that. It is my first visit to Austria and I very much hope that it will not be the last.

We have heard some very interesting and stimulating presentations so far and I am sure we will hear many more. I would like to congratulate the organisers for their initiative, for the excellent programme and, not least, for all their hard work.

I have been asked to speak on "Non-European Initiatives and Systems".
The non-European focus is very appropriate because of course both tourism and technology are worldwide industries. Understanding key trends and developments, not just in Europe, but in the intercontinental marketplaces, has to be central to any European discussions.

Product characteristics such as beautiful nature, excellent facilities, good service and businesses which reflect the individuality of their owners are central to the attractiveness of many European destinations. But no destination can prosper on these qualities alone. The first rule of marketing is to focus on what the customer requires and the second is to reach out to and to provide for that customer more effectively than one's competitors.

This is where electronic marketing comes in. Firstly many of our potential customers come from North America or the rapidly growing Pacific Rim economies. Secondly we have much to learn from the techniques and initiatives employed in those parts of the world - by destinations, by product vendors and not least by resourceful and imaginative intermediaries. These techniques reflect the highly competitive technological and business environment within which their users operate.

In my time today I would like therefore to do three things: to look at the factors behind the emerging electronic marketplaces;
to consider some of the ways in which the major players are exploiting the opportunities that electronics provide;
to suggest some lessons which we should draw from these developments.

What are these electronic marketplaces? You will note I just referred to "emerging" electronic marketplaces. This is because I do not believe that we yet have any true electronic marketplaces in the tourism industry. However the United States domestic airline industry comes close to it.

95% of all US domestic air travel is on discounted rather than full fare tickets. Fares are filed, distributed and accessed electronically through the airline CRS systems. Reservation requests can be made by e-mail, cross-checked against company travel policy and confirmed and paid for without human intervention, in a complex but increasingly seamless process.

The travel agent's PC-based software can then automatically check and re-check flight and fare availability, to take advantage of even lower fares filed closer to departure date. Management reports can then be generated showing achieved savings. Finally tickets can now be issued through Electronic Ticket Distribution Networks (ETDNs) for customer collection at points far removed from airline, agency or customer premises.

These airline seats have almost become a commodity traded like currencies. We don't yet have futures in airline seats but we do have speculators (called consolidators) and the prices fluctuate with amazing speed and complexity. The use of electronics is central but the characteristics of the product and its marketplace are crucial. The main distinguishing features of airline tickets (physical location, route, departure time and price) fit easily into the still rigid formats of airline computer systems. The US marketplace is largely unregulated and airlines, travel agencies, their technical suppliers and their customers are all highly entrepreneurial.

Contrast the situation for the majority of tourism products, both here in Europe and in other parts of the world. It is quite different. Tourism products are characterised by their individual location, their individual facilities, their individual appeal, their individual ownership and their individual trading basis. This individuality is both an asset and a problem. It is an asset because it is what many customers want. It is a problem because individuality and databases don't mix very well. This restricts the customer's access to the product and the product's access, through the electronic distribution networks, to the customer.

What can we do to reconcile the asset with the problem? We know the international travel and tourism industry is increasingly using electronics, both at the point of sale and for marketing and distribution. What lessons can we draw from what is happening in other parts of the world?

When considering these issues in a major study for the Pacific Asia Travel Association last year I described the situation as follows "The airline CRSs are the only major existing travel related network. Technology costs are continuing to fall. The CRS systems do not yet supply an entirely satisfactory method for the effective sale of leisure products by travel agencies. But, these constraints apply even more to alternative distribution channels. Major vendors are increasing their efforts to take advantage of the distribution and sales opportunities that the airline CRSs provide. This activity is encouraged by many international initiatives to develop technical and commercial standards. The use of the CRSs to deliver leisure related information and sales facilities, though relatively piecemeal and ineffective to date, can therefore be expected to increase sharply."

In the eighteen months since those words were written developments have been as I forecast. But there is a bigger world out there. We are seeing a media explosion, with rapid developments in communications technologies, with databroadcasting, satellite, cable and ISDN jostling for position in both consumer and business markets. Computing is becoming both mobile and multi-media. But I believe that the single most significant development is the move toward real functional integration at the chip level.

Of course so-called integrated systems exist now. But they consist of distinct elements bolted together, needing complex protocols and standards for their apparent integration and in practice are dependent on human beings to make them work at all. The incorporation of integrated functionality at the core level, the chip itself, will have an immense impact but apart from the (hitherto disappointing) Personal Digital Assistant it isn't here yet. And as has been so frequently said, applications follow devices.

In considering the strategic positioning of the European tourism industry and its technical suppliers it is surely essential to look at some of the applications already in place in the travel world and see what we can learn from them.

Taking the USA first - the home not of the original CRSs - what do we have? An enormous single market, with a single language, currency and legal system. Its people have the incentive and the ability to travel. They do so in a largely unregulated and highly service oriented marketplace. Most primary suppliers of transport and accommodation are large companies and intermediaries such as travel agencies are highly automated. The public sector role (with the exception of some Convention Bureaus) is muted in comparison with many European countries.

This competitive marketplace has produced a rich flora of IT applications with particular focus on business efficiency and customer service, highly relevant to public authorities as well tourism businesses in Europe.

One such application uses the airline Passenger Name Record (PNR). The PNR identifies the passenger and his journey as well as providing accounting and management information to the many parties involved. Many US travel agencies operate Customer Databases which record client requirements, such as non-smoking seats or a particular hotel preference.

Some travel agency software packages can link the two for administrative reasons, but what if it were possible to link both the PNR and the associated customer database to a Destination Database? Bespoke information could then be provided for each traveller's particular itinerary. Opera enthusiasts travelling to Vienna would receive information on opera (and the travel agency an opportunity to sell opera tickets), skiers would receive information on skiing and so on.

This may sound like a pipe dream but a product already available in the US does just this. Its name is Worldview Automated TripPlan Software (WATS). WATS links the destination data Worldview already supply to agency held Customer Database details. Customised reports are produced at a cost varying from US$9 to US$6 depending on monthly volume. That's quite an advance on receiving a paper slip attached to your ticket showing check-in times but little else.

Another application is the automation of customer/agency communications. The giant American travel agency chains such as Amex and Rosenbluth have developed sophisticated E-mail systems for handling corporate travel requests. Partly as an element of their own drive to cut staff costs and partly as a necessary service to clients already using E-mail for other purposes.

CD-Rom based services are flourishing. Since October a new service in New York, World Travel Online, even enables its users to download video-clips and other destination data from a dial-up database service to their own PCs. Travel agents can download the software via modem.

Vendor applications are multiplying with several examples of system integration, even between entirely separate companies. Avis and Radisson Hotels now provide combined check-in at certain locations. Collect your car at the airport and receive your hotel card key at the same time. A highly attractive alternative to the astonishingly lengthy check-in queues that sometimes arise.

The driving forces behind these developments are commercial but an essential facilitator is the skill levels of the companies involved. Skill is required for effective exploitation, which is what can turn two and two into five.

What will happen with the enabling technology of the ATB2 ticket and boarding pass? ATB2 was initially driven by airline requirements. But now it is there I believe that the most exciting ATB2 developments will come from the commercial opportunities that it opens up for the multi-national non-air vendors.

These companies are currently focusing on branding, yield management, quality customer service and highly targeted marketing. Their loyalty is to their own profits and market share, not to the region or country within which their individual hotel or car rental outlets operate.

These companies can already integrate their own Product Databases with Promotional Databases and Customer Databases. Consider the competitive advantages they can achieve if they can really integrate their own marketing with those of complementary partners. The necessary building blocks for this are now in place - system integration at chip level, enabling technologies such as the ATB2 standards, commercial expertise and skill in exploiting IT applications.

This scenario raises some fundamental issues for those responsible for destination marketing. How will destinations and smaller businesses maintain their market share if the massive power of technology is deployed effectively against them by multi-national corporations. What role should the public sector play? How can we avoid destructive competition between economically weak parties for a share of a declining cake?

We have already heard from Mr. Haines about the background to the development of Destination Databases. I would like to look at some examples of activity in this field from the USA, Canada and Australia. I have already spoken about the vibrant private sector activity in the USA. One might expect that the same opportunities could be exploited by the public sector there but in fact the number and scale of initiatives is relatively modest.

In part this is due to the structure of the US travel and tourism industries and in part to the relatively restricted role of the public sector in general. Even when regional reservation and information services have been established under the wing of a Visitor and Convention Bureau, only one of these (the Kissimmee-St. Cloud) claims a six-figure reservations total. It's helped by the presence of DisneyLand as well as a 4% local room tax as a source of funding!

Moving East, the Caribbean Hotel Association set up the CHARMS reservation service in 1990. The objective was to reduce the substantial distribution costs incurred by Caribbean hoteliers using the established "representation" companies in the key US marketplace. This can cost up to 30% of rack while essentially only providing a primitive form of "store and forward" service. However, despite several years of effort and considerable investment by the major telecommunications company which initially backed CHARMS, neither subscribing hotels nor users reached commercially viable levels. The CHARMS service was recently taken over by Robert Reid, a Utell subsidiary, and is therefore effectively using (and paying for) a private label service from an existing player.

Away from Caribbean sunshine there is a major North American destination with a strong public sector - Canada. As well as a national tourism organisation the various states have traditionally maintained separate tourism promotion organisations. In the Destination Database context this has resulted in the development of a number of publicly funded and operated information and reservation services.

At the state level these are primarily targeted at the domestic tourist, with an increasing focus on integrating information services with the sales function. The longest established service in the Check-Inn operation in Nova Scotia, currently in the process of up-grading to a second generation system. At the national level Tourism Canada has been able to piggy-back on a federal export promotion database, the Business Opportunities Sourcing System (BOSS).
The tourism section of the BOSS database contains detailed information on Canadian tourism products suitable for international tourists and is particularly targeted at inbound tour operators.

Travel agency access to the BOSS data has recently been substantially improved through an agreement with Montana-based Applied Information Services who maintain several leisure databases on the main airline CRSs.

The largest "public" Destination Database though is to be found on the other side of the world, in Australia. In system activity, number of employees and in turnover the Queensland Travel and Tourism Commission's ATLAS dwarfs all others. It is used on a bureau basis by some of the other Australian states and the software has also been intensively marketed worldwide, including a sale to the now defunct British BRAVO company.

New South Wales, now preparing for the 2000 Olympics, operates a more information oriented service, NEWTRACS, though it is fast becoming a fully-fledged reservation service as well.

In the Pacific-Asia region an interesting development is the way in which individual tour operators, of which the best known is Jetset, are expanding their internal product databases into what are effectively multi-national Destination Databases. Access to these is becoming ever more widely available and, similar to the airline CRSs, such operations are becoming businesses in their own right.

What lessons can we draw for the European tourism industry and especially for public authorities from this exciting but rather mixed bag of developments?

1. It is clear that the march of electronics is here, and here to stay.

2. It is clear that the big players, especially the multi-national are well-equipped to exploit the marketing opportunities that electronics bring. They are doing so and they will increasingly do so.

3. It is clear that neither SMEs nor the public sector are well-positioned to exploit these marketing opportunities.

4. But it is also clear that unless both SMEs and the public sector can maintain their competitive position vis-a-vis multi-nationals and alternative information providers respectively that both risk being disconnected from the marketplace.

I will make two quick observations. In the public sector, particularly at a national level, there is often too rigid a demarcation between the marketing and information functions. Product data has often been (partially) computerised but with insignificant regard to the marketing applications. At the same time the marketing people have ignored the very real opportunities that electronics can bring them. Perhaps this comes from being "non-commercial" and service rather than customer-led.

Secondly, there is a danger of being seduced by all the sexy whizz-bang elements. True, the really new developments are exciting and illuminating, but like fireworks they are expensive and many will fade before our very eyes. If we can't even get local databases or CRS distribution properly organised, how can we expect to manage leading edge applications.

These cautionary words though do not mean that we should hold back or remain aloof from these development - far from it. It is above all clear that public authorities in Europe have a great responsibility to their constituents - the tourism businesses in their countries, regions or cities. In turn these businesses cannot possibly cope alone with the explosion of activity that we see amidst this entrepreneurial chaos of creation in the world of electronic marketing. In order to provide the best possible levels of customer service and to reach out to the worldwide marketplace they need the support, advice and cooperation of the public authorities.

My recommendations therefore are that:

1. the public sector must develop its knowledge base - not just through such excellent and timely events such as ENTER, but on the basis of a conscious and structured programme.

2. this cannot be done on a regional or even national basis - it will therefore demand cooperation between different European authorities. I cannot see why this should in any way be contrary to their constitutions or objectives. They are after all the representatives of their national constituents, and especially the SMEs.

The march of electronics brings common issues which affect us all - knowledge and cooperation will enable us to prosper.

Ladies and gentlemen - my thanks for your attention and I look forward to many more interesting discussions.

PROCESSING TRAVEL QUERIES IN A MULTIMEDIA INFORMATION SYSTEM

W.J.Austin*, E.K.Hutchinson[1], J.R.Kalmus[1], L.M.MacKinnon*, K.G.Jeffery[1], D.H.Marwick*, M.H.Williams* & M.D.Wilson[1]

* Dept. of Computing & Electrical Engineering, Heriot-Watt University, Edinburgh EH14 4AS, U.K.
[1] Systems Engineering Division, SERC Rutherford Appleton Lab., Chilton, Didcot, OXON OX11 0QX, U.K.

Abstract

This paper provides an overview of a multimedia information processing system which will be applied to the tourism industry. It concentrates on the part of the system architecture which is responsible for selecting and retrieving multimedia data from remote and local heterogeneous data sources, and in particular, on the modules responsible for understanding and providing a consolidated answer to a user's query. The understanding of queries requires the representation of information at several different levels and a communications language which is sufficiently flexible to represent user queries and subqueries at those different levels.

Introduction

MIPS (Multimedia Information Presentation System) is an Esprit III Project (P6542) concerned with the retrieval and presentation of multimedia data from heterogeneous data sources. It addresses the problems of information overload which are often associated with multimedia systems. The MIPS project will produce a software demonstrator for the tourism industry which supports:

- the integration of multimedia information including text, graphics, video, sound, etc, in a uniform display style;
- the integration of information from heterogeneous distributed databases as answers to user queries which may be complex;
- the tailoring of the information to be presented to the domain, task, user and stage in the dialogue; and
- the implementation of the HyTime standard for storage and navigation of hypermedia documents.

A user can browse hypermedia documents resembling holiday brochures to find towns they would like to visit, hotels where they might stay, and activities they wish to undertake. They can also call upon remotely located databases containing assets such as: video tours of towns and hotels; excerpts from television reviews of holidays; and up-to-date information on local events. The MIPS system will be able to present diverse information from local CD stores on the same screen, (e.g. the Michelin, Fodor, or Time Out guides), or background information from atlases and encyclopedias. This would normally require access to libraries of books.

It will not be necessary to encode the large volume of information derived from different local and remote data sources into a single standard such as CD-I or Sony Bookman. Rather, the information can be accessed from a large number of heterogeneous sources and unified into a single locally stored hypermedia web using the recent HyTime standard. This hypermedia web can then be browsed through a consistent interface presentation style which is tailored for each task and user.

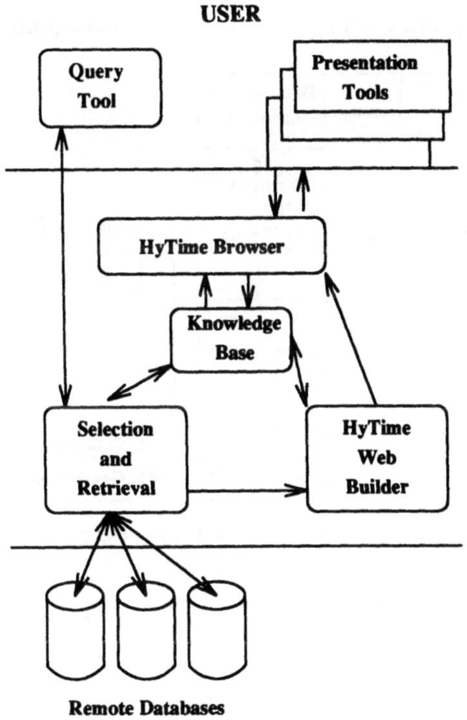

Figure 1: An overview of the MIPS architecture

The overall structure of the MIPS system is illustrated in Figure 1, as per [1].

The Presentation Manager (PM) / HyTime Browser directs the presentation to the user, through the Presentation Tools, according to an application description which is encoded as HyTime [2] and SGML [3] documents, stored in a HyTime Store. When this application description is not statically complete, the PM uses the services of the HyTime Web Builder (WB) to expand it at session time [4]. The Selection and Retrieval Tool (SRT) decomposes a query (arising from the WB) into simpler ones suitable for the Remote Databases and aggregates the answers into a meaningful consolidated answer [5]. When the query is incomplete, the SRT activates the Query Tool (QT) to enable the end-user to refine the query via clarification subdialogues [6]. Finally, the Knowledge Base (KBS) is the source of information about the domain, the task and the user. It supports the functionalities of the PM, the WB, the QT, and the SRT [7]. This paper concentrates on the high level components of the SRT.

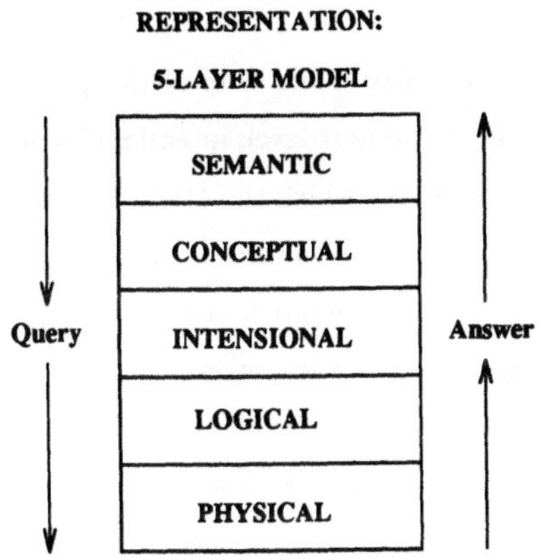

Figure 2: A simple 5-layer representational model

The authors are involved in the development of the selection and retrieval component of the system which will:

- decompose a query into an equivalent set of subqueries;
- choose the appropriate source(s) of data to answer these subqueries;
- translate queries into the format required for that source; and
- assemble the query results into a consolidated answer to the original query.

A second area of ongoing research work is in using the knowledge base to build the hypermedia web from the retrieved information and to tailor its presentation to the task and user.

A Representational Model

In order to satisfy a user query, processes of query elicitation and interpretation are initiated. The query is transformed into a set of subqueries, each intended for a specific external database. These processes can be mapped onto the 5-layer model of representation illustrated in Figure 2 which is an extension of [8].

The semantic layer aims to represent the user's purpose; the conceptual layer carries a representation in terms of an entity-relationship-attribute model of the particular application domain; at the next level, intensional representations of the databases about which the MIPS application has information are applied to the processes to constrain further the set of subqueries generated; the logical representations are equivalent to expressions in external query languages; physical representations are expressed in the external query languages themselves. At each level, some richness of representation is lost, but the relevant details are stored in order that the richness can be recovered as the answer satisfying the original query is constructed.

The conceptual representation of a query contains expressions closely associated with the application domain representation within MIPS. To answer a user's query successfully, MIPS reasons about objects and sets of objects (for instance in the tourism domain, hotels or flights) as well as values or sets of values (e.g. hotel prices or flight times).

Retrieving Query Data

The selection and retrieval component of the MIPS architecture takes a user's query, clarifies the user's requirements and generates a set of equivalent subqueries which can be addressed to appropriate remote data sources. Each individual subquery is then converted into the DBQL appropriate to an external data source and dispatched to that data source. This latter functionality is supported by a separate External Data Access module. Once data have been retrieved from the external sources by the External Data Access module, they are assembled into a consolidated response to the user's original query [9, 10]. This paper concentrates on the decomposition and clarification of the user's query and construction of a consolidated answer as supported by the Query Analysis submodule and the Answer Assembly submodule, both submodules of the SRT, respectively.

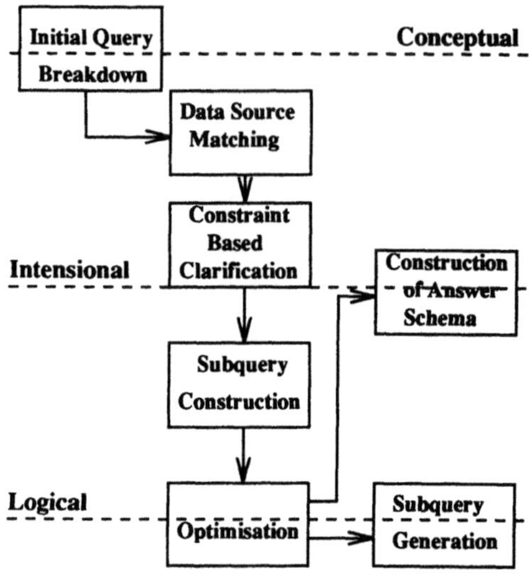

Figure 3: Mapping query analysis onto the 5-layer model

An Example of Query Analysis

The processes of breakdown and clarification maps onto the five layer model as shown in figure 3.

These processes and assembly of the consolidated answer can be illustrated by considering the query

> "Identify package holidays from Glasgow to Crete in June for 2 weeks for 2 adults and 2 children costing less than £1000."

The initial breakdown of this query identifies the main components of the query and builds a graph which represents their inter-relationships. This graph is then matched against the external data sources during a dialogue with the KBS. Initially the matching phase attempts to match the entire query to individual, discrete data sources (e.g. a tour operator's database of package holidays) . If the matching process is unable to find sufficient such data sources, based on an application-specific threshold determined locally, then individual subqueries are identified and matched against the data sources (e.g. separate databases of flights and accommodation). After identifying suitable data sources, KBS rules and heuristics can be used to attempt to match on value, e.g. the KBS might identify other UK airports as suitable starting points for the package. Thus intensional level subqueries might be generated for packages to Crete from Glasgow, Newcastle and London. Additional subqueries would be generated for travel from Glasgow to the other UK airports.

Once a subquery has been matched with a data source, further constraint-based clarification rules attempt to match the query constraints with the data fields in the matched data source. This results in a set of clearly bounded intensional level subqueries which are converted into logical level subqueries intended for different types of database: the same basic subquery may be represented differently for different external data sources (e.g. the UK departure point associated with an external database's 'Departure' field might be 'LHR' in a flight database and 'London Victoria' for a coach database). To mimimise the delays associated with access to external databases, optimisation strategies are applied during overall subquery generation. Further optimisation strategies are applied at the individual subquery level.

Following optimisation, the subqueries can be sent to the external data access processes where they are converted into the appropriate DBQLs and despatched. An intensional structure which contains an answer schema specifying the type of data expected, the structure of the subqueries sent to the external data sources and any constraints and operations which must be applied across the retrieved data is also constructed at this point [12]. This is used to guide the construction of a consolidated answer to the original query.

In the query example given here, the construction of a consolidated answer may involve the combination of separate flight, accommodation and transport costs: the user's cost constraint can *only* be applied after the data has been retrieved. In addition, the answer schema may specify that the packages to be presented to the user should first be sorted according to cost and then according to departure date, this may be done partly at the remote database site and partly within the MIPS system after information has been retrieved from all appropriate external data sources.

The answer schema is normally specified by the Web Builder. In the current example, it may originally have specified a timetable type structure with additional tables for accommodation and any associated multimedia assets. This will have been extended to deal with the subquery relating to the cost of the additional internal UK travel. The modified answer schema is supplied to the KBS to allow a new web structure to be built dynamically.

Assembling an Answer to a User Query

The production of a consolidated answer is performed by the Answer Assembly submodule. The main task of this submodule is to recover the richness of representation which was lost during query breakdown and clarification before a response to the user's query is provided to the Web Builder. The answer schema provides the intensional level information which allows the data in the subquery responses to be linked into an overall query answer at the conceptual level. The functionality of the Answer Assembly submodule can be broken down into three stages:

1. Structuring subquery responses from the External Data Access module guided by the intensional structure provided by the Query Analysis module.

2. Application of those user constraints and functions (e g sort, average, min, max) which can only be applied after the data has been retrieved.

3. Assembly of the consistent and constrained data into a consolidated answer to the user's query at the conceptual level.

Matching Subquery Responses As subquery responses arrive from the External Data Access submodule they are built into intensional level storage structures from which the consolidated answer is constructed. In the package holiday example there may be storage structures for flights, accommodation and transport. The Answer Assembly submodule checks each new response for consistency with those which have already been received. Any inconsistencies are referred to the KBS for a decision on which response to accept (e.g. due to a transposition error, the cost of a flight from Glasgow to Crete in the Glasgow Airport database is £819, whereas the same flight in the carrier's database costs £189). Where consistent responses to the same logical query are received they are merged to form a single entry in the intensional structure, thus reducing the amount of data which must be stored.

Applying Constraints and Functions To allow the application of constraints and functions to the retrieved data, the Answer Assembly submodule needs information on: the subqueries and fields involved; the types of the constraints; the inter-relationships between constraints; and the priorities of the constraints.

The Query Analysis submodule is responsible for identifying those constraints which cannot be applied until the data has been retrieved, (e.g. the combined cost of separate flights, accommodation and transport in the Crete example). It can also add constraint order information to the structural information supplied to Answer Assembly submodule. Domain and user model information are also required: both to ensure that constraints are not applied too vigorously (e.g. applying a cost constraint which excluded all responses), and to determine priorities when there are no explicit user priorities. For example there is probably no point in retaining the cheapest available package holiday if there are insufficient seats for all members of the travelling family.

If the constraints are insufficient to reduce the amount of information to a level which can be displayed, further constraint-based data reduction is required. The decision to seek modified or additional constraints is taken by the KBS using information from the user and domain models and information on the database responses supplied by the Answer Assembly submodule. If the KBS can provide such constraints to the Answer Assembly submodule, these are applied. If the KBS cannot provide further constraints, the KBS and Answer Assembly submodule generate a clarification subdialogue which invites the user to provide further constraining information (e.g. in our example, the user being asked to provide specific dates of travel).

Assembling the Consolidated Answer After the merging of consistent data and the application of user constraints and of further query processing, the data which remains in the intensional storage structures are used to construct one or more consolidated answers to the user's original query. This process is guided by the answer schema, with the support of the user and domain models held by the KBS. Where it has not been possible to populate the intensional structure fully, the answer schema is modified to reflect the missing information.

The process of extracting information from the intensional structure using the answer schema results in one or more answers to the user's query at the conceptual level. These are encoded in a standard structure data format and passed to the WB (e.g. A timetable of flights from U.K. to Crete, with an associated accommodation table, for the specific dates identified, within the identified cost constraint.)

Representing and Communicating Queries

The Internal Representation Language or IRL is used as the medium of communication between the major modules of the MIPS system identified in Figure 1 [12]. It performs the same task between submodules within the SRT. Two aspects of the IRL are important in this respect: an applications communication protocol, which remains constant across the architecture and provides an envelope for carrying messages in different forms; and a message content, which supports the functionality of the particular module and submodule interfaces involved; viz:

1. breakdown and clarification of queries into sets of subqueries;

2. interpretation and manipulation of retrieved data; and

3. the server role of the KBS throughout the architecture.

The interfaces described in the architecture fall into three families, each relevant to one of the three areas of functionality identified above. In order to be sufficiently rich and flexible to support the varying functionality required across these three families of interfaces, three dialects of IRL are defined. This paper concentrates on the dialect of the IRL which supports the breakdown and clarification process. This dialect is called the Query Dialect (QD).

The global structure of the IRL is represented by a message header which supports the application communication protocol, and a message body which supports the underlying functionality of the module for which the message is intended. The message header identifies a user id, machine id, source, destination, message id, and time stamp; this is judged sufficient to support an effective communications protocol for the purposes of MIPS.

The message body contains two required fields, MessageInfo and MessageContent, and an optional field for processing constraints. The MessageContent field depends crucially on the underlying functionality of the particular processes which are being supported i.e. on which of the three dialects of the IRL is being considered.

The MessageInfo field identifies the type of the message and a query identifier which is used to identify all MIPS communications which relate to the satisfaction of a particular query. Four message types (query, assertion, command and acknowledgment) have been identified, these reflect a model of communication [13] which is currently believed to be sufficiently rich for MIPS.

Processing constraints allow non-functional requirements, such as access cost and response time to the process of retrieval from external data sources, to be attached to the query. These can influence the breakdown and clarification process, e.g. by restricting the set of external data sources which may be accessed to satisfy the query. Other constraints relevant to the selection and retrieval process include user security thresholds, delivery platform capabilities, the reliability of data from particular sources, and current availability of data sources. Such constraints may be applied by an application builder, who will use the MIPS Tools identified in this paper to build a MIPS System for a particular application in exactly the same way as the project will build a demonstrator for a tourism application, or a system configurer, who will use configuration tools to install an application- specific MIPS System for a particular domain, country, site or user.

The Query Dialect of the IRL

The role of the Query Dialect (QD) is threefold. It communicates queries between QT and SRT, clarification subdialogues between QT and SRT, and parts of the complete query (i.e. subqueries) between the submodules of SRT. The submodules involved in query breakdown and clarification and despatch require different levels of expressivity from the QD. These can be seen to map onto the 5-layer representational model.

Message Content of the Query Dialect

The MessageContent field of the QD contains a message formula (identifying the individual elements of a query or subquery and the relationship between them) and an optional answer schema representing the type-description of the retrieved data set for the complete query. The answer schema also contains logical level structural information to allow the retrieved data to be built into an appropriate conceptual level answer.

The specification of the QD has been determined by focusing on the breakdown and clarification process and by analysing a set of user queries which a MIPS application will be expected to handle. This top-down approach has been complemented by a bottom-up approach which considers the types of data source to be accessed.

<u>**The Message Formula**</u> The QD is based on a typed first order predicate logic which represents the message content using an object-attribute-value model. The content of a query in the QD is given by a conjunction of expressions which: (1) declare, type and quantify variables bound to objects and attributes; (2) declare object-attribute relationships; and (3) declare query constraints by the application of functions and of logical, comparison and second order operators.

The message formula represents the 'core' of the query elicited from the user or passed by the HyTime Web Builder and is interpreted in the context of the answer schema (if it exists) and the non-functional requirements expressed in the processing constraints. It supports the representation of a query:

- at the conceptual level, as received from the QT;
- at the intensional level, during the breakdown and clarification process; and
- at the logical level, (i.e. after it has been decomposed into subqueries to be directed to different databases).

<u>**The Answer Schema**</u> The answer schema defines the representation of the expected answer by binding variables denoting objects and attributes in the message formula with media and representational devices known to HyTime and the KBS. It can also identify functions to be applied over the returned data set, (e.g. a SORT function could be applied over a set of returned values or tuples). Such functions could also be applied at an external data source if such functionality is supported and is appropriate for a particular query.

The answer schema can support the breakdown and clarification process by constraining the set of databases to be accessed. It also specifies the form of the consolidated answer which will be passed to the Web Builder.

Summary

The MIPS project involves the creation of a tool set based around the ISO Standard Generalised Markup Language (SGML) (ISO 8879) and the new ISO HyTime (ISO 10744) standards, which allow the user to obtain and present distributed heterogeneous multimedia information from a variety of sources in a controlled, timely and cost-effective manner. The MIPS project addresses the problem of information overload by filtering and prioritising multimedia information before it is presented to the user. The viability of the project will be illustrated by using the tool set to build a demonstrator intelligent tourist advisor.

This paper has described the engineering processes underlying the selection and retrieval module, one of the main components of the MIPS tool set. A 5-layer representational model was introduced and used to explain the processes involved in two submodules of the SRT. The first of these is the Query Analysis submodule, which takes a user's query, clarifies the user's requirements and generates a set of subqueries which can be addressed to appropriate remote data sources. The second is the Answer Assembly submodule, which takes data retrieved from various external data sources and assembles a consolidated response to the user's original query. This process involves the application of those user constraints and second order functions which can only be applied after the data has been retrieved.

The queries and subqueries involved in these processes are represented and communicated via the Query Dialect

(QD) of the Internal Representation Language (IRL), which is the medium of communication between the major modules of the MIPS system. The QD has three components:

- an applications communications protocol (consistent across the dialects of the IRL and the MIPS architecture);
- a message formula, based on typed first order predicate calculus, identifying the individual elements of a query or subquery and the relationships between them; and
- an optional answer schema, which represents the type-description of the retrieved data set for the user's original query.

A demonstrator system is planned to be in place by the latter half of 1994.

References and Bibliography

1. MIPS Consortium, *The Definition of the MIPS System Volume 1 - The Detailed Architectural Design of the MIPS System*, EC ESPRIT III 6542 MIPS D.2.2.2 V.1

2. ISO/IEC JTC1/SC18/WG8, *Information Technology - Hypermedia/Time-based Structuring Language (HyTime)*, ISO/IEC 10744:1992(E).

3. Goldfarb, C.F., *The SGML Handbook*, Oxford University Press, 1990.

4. MIPS Consortium, *The Definition of the MIPS System Volume 3 - The Detailed Functional Specification of the HyTime Modules*, EC ESPRIT III 6542 MIPS D.2.2.2 V.3

5. MIPS Consortium, *The Definition of the MIPS System Volume 5 - The Detailed Functional Specification of the SRT Module*, EC ESPRIT III 6542 MIPS D.2.2.2 V.5

6. MIPS Consortium, *The Definition of the MIPS System Volume 2 - The Detailed Functional Specification of the Interactive Modules*, EC ESPRIT III 6542 MIPS D.2.2.2 V.2

7. MIPS Consortium, *The Definition of the MIPS System Volume 4 - The Detailed Functional Specification of the KBS Module*, EC ESPRIT III 6542 MIPS D.2.2.2 V.4

8. ANSI/XS/SPARC *Interim Report from the Study Group on Database Management Systems*, in Bulletin of ACA-SIGMOD, 7(2), 1975.

9. Sheth, A.P. and Larsen J.A., *Federated Database Systems for Managing Distributed, Heterogeneous and Autonomous Databases*, in ACM Computing Surveys, 22(3), 1990

10. Bell, D. and Grimson, J., *Distributed Database Systems*, International Computer Science Series, Addison-Wesley, 1992

11. Fonkam M.M. and Gray W.A., *Employing Integrity Constraints for Query Modification and Intensional Answer Generation in Multi-Database Systems*, in Lecture Notes in Computer Science, 618, 1992

12. MIPS Consortium, *The Definition of the MIPS System Volume 6 - The IRL Definition*, EC ESPRIT III 6542 MIPS D.2.2.2 V.6

13. Chafe, W. L., *Meaning and Structure of Language*, University of Chicago Press, Chicago, 1970.

A HYPERMEDIA TOURIST GUIDE

A. Tsalgatidou, M. Spiliopoulou, K. Apostolaki, I. Roussou, M. Hatzopoulos

University of Athens, Dept. of Informatics,
TYPA Buildings, ILISIA GR-157 71, Greece

Abstract

A hypermedia model is presented for the management of extendible multimedia information envisaged for tourist applications. The information is modelled according to the object-oriented methodology and organised into aggregation and specialisation / generalisation hierarchies, containing data that can be further enriched by authorised users - typically travel agents. The end-user conceives a hypermedia network, in which visited nodes are traced and navigation paths can be constructed on the fly.

1 Introduction

Tourist applications present an interesting case in the development of information systems, due to the multitude of tasks that have to be performed and the wide range of facilities that have to be provided by such systems. The demands put by the information rich and highly interactive tourist guidance environment, cannot be handled by conventional development techniques and alternate solutions have to be sought in the emerging technological area of hypermedia.

Hypermedia systems are complex information stores with flexible structure, often comprising of thousands of links and nodes, which enable the user to freely navigate through these nodes or to follow a guided route predefined by the system author. Such systems are very useful for tourist applications. Additionally, hypermedia systems have been found suitable to fields such as office automation, medicine, education and training [11]. From a knowledge point of view, these systems comprise mainly of three components [12]: *organisational knowledge*, which describes the ways knowledge is organised in a hypermedia system, *domain knowledge*, which is composed of rules and facts about the application domain, and *contextual knowledge*, which describes the way that information in the hypermedia will be used.

An important issue in the hypermedia application development is the need of new design models specific to the features of hypermedia. The various hypermedia development environments, like Guide™, g-IBIS [5], HyperCard™, KMS [1] etc. that have emerged in the market, use different approaches and design models. Thus, HyperCard and Guide use linear structures as building blocks for the creation of hypernetwork structures. KMS uses hierarchical structures to organise the hyper-documents, but it also allows cross-hierarchical links, inducing in this way a complex topology in the hypernetwork. g-IBIS explicitly models the semantics of the domain under study, by assuming a well defined theory of the design process and by providing a set of specific node and link types that represent conceptual objects in the domain model. The design of hypermedia applications is better handled by the HDM methodology [7] which follows an *authoring-in-the-large* approach. HDM allows the description of hypermedia applications in terms of a *schema* which defines the structural, the navigational and the semantic properties of a class of applications, an *instance of a schema*, which defines the actual information structures according to the schema prescriptions, and *the access structures*, which define the entry points for navigating in the hyperdocuments along predefined paths. According to this approach, HDM primitives are totally independent from specific development/ delivery environments; thus, the same HDM description of an application, can be compiled towards different hypermedia environments, e.g. HyperCard, KMS etc.

Known problems of hypermedia systems are the cognitive load, the user disorientation, and the possibility for the user to be lost in the hyperspace of links [4]. However, if a considerate approach is followed for the development of such a system, these problems may be moderated. It has been demonstrated [6] that knowledge based approaches to organising hypermedia, may benefit users in finding information in goal directed activities. Other approaches to solve the disorientation problem concentrate to the user interface [13][17] and textual analysis [15]. A recent approach to this problem, still under research, is the use of authoring tools based on hypermedia structural analysis [3].

It has become apparent now that, the use of hypermedia technology may significantly contribute to the development of sophisticated tourist applications. When dealing with services offered to tourists by tourist agencies, the most noticeable requirements are the storage, linking and the presentation means of the related information, which may be in the form of text, image, video, graphics, animation or sound. Another demanding requirement is the interactivity that has to be offered to the user. The goal is, on one hand the creation of a complete, vivid and pleasant description of the offered holidays and excursion programs - something that cannot be achieved in any printed brochure - and on the other hand, the provision of means to let the tourists freely create their personalised tour.

The flexibility and the adaptability of the user interface is a very important issue stemming from the fact that, tourists are not always certain of what exactly they want to do and their interest evolves as they are collecting more information for the various places. Typically, a travel agent, in the beginning of a session with a tourist, will not be able to assert what s/he may wish. The tourists' needs and preferences are actually acquired while the agent presents the various activities and events that take place in a certain area, the interesting sites to be visited, information about accommodation, transportation etc. The agent may even propose certain package tours and solutions to be taken. However, tourists may not be satisfied by the offered options.

In computer-assisted travel agencies, tourists may interactively create personalised tours. They can also easily derive versioned tours and modify existing ones, so that they better suit their needs and interests. It has to be noted here that, the interactivity which has to be offered by a computer-based tourist guide does not replace the human agent. Instead, the agent's role becomes more specific and her/his productivity is increased: s/he may help tourists to organise their journey, after they have created a coarse or a detailed travel schedule, or s/he may provide information and advices beyond the ones offered by the computer. Thus, a human agent spends much less time with each tourist and has more time to deal with other activities like gathering information about other places, organising more sophisticated tours, or spending more time to better understand the needs of customers.

Exploiting the facilities offered by this technology, we have developed a **Hyp**ermedia **T**ourist **Guide**, denoted hereafter as **HTGuide.** This system models all relevant multimedia information according to the object-oriented paradigm and organises it into a hypermedia network. It has been developed on a Macintosh platform using HyperCard and satisfies the following requirements:

- it models and maintains all the relevant multimedia information
- it has an appropriate user-friendly interface for two types of users: the travel agent and the tourist
  - the agent may extend the model on the fly, so that
    - to add new information and keep the database up-to-date
    - to customise it to the personal interest of the tourist
  - the tourists are able
    - to explore the multimedia information by navigating the hypernetwork
    - to interactively create their personalised tour
    - to observe their personalised tour, as a simulation of the desirable journey through the interest sites they have selected.

The following section presents the object-oriented data model of HTGuide and analyses the maintained information. Section 3 describes the user-interface of the system presenting the information retrieval mechanisms available to the user. The extensions that can be performed on HTGuide are discussed in section 4, while section 5 briefly describes the implemented prototype. Finally, section 6, concludes the results of this work.

2 The HTGuide Object-Oriented Model

2.1 Outline of the Tourist Information Modelling Mechanism

At the presentation (external) layer of the HTGuide model, information may be classified into two categories: the first one refers to information which presents the tourist attractions and the second describes the facilities of the attractions such as accommodation, transportation etc.

The storage (internal) layer of HTGuide has also two categories of information: the unstructured information forming aggregates and having properties of non-conventional nature, such as images, graphics, sound and textual documents and, conventional database objects describing well structured information entities with numerical and string properties.

The high level objects in HTGuide correspond to the geographical analysis of a country, i.e. they are districts, regions and towns, where isolated sites of interest (like ancient cities) also appear at the town level. According to this analysis, a country is a composite object consisting of regions, while a region is an aggregation of towns and sites. So, high level information is modelled as an *aggregation* hierarchy. A second information classification scheme is a *specialisation* hierarchy. In this hierarchy, an object belongs to a class and has a number of properties, which are either defined in this class or inherited by its superclasses. Properties range over domains that may be either primitive ones like integers, floats, strings, or other classes.

The information manager handles the mapping scheme of objects so that users see names meaningful to them, without being concerned about their internal representation. The same facility will be used for the development of a multi-lingual interface of HTGuide. Names are not unique within the application, but the name and the type of an object constitute a unique key.

2.2 Aggregation Hierarchy

The aggregation hierarchy of HTGuide is presented in Fig. 1. The nodes in this aggregation hierarchy are classes. The objects of these classes are composed of objects of classes of the level directly below it. The database of HTGuide contains one object per country; this object is composed of lower level objects, the districts, which are in turn composed of regions. The towns and other sites of a region constitute a region object.

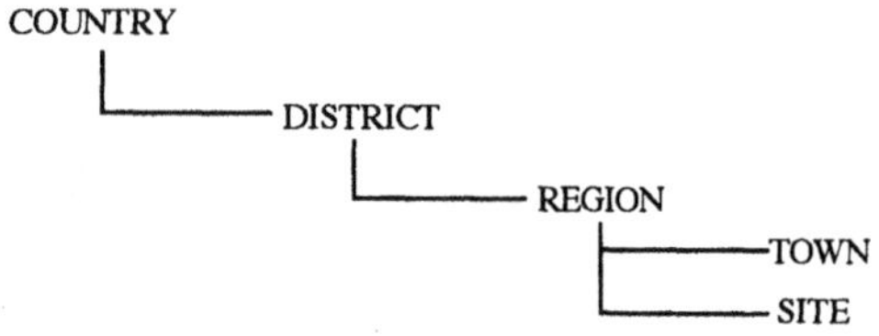

Fig. 1. The aggregation hierarchy of HTGuide

The objects of the classes constituting this aggregation hierarchy are also denoted as *geographical objects* hereafter. Each geographical object is accompanied by a visual presentation, which, for the three upper levels of the aggregation hierarchy is a map and, for the leaf level is a picture. According to the naming mechanism of HTGuide, a geographical object has a name which is the name of the area it describes. Its visual representation has the same name, enabling in this way, the automatic linking of an object to its map/picture

2.3 Specialisation Hierarchy

The specialisation graph of the HTGuide prototype is presented in Fig. 2. This graph is a tree of classes, where each class, except from the root, has one parent.

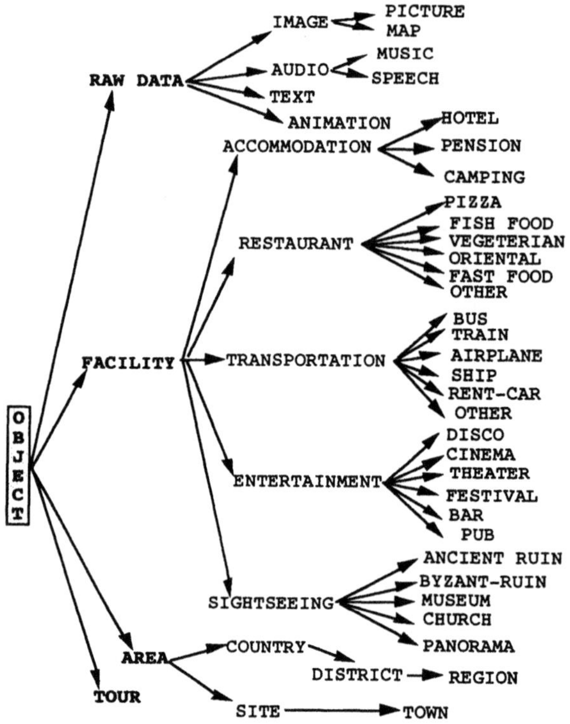

Fig. 2. The specialisation hierarchy of HTGuide

The subhierarchy rooted at the class **Country** contains the aggregate objects on which the presentation mechanism of HTGuide is based. The objects belonging to the subhierarchies rooted at **Facility**, **Image** and **Text** classes, are properties of the geographical objects in this subhierarchy.

The class **Tour** contains paths over the hypermedia network, which can be either constructed by the user on the fly or be created by the travel agency and suggested to the users.

2.4 Property Graph

Values of properties of objects are other objects, which may belong to a class of the specialisation hierarchy or range over a primitive domain (integers, floats, strings), omitted from the application schema. Thus, classes are connected to the domains of their properties which are other classes. In this way, a (disconnected) *property graph* is constructed, the nodes of which are the classes appearing in the specialisation hierarchy. The links between them are named after the names of the properties; the source of a link is the class where the property belongs and the target of a link is the domain of this property.

Part of the property graph of HTGuide is presented in Fig. 3, where only the most important properties of the selected classes are shown. When the value of a property is a list of objects of the domain, then the property name is enclosed in curly brackets, as in {map of sightseeings}, denoting that the value is a set of **Map** objects. It is worth to note here that, the value of the property 'content' in class **Text** can be either the text itself or the name of the file containing the text. The value of the 'content' property in the **Audio** and **Image** classes (the latter is not shown in this graph), is always a filename.

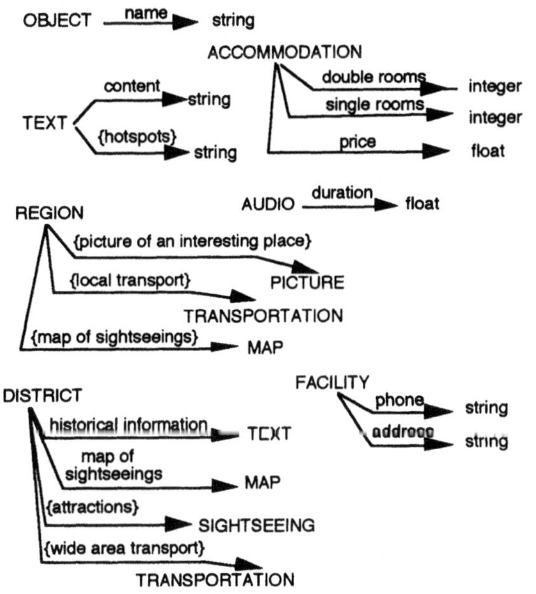

Fig.3. Part of the property graph of HTGuide

3 Information Retrieval in the HTGuide User Interface

The HTGuide interface assumes the form of a country map with submaps. The user may navigate through the hierarchy of maps by traversing the links which connect related information pieces. The possible ways of exploring information are described below. Whatever way is used, the tourist has the impression of visiting the areas of interest and thus performing a simulation of the actual excursion on the computer. The travel agent may use this effect to suggest one or more alternative trips, which can be defined as described in the next section.

3.1 Traversal of the Aggregation Hierarchy

The exploration of information maintained in HTGuide is performed by traversing the aggregation graphs, which connect each geographical object to its components, as shown in Fig. 1. A user session starts with a country map containing the districts it consists of. The districts on the map are hotspots, i.e. areas of the display where mouse events are captured. The event recognised by a hotspot on the country map triggers the traversal of an aggregation path, emanating from the **Country** object and pointing to the related **District** component corresponding to the hotspot area. The result of this, is the presentation of information for the selected district. The tourist may select an interesting region within the district and an interesting site or town within the selected region, in a recursive way.

Towns and sites of interest also appear as hotspots on the maps of a region. At the site/town level of the aggregation hierarchy, the tourist may obtain information like pictures, road maps of the town, information about transportation, accommodation, etc. by activating the attached hotspots and buttons.

The traversal of the aggregation hierarchy is intended as an aid to a tourist who has no or very little knowledge on the country of interest and wishes to explore the maintained information, obtaining gradually more detailed data, before deciding on the specific areas to be visited. The HTGuide interface allows the traversal of the aggregation hierarchy in two ways; namely, (i) in the reverse direction of aggregation graphs so that the user may return to a higher-order composite and select another component to study, and (ii) in breadth-first order, so that the sibling objects at each level are visited, before an in-depth study of the components of a geographical object takes place.

3.2 Free Navigation in the Hypernetwork and Direct Access to the Nodes

The method of traversing the aggregation hierarchy is not appropriate if the tourist is interested in visiting specific places of the country of interest. The HTGuide interface provides an alternative method which allows a user to freely navigate through the hypernetwork. This free navigation is facilitated in two ways, namely by direct accessing nodes using the naming mechanism of the HTGuide model and by providing visual representation of links in the form of hotspots.

In this way, the tourist may provide the name of the area of interest and retrieve all objects under the same name. These objects may be presented to the tourist in many forms like pictures, maps, text, animation, sound, music etc. Furthermore, if the textual information on an object contains explicit references to other objects, the tourist may freely navigate these links and retrieve all related information. For instance, if the historical description of a site contains references to other towns - not necessarily in the same region - which have sightseeings of the same period of time, with these references defined as hotspots, the user may traverse these links by activating the hotspots and retrieve the information related to the referenced towns.

3.3 Construction of Paths

HTGuide provides the possibility of 'virtual' trips according to the routes created by the users, during their navigation over the hypernetwork. In order to assist the tourist in constructing the route of a desired trip during navigation, HTGuide offers a path marking mechanism: when a user visits a node describing a place (district, region, town or other site) which may be visited during the actual trip, this node is marked for reconsideration.

The HTGuide interface 'remembers' these nodes and attaches them to a list of nodes marked so far. If a node is visited more than once, only the most recent visit is recorded. This mechanism is available to the user, who wishes to trace back his/her exploration of the hypermedia network. The path of visited nodes can be recollected later on, to serve as the initial plan of the journey. This plan can be further filtered and a human agent may help in fixing details on its materialisation.

Further developments are considering more sophisticated methods for the path marking mechanism, as the one proposed in [8].

4 Customisation facilities

Since there is no model that can satisfactorily cover all needs for an application, the possibility of customisations performed during the lifetime of the application must be incorporated in the model. The HTGuide model allows a number of modifications in the tourist database to be performed by non-expert users. The user who will perform the modifications is expected to be typically the travel agent.

The updates on HTGuide fall into two categories. The first one concerns customisations of the interface, by creating hotspots and suggesting paths over the hypermedia network, corresponding to suggested tours. The second one concerns modifications of the database, both in terms of regular updates in order to add new hotels and restaurants, to modify prices or other characteristics etc., and in terms of adding, modifying and deleting geographical objects.

More specifically, hotspots are certain areas on the screen that can capture mouse events and trigger actions by traversing predefined links. HTGuide provides the facility to the user to automatically generate such hotspots as well as the corresponding links. In this way, the user may relate already existing objects and customise the interface according to his/her interests and according to his /her way of viewing things.

The path construction mechanism, described in subsection 3.3, is used both by the tourists for the creation of their personalised tours and by the travel agents in order to prepare suggested tours for their clients. HTGuide lets travel agents create a portfolio of solutions to be produced for different categories of tourist groups according to their specific interests.

Fig. 4 depicts an animated map of a suggested tour. The interface is written in Greek, as the developed prototype was tested by Greek tourists. The edges of the path are being constructed dynamically, during an audible short description of the places suggested to be visited. At the bottom of the right side, there appears a list of keywords on the type of places that may be visited. It can be seen that in this figure, two keywords have been clicked on, namely Archaeological sites (Αρχαιολογικά μνημεία) and Continental Greece (Ηπειρωτική Ελλάδα). The suggested tour has been constructed according to this selection.

The second category of updates, i.e. the modifications on the HTGuide database, refers to the updating of information of the facilities attached to already existing geographical objects, as well as to the creation of new geographical objects or their deletion. The former case corresponds to conventional database operations, e.g. when a new pub has opened in a town, it must be added to the value of the {entertainment} property of the town object. In the latter case, the geographical objects must be processed according to the principles of composite object manipulation, as they belong to an aggregation hierarchy. Thus, the creation of a geographical object requires that the higher order composite, to which it belongs, already exists.

generated externally to HyperCard^{TM} in a format supported by HyperCard. The prototype is a tourist guide for Greece, and is operational under HyperCard.

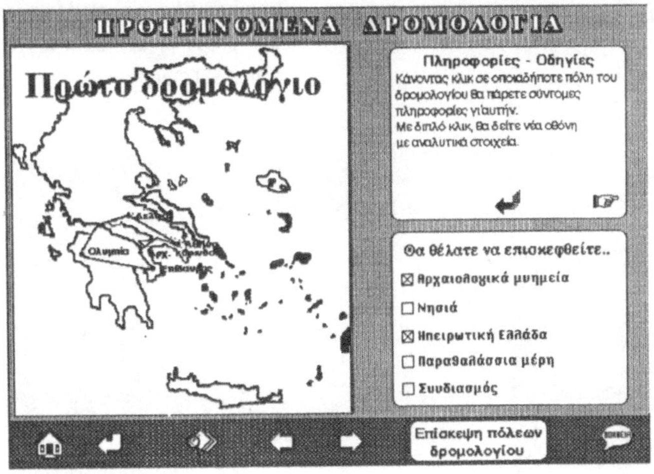

Fig. 4. A suggested tour on archaeological sites on the continental part of Greece

As regards the deletion of a geographical (composite) object, other than a Country object, it does not take place as in most conventional applications, i.e. it does not imply the elimination of all its components. Rather, when a geographical object O is deleted, its components become directly attached to the composite, to which O initially belonged. In terms of the aggregation hierarchy of Fig. 1, this policy means that the deletion of an object belonging to a non-leaf class implies the *elimination of the object's name*: the object cannot be accessed by the HTGuide retrieval mechanisms, but it still serves as a dummy container of its components. However, the deletion of a **Country** object results in the elimination of all its components.

5 A Prototype Implementation of HTGuide

A prototype of the proposed HTGuide model has been implemented on a Macintosh platform using MacroMind Director^{TM} for the construction of the animation sequences and for audio-visual synchronisation. The object-oriented data model, the interface, the naming mechanism and the automatic linking facility have been developed using the HyperTalk language. No knowledge of HyperTalk is required to perform the activities described in the previous sections. The multimedia data intended for usage in HTGuide must be

In the current implementation, author-defined hotspots are supported both for textual items and for images, but the end-user may define only textual hotspots.

Properties ranging over the subhierarchy rooted at the class **Facility** are implemented as components, i.e. objects of this subhierarchy of classes only exist within the geographical objects they belong to. This approach facilitates local updates over global ones, since the tourist agency is expected to modify individual facilities attached to a given geographical object, rather than update the same property of all objects appearing as facilities to any geographical objects in a global way.

Fig. 5 and Fig. 6 depict the cards presented to the HTGuide user for the region and town objects. Fig. 5 shows the region of Chania in the island Crete and Fig. 6 shows all the facilities provided by the city of Chania.

The buttons at the bottom of the card in Fig. 5, serve for the activation of the HTGuide direct access mechanism, for the traversal of the aggregation hierarchy towards sibling and towards higher level nodes, for the usage of the history and for the activation of the on-line Help. The small map at the upper left-hand corner serves for accessing other geographical nodes at the same level of the aggregation hierarchy. Finally, on the central map in Fig. 5, each textual item is a hotspot for direct access to the geographical object with the same name. On Fig.

6, the button for the display of the {food} property is activated, presenting a menu of selections of the subclasses of the class **Restaurant**, to which the objects of this set belong. The user is prompted to select objects of a subclass, whereupon the list of the restaurants in this subclass will be presented.

6 Conclusions and Future Work

The development of tourist multimedia systems has become lately very active and a number of systems offering guidance to tourists have started to appear [9, 14, 16]. Along these lines, this paper presented a **H**ypermedia **T**ourist **Guide** system, called HTGuide.

Fig. 5. Region object for the Chania region in Crete

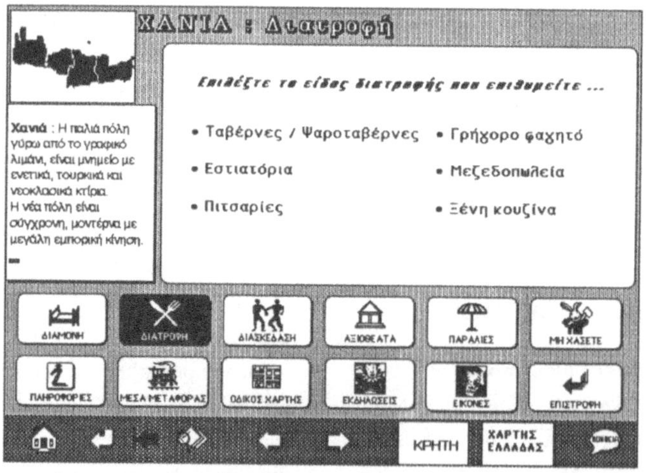

Fig. 6. Facilities provided by the Town object for the city of Chania

The main advantages of HTGuide are its user-friendliness, its interactivity, its openness and extendibility and its provision of a model suitable for the design of multimedia tourist applications. HTGuide also proposes two classifications of information at the higher level of design (tourist attractions and facilities), which help in the automatic creation of links and in the maintenance of the database schema.

The requirements for developing the HTGuide prototype have been collected by interviewing its potential users (i.e. travel agents and tourists). The prototype has been tested by a large number of Greek tourists (hence, its Greek language interface) in large tourist agencies in Athens and it has been updated according to the obtained results. Further development of the prototype will include a multi-lingual interface.

Currently we are working towards the development of a conceptual language for the formal expression of the concepts and the relationships between the conceptual entities defined in the schema. This language will model clearly real-world objects belonging in the tourist domain. The same model will also be used in checking integrity and completeness constraints during the instantiation of new tourist applications.

Future work involves the incorporation of HTGuide in the communication infrastructure of the constraint-based tourist guidance system MaTourA [9]. HTGuide will then be used to automatically generate user interface agents. Following this approach, it will then be possible to use real-world data, stored in large distributed tourist data bases, as they are becoming accessible by the information retrieval agent of MaTourA.

References

1. Acksyn, R., McCracken, D. and Yoder, E.: KMS: A distributed hypertext system for managing knowledge in organisations, *Comm. ACM* 31, 820, 1988.

2. Berk, E. and Devlin, J. (eds.): *Hypertext/Hypermedia Handbook*, McGraw-Hill, 1991.

3. Botafogo, R.A., Rivlin, E. and Schneiderman, B. : Structural Analysis of Hypertexts: Identifying Hierarchies and Useful Metrics, *ACM TOIS* 10, 142, (1992).

4. Conklin, J. : Hypertext: An Introduction and Survey, *IEEE Computer*, September 1987, pp. 17-41.

5. Conklin, J. and Bageman, M.L. : g-IBIS: A Hypertext tool for exploratory policy discussion, *ACM TOIS* 6, 303, (1988).

6. Fischer, G. and Morch, A. : JANUS: Integrating Hypertext with a knowledge-based Design Environment, in [10].

7. Garzotto, F., Paolini, P. and Schwabe, D. : HDM - A Model Based Approach to Hypertext Application Design, *ACM TOIS* 11, 1, (1993).

8. G. Gyftodimos and M. Spiliopoulou. Ariadne's cord as reorientation tool for the exploration of a hypertext network in Greek, *Proceedings of the 3rd Panhellenic Conference on Informatics*, pp. 298-312, Athens, Greece, *1991*.

9. Halatsis, C et al. : MaTourA: Multi-Agent Tourist Advisor, *Proceedings of ENTER'94*, Springer-Verlag, 1993.

10. *Proceedings of Hypertext '89 Conference*, Pittsburgh, Pa. Nov. 5-8, 1989, ACM, New York, 1989.

11. Jonassen, D.H. and Mandl, H. (eds.) : *Designing Hypermedia for Learning*, Springer-Verlag 1990.

12. Littleford, A. : Artificial Intelligence and Hypermedia, in [2] pp. 357-378.

13. Marshall, C.C. : Guided Ttours and on-line presentations: How authors make existing hypertext intelligible for readers, in [10], pp. 15-26.

14. Plaisant, C : Guide to Opportunities in Volunteer Archaeology: Case Study on the Use of a Hypertext System in a Museum Exhibit, in [2], pp. 498-505.

15. Salton, G. *Automatic Text Processing*, Addisson-Wesley, Reading, Mass, 1989.

16. Stamatopoulos, P., Karali, I., and Halatsis, C. : PETINA - Tour generation using the ElipSys inference system, in *Proceedings of the 1992 ACM/SIGAPP Symposium on Applied Computing*, Vol. 1, pp. 320-327, 1992.

17. P.T. Zellweger. Scripted documents: A Hypermedia path mechanism, in [10], pp. 1-14

TIS/MM
- PORTUGAL -

*Gerald Quirchmayr * and Reinhold Schimak ***

* Forschungsinstitut für Anwendungsorientierte Wissensverarbeitung (FAW)
Abteilung für Verwaltungsinformatik
Johannes Kepler Universität
Altenbergerstr. 69
A-4040 Linz
Austria

** Institut für Informatik
Abteilung für Informatik in Wirtschaft, Verwaltung und Gesellschaft
Johannes Kepler Universität
Altenbergerstr. 69
A-4040 Linz
Austria

ABSTRACT

The objective of our paper is to demonstrate in how far multimedia systems can contribute to improving traditional tourist information systems by adding additional valuable information such as convincive images of holiday resorts and accommodations. In addition to this advantage, multimedia technology can also help to improve existing user interfaces.

INTRODUCTION

In the domain of tourism there are several systems available on the market, almost all of them focusing on managing the internal data of travel agencies. Systems directly supplying the customer with information about the destination are however scarce.

figure 1: coast of lisboa

Integrating the classical "booking systems" with multimedia systems containing images and videos of resorts, accommodations and other important issues, such as the culture and history of a country (region, city). This add-on will definitly make the existing systems more flexible and usable for direct customer consultation.

Another idea is to use them as replacement for traditional print media. Figure 1 gives an impression of how we have tried to implement an advanced user interface satisfying the above-mentioned demands.

Summarizing we state the following requirements:

- an easy to handle system, i. e. user interface.
- a system which can be used as a selling assistant in tourist offices.
- a stand alone version
- an add-on to traditional tourist guides

The System Concept

In order to be able to use the system in two forms, as a stand alone version in travel agencies or as add-on to traditional tourist guides (or even as a replacement) on CD-Rom we have had to choose standard DOS-Tools, such as Asymetrix MS Toolbook, Windows 3.1, and dBase IV files as basis for the implementation [1] (see figure 2).

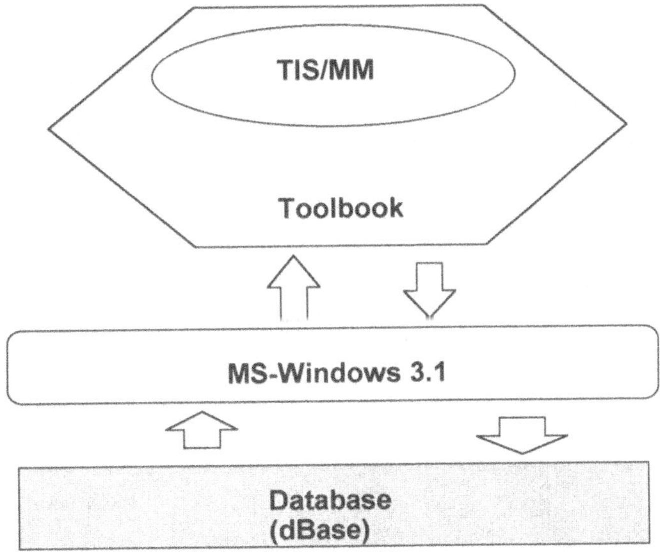

figure 2: system components

The reason why we have choosen Toolbook simply is it's cheapness compared with other multimedia software and that it does allow the creation of runtime versions.

In order to meet the organizational requirements concerning the maintenance of TIS/MM - Portugal, we propose the following structure (similar to CITY Info) [2]:

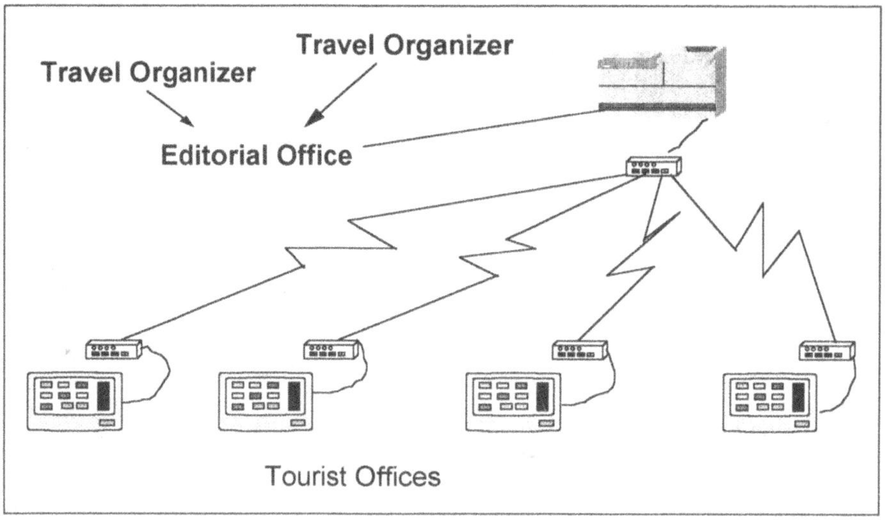

figure 3: network organization

Several travel organizer send their informations to an editorial office managing the data. The system in the tourist offices will be updated by regulary modem communication.

DESIGN AND IMPLEMENTATION

The major requirements on such a system are almost obvious: it must be easy to use and maintenance should not cause any problem. That is why we have designed our system in a way that it is formed around a shell providing an easy to use interface. Maintenance of the textual information is therefore done via a simple dBase IV interface. Images are imported from Kodak Photo CDs.

The information available in the system can be classified as follows [1]:

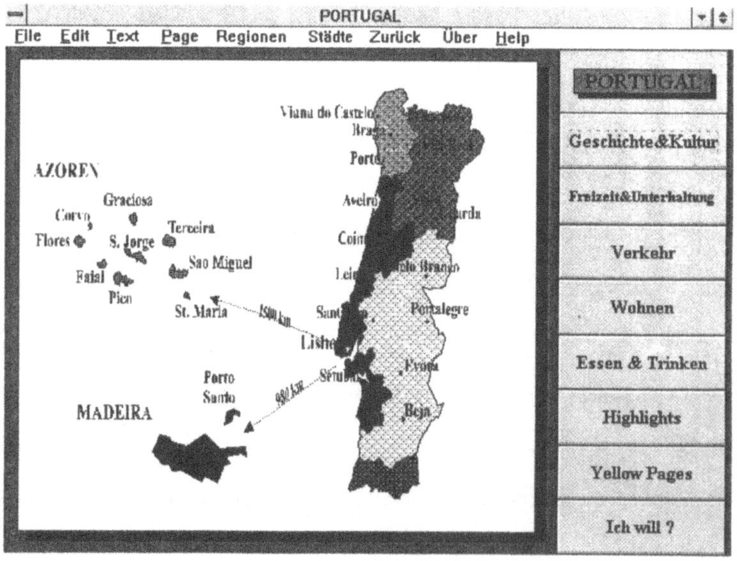

- history and culture
- leisure and events
- traffic information
- accommodation
- restaurants, pubs and bars
- highlights
- yellow pages
- keywords allowing some basic information retrieval

figure 4: user interface

The user has three opportunities to enter the system:

- menuitems,
- maps and
- index.

To make the system flexible and adaptable it is organized in a way that information is grouped by countries, regions and cities, an approach which allows us to provide the user with a sort of zoom function.

The structure of the system consists of two parts. First, the hierarchical structure as shown below:

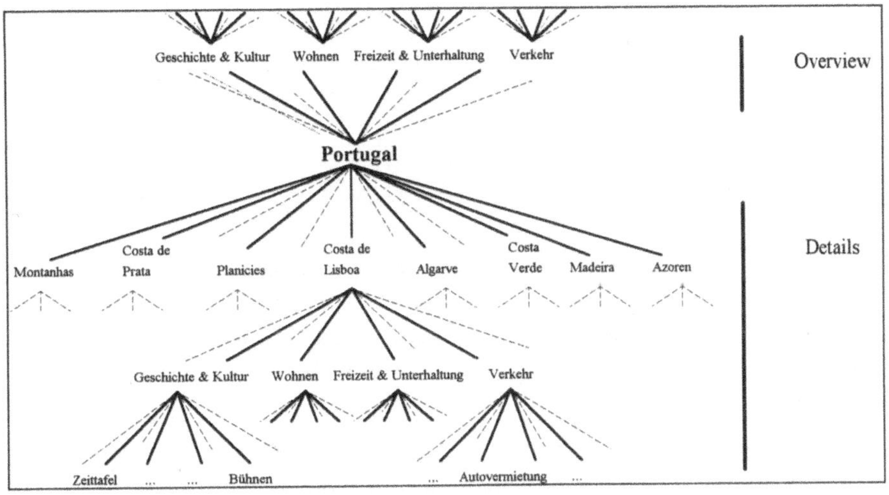

figure 5: hierarchical system structure

Second, the cross references between the several parts of the system:

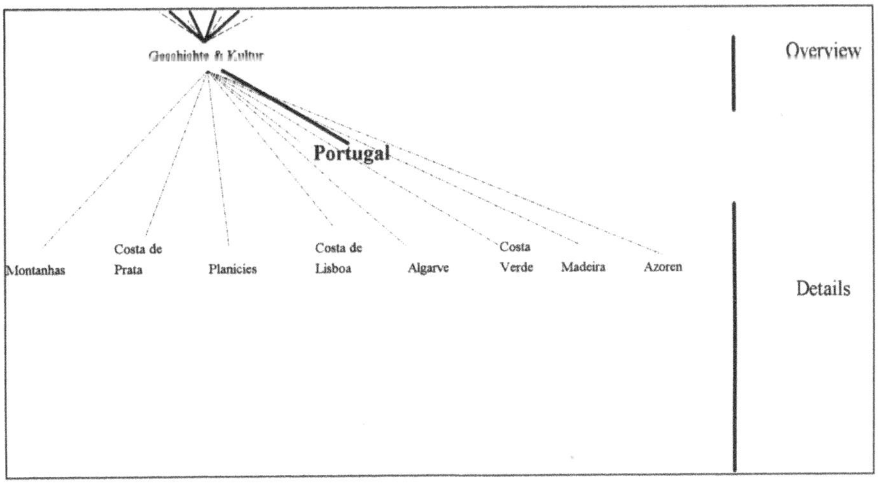

figure 6: cross references

These two structures should be realized in one system. The following figure demonstrates the combination of the two structures shown above [1].

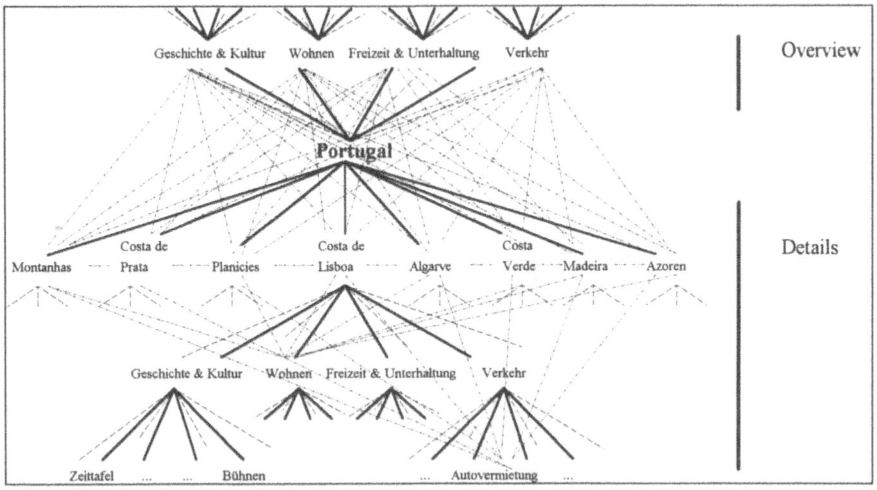

figure 7: hierarchical system-structure with cross connections

The solution is a matrix [3] (fig. 4, fig. 8), organized in rows as classifaction points, in columns as region and citys. Classification points describes the local selection in user interface. The menubar specifies the columns of the matrix (global selection).

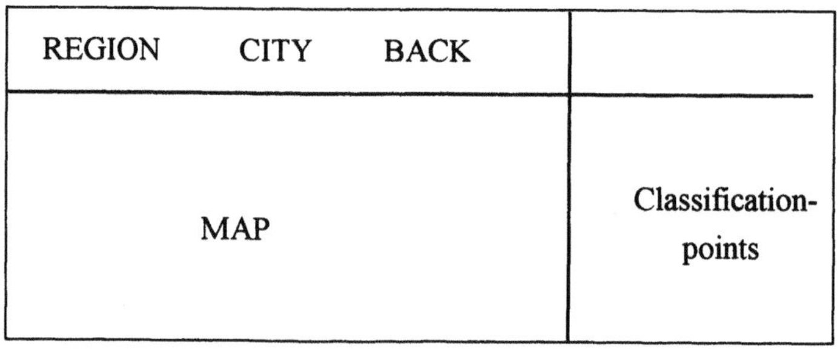

figure 8: matrix-organization

The screen-shoot of the user interface (fig. 4) presents the map of Portugal, the menubar with the items "Region", "Städte" and "Zurück" and on the right hand the classification points (history and culture, leisure and events, traffic information, ...)

FUTURE DEVELOPMENT

The current version of the systems aims at providing customers in travel agencies with additional information. The Portugal-prototype has first been presented at "Viennas Tourist Fair" (Ferienmesse Wien 1993).

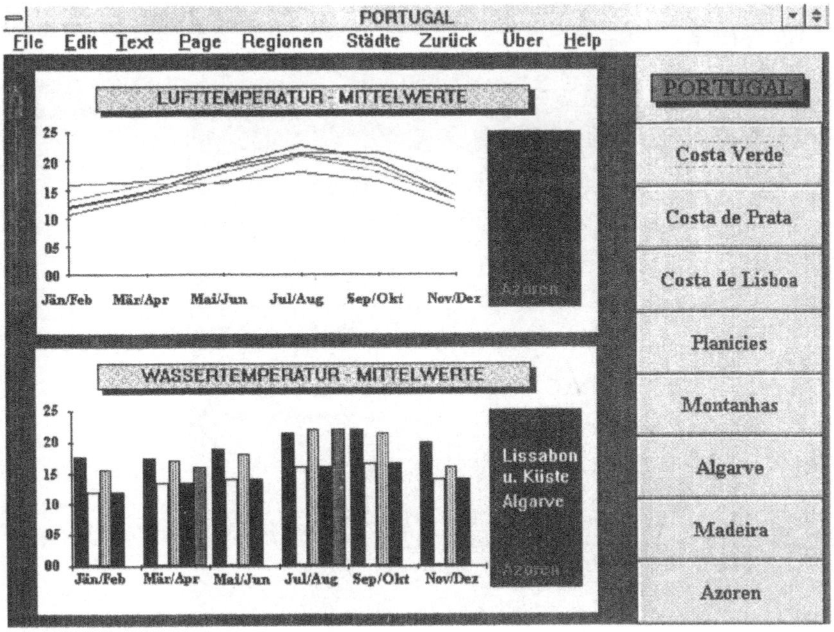

figure 9: table of climate

It is planned to produce CD-Rom versions as soon as the prototype has been tested during one or two seasons. If the storage capacity available at travel agencies does allow it, videos and animations will be added in the next version.

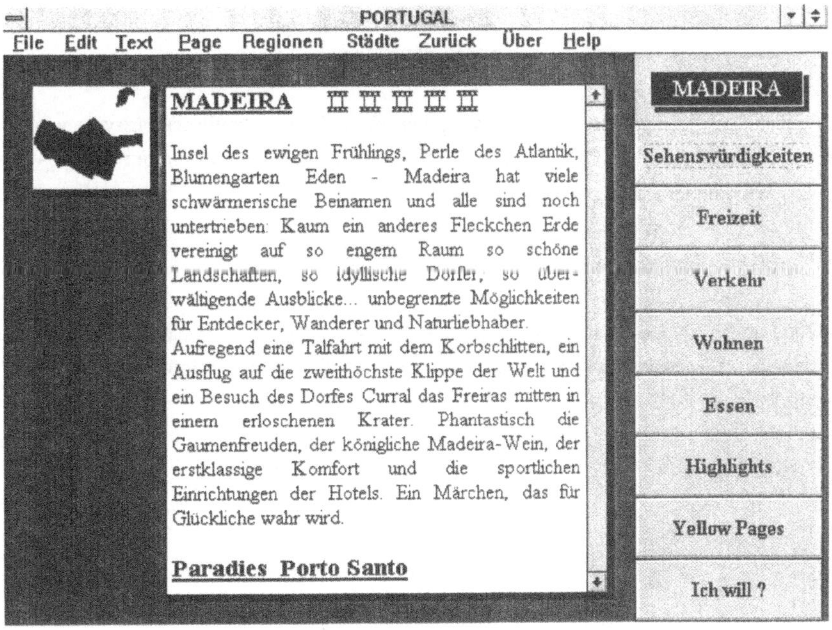

figure 10a: highlights

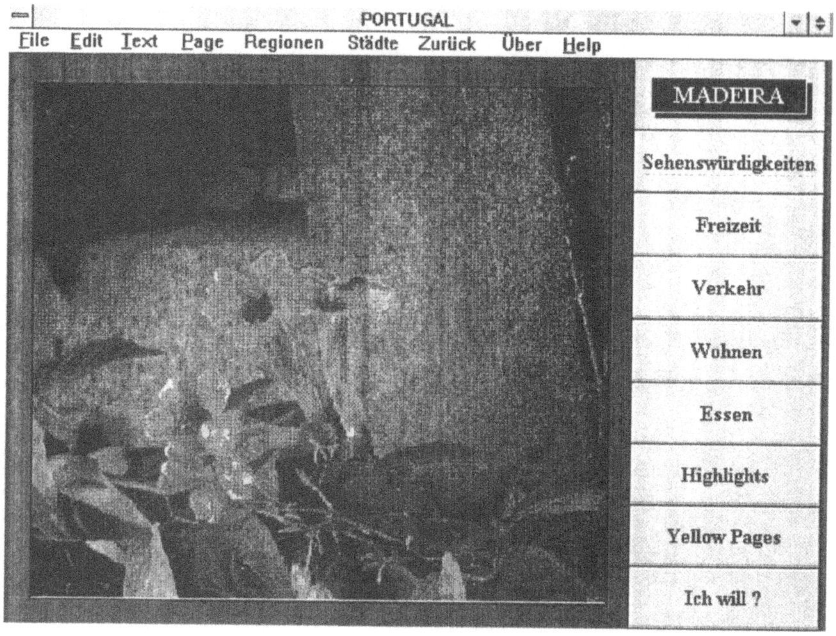

figure 10b: highligths

REFERENCES

[1] R. Schimak; "Grundlagen, Komponenten und Konzeption eines Touristeninformationssystems auf Basis von Multimedia (TIS/MM)", thesis at Uneriversity of Linz, Institut für Informatik, Abteilung für Informatik in Wirtschaft, Verwaltung und Gesellschaft, 1992 - 1993, under review.

[2] City Info, "TIP?!TAP - Die Software", Eigenverlag, Wien, 1992

[3] R. Denzer, Dialogue Shifts - A New Paradigm for the Visual Presentation of Complex Environmental Data, in: R. Denzer, G. Schimak, W. Haas (eds.), Visualisierung von Umweltdaten 1992, 3. Workshop, Schloß Zell an der Pram, Dez. 1992, pp. 36 - 37, Informatik Aktuell, Springer, 1993

CAN TOURISM BE REPLACED BY VIRTUAL REALITY TECHNOLOGY?

Sabine Musil and Georg Pigel

Vienna User Interface Group, Lenaugasse 2/8, A-1080 Wien

Abstract

There is no doubt that Virtual Reality (VR) technology will be exploited by the entertainment industry. In this paper we will discuss the trend towards a more and more artificial environment in which to consume our spare time, a trend which is enforced by public panic of a polluted nature. In this context we will show the visions VR technology offers, its strengths and its defeciencies. In our conclusions we will attempt to answer the question of the title.

Introduction

Imagine it is Friday in the year 2010. After a hard business day you want to do something for your fitness before finishing off your balances. You decide to tour with your bicycle through the Alps. But instead of driving to a holiday resort somewhere in the Tyrol you just go into the next room, turn on your computer, choose a program, put on a strange helmet, sit down on your hometrainer and start pedaling. Up the slopes and down the hills in the beautiful countryside of Austrian mountains. The sun is shining and you can regulate the wind by turning a knob on your handle bar. After two exhausting hours you climb down from your bike and go back to work.

An event like this is not as far away from reality as it may seem. In the past few years a new direction of information technology has emerged from the brains of some people, that first were considered lunatics, but then convinced with their ideas. What we mean is Virtual Reality (VR).

Virtual can be defined as "being in essence or in effect, but not in fact" and reality is defined as "a real event, entity of state of affairs". Insofar we could paraphrase virtual reality as "a fact or real event that is such in essence, but not in fact." [16] What we are talking about is a kind of human computer interface, that goes beyond the traditional interaction devices and also beyond the common human-computer interfaces. It takes up new interaction devices like the DataGlove, head mounted displays and even whole data suits and adds a new dimension to interfacing, namely that of being able to move around consciously in something that looks like reality, but isn't.

The trend to use such virtual realities instead of the real thing can be seen in a lot of areas. Partly panicked by a more and more polluted environment, partly because of social isolation people turn to second hand experiences.

In the realm of sports more and more people use machines and equipment to perform various disciplines indoors that are normally carried out outside. There exist the hometrainer to cycle, a sort of band conveyor to jog, a rowing machine to row and there is even a machine to climb stairs. Latest developments provide the sportswoman with a facility for indoor golfing and also indoor skiing

[17]. In addition to just making exercising possible the equipment used for these two disciplines offers some kind of real nature simulation. Virtual reality researchers have taken up this field, too and have carried on these ideas. A sports and fitness playhouse is presented in [19]. Autodesk has developed an environment for cycling tours where the cycle just like in the movie E.T. takes off if it is fast enough ([9]).

Another real thing that is replaced by a machine is the sun. As he becomes more dangerous every year caused by the growing ozone hole, but people nevertheless want to be tanned, they turn to solariums to achieve the desired level of bronzing. Some refuse the sun completely and prefer the loneliness in the blue lights of the fluorescent lamps to a day in the sun with friends. The logical continuation of that trend would be virtual beaches. Steps in this direction can be seen with holiday resorts like the Vienna City Club, with its artificial tropical shore.

Even the most natural thing in the world, sex, is experiencing a shift to virtual spheres. People no longer seek their satisfaction in a real relationship but prefer rubber maids, porno videos, peep shows and dial-a-porns. Partly this trend may be caused by the rising of AIDS, but to some extent this is also a sign of our inability to communicate in a time when worldwide communication has been made possible and it only takes some seconds to transport a piece of information from one pole to the other. Possibly we are overwhelmed by the mass of information and communication that we do not want to take the troubles of establishing communication and relationships in our sparetime, either. Also this area has been given attention in the virtual reality community. Teledildonic has become a well known term and is presented in [14].

Our last example area brings us back to tourism and was more or less the motivation to write this paper. Today people no longer feel the need to really seeing places. Often a video or a plastic copy is all they want to get an impression of a certain place. This trend is, for us surprisingly, supported by the tourism industry itself. When one books a journey often a video of the chosen place is shown while the paperwork is done. Theme parks are becoming more and more fashionable because there it is possible to visit far off places, but still staying more or less at home. As for virtual reality this trend opens up a vast playground. The virtual holiday trip to the African jungles or even to Mars is something that can be done very easily and, if cheap enough, will offer the joys of such trips to people, who normally wouldn't be able to afford them.

This paper tries to show the chances and risks such virtual realities are offering for tourism. In order to do so we start with painting a picture of a recreation center of the future which serves as an example of how a virtual reality could be used for tourism purposes. Then we explain the necessary technology to produce such an experience, its abilities and shortcomings today, and finally we talk about what virtual reality offers for tourism and what tourism can do for virtual reality. We also will put an eye on the dangers that this new technology is bringing along. Conclusions will round the paper off.

Scenario

In this section we want to give an impression of what could be done with virtual reality. We describe a possible scenario of a next generation' s recreation center.

It is Sunday afternoon in July. Ruzlan and his girlfriend Miriam are sitting at home in Hamburg, watching TV, bored and upset. Suddenly Ruzlan proposes to go rafting and Miriam, not astonished at all, simply nods and agrees. They discuss about which course to choose this time. To cross the Klondike or the Ötztaler Ache would attract them but why not have something real exotic for a change? Still undecided they get up and go to the "Exotic Center", the leading house for exploring nature at its exciting side, throw in their coins and enter a cabin.

In the red subdued light of the cabin they see the equipment needed for virtual fun: A suit with numerous senders and sensors which allows the virtual reality system to track down their movements with an accuracy of only a few millimeters, the head mounted display and the sound system, which is hidden inside a helmet, looking very much like the ones motorcyclists are wearing. All data are transmitted wirelessly, so that the actors have more freedom in their movements. Ruzlan and Miriam put on their helmets. Immediately they are inside the virtual reality system. An incredibly soft voice which could be of either sex welcomes them and instructs both actors in how to put on the VR suits. Then Ruzlan and Miriam are asked to get hold of the tactile feedback system.

This feedback system consists of two handles for the hands and a pair of large boots, into which the actress steps and which she then wears like overshoes. The last part of the tactile feedback system is an elastic rubber band, which is tightened when neccessary to give the actress the impression of sitting, but also to make sure the actress does not fall down and gets injured during a VR session. So one actually gets tactile feedback on the hands, the back and the feet only. Nevertheless this is enough to provide a very realistic feeling, as all other tactile sensations are present through the actress's imagination, too. More sophisticated tactile feedback systems have been tested such as suits which get harder and softer by either filling little cells inside the suit according to the simulation or by special materials which stiffen when under electric current. But these systems have been rejected by most people who do VR only for fun as they felt cramped, especially if tactile feedback was given to the head to produce a feeling of acceleration. Besides, such special tactile feedback equipment must be tailor-made to the actress's body to get the full use out of it, and therefore has proved not to be very practical for public recreation centers.

Ruzlan and Miriam have been in VR before, so they do not need the instructions. The next step in starting the VR is to select one's personal appearance in cyberspace. The actresses in VR see each other not in reality but as part of the simulation. Therefore each actress can select her looks and clothes but even voice, sex and physical strength at will. Anyway, as creating a full VR character is very complicated and time consuming, the actresses are only allowed to choose a basic character and to make minor modifications to it such as changing the colour of hair and eyes, or the clothes worn. It was fashionable for some time to appear totally naked in the simulation, but in a strange alliance women's lib movements and the Christian churches together pushed a law which declared such interesting variations unethical and prohibited.

After selecting their characters Ruzlan and Miriam still cannot make up their minds on which river to choose. So they let the random generator create the river, which has the exciting advantage, that river and landscape will change after each winding. And off they go! They hear the roaring of the water, they see rocks and cliffs avoiding them only some inches, and they feel the raft thrown up and down by the enormous forces of the current. After fighting against nature with all their strengths, Ruzlan and Miriam seem to have made it to calmer water, when suddenly there is a rock in the middle of the river and the raft hits it! Our actors feel a strong blow, they hear the sound of breaking wood, and all at once find themselves in the midst of white boiling water, grasping for air. They are taken away by the floods and seem to faint. But then the sounds calm down and the incredibly soft, sexless voice announces the end of the trip. It congratulates our actors to their skills in rafting and, not without stating how glad the VR system would be to meet its favourite participants again, Ruzlan and Miriam are instructed in how to release the tactile feedback equipment and how to take off suits and helmets. Then our heroes leave the subdued red light of the cabin. Still moved by the exciting dangers they just have survived, by the strong impressions of rocky stiff mountains and the masses of roaring water Ruzlan and Miriam leave the 'Exotic Center' to take a deep breath in the warm air of a midsummernight in Hamburg.

How Far Away? - Today's VR Technology

In this section we want to describe what today's typical virtual reality equipment looks like, what it is still lacking and into which direction future research in this field will go.

There is one stream in VR research which claims to be able to create an artificial reality not with gloves and goggles but by filming the actress and displaying her image on the screen. These VR environments are called unencumbering. The 'guru' in this line of VR is Myron W. Krueger, an example environment would be VIDEOPLACE [8]. This technique is very much suited for bringing a kind of VR experience to the broad audience as there is nothing to hold, nothing to wear and no wires.

Another kind of VR, which is the one we have used for our scenario, are the physically involving artificial realities. Most of the basic work in this area was driven by military research for developing flight simulators, head-up displays and 'virtual cockpits' [5].

Such a VR sytem typically consists of a number of hardware devices:

♦ A head mounted stereoscopic display. The Private Eye, a widely used monitor for head-mounted displays, provides a resolution of 720 x 280 pixels in black and white. The size of its display is 3.9 inches in the diagonal by a weight of 2.25 ounces. Two such devices are fixed in a helmet. The display must completely fill the user's field of vision to give a convincing feeling of presence in VR. A head-mounted stereoscopic display such as VIEW [4] supplies a field of vison of 120 degrees both horizontally and vertically, with up to 90 degrees overlap in the binocular fields.

♦ The tracking system is needed to record motions of the head to compute the actress's position and the direction she is looking into. The most popular tracking device, the Polhemus 3Space Isotrack [13], senses changes in a magnetic field and reports spacial position and angle of the head 60 times a second. But as this system has a rather limited working range and is very sensitive to interferences other possibilities such as optical tracking systems are under exploration [20].

♦ A glove is used as input device for position and gesture information. It reports hand position and finger bend. The first commercially available glove device was the DataGlove by VPL Research [18]. The DataGlove uses fiber optics to determine finger bend and a Polhemus tracker to determine hand position. This technology is not suited for mass production and therefore quite expensive. Nevertheless the entertainment industry produces such gloves as input devices for video games, e. g. Mattel manufactures the Power Glove which uses variable resistance material for finger bend, and ultrasonics for hand position [12]. The Power Glove is a cheap device but offers less accuracy than the DataGlove and therefore only allows to record a more limited number of gestures.

♦ The last, but not least devices needed for VR are one or more high performance workstations for performing the computations. Typically Silicon Graphics machines are chosen for their high performance graphics facilities. There are research reports claiming to have enough computing power with one 20 MHz 386-based IBM PC, but personal experiences with a SPEA PC based VR system let us doubt the quality of such solutions. Most researchers have to use one or more workstations to achieve good performance [1,3,15].

All this provides the actress in virtual reality with the possibility to see stereoscopic pictures according to the movements of her head and allows gesture input by e. g. pointing with the finger into a certain direction, dropping down menus by a snip with the fingers, or selecting by rolling the hand.

Still there are enough crucial problems to solve:

♦ It is not usual to record the motions of the eyes, it is always the full head that is tracked. This means that in order to take a look to the side in VR you have to turn your head instead of only moving your eyes as you are used to in natural life. As trivial as this problem seems to be, as annoying it is in practice as it violates natural behavior very hard. An example for research in this field can be found in [7].

♦ Despite the consequent development of faster and faster hardware it still is a problem to achieve a satisfying frame rate (i. e. the rate in which the displayed pictures are updated). Researchers claim a satisfying frame rate of twenty to thirty-two frames a second to be a lower limit. This is more important than realistic pictures [12].

♦ Today's VR equipment does not allow free movements. This is due to the limited range of the tracking system and to the number of cables and power supplies the helmet and glove require. Users still have the feeling that they are reducing their personal freedom when they put on VR equipment.

♦ A direct consequence of the restricted freedom of movements is the problem of how to move through virtual space. You cannot simply walk through the virtual space, as the real room in which the experiment is performed is limited to a few square meters. Today's solution normally consists of the actress navigating through VR by standing on a vehicle and pointing into the direction she wants to go. If the user wants to view an object which is in the range of the vehicle, she may walk over to it. The limits of the vehicle are normally displayed by a railing that cannot be passed.[12]

♦ The most important problem still to solve is that of tactile feedback. Today's research tries to develop force-feedback for the hand wearing the gesture input device, the glove [0], or lets the actress feel the texture of surfaces with her hand [11]. All of these approaches have in common that they are limited to give feedback only to one hand and that the devices are not more than inconvenient baroque mechanical prototypes.

Anyway, in our opinion the problem of force feedback will be solved for specific applications (for bicycling for example) in the next years, but a force feedback device for the whole body that can be used by general VR applications is not in sight yet.

Despite all these problems mentioned above we think that VR technology is far enough developed to be taken seriously and that due to the dominance of graphical information in human reception existing technology can produce impressive applications.

VR vs. Tourism

In this section we want to discuss the possibilities of using virtual reality for tourism purposes, talk about the possible synergies but also keep an eye on the dangers that such developments are constituting to tourism in the way that we know it today. We will give an overview of possible areas where VR could be used to serve tourism and also talk about the advantages and disadvantages of such applications.

A first possible application area is some kind of adventure trip like the one that we have described in our scenario. One could be enabled to climb a dangerous mountain, to traverse a mysterious cave, to parachute from 10 km height or to raft through dangerous waters. The advantage of doing such trips in this way is that they are not dangerous at all and nevertheless can provide the user with the possibility of accidents and catastrophies any time they want. We think that this is a very important aspect. Today people more and more want to test their limits in their sparetime. They search for extreme disciplines like free climbing and bungee jumping. But very often people are not well trained when they do these things and so there regularly happen accidents. VR technology can help to overcome these dangers to some extent. On the one hand it can possibly check the user's body functions like heartbeat and bloodpressure and turn the system off if the values go beyond certain limits. On the other hand the system makes sure that you will survive the virtual catastrophies it initiates. You can drown three times a day if you want, but return home in the evening anyway.

Another kind of adventures are of visits to savage areas like the jungles of South America, the deserts of Africa or the deep sea. Again, these adventures are not dangerous and still have another advantage: if they are cheap enough they provide experiences to a lot of people which normally they could never afford and probably also shouldn't be able to afford in order to preserve the nature. In this way information technology becomes an environmentalist.

If we spin on this idea of adventure trips we must also think of adventures in outer space, fairy worlds and other time periods. A trend towards having such trips can be seen in the rising popularity of role games with a narrator and adventure games on the computer. Virtual reality could provide the people with the best possible simulation of such worlds and even could replace the now necessary narrator and the need for rolling dice.

All these possible adventures have one thing in common. They replace conventional theme or adventure parks. In our opinion it makes no sense to open such parks any longer because they will be superseded by virtual theme parks in the near future. People will prefer the latter ones as they offer the better simulation and are not weather dependent.

Another application area of virtual reality for tourism purposes are educational leaves. One could visit the ancient Rome, Vienna during the reign of Maria Theresia or walk through the Salzburg of Mozart's time. Of course such a trip can't replace the visit to the town or regions completely but it can enrich the impressions of the sight. We can think of two kinds of tours. Either the user explores the area by herself or she makes use of a guide. The concept of guides serving as interface agents has already been adopted by HCI researchers for Multimedia interfaces, e.g. by [10], and it is only a small step from there to virtual reality. Guides can have certain features, which causes the same tour made with different guides to be different. The user can select the guide she wants according to her interests and in this way construct her personal tour.

This kind of sightseeing is superseding the normal one, because it allows the participant to be more directly involved. It is very nice if a guide tells you that this or that has happened here some hundred years ago, but it is a much greater experience if you can 'virtually' take part in that event.

One further application area has been mentioned already in the introduction: sports. A lot of disciplines can be simulated with virtual reality, again presenting riskfree joys, but also providing nothing more than can be found in reality. Insofar we do not like the idea of virtual skiing, cycling etc. Things like that truely make sense if one uses them to be independent of the weather or the season, but there remains the question if virtual reality shan't better be used for application areas where it can provide more than reality (e.g. the flying bicycle) or where it increases the usability of reality significantly (for example by making it harmless).

Similar things are valid for the last application area we want to mention, virtual beaches. Imagine people wearing goggles that show them pictures of beautiful sandy beaches, lying in the 'sun' of the solarium attached above them and swimming in a little pool that simulates them the Mediterranean. If this illusion works, it is doubtable if people will still feel the need to go to Italy, Spain or the South Sea, especially if these virtual experiences are cheaper than the real ones and still provide the same feeling.

Looking at all these examples virtual reality seems to offer the following things to tourism:

- ♦ it opens up the possibility to see places that one normally couldn't visit, such as outer space, or shouldn't visit, such as the Antarctica. If these virtual trips are cheap enough they will open a new dimension for tourism as there certainly would have to emerge a new economy branch that produces these experiences.
- ♦ it allows journeys through time and thus giving the tourist an additional means of exploring a certain sight. If used with guides there also is the chance of giving such a tour a certain motto that will meet the user's interests as far as possible.

♦ it makes adventures harmless and so reduces the risk of accidents as people won't try the real thing if they are only curious. Climbing a virtual rock is of course putting the climber at a much lower risk of meeting with an accident and with that she is saving her life and the lives of possible rescuers.

But there are also some aspects of virtual reality that are a danger to tourism and the human being as *ens sociale*:

♦ it could replace the need to actually visit a place as the impression one can get of a place virtually is as good as the real one.
♦ it could withhold people from travelling as virtual journeys are more comfortable and possibly also cheaper.
♦ it could destroy people's ability to deal with reality. As everything they do becomes harmless they cannot judge the risks and consequences of their actions any longer. It could become difficult to tell the game from reality.

Nevertheless virtual reality will never be able to replace tourism completely for the following reasons. On the one hand virtual realities will in our opinion never be able to replace the feeling of being in nature and seeing, hearing, feeling and breathing an environment that is real and not coming out of the can. Insofar regional tourism experts should rely on selling this general experience and not try to advertise certain events or sights that can be easily made up by computer technology.

On the other hand virtual reality environments are never a real social event, the person that is using them is always alone with her data glove and head mounted displays. Although there exist virtual realities that are built for two or more [1,2], we definetely believe that this is not the same as being together in reality. VR not only offers new experiences, but also a gateway from reality into a land of dreams. It is undoubtably more exciting to be a hero in a tailor-made environment than to face problems with real human beings who have the annoying feature of not always being of the same opinion. The ability to cope with your social environment could get lost by heavy use of VR technology. You could become lonely, isolated and unable to communicate although you are connected with a vast cyberspace.

Real tourism instead is a social event. Tourism managers should try to stress that feature in their advertisings in order not to be overrun by technology.

Conclusions

Summing up all our thoughts we can state that tourism for the broad masses (adventure holidays) in an artificially styled environment a'la Disneyworld (theme parks) will in the long run not be able to stand a chance against VR, no matter if it is more entertainment centered (Fantasyland) or more culturally teaching centered (Historyland). Creating artificial homogeneous environments is exactly what VR will be able to do best, with the advantage that each visitor of such a virtual space can be a hero and take part in adventures that will never be possible in the most exciting park she visits without endangering the tourist's life. But endangering the tourist's life can never be good for the offering part, as the tourist wants to have the thrill without risk. Therefore in selling adventures VR will be superior to 'real' tourism (and probably cheaper, too).

A tourism country should not try to sell itself as a show stage where the visitor can have the most exciting adventures and enjoy herself being a hero, but has to present itself as a complex environment where the natives also got other troules than to 'joddle'' on the mountain tops the whole day long.

These are the things VR is not able to do. Insofar we can answer the question of our title by saying that VR can enhance and augment tourism, but will never be able to replace it completely.

References

1. C. Blanchard, S. Burgess, Y. Harvill, J. Lanier, A. Lasko, M. Oberman, and M. Teitel. 'Reality Built For Two: A Virtual Reality Tool'. In: ACM SIGGRAPH 1990 Symposium on Interactive 3D Graphics, pp.35-36, March 1990.
2. C. Codella, R. Jalili, L. Koved, J.B. Lewis, D.T. Ling, J.S. Lipscomb, D.A. Rabenhorst, and C.P. Wang. 'Interactive Simulation in a Multi-Person Virtual World'. In: P. Brennersfield and J. Bennet, Eds., Striking a Balance, CHI'92 Conference Proceedings, pp.329-334, ACM, Addison-Wesley, 1992.
3. S. Fisher, E.M. Wenzel, C. Coler, and M.W. McGreevy. 'Virtual Interface Environment Workstations'. In: Proceedings of the Human Factors Society- 32nd Annual Meeting, 1988.
4. S.S. Fisher and J.M. Tazelaar. 'Living in a Virtual World'. Byte, pp.215-221, July 1990.
5. T.A. Furness and D.F. Kocian. 'Putting Humans Into Virtual Space'. In: Proceedings of the Society for Computer Simulation - Aerospace Conference, pp.214-225, San Diego, CA, 1986.
6. H. Iwata. 'Artificial Reality with Force-feedback: Development of Desktop Virtual Space with Compact Master Manipulator'. Computer Graphics, Vol.24, No.4, pp.165-170, August 1990.
7. R.J.K. Jacob. 'What You Look at Is What You Get: Eye Movement-Based Interaction Techniques'. In: J.C. Chew and J. Whiteside, Eds., Empowering People, CHI'90 Conference Proceedings, pp.11-18, ACM, Addison-Wesley, 1990.
8. M.W. Krueger. 'VIDEOPLACE-An Artificial Reality'. In: CHI'85 Conference Proceedings}, pp.35-40, ACM, 1985.
9. M.W. Krueger. Artificial Reality II. Addison-Wesley, 1991.
10. B. Laurel, T. Oren, and A. Don. 'Issues in Multimedia Interface Design: Media Integration and Interface Agents'. In: J.C. Chew and J.Whiteside, Eds., Empowering People, CHI'90 Conference Proceedings, pp.133-139, ACM, Addison-Wesley, 1990.
11. M. Minsky, M. Ouh-young, O. Steele, F.P. Brooks, and M.Behensky. 'Feeling and Seeing: Issues in Force Display'. In: Proceedings of the 1990 ACM Symposium on Interactive 3D Graphics, pp.235-244, Snowbird Ut., 1990.
12. R. Pausch. 'Virtual Reality on Five Dollars a Day'. In: S.P. Robertson, G.M. Olson, and J.S. Olson, Eds., Reaching Through Technology, CHI'91 Conference Proceedings}, pp.265-270, ACM, Addison-Wesley, 1991.
13. F. Rabb, E. Blood, R. Steiner, and H. Jones. 'Magnetic Position and Orientation Tracking System'. IEEE Transaction on Aerospace and Electronic Systems, Vol.15, No.5, pp.709-718, September 1979.
14. H. Rheingold. Virtual Reality. Summit Books, 1992.
15. C. Shaw, J. Liang, M. Green, and Y. Sun. 'The Decoupled Simulation Model for Virtual Reality Systems'. In: P.Brennersfield and J.Bennet, Eds., Striking a Balance, CHI'92 Conference Proceedings}, pp.321-328, ACM, Addison-Wesley, 1992.
16. M.B. Spring. 'Informating with Virtual Reality'. In: S.K. Helsel and J.P. Roth, Eds., Virtual Reality, Theory, Practice, and Promise, pp.3-17, Meckler Publishing, 1991.
17. Time International Magazine. 'Hot Stuff!, From the land of high-tech gizmos, more Techno Toys'. December 1992. p. 51.
18. VPL-Research. DataGlove Model 2 Users Manual. 1987.
19. R. Walser. 'Elements of a Cyberspace Playhouse'. In: S.K. Helsel and J.P. Roth, Eds., Virtual Reality, Theory, Practice, and Promise}, pp. 51-64, Meckler Publishing, 1991.
20. J. Wang, V. Chi, and H. Fuchs. 'A Real-time Optical 3D Tracker For Head-mounted Display Systems'. Computer Graphics: 1990 Symposion on Interactive 3D Graphics, Vol.24, No.2, pp.205-215, 1990.

ANATOMY OF A MULTIMEDIA PROJECT: APPLYING MULTIMEDIA TO PUBLIC TRANSPORT AND TOURIST INFORMATION

Dermot Rogers

MTI, Multimedia Centre, Trinity College Dublin

Abstract

This paper sets out the describe the design and development process, and features of a multimedia public information system, the Passenger Route Finder (PRF), which was developed by the MTI Multimedia Centre in TCD for London Underground Limited (LUL). While dealing with some technical aspects of the project, the paper will concentrate on the system's design, the nature of the development team and our experiences of developing such a system for a commercial client to a tight schedule.

Background

The Multimedia Centre in TCD has developed an interactive multimedia point of information system for London Underground. The touch screen system offers real-time routing, tourist information and a guide to the system's map, tickets and barriers.

The London Underground system is the longest metro system in the world with over 300 destinations and 13 intersecting and branching lines. Passengers navigate the system with the aid of the famous Underground map. Some people do so instinctively, but for many it takes time to learn and even then routes are often planned on the basis of incorrect assumptions.

Over 5 years ago London Underground's market research identified the need for a system which would provide passengers with an "intelligent" routing and general information system. Delays caused by travellers who are unfamiliar with the Underground system causes problems and frustration for other passengers and staff. They felt that a well designed point of information system would not only eliminate such problems but could also lead to more efficient use of the Underground by passengers in general. Additionally such systems are regarded as being an inevitable part of passenger information in the future.

Two previous attempts to produce similar Passenger Route Finder (PRF) systems had been unsuccessful. The business area responsible for the PRF had until March 31st 1993 to use the available budget for developing a prototype system, or face the loss of the budget allocation. In August 1992 the Multimedia Centre proposed a design, and in October a contract was awarded and work began.

Given the short time available to develop the PRF, London Underground's preference was to have a single supplier for both the software and hardware. The Multimedia Centre therefore undertook to design and develop the entire PRF system.

Functional Overview

The Passenger Route Finder (PRF) is multilingual, offering French, German, Italian and English text. Users have full flexibility in their choice of information and language at all points in the system. The PRF has three main offerings: the Routefinder, the London Explorer and About the Underground.

Routefinder

This allows passengers to pick any station destination in the London Underground system, and then generate the optimum route at that time to that destination. The Routefinder plots the route as an overlay on the system map, summarises the route in linear form alongside, indicates the estimated journey time and offers a detailed printout of the route. The printout contains all stations and line changes, platform and direction details plus time, date and walking directions if required. The passenger uses the printout as his/her private travel guide to their destination.

Their are 13 intersecting lines in the Underground system serving 260 stations. The frequency and availability of the service varies substantially particularly in stations distant from the centre (for example some stations offer peak hour service only) so the routing algorithm at the core of the system is very complex as is the database which stores the complete timetable for all stations.

London Explorer

This allows passengers to select destinations from six categories (famous sights, galleries, museums, parks & sports, shopping, entertainment). For each destination there is a full colour image, a street map section showing the sight's position and general information such as opening times, attractions and nearest Underground stations. Users can then choose to be routed to the sight.

On choosing the routing option in the London Explorer, a large map showing the walking route from the nearest Underground station to the tourist sight is plotted plus the rail route summary and "outlink" walking information to the sight. This route can then be printed as with the Routefinder option.

There are 50 tourist sights currently available in the PRF. This represents the major tourist attractions in the London area. However there is no limit to the number of sights that could be included. The target number of 50 is a factor of the time available for the development of the system (gathering accurate sight information requires some effort).

About the Underground:

This provides passengers with a guide to the range of tickets and fares on the Underground, the operation of ticket machines and ticket barriers, and the interpretation of the system map. It is a comprehensive interactive subsection which is illustrated extensively with still and animated images.

London Underground offers a relatively complex system of fares and ticket types, and two different sorts of ticket machines. The PRF offers an overview of these options in addition to practical information such as map interpretation, and barrier negotiation. The information can be easily modified as required or increased if new fare systems or tickets or additional services are added.

Technical Overview

The PRF consists of :

Hardware

486 PC,
21" monitor,
thermal printer,
robust aluminium cabinet
toughened glass screen protection
touch screen system
vibration alarm
paper low and paper jam alarms
thermostats
voltage controllers
high security locks

Software

C++
Codebase
"firmware"

The hardware elements were specified by the Multimedia Centre in accordance with London Underground's stringent safety and security guidelines. The cabinets' construction was sub-contracted to an Irish company which specialises in touch screen systems.

The PRF software was initially intended to be developed using existing authoring systems.
Author ware and Toolbook were analysed for suitability and subsequently rejected because they couldn't offer the required user response time of <3 seconds. As a result we developed parallel versions in C++ and Visual Basic. The C++ version was favoured for delivery to London Underground.

The database containing the details of the Underground timetable and station information, and the routing algorithm were supplied in a raw form by London Underground for adaptation into the PRF software.

Design Issues

The key to successful development and implementation of any multimedia system is design. There are three elements of the PRF which I would like to discuss: screen and interface design, software design and hardware design.

Screen and Interface Design

The function of the PRF is to communicate complex time sensitive information to a diverse group of passengers of differing ages, nationalities and technical understanding. To allow such people to interact with a complex software system in an uninhibited manner required a design that was attractive, intuitively understood and minimised contact with the unit so that other people would be encouraged to use the system. Additionally the corporate design standards of LUL needed to be paramount so that all colours, texts, symbols and information formats were consistent with information presented in different media (e.g. posters, signs) in other Underground locations.

The interface design objective was to meet LUL's corporate design standards and to enable users to access routing, tourist or general Underground information rapidly and flexibly. Having designed the simplest and quickest information flows for users, all other screen design issues were left to our graphic designer. His role was central to ensure that the PRF would be simple and attractive to use. This policy of graphic designer led interface design is central to the development policy of the Multimedia Centre.

Passengers interact with the unit by using a touch screen. No alphanumeric entry is required, passengers simply the touch of the appropriate screen area. From the idle state screen to a routing print-out requires 5 touches. Typically, when the PRF is in regular use, the number of touches required would be less due to current users being able to take advantage of previous users choices.

All screens have some common elements for example, the language choice and start again buttons. Each screen has unique characteristics but button shape, coloration and location is consistent so that users always know what part of the screen to touch.

The staff interface of the PRF enables London Underground personnel to carry out a variety of functions such as:

- change the database files
- gather statistics on use by passengers
- test the hardware and software components
- change the "home" station
- alter the system configuration e.g. include advertising, English only option, alter time to Idle state screen
- examine the error log

The PRF software is currently updated, tested and analysed locally. All of these operations are carried out using a special "key" diskette. The software design however caters for remote operation either via modem or local area network.

The staff interface of the PRF is a Windows interface which is accessible only when the cabinet has been unlocked and when the authorised staff member use the special "key" diskette. This first version of the staff interface assumes that the staff have Windows experience. However the plan for the second version is develop a highly intuitive interface similar to the passenger interface. Unfortunately the short development time available was factor in this decision.

The frequency of updating the system is unknown. It will be necessary to update the database as the passenger timetable alters. It may be necessary to add new or omit existing stations. The tourist sight information may change or be increased. This is very simply done by using the staff interface. Ideally a system such as this should be remotely controlled so that all operational units can be updated immediately to reflect changed service, even if it is only short term change. There is no technical obstacle to doing so. It was not implemented in this version of the PRF because it extended beyond our initial brief which was largely time limited. It is our hope that London Underground will request us to so in the relatively near future.

Having designed the interface and the cabinet to allow access to the routing and tourist information, we had to ensure that we had all of the maps, images and text required by the system, especially for the tourist sights. This did not present a major problem. Most sights were happy to supply us with material without copyright risk. However some images supplied were not of sufficient quality so we had to face accessing images from a slide library or shooting them ourselves. Slide library charges vary greatly. For our initial PRF installation sites we are happy to bear the cost, but for larger numbers of sites it would be more cost effective to shoot all relevant shots, about twenty in all, ourselves.

It is worth noting that while the interface, software and hardware design are critical issues, it is also important that developers of point of information systems should address such issues as copyright, access to materials and quality early in the project. If the images or materials supplied are of poor quality it will have a negative impact on the success of the system. Again this is an area where our designer has control.

Software Design

The programming team's function is to implement the interface design and to ensure that the programs are robust and efficient. It is a credit to our programming team that they acknowledge this role enthusiastically. Additionally they needed to design an interface for the LUL staff who would be involved in maintaining and testing the PRF.

Our programming team's expertise is in software design and implementation of the interface design without compromise. Future flexibility is the key element in our approach to each project. For example in the PRF project we have designed for on-line control and updating, maintenance and testing of the system by non-technical personnel and modification of functionality e.g. addition or expansion of user options and information sources/formats.

In addition to preparing for future developments of the PRF system, the code was designed so that it could be easily modified for use in other similar applications. Much of the code is re-usable, indeed some elements of the PRF system could be easily developed into generic software products. Since completing the PRF software, some elements of the code have been used in a point of information system developed for a gallery application.

Another significant element of our software design approach is cater for multiplatform delivery. Already we have ported an earlier application developed in the Apple environment to the PC environment and more recently we have ported from PC to Apple.

Hardware Design

In simple terms the PRF hardware consists of a PC in a box which serves as a suitable platform for the touch screen while also ensuring that the PC is protected from environmental threats such as vandalism, water, humidity, electromagnetic interference, fire etc. The unit had to comply with LUL's safety and technical standards while also allowing and encouraging the public to use the system. Of the eight companies we approached who claim to specialise in the supply of such units, only 2 were able to meet the technical requirements.

The cost of the cabinets was such that the PC hardware amounted to less than 20% of the total hardware cost. The extra cost arose from the non-PC components such as:

3 mm thick aluminium outer construction with internal shelving
A line voltage controller
Seals around all external access points
High security locks
Thermostats
A vibration alarm
A test panel
A high spec. thermal printer
An infra red touch screen system
A toughened glass touch surface

Designing and building a unit such as this takes a relatively long time. We sub-contracted the job in January for delivery in mid-March. We should have sub-contracted the job at the earliest stage of the contract as the delivery of the unit almost put our main contract with London Underground in jeopardy due to small slippages and technical problems. Unlike software, hardware problems cannot be quickly fixed using the same raw material. If the metal is the wrong shape or doesn't work according to plan, it needs to be re machined, not recompiled.

Commercial Aspects

The development of the PRF units had many technical objectives, all of which were achieved. However the success of such systems in the longer term depends on their commercial viability. Units such as the PRF can be relatively expensive, especially if they are to be sited in environmentally demanding locations such as the London Underground. It is highly desirable therefore that such point of information systems can be financially self supporting. This issue was recognised by us and London Underground at the outset of this development. Therefore, for example there is an option to display a dedicated sponsored idle state screen to gain advertising revenue. The cabinet itself could be painted to reflect sponsorship. The tourist sights could pay for inclusion in the system. All of these options are possibilities which are being explored by London Underground. Currently the PRF is an entirely free service without advertising.

Next Steps

Having successfully installed two units in London the reaction has been superb. From a technical, aesthetic and most importantly, a user viewpoint the PRF has been greeted enthusiastically. The next possible steps in developing the PRF are:

- introduce central control through LANs and modem control
- increase the number of sites using the system
- increase the number of tourist sights
- add new services to the system
- seek sponsorship and or advertising revenue
- adapt for visually disabled users
- produce a hand held version
- make available to desk-top users
- develop similar systems for other organisations

Conclusion

The success of our proposal to London Underground for the development of the PRF, and for its subsequent positive acceptance by users was due to the importance given to the graphic designer in our group. Programming and construction expertise is obviously important, but without the input of a graphic designer the impact and appeal of the system would be lost.

Our experience with this project has led us to the following conclusions:

Retain the input of a graphic designer in all aspects of the project.

Weak development tools are prevalent in multimedia so we are developing in languages such as C++ and Visual Basic.

Don't underestimate the difficulty in developing hardware units for point of information systems. They should be given the same priority as software.

Commercial viability is an important issue which should be addressed from the earliest stages of the project.

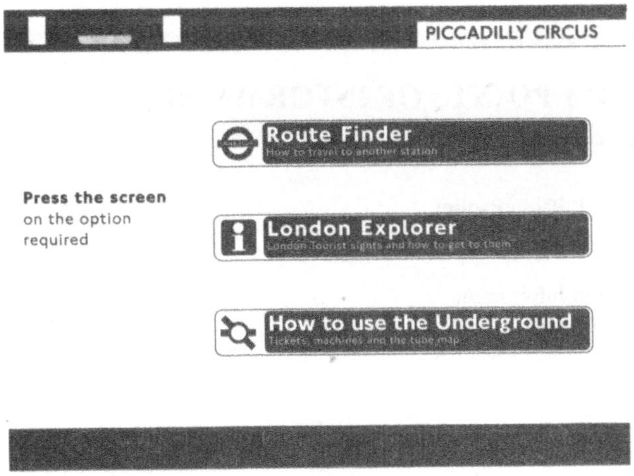

Primary screen with basic options

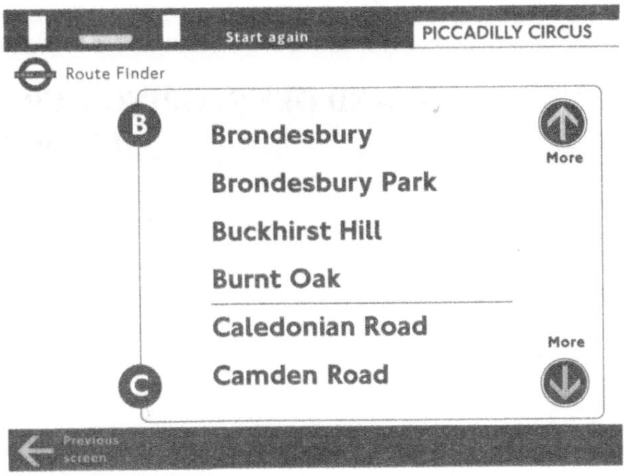

Selecting a station

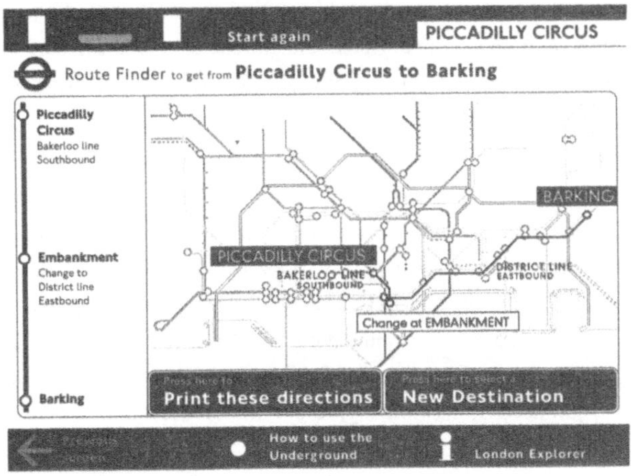

Route Finder

Tourist Sight in German Language mode

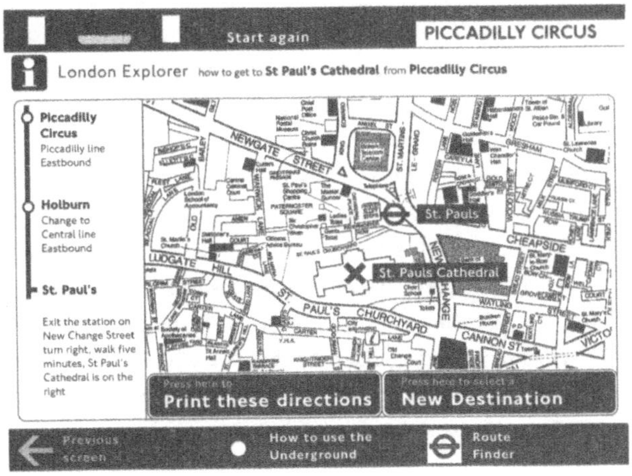

How to get to the Tourist Sight

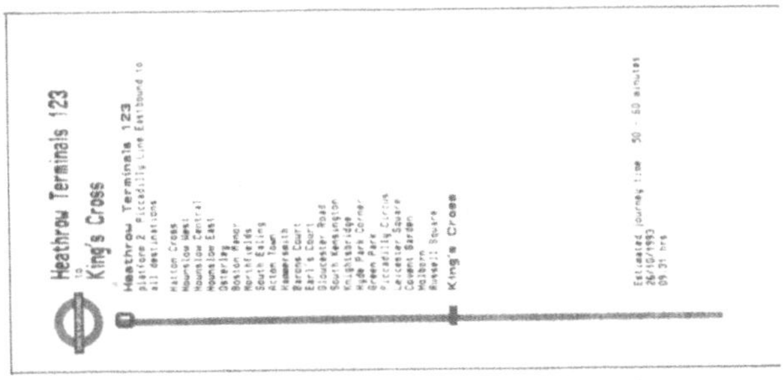

Sample Printout

USING AND DEVELOPING HYPERMEDIA POINTS OF INFORMATION: LESSONS LEARNED

Franca Garzotto, Luca Mainetti, Paolo Paolini

Department of Electronics and Information
Politecnico di Milano, Italy

Abstract

From the experience gained in evaluating several existing Hypermedia POIs (Points of Information), and from our own development work in this field, we have identified some critical issues in designing this class of systems. This paper briefly presents these results, by outlining the major stages of POI design and by discussing their impact on the quality of the final system. These concepts are exemplified by presenting the design choices in HyperMilano, a full size hypermedia POI developed at the Multimedia Laboratory of Politecnico di Milano.

1. Introduction

Since multimedia and hypermedia technology has become popular and largely available on the market, it has been intensively exploited for computer-based Points of Information (POIs for short). This class of software applications have become more interactive, more sophisticated, and richer of impressive visual effects. However, if multimedia and interactivity make a POI more appealing for end users, on the other hand non necessarily they imply an improvement in quality, usability, and utility of the system. A bad use of multimediality and interactivity might be the main source of failure of an Information Point, or might largely reduces the advantages the users could take from consulting the system.

The authors of this paper have informally conducted a small scale exploratory investigation on several hypermedia POIs available in public sites in Europe and the US. - museums, scientific conferences, commercial exhibitions, fairs, banks, airports, train stations. A qualitative evaluation of these systems has been done, in terms of quality of layout, quality of navigation and interaction facilities, easiness of use and quality of the information "message".

While a limited number of these systems were quite good, most of them were disappointing. After few minutes of playing, we simply felt lost and had to restart the session from scratch; after half an hour, we had seen a lot of video clips but had learnt almost nothing about the subject(s) of the POI, spending our time in trying to understand the rationale of the system, the meaning of the various buttons, and the actions we were doing with them.

Some major problems were common to the latter POIs:

- *an excessive amount of active media* - video, sound, animation - *with shallow information content*: active media were mostly conceived as *technological effects* to impress the audience. If it is true that the communication power of video, sound, and animation is typically higher that pure text, an excessive use of these media can be disturbing, confused and confusing, especially if the quality of their information content is low.
- *A poor organisation of the material*: the material was too fragmented in some parts, too long in other parts; the criteria adopted to organise it were obscure; many links did not have a clear meaning; links were not defined when the user would need them; there were to many links in some situations; the interplay of different media (e.g., the synchronisation of text and video) was inconsistent.
- *Inconsistency in lay-out*: lay-out elements with the same meaning - buttons standing for links of the same type or active areas on the screen standing for the same functionality - had different uses and representations in different nodes.
- *Lack of asymmetry in functionality's*: Some operation were available in some situations but were omitted in some similar cases, where instead a user would expect them (e.g., "stop" or "restart" were not provided on all videos).

- *Inconsistency in navigation mechanisms*: we did not find the proper links when we expected them, by analogy with similar situations; history based navigation (e.g. trace and backtracking, which allow to return to previously visited nodes) had a confuse meaning[1].

On the other hand, the POIs we enjoined more all share the following features:

- good *balance* in the use of the *various media*.
- Good *quality* of the content.
- *Simple*, but *clear* and understandable, *organisation* of the content.
- *Consistency* in the way material was *fragmented*, *interrelated*, and *presented* on the screen.
- *Consistency* in the presentation of the various *functionality's*.
- Clear *meaning* of links and functions (sometime provided with explicit *explanations*).

As a consequence, the degree of acceptance and utility of these systems was potentially high. In fact, POIs address a particular category of user, who very seldom are experienced in computers, and for whom it's extremely important that the system is predictable in his behaviour and navigation structures, so that there is a limited risk of getting lost. The POI user must find very easy to understand what the system is about and how to use it. Enforcing the above features, however, is not easy. It requires that the application is thought out in depth, carefully planned, and developed in a rational, systematic way. In other words, the degree of usability, acceptance, and utility of a POI are largely dependent on the *quality of design* (at least as much as on the quality of the technology used).

2. Critical Issues in Designing a Hypermedia POI

Hypermedia design is the task of planning a hypermedia application at the logical level, as much as possible independently from implementation constraints, i.e., hardware and software requirements. From our experience, the design process of a POI can be described by the following set of (interdependent and non necessarily sequential) tasks:

- *Authoring in-the-large*
  Partially analogue to logical data base design, this phase defines the basic classes of information, their representation structures (e.g., sequences, trees), and the various categories of connections (i.e., relationships) among them.
- *Authoring-in-the-small*
  This phase produces the actual content of information units, i.e., text, images, video clips, formatted data, etc., that will fill the proper representation structures defined in the previous phase. When active media are involved (e.g., video, animation, sound, etc.), this phase defines also the local behaviour of these information elements when activated. For example, it specifies if the play of a video clip is under the user's control (e.g., the user is allowed to stop, pause, or restart it) or not, or if a video and the corresponding text must be synchronised.
- *Navigation design*
  Rather than being an arbitrary network of multimedia information, the set of connections and paths of a POI should follow regular, recurrent patterns, in order to make the navigation environment more predicable and less disorienting for the end user. In addition, free navigation should be complemented with guided navigation, i.e., mechanisms that lead the user across simplified structures in a rigid manner, and have the purpose of providing an easy, simplified navigation environment to the users. Typical examples of guided navigation are provided by guided tours, first defined in [7].
  This phase defines the navigation patterns of free and guided navigation available in the hypermedia information point. In addition, facilities that support navigation are also defined in this phase. Some examples are the graphical display of the structure of the network [6], which helps the user in constructing a coherent mental representation of the application, or trace mechanisms, which allow to keep track and inspect the navigation history of a session.
- *Access mechanisms design*
  Pure navigation might need to be integrated with other access mechanisms, e.g., text-based search and similar Information Retrieval mechanisms, or query based access. In fact, POI users might have heterogeneous goals. Sometime they do not have a clear feeling of what information they are looking for, and need exploration based access to

[1]For example, the command "previous node", performed twice from the N-th visited node X, sometime return the user to X, sometime move to the (N-2)-th visited node.

information; sometime they do know precisely what they are looking for, and need more direct ways to access information.

- *Design of additional gadgets*
  A hypermedia POI, in a broader sense, might include a number of functionality's that are non strictly dependent on the navigational nature of the application. In general, they depend on the application domain and the needs of end users, who might require, for example, a printing facility on the visited node(s), integration with external, pre-existing applications (e.g., reservation facilities) and similar options.
- *Layout design*
  This phase defines how the content and the various information structures are visualised on the screen, and concerns with the aesthetic appearance on an application. For example, this phase defines how links are visualised (e.g., through active icons), where they are positioned, how the content must be formatted and arranged on the screen, etc.. Lay out design should convey as much as possible the intended semantics of the information structure(s) displayed on the screen, adopting, visual effects (e.g., background colours) that make explicit the distinctions among different classes of information objects and different meaning of links.

We should remark that the above design tasks, here described in a general perspective, are user driven, i.e., the specific decisions taken during the various phases strictly depend on the type of user and on his specific features and requirements. We will exemplify the design process by presenting HyperMilano, a hypermedia information point about Milano, developed at the Multimedia Laboratory of Politecnico di Milano.

3. An Example: HyperMilano and its Design Model

Before discussing the specific decisions taken in the design of HyperMilano, we will briefly introduce its design model, HDM[2]. HDM is a sophisticated and complex design model, and provides extremely rich modelling facilities (only part of which has been exploited in HyperMilano). In HDM, a hypermedia application is described by a set of structured information segments, called *entities*, and a set of connection structures of various categories, called *webs*, that glue together entities, or portions of entities, or other webs. HDM entities and webs are typed, and the collection of their types is defined in the *application schema*.

An entity is a structured segment of information, that represents a physical or abstract object (e.g., a shop, a museum, a monument). Entities are organised sequences or trees of components.

A component consists of a set of *units*, each one representing the same piece of information under a different *perspective*. A perspective defines the type of a data content, e.g., text, video, picture, formatted data, or its rhetorical style, e.g., "for beginner", "for specialist", or the language, e.g., Italian, English, French.

Entities are grouped into *entity types*. An entity type describes a class of domain objects (e.g., Monuments, Hotels, Restaurants). All entities of the same entity type have the same *structure*. A structure describes the organisation pattern of components and units within entities.

HDM supports several categories of webs; each one has a different representational role and different navigational semantics. Webs are grouped in types.

Application webs express domain relationships among components, entities, or units, and can be navigationally interpreted as a traditional hypertext link. A monument, for example, is *located-in* a given town area.

Index webs (indexes, for short) glue together a set of objects of interest to the users. An index has always a centre connected to the index items, which can be objects selected according to arbitrary criteria (say, for example, the index "Our favourite restaurants"), or can identify a subclass of objects that share some common properties or relationships (say, the top ten hotels, the Renaissance buildings, the monuments closed to Duomo, etc.). Thus indexes allow to introduce non intrusive classifications, without modifying the schema.

Indexes are mainly used as entry points to the application. The typical navigation on an index is from the centre to an item. Once the user has reached an item, he can return to the centre in order to select another item, or start any navigation pattern

[2]For lack of space, we will only summarise here the most relevant aspects of HDM - Hypertext Design Model; details can be found in several published papers (see for example [1] [2] [3] [5]).

available from that item. Examples of indexes will be described in the section 3.3.

Finally, HDM allows to define webs that have a linear *guided tours* semantics. Linear guided tours have the purpose to lead the user across a list of items in a linear manner. They are composed by a sequence of *existing* elements, called *items*, that are intended to be traversed linearly. Guided tour navigation starts from the initial item. From here, the user can navigate to the first destination, and from each element to the *next* element, to the *previous* element, the *first* element, and to the *last* element. Most important, while a user is located on a guided tour item, perspective, structural and application links outgoing from the current node *cannot be traversed*. They are inhibited (hidden to the user, or visible but disabled), unless the guided tour is explicitly *suspended*. Only from a suspended guided tour can the user activate these links, and reach any node, (directly or indirectly) connected to his current position. At any point, during this exploration, the user can *resume* the guided tour from the item at which it was suspended, and restart his linear navigation from here[3]. If the user desires to stop guided navigation, he can either *stop* or *close* the tour. With a stop command, the reader is left in the current position, but the commands of the guided tour cannot be activated any more, while all links outgoing from the current node become active. With a close command, instead, the reader returns to the guided tour centre, still deactivating the guided tour.

3.1 Authoring in-the-large of HyperMilano

HyperMilano provides information about the most interesting aspects of Milano, including *monuments*, *shopping*, *restaurants*, *clubs* (i.e., night sites or entertainment places), *hotels*, *geographic areas*. These are the classes of information objects, i.e., in the HDM terminology, the entity types of HyperMilano[4]. Each topic, but geographic areas, is described by a fragment of text, and a small set of basic data (opening hours, address, phone-number, etc.). Whenever available, the description also includes a picture or a sequence of pictures and a short video. Geographic areas are described by a map. In addition, HyperMilano has been conceived as a bi-lingual application, i.e., text, picture annotations, and voice comments to videos, are available in Italian and English.

The resulting entity types are graphically depicted in Fig. 1a. For HyperMilano, all entities, but areas, are structurally *sequences* of components. Areas are made of a single component.

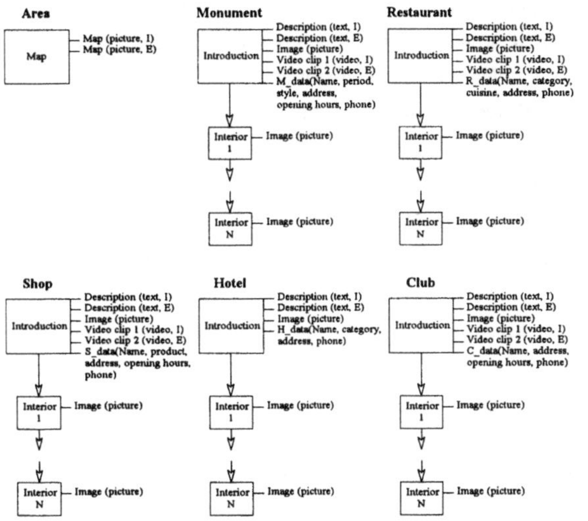

Figure 1a - Entity types of HyperMilano:
bolded terms denote entity type names; rectangles denote components; a name inside a rectangle denotes the role of the corresponding component within the entity; perspectives of a component are specified outside the rectangles (I = Italian, E = English).

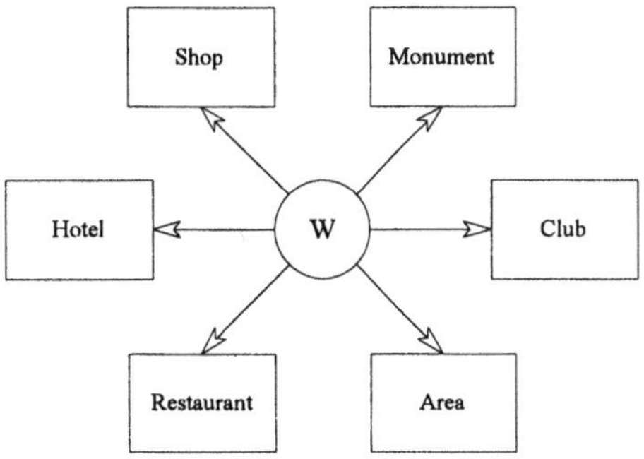

Figure 1b - Web type of HyperMilano

[3]The implementation of guided tours requires a sophisticated definition of the run time model of navigation, which must dynamically keep track of the navigation status. The interested reader is referred to [4] for details.

[4]Other classes of information could have been included (e.g., "history") as well as more fine-grained entity types (e.g., replacing "monuments" with "museums", "churches", "palaces", "fountains", etc.). We chosen the above mentioned entity types they seemed to be more intuitive for the "average" tourist, and because most of the guide books about Milano organised their content in a similar way.

The only application web (W) of HyperMilano connects geographical areas to the restaurants, shops, monuments, hotels, clubs located-in that area (see Fig. 1b).

3.2 Authoring-in-the-small of HyperMilano

For collecting the actual material stored in HyperMilano, we mailed approximately one thousand letters to the most significant hotels, shops, restaurants, entertainment places, in town, explaining the project and asking for explanatory material about them. Approximately 80% of them replied, sending us descriptions, high quality pictures, or brochures about their sites and their products. The visual material was scanned or captured with a video camera, and stored in HyperMilano. The textual material was partially re-edited and translated in English if necessary, in order to provide a uniform style to all the descriptions, and inserted in the root components of the corresponding entities (together with a picture, when available, and the formatted data).

As far as artistic and historical information about museums and monuments, we collected material from a number of existing guide books, from specialised books (some of them offered by the Municipality of Milano), again re-arranging the content for uniformity of style (and to avoid copyright problems). Videos sequences were extracted and partially re-arranged from commercially available video tapes.

3.3 Navigation Design of HyperMilano

Several navigation patterns are available in HyperMilano:

- *perspective navigation*: this is the navigation from a node to the node storing information about the same component but under a different perspective. In HyperMilano, perspective navigation allows to move from a node storing the English presentation of an "object" (restaurant, shop, monument, club, hotel), to the node storing the same content description in Italian or to the video describing the object, in Italian or English of the two languages, and any other way around.
- *Structural navigation*: this is the navigation across nodes of the same entity. In HyperMilano, this consists into moving from an "object" description to its interiors (see the structure of Entity Types in Fig. 1a), and backward.
- *Applicative navigation*: this is the navigation on the links resulting from the application web depicted in Fig. 1b. It allows to move across "objects" located in the same area (e.g., from Central Area to Duomo Cathedral, or to Rinascente Department Store, from here to La Scala Theatre, from here to Savini Restaurant, or back to the Duomo, etc.).
- *Index navigation*: according to the semantics of indexes in HDM, index navigation consists in selecting an index item from the centre, and eventually returning to the centre (or continuing any navigation available from the current item). HyperMilano provides an Index of Topics which lists all entity types of the schema (Monuments, Hotels, Restaurants, Shopping, Areas, Clubs). The items are indexes in turn. Each of these sub-indexes allows to select and to access any entity of the corresponding type, but for the Area index. Once a specific area is selected from the Area index, a further sub-index is activated.

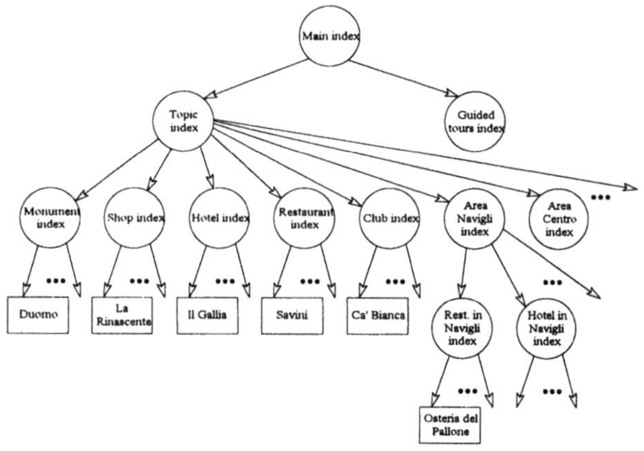

Figure 2 - Nested Index Structure of HyperMilano

This shows a list of topics (again, restaurants, shops, etc.), and points to an index for each topic, listing all the restaurants (res., hotels, monuments, etc.) in the current area. Finally, any of this places can be selected from here. These nested indexes of HyperMilano are described in Fig. 2.

- *Guided tour navigation*: metaphorically, guided navigation in HyperMilano would correspond to visit the town strictly according to the plan proposed by a guide book, or under the guidance of a human guide.

Three guided tours are predefined in HyperMilano: a video-based *cultural tour* (essentially, a sequence of video elements about the most relevant artistic and historical monuments and buildings in Milano); a *shopping tour* across the most elegant shops in Milano, and a *hotel tour*. The latter ones are mainly based on pictures, textual descriptions, and data. During navigation on these tours, all guided tour commands prescribed by HDM are available to the user. Guided tour navigation can be also performed on user defined guided tour (see section 3.5).

3.4 Access mechanisms in HyperMilano

Beside free or guided navigation, HyperMilano provides query based access. By invoking a simple Query-By-Example editor, the user is allowed to specify properties of the objects of interest (e.g., all restaurant that serve Milanese cuisine, accept VISA or AMEX credit card, are moderately expensive, and are located in the Duomo Area or in Navigli Area), and to retrieve the corresponding objects. One of the most innovative aspects of HyperMilano, however, is that query and navigation can be interplayed. In fact, not only the result of a query can be just inspected in a list, but it can be also used as a *navigational structure*, index or guided tour, as wished. In the former case, the result is interpreted as an entry point, to access any of the objects retrieved by the query, and eventually to navigate from there to any related node. In the latter case, the user can navigate sequentially from any item to the previous and the next one, according to the guided tour semantics. Query results and their navigational semantics are temporary structures. They can be made persistent with an explicit command by the user, and reused in a later exploration of HyperMilano.

The QBE interface of the query editor, and the display of results, are depicted in Fig. 5 and 6 (section 4), which show a query on monuments and its result, interpreted as a guided tour.

3.5 Additional Gadgets of HyperMilano

Additional gadgets of HyperMilano include:

- a *guided tour editor*, which allows the user to can create his own (linear) guided tours, by marking the nodes of interest. Marked nodes are collected in a list that can be modified by changing the order of items or deleting some of them.
- The *parallel processing of guided tours*, which allows opening several (built-in or user defined) guided tours at the same time.
- The *phone connection* to any place in town presented in the system. By activating a "Telephone" button, the user can call the place where he is actually located in HyperMilano, and communicate via microphone and speakers, or via a telephone.
- The possibility of *printing* the current node or the sequence of nodes in the current guided tour.
- *Active maps*, that, upon request, display a portion of the city map the position where an object resulting from a query is located.

3.6 Lay-out design of HyperMilano

The following pictures shown some layout decisions in HyperMilano. Fig. 3 shows the root node of an object of type Monument (the Church "Santa Maria delle Grazie").

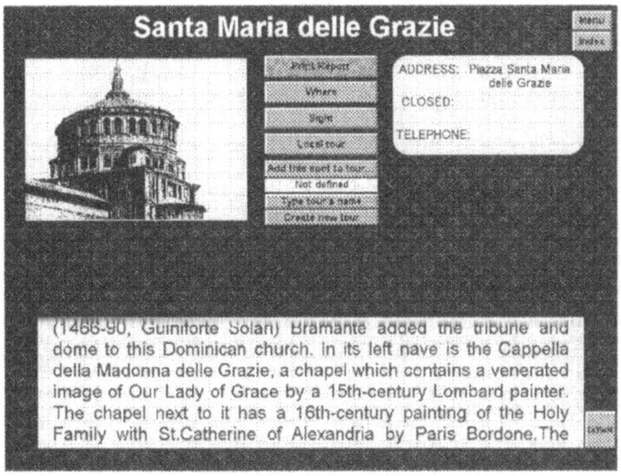

Figure 3 - The root node of a monument of HyperMilano

The node displays three units (in English): the short textual description, the main picture, and the data. On the right up corner, the buttons "Menu" and "Index" allow to perform index navigation, and returning to the Main Index and to the Index of Monuments respectively. In the centre of the picture, the print report button activates the printing of the current node. The "Where" button allows to perform applicative navigation to the area where the monument is located. The "Local Tour" button allows to access the sequence of pictures that describe the monument interiors. The button "Local Tour" and all buttons below, usually hidden and activated upon request, manage the creation of personal guided tours by the user. Hidden in the picture are explanations of the meaning of each buttons.

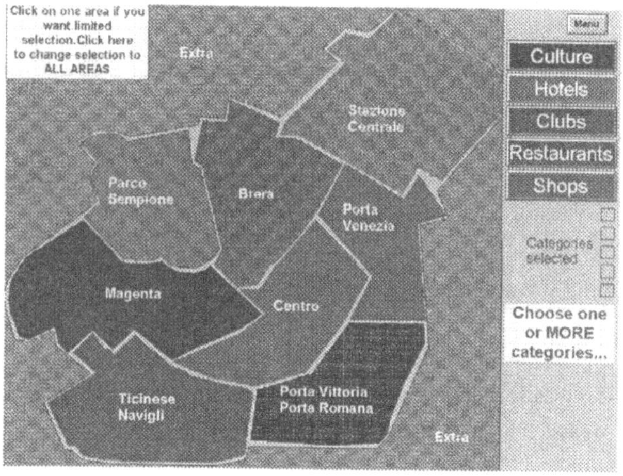

Figure 4 - The index of topics of HyperMilano

Fig. 4 presents the Index of Topics. Fig. 5 shows the QBE interface, with the specification of some attributes on Monuments.

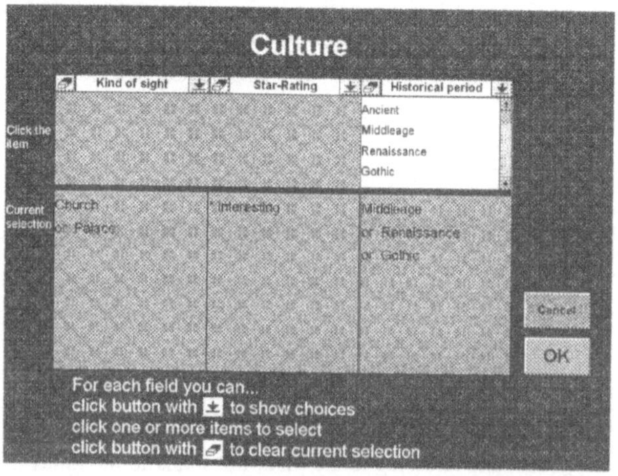

Figure 5 - The QBE interface of HyperMilano

The results of a query, to be interpreted as a guided tour, appear in Fig. 6.

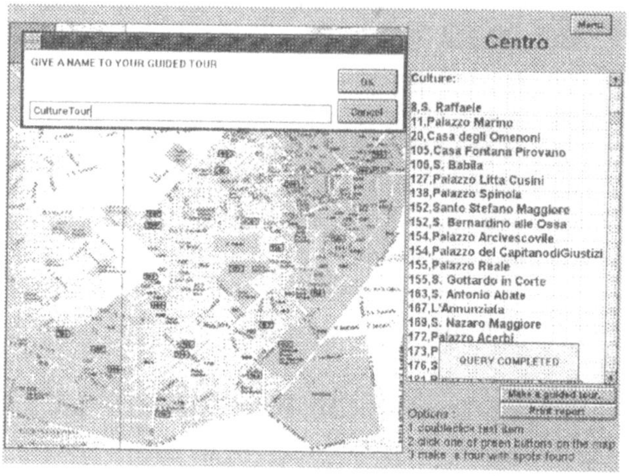

Figure 6 - The results of a query in HyperMilano

The list of retrieved monuments is on the right, the active map (see section 3.5) is on the left, and a dialogue box allows the user to assign a name to the personal guided tour.

4. Implementation Issues

HyperMilano has been initially developed for the 2nd ACM European Conference on Hypertext and Hypermedia (held in Milano in December 1992), where it was available to all participants. After that event, which provided a serious test to the work, the application has been significantly improved, with the purpose of being located in protected public areas (e.g., the Gallery, the City Hall), hotels, or department stores, for free consultation by Italian and foreign tourists and casual visitors of the town.

The system currently runs on a PC 486 with 8Mb of RAM and 40Mb of Hard Disk, a Super VGA screen (1024x768x256 colours)[5], and speakers. A dial board, a telephone or a microphone, support the phone connection.

Video and full size still images are stored on and managed by an analogic WORM, controlled by user through (the buttons of) HyperMilano. Small size pictures, presented in nodes with text

[5]This configuration is needed to ensure the display of high quality pictures.

and data (see Fig. 3), are displayed on the PC screen. Full size pictures and video are projected on a RGB monitor connected to the WORM, and are shown in parallel with the screen when activated.

HyperMilano is implemented in Toolbook (Asymetrix). A set of Windows DLL's, implemented in C++, provide the interface to the WORM. The current implementation includes 15 minutes of full motion video, 1200 pictures (most of which stored on the WORM), and 868 nodes. So far, the English version only is available.

5. Conclusions

This paper has presented the lessons we learned from evaluating some existing hypermedia Points of Information and from our own development work in this field. Even if the current technology invites the developers to concentrate on strictly technological aspects, i.e., on multimedia capturing, storage, and display, we claim that the conceptual phase is at least as important as the implementation phase, if we want to support a systematic, engineered approach to the development of hypermedia Points of Information. To exemplify this philosophy, we have outlined our view of the design process, and we have discussed it in practice by presenting a full size hypermedia Information Point about the city of Milano. Our approach has been experimented to other classes of Hypermedia systems, and has proved to be extremely effective as well.

Acknowledgements

The work presented here has been partially supported by the European Commission within the ESPRIT III program (Project HYTEA - P5252), the ESPRIT IV Program (projects HIFI - P6532, and MINERS - P6530) and by the Prometheus Program of Politecnico di Milano. We especially thank A. Bernesco, M. Cecchet, E. Gatti, G. Masolini, and R. Molinari, for their collaboration in the development of HyperMilano.

References

[1] Garzotto F., Paolini P., Schwabe D., Berstein M.: Chapter 13: Tools for Designers, The Hypertext/Hypermedia Handbook, Berk E, Devlin J. (eds.), McGraw Hill, New York, 1991

[2] Garzotto F., Paolini P., Schwabe D.: HDM - A Model for the Design of Hypertext Applications, Proc. HT'91 ACM International Conf. on Hypertext, Dec. 1991

[3] Garzotto F., Paolini P., Schwabe D.: HDM - A Model Based Approach to Hypermedia Application Design, ACM Transactions on Office Informations Systems, Vol.11, N.1, Jan. 1993

[4] Garzotto F., Mainetti L., Paolini P.: Navigation in Hypermedia Applications: Modelling and Semantics, Journal of Organizational Computing (to appear), 1993

[5] Schwabe D., Caloini A., Garzotto F., Paolini P.: Hypertext development using a Model-based Approach, Software Practice and Experience, Vol.22, N.11, Nov. 1992

[6] Thuring M, Haake J.M., Jannemann J.: What's Eliza Doing in the Chinese Room? Incoherent Hyperdocuments - and How to Avoid Them, Proc. HT'91 ACM International Conf. on Hypertext, Dec. 1991

[7] Trigg R.H.: Guided Tours and Tabletops: Tools for Communicating in a Hypertext Environment, ACM Transactions of Office Information Systems, Vol. 6, N. 4, Apr. 1986

DEVELOPMENT OF A CD-ROM-BASED MULTIMEDIA-APPLICATION IN AN OPEN SYSTEM ENVIRONMENT

Kornél Szabó, Peter Stucki
Martin Blatter, Peter Simeon, Martin Ruff
Claudine Horezky, Kurt Pauli

MultiMedia Laboratory, Computer Science Department, University of Zurich,
Winterthurerstrasse 190, CH-8057 Zurich, Switzerland
Tel: +41 1 257 43 46, Fax: +41 1 363 00 35
E-Mail: {szabo, stucki, blatter}@ifi.unizh.ch
E-Mail: {simeon, ruff, horezky, pauli}@amiga.physik.unizh.ch

Abstract

This experience report describes the preconditions and methodology for the development of a CD-ROM-based multimedia application. By means of a prototype application different aspects and problems are discussed that must be considered during the development of a CD-ROM-application. Finally, this paper will present possible scenarios for CD-ROM-based information systems in tourism.

Keywords: CD-ROM, CDTV, multimedia, information systems, man-machine-interface, project management, open systems.

1. Introduction

The successively increasing computing power and storage capacity of low-cost computer systems made it possible that applications could be realized which integrate different media such as text, image, graphics, voice, music, computer animation, or video. Multimedia applications could therefore be considered as a real alternative to classical means of sales support such as color brochures, catalogues or videos in tourism. Their strengths lie mainly in the interactivity and dynamics of information presentation. The aim of this work was to get a deeper understanding of the CD-ROM development process by putting special emphasis on project management and technical requirements.

2. Prototype-Application as Object of Analysis

By the help of a prototype application, answers to questions that may appear during the development of CD-ROM-based multimedia applications were to be worked out. The aim was to implement several partial aspects of a possible *point-of-information-system* (pois) for the Zurich Airport in cooperation with the airport management. This prototype application integrated as much multimedia elements as possible, like text, image, animation, video, voice, or music as possible, and use a CD-ROM as a storage medium. Such a *pois*, in its functionality as an information store, had to offer different kinds of requested information about the Zurich Airport to arriving tourists and businessmen. This system´s main feature should be in its easy of use and in a short training period for inexperienced users. A further goal was the development of a consistent user-interface. An adequate design of the user-interface can be achieved by respecting user-interface design guidelines during the application development process. Some of such design guidelines are described in [1] or [2]. To make the prototype application available to a wide range of users a low-cost hardware platform was chosen. Another requirement for the development environment consisted in its device independency and, therefore, portability across different system platforms.

3. Open System Environment as a Development Platform

The development of advanced multimedia applications needs adequate environments for experimenting with different media types, representations or formats and for working out new multimedia concepts. An efficient integration of new IO-facilities, workstations and network components requires an open system environment that is mostly realized by a local area network. The openness of a system consists of features like portability, extendibility or transparent data access. Important functional building blocks in the development of CD-ROM-based multimedia applications are data acquisition, data processing, data format conversion and authoring of the target application with an authoring system. To support data acquisition and processing, self-written or externally acquired software tools and different input devices, such as a color scanner or a video camera, are used. The manifold media types and data to be processed require a functionally flexible hard- and software environment. Many development environments combine multiple hard- and software tools to accomplish these functional requirements for the development of multimedia applications. During the implementation of the described CD-ROM application, IO-devices and UNIX workstations have been connected through an Ethernet network. The workstations served for data acquisition and data processing. A low-cost personal computer was also connected to this network. After processing, data was transfered to this personal computer and integrated with a self-written authoring program to a multimedia prototype-application. Finally a CD-ROM player was used to verify the produced master-CD before CD-ROM production.

4. Methodology

The methodology for the development of a CD-ROM-based multimedia application closely follows a standard software life-cycle model as described in [3] or [4]. Essential for the success is a systematic proceeding and permanent keeping in view of the target system's requirements during the development process. The methodology shown in figure 1 was used as a development model. The different development phases will now be described.

4.1 Requirements Analysis

The requirements analysis phase consists in the clarification of technical constraints for the development platform and the target application system. Additionally, the necessary personnel assumptions for the implementation of a CD-ROM-application have to be organized. After a detailed evaluation of existing CD-ROM systems, CDTV[1] of Commodore was defined as the target system. This decision was made because other platforms would have meant to high investments for the development environment. The development platform was an Amiga 3000 with 2.2 GB harddisc memory, 18 MB RAM and a TCP/IP network adapter card for networking. The infrastructure of a multimedia laboratory served mainly for data acquisition and processing of digitized pictures. A main focus during requirement analysis was the make-or-buy decision concerning the authoring system. Because of the heavy resource requirements of existing authoring systems for the Amiga platform (e.g. huge memory consummation, poor performance in information access, run-time player license fees for each application copy), a new authoring program was implemented. Similar problems of existing authoring systems caused a new implementation of the authoring system for the development of "Multimedia Graubünden", a tourism information system described in [5].

---

[1]Commodore Dynamic Total Vision: multimedia system for audio and video discs (Commodore, Inc.)

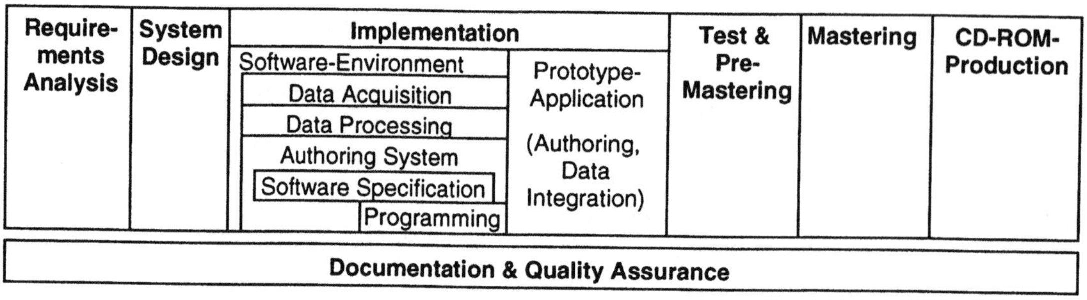

Figure 1: Methodology chosen to develop a CD-ROM-based application.

4.2 System Design

During the system design phase of CD-ROM-based multimedia applications, first there has to be created a story board for the interaction sequences and features of the final application, similar to movie productions. This includes designing the structure and interaction mechanisms of the application. To ease program navigation and shorten the operation training period for the user, consistent design guidelines for the application structure have to be defined. The user should understand the operation of the system in a short period of time (some seconds). This postulate evolves out of other experiences like the one described in [5]. Similar user interactions should cause similar system feedbacks. English was chosen as application language to make the application available for a broader range of users.

The architecture of the prototype application consists of two main elements: An introduction about the application domain accompanied by music and a main part containing pages with the information objects. Because of restricted possibilities of information presentation on 2D screens it is necessary to split the amount of information and present it in several pages or chapters. A way to realize this is by a hierarchical structure as it can be found in many hypermedia applications. Information access is done by a hierarchically organized index in form of menus and an alphabetical index in form of a glossary.

4.3 Implementation

4.3.1 Software-Environment

After the design phase the defined data objects, that will be integrated in the final application, have to be generated or acquired. Image documents were digitized by a color scanner with a resolution of 400 dots per inch or by a video camera. A graphic board was used for digitizing single video images for further processing. The processing of animation sequences and color images was done by special, self-written conversion and image processing programs. Text, that is presented in the final prototype-application, was entered manually. Different utility programs for storage optimization, data format conversion or image data compression helped reducing the amount of data resulting from digitizing video sequences and lead to an efficient management of scarce memory space. Voice and sound was digitized by a digital audio tape.

Disadvantages of existing programs such as high memory allocation or slow information access mechanisms caused the implementation of a completely new authoring system. Several requirements needed to be fulfilled by this new authoring system. The most important ones are presented in table 1.

- direct compilation of code for better runtime performance
- minimal memory allocation (at the most 70 KB)
- functions for image presentation (different sizes and color depths, special effects)
- 8 and 16 bit sound playing
- support for user-interface elements like buttons etc.
- command stack mechanism similar to the one used in HyperCard for backward navigation in dialog sequences
- remote control panel support on CDTV-platforms
- mouse support
- playing of computer animations directly from memory
- playing of CDXL-animations directly from CD-track

Table 1: Important requirements for a modern, CDTV-based authoring system.

An authoring system that meets these functional requirements was realized on the base of a self-written multimedia program library and by a top-down specification and implementation strategy.

4.3.2 CD-ROM-based Prototype-Application

The authoring or integration of the acquired, generated and processed multimedia data to a CD-ROM-based prototype application was done by the help of the authoring system. The different multimedia information units were combined to a hypermedia application in a hypertext-like manner. Buttons, as interaction elements, allow the access of information nodes.

4.4 Test and Pre-Mastering

Besides system design the testing phase is another very important part during the development of CD-ROM applications. As a WORM (Write Once Read Many) the writing of data onto the master CD can be done only once. Therefore adequate testing tools and emulation software has to be used for debugging and correcting errors that have not been eliminated by quality assurance techniques. Successful testing and quality assurance during the development process avoid many problems that may occur in the mastering phase. Nonrecognized errors would cause unwanted costs and time-related delays for the production of the master CD. After testing, the final application was written as a pre-master version onto an exabyte tape in ISO 9660 level 2 format. This data format standard is specially designed for the specific features of CD-ROMs such as high storage capacity or long data access time and can be used from different computer platforms.

4.5 Mastering and CD-ROM Production

Based on the master CD the final CD-ROM copies will be produced. The maintenance of CD-ROM-based applications differs from classical software engineering processes in the aspect, that the focus is not in the maintenance of the software itself, but in the updating of information entities in the application. The updating interval depends on the application domain and may timely vary. The production of a new CD-ROM application release is also dominated by economical constraints. The distribution of a new release means a new mastering-production-cycle and therefore additional costs for the CD-production. Such additional costs do not occur in traditional software products. Finance analytical models could help in determining the effective costs of the CD-ROM development and production process and calculate the optimal amount of CDs to produce and time for the mastering-production-cycle.

5. Scenarios for CD-ROM-based Multimedia-Applications in Tourism

In tourism a CD-ROM-based multimedia application could be applied as a part of a *point-of-information-system* (pois) for an airport. Such a *pois* would offer information about the airport and its infrastructure to arriving tourists in form of an electronic information desk. Besides that, travel offices could be supplied with such information desks. The CD-ROM application would visualize static, rarely changing information like the location of restaurants or taxi stands. Additionally other applications could offer dynamic, often changing information such as departure times or delay messages. In a stand-by mode a TV newscast would be broadcasted as a third application. A possible configuration setup for such a *pois* is presented in figure 2a).

Input devices such as a keyboard, a trackball and a touch-screen give the *pois*-user the possibility to pose queries interactively and visualize information on a high-definition color screen. The visualization of information and the user guidance is supported by sound and music sequences, coming from two stereo speakers. Inside the electronic information desk a CD player with a CD-ROM, that contains the CD-ROM-based multimedia application, is integrated. Dynamic information is downloaded from a central host computer to the information desk through a network and presented on the screen by a terminal emulation program. The presentation of the TV newscast can be realised by a desktop video board. Switching between the three applications is enabled by the multitasking capabilities of the integrated low-cost personal computer.

Another scenario of use for a CD-ROM-based information system can be found within the home consumer electronic market. By the help of well established distribution channels, users may buy CD-ROMs, that store information about special holiday destinations, for interactive holiday prototyping or entertainment purposes. Such CD-ROM applications offer competitive price performance ratio and are therefore a serious alternative to conventional advertising media like brochures or video tapes. In our case a standard CDTV configuration would serve as a home equipment setup. This setup contains a CDTV player with 1 MB of memory (for operating system and applications), a TV color monitor and a remote control unit for interactive control of the CDTV player (see figure 2b).

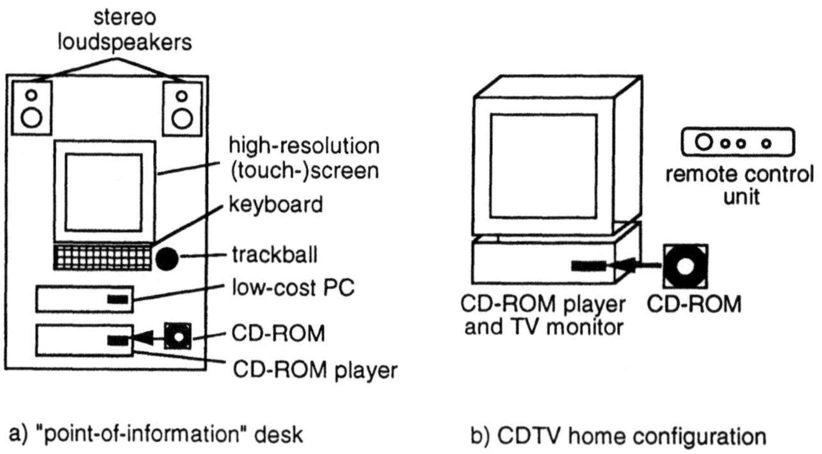

Figure 2: Schematic presentation of an electronic *point-of-information* desk and a CDTV home configuration.

Finally a CD-ROM-based information system could be applied inside an aeroplane. An air-passenger could query different kinds of information about the flight destination for easier and faster reach of his destination point. Some airlines are already experimenting with such scenarios.

6. Conclusions

A main finding during the implementation of the CD-ROM-based prototype application was that a lot of problems can be avoided by a systematic methodology and a well constituted development infrastructure. A lot of time and costs spent for development can be saved by the usage of adequate techniques, software tools and peripheral devices for data acquisition and processing. These requirements help minimizing or even eliminating unwanted revision cycles in the test phase. The development of an own authoring system allowed using the available resources, such as memory space or computing power, on the target system efficiently and meet economical constraints.

Another aspect that may cause difficulties in developing CD-ROM applications are copyright restrictions. The legal status of CD-ROM applications is often uncertain. This may cause immense costs because of unpretended violation of copyright claims. Because of that, using public domain image and sound data or own productions (digitized pictures, self-implemented animations, music and voice recorded in own sound lab) would be regarded as more advantageous until legal aspects are clearly defined. The development of applications, where the user-interface and man-machine-interaction is a main focus, requires corresponding knowledge in the development team, as pointed out in [6]. The development of interactive multimedia applications requires, besides computer specialists, also human factors specialists, artists, composers and teaching specialists, who design the user-interface for effective meet of user profiles.

7. References

[1] A.Marcus, "Designing Graphical User Interfaces", UNIX World, September 1990.

[2] Shneiderman B., "Designing the User Interface: Strategies for Effective Human Computer Interaction", Addison-Wesley, Reading (Mass.), 1992.

[3] Zehnder C.A., "Informatik-Projektentwicklung", Teubner Press, Stuttgart, 1986.

[4] Pomberger G., "Softwaretechnik und Modula-2", Hanser Press, Munich, 1987.

[5] Fischer A., "Fast wie im richtigen Film", MacWorld Switzerland, June, 1992.

[6] Gloor P.A., "Hypermedia-Anwendungsentwicklung", Teubner Press, Stuttgart, 1990.

HYPERTOUR: A HYPERMEDIA ECOTOURISTIC INFORMATION SYSTEM FOR THE NATIONAL PARKS OF COSTA RICA

Erick Mata-Montero
Centro de Investigaciones en Computación
Instituto Tecnológico de Costa Rica
emata@cic.itcr.ac.cr

Alejandra Corrales-Madrigal
Centro de Investigaciones en Computación
Instituto Tecnológico de Costa Rica
acorrale@cic.itcr.ac.cr

Abstract

HyperTour is the first hypermedia touristic information system developed in Costa Rica. Its main goal is to promote sustainable ecotourism to this country. Its scope is limited to the Costa Rican National Park System, which includes more than 12% of the national territory. This effort is a first step in the development of a comprehensive national touristic information system.

Introduction

Multimedia is a computer-centered technology that allows the capture, edition, organization, and presentation of information in different media (text, sound, static images, and dynamic images). Hypermedia, is a particular case of multimedia in which the information is broken down into pieces and modelled with a directed graph. Each node of the directed graph corresponds to a piece of information (text, sound or images) and arcs connecting a node u to a node v define an access link (navigational button) from node u to the information in node v. This simple scheme permits the organization and presentation of considerably large volumes of information in a very friendly and effective manner. Besides, hypermedia systems allow fast non-linear user-controlled access to information and can be implemented in relatively inexpensive microcomputers. These characteristics make hypermedia systems ideal for touristic information systems, especially in the areas of promotion and development [1].

Costa Rica is a country that has several important touristic attractions. For example: a consolidated National Park System that includes more than 12% of the national territory, thousands of species of animals and plants (more than Canada and the USA together), tropical dry, rain and cloud forests, beautiful white, black and shell beaches on two coasts, and many other natural attractions. These natural attractions along with a renowned political stability, excellent weather, a small territory (50,900 Km^2) and very good communication technology (there are telephone and electricity services in virtually every town) have generated a touristic boom without precedent in this country. The tourism industry is expected to bring $400 million in foreign currency in 1993 and is currently second to bananas as the nation's leading industry [2].

Understandingly, ecotourism is one of the priorities of the Costa Rica Tourism Board (ICT), the government agency in charge of administering and defining tourism policies (the ICT has the de facto status of a ministry). Considering this priority and the facts mentioned in the preceding paragraphs, the Center for Research in Computer Science (CIC) of the Costa Rica Institute of Technology signed an agreement with the ICT to carry out an in-depth study of the potential uses of multimedia technology in the Department of Promotion and Development of the ICT. In addition to the study, the CIC is developing HyperTour: a hypermedia ecotouristic information system for the national parks of Costa Rica.

We have already implemented a prototype of HyperTour with full functionality. The user interface has been completely defined and implemented. This prototype includes information of ten national parks. By December 1993, the information of the remaining ten parks will be included and HyperTour will start operating in several information booths.

Goals of the project

1. To develop an information system about the National Parks of Costa Rica. It should include graphics, sound, and text to describe the flora, fauna, geography, climate, lodging facilities, and services in each of the parks.
2. To promote sustainable ecotourism to Costa Rica with a kiosk application that uses multimedia technology.
3. To prove with a concrete example that multimedia technology is a viable alternative for the activities of the Promotion and Development Department of the ICT. The success of HyperTour will be crucial to justify the development of more comprehensive touristic information systems by the ICT and the CIC.
4. To prove that Costa Rica has the "know how" to develop state of the art multimedia information systems according to our own needs.

Technical characteristics of the project

HyperTour has been developed for the MacIntosh platform. We used HyperCard 2.1 to create the hyperdocument and Macromedia Director to develop the animations. Besides, as color images are used in every screen of the hyperdocument and HyperCard has very limited facilities for color (only the "picture" XCMD), we used other XCMD's such as "playMovie" to display Macro Mind Director files and "QTPict" for color images compressed using QuickTime [3].

HyperTour has been developed on a Quadra 800 computer but runs on any color MacIntosh computer with at least 4 Mb of RAM, a 13" color monitor with touch screen, and 120 Mb of hard disk.

Structure of the hyperdocument

HyperTour is a hyperdocument that consists of on 113 nodes (cards). It starts with a ten second color animation that presents two toucans flying around. At the end of the animation the user may select the language in which the information will be presented (see Fig. 1). If, after ten seconds, the user has not clicked on any button to choose a language, HyperTour takes control again and presents one of three animations selected

Fig. 1 First screen of HyperTour.

randomly from: the animation that shows two toucans flying around, an animation giving credit to developers and sponsors of this system, and a color digital video clip that displays some of the natural beauties of our national parks.

When the user selects a language, HyperTour takes him to the "home" node (see Fig. 2). The home node presents a map of Costa Rica in which the regions corresponding to national parks are buttons. Each of these buttons reacts by displaying and saying the name of its corresponding national park The name of the park is pronounced with Spanish accent so that tourists learn how to pronounce it if they need information from a local person. In addition, the user can click on any of three navigational buttons that appear at the bottom of the screen. The leftmost button leads to a node in which the names of the national parks are displayed in alphabetical order (for users who know the name of a park but do not know where they are located in a map). The middle button provides context-sensitive on-line help. Finally, the rightmost button "transports" the user to the park selected on the map (see Fig. 3).

Fig. 3 shows the node corresponding to a particular park. In the background, HyperTour presents a five second sound typical of the region (e.g., birds singing) and a gray tone picture representative of the park. The sound is a short one and the picture is in gray tones for aesthetical reasons and because we wanted to keep them as unintrusive as possible. At the bottom of the screen, HyperTour presents two rows of buttons. The top row includes buttons to display graphical and textual information about ecological and administrative facts: climate, geography, general information, flora, and fauna. The bottom row includes buttons to display graphical and textual information about hotels and restaurants, as well as a button to return to the home node and a button to get context-sensitive on-line help.

On-line help is always context sensitive. It is provided by showing the layout of the node the user just came from and inviting the user to click on any button about which help is needed.

Impact

1. HyperTour is the first system of its kind in the Central American and Caribbean region. It will be used in information booths in Costa Rica and in international fairs. It is therefore, expected to have an important impact in changing the way the ICT promotes sustainable ecotourism in the country and outside of it.

2. HyperTour is the first step in the development

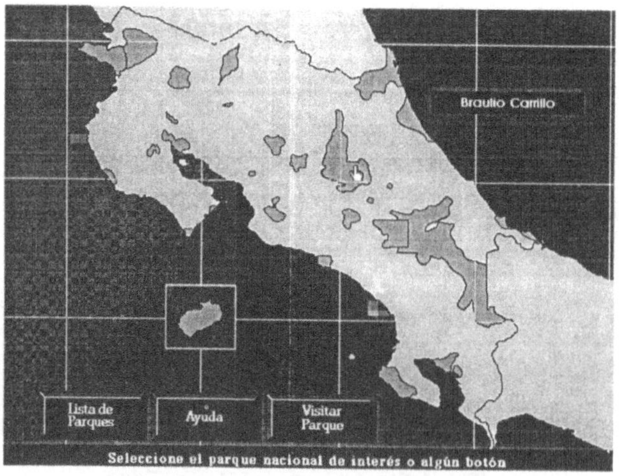

Fig. 2 Home node of HyperTour.

Fig. 3 Braulio Carrillo Park node.

of a comprehensive national touristic information system. By December 1993, the CIC will have also finished the study of the potential uses of multimedia technology in the Department of Promotion and Development of the ICT. The conclusions of this study along with the development and implementation of HyperTour will determine the way this comprehensive touristic information system will be designed and implemented.

3. HyperTour is also the first step in the development of a hypermedia system to teach children about ecology and the national parks of Costa Rica. This other system will operate in the National Children's Museum. Most of the pictures and textual information will be reused but the interface will be adapted to the new audience and to new design goals.

References

[1] Mata-Montero, E. HyperTour: A Touristic Information System for Costa Rica. Technical Report. CIC-RT-15-92. Center for Research in Computer Science, Costa Rica Institute of Technology (1992).

[2] The Tico Times 1992-1993 Visitor's Guide. San José, Costa Rica.

[3] Odio, S. Incorporating Color in HyperCard 2.1. Technical Report. CIC-RT-5-92. Center for Research in Computer Science, Costa Rica Institute of Technology (1992).

AN ADVICE SYSTEM FOR TRAVEL AGENTS

Prof. dr. K. VANHOOF, drs. I. MOLDEREZ
Dep. Bedrijfskunde LUC

LUC Universitaire Campus
3590 DIEPENBEEK BELGIUM

In the tourism sector it is often impossible for an travel agent to answer all the specific questions about destinations in a certain area. The tourist expects an expert in front of him, but a travel agent can't know everything about all the holiday resorts. The travel agent needs a tool to give better advice to the tourist. Together with the students of the special licentiate in Tourism at the Limburg University Centre, faculty of Applied Economics, we have constructed such an advice system. It should lead to an improvement in the quality of advice given to the tourist who is looking for the appropriate holiday destination.

1. The problem domain

In the tourism sector a customer is often seeking for expert advice. When explaining his particular problem a customer expects a clear answer from the travel agent, before he will do business with the agent. This is surely true in the case of holiday bookings. Most of the time the travel agent is not deeply interested in the wishes of the customer and only asks him some questions about the destination, the period and the accommodation. With this information he is able to select the right operators' brochures. After some explanation about the price charges, the customer goes home with a lot of brochures but also with his unsolved problem. The reason for the agent's behaviour is very simple. A travel agent cannot answer every specific question like 'Are there nice bicycling facilities in Nieuwpoort or 'Is Wenduine a childfriendly place?' without using a certain tool. Probably most of the information needed is contained in some brochure, but also for the travel agent it is hard to find the right information. The conclusion is that tourists demand more complete and relevant information then agency personnel are accustomed to provide.

A tool that raises the counseling quality can result in a strategic differentiation from competitors. We have devised a tool for specific advice relevant to our home country: 'Which Belgian seaside resort is the most appropriate for my holiday?'

Belgium is divided in 5 tourist regions: "Coast", "Ardennes-Meuse", "Historical Cities", "Campine" and "Other Places". According to the number of nights spent, The Belgian Coast is the most import tourist region in Belgium. This evolution hasn't changed since 1960 , although the relative importance has been declining .

The Belgian Coast is mainly visited by Belgians. In the first place Belgians prefer villas and flats. This type of accommodation is rented mainly by property agents who don't cooperate with travel agents.

According to recent studies (WES 1988-1989), Belgians are very individualistic with regard to travel agencies. In 1989 79% prefered to organise their own holiday to the Belgian Coast and only 21% chose for a travel agency. These percentages differ strongly for foreigners, according to the "Westvlaams Ekonomisch Studiebureau" (WES), the most important survey-office in Belgium, specialised in studies about the Belgian Coast.

If we take a look at the elements that influence the Belgian tourist in choosing the Belgian Coast as his holiday destination, we can conclude (WES 1988-1989) that commercial factors are not that important. The most influencing elements are friends, family and previous experiences. Again, this situation is quite different from the one existing with foreign visitors.

Taking these situations into account one could say that an advice system isn't very useful for Belgian tourists because they rarely consult a travel agency. However, the system can also be of great use to the tourist offices who have to give information about the different seaside resorts. Speaking from experience, they are frequently consulted. The advice system can also be an interesting tool for property-agents and for travel agents who have to advise the foreign tourists who like spending their holiday on the Belgian Coast which consists of 10 Coast Communities, namely Knokke-Heist, Zeebrugge, Blankenberge, De Haan, Bredene, Oostende, Middelkerke, Nieuwpoort, Koksijde en De Panne. The brochures, developed to attract the tourists, mention 13 seaside resorts. They also include Wenduine (part of the community De Haan), Westende (part of the community Middelkerke) en Oostduinkerke (part of the community Koksijde).

2. An advice system as solution

The 13 seaside resorts mentioned above all have their own characteristics and an advice system can help to choose the seaside resort that is most appropriate to the tourist's wishes. In order to reach this goal the system has to support the full decisionmaking proces. Many models of this proces have been proposed in the literature . They all have one characteristic in common : they break up the decisionmaking proces into a number of phases or steps. The three-phases model developed by Simon (SIM 60) has become famous and is referred to widely. He distinguishes the following phases:

1: the intelligence or information gathering phase
   problem capture and generation of alternatives
2: the processing phase
   for each alternative a solution or outcome is derived
3: the choice phase
   the solution' are evaluated

So the aim of the first phase is to determine the customer's wishes and expectations. This is implemented by a questionnaire. First, it helps the travel agent to structure the conversation, reminding him/her of relevant aspects for a succesful consultation. Second, it forces the client to express wishes. It is however possible to give more than one answer on a specific question or not to answer at all. These features are implemented in the system by multi-compound items and by default values. The possibility of reasoning with probabilities or certainty factors is not implemented. The answers fill in a hierarchical data structure of objects that tries to describe the desired holiday. However, this list of questions is not a static list but a dynamic one. Depending on the answers given and on the data contained in the objects, questions will be asked. For example if the client is not sporty at all, no questions will be asked about typical sports. If the client is sporty and he/she decided to enjoy the Belgian coast, no questions will be asked about mountain climbing.

In our prototype the generation of alternatives is not a difficult task. We start from a fixed and limited set of Belgian seaside resorts. A certain place will be eliminated during consultancy if the client has a specific requirement. (For example sea fishing is not available in place B). After this phase we have a good idea of the holday desired and we also have a list of candidate resorts.

The next step is to structure the supply side. The information available in tour brochures, VVV brochures has to be collected and put into a database appropriate for counseling purposes. In the prototype the structure is the same for every seaside resort. This is, however, not a requirement; at this stage it was sufficient. The specific information was obtained by sending questionnaires to the Tourism Offices of the different resorts. The advice system should rank the candidate resorts. This can be done by two strategies. The first strategy is to scan the candidate resorts and to evaluate them quantitatively. The second strategy is to differentiate between candidates by looking for attributes that separate groups of places. For both strategies we need to match the information of the resorts with the attribute values of the holiday desired. Some times this is straightforward (for example the client is a family with young children and the place is car-free with a large beach), sometimes it is more subjective. Theoretically, the strategy of differentiation is preferable, but in our case the different seaside resorts are not distinctive enough to apply this strategy. So we used the strategy of linear scanning for the second phase to evaluate the alternatives. For the last phase of the decision-making process we just show a ranked list of the possible places with the evaluation marks.

3. Expert system technology

Expert system shells are very well suited for building advice systems. We chose the objectoriented expert system shell Level 5 Object for flexibility reasons. Level 5 offers control, functionality and flexibility by combining the versatility of object-oriented techniques with powerful multiple inference techniques in a flexible windows environment.

Objects or frames serve as a kind of template for holding related clusters of data, facts, rules, hypotheses, or any other knowledge in a single conceptual unit. Frames use slots to hold information about an item or object. Each slot, in turn, is made up of facets. One facet contains an attribute while another contains the values, facts, rule, procedure, or pointers associated with the attribute. Still other facets can contain meta-information about the information in the slot.
This information usually covers the object's attributes and values, as well as procedures and pointers for getting data and information from other frames in the knowledge base. Frames may also contain rules and questions involving information in the frame. They may even contain default values (values assumed when no other values are available). Frames can be linked to other frames to form a frame hierarchy. For example, pointers and procedures can direct the system to search other frames for related data. They can even be manipulated by the inference engine to draw information from other frames.
One method of representing objects is by frames with or without inheritance. The objects can form a semantic network that takes advantage of the property of inheritance. Objects can inherit properties from other objects. The ability to build quickly more specialized objects from more general ones offers a significant productivity advantage. With this feature you can

implement very easily the different characteristics or attributes of different bath places.

In the application we need a knowledge base that matches the holiday desired with the seaside resorts available. IF-THEN rules are the most common way to represent knowledge in current knowledge based systems. Such rules contain premises or conditions in the IF clauses and conclusions in the THEN clauses. These rules differ from similar rules in conventional computer languages in that they can be modified more easily to meet changing needs. Systems that use this knowledge representation are called rule-based systems. Rule-based systems (and other kinds of knowledge based systems) can also ask users' questions about the information needed to deal with specific problems during consultation.

How do the data and knowledge components communicate with each other? For example, how does the expert system decide which rules or objects in the knowledge base apply to the situation currently described ? This is the task of the second major component of an expert system: the inference mechanism. As its name suggests, the inference mechanism compares the known data with the information in the knowledge base and decides which information in the knowledge base applies to the data.

The proces of testing or "firing" rules in an optimal sequence is aided by two major inferencing techniques : forward chaining and backward chaining.

In forward chaining, the information in the data base is compared with the IF part of the rules in the knowledge base. If a rule is found whose IF part matches the information in the data base, the rule fires, that is, the rule's THEN part is added to the data base. The procedure repeats until all possible conclusions are drawn.

In backward chaining, the system forms a hypothesis that corresponds to the THEN part of a rule or set of rules in the knowledge base and then attempts to justify it by searching the data base to establish the facts appearing in the IF part of the rule or rules. If succesful, the hypothesis is established and the expert system reports its results.

The difference between backward and forward chaining is basically one of beginning with the data (facts in the data base) and beginning with the goal. For this reason, forward chaining inference mechanisms are sometimes referred to as "data- driven", while backward-chaining inference mechanisms are called "goal-driven".

In an object-oriented knowledge base, the pre-established patterns of inheritance within classes of objects trigger certain actions or events to occur within the expert system. Once invoked, these objects might then call specific functions or rules into action to reach a specific result or conclusion.

For example, you could place a rule (demon) in an attribute that would automatically fire whenever the value of that attribute is altered. The use of demons that wait for values to change and then spring into action is often referred to as action-oriented programming. Demons can also force the inference engine to react. The result is that a system can start using a backward-chaining, goal driven approach but can change midstream to a forward chaining data driven model. This technique results in a highly flexible procedurally based system that can respond dynamically to new situations.

4. Design and implementation considerations

In the advice system we used the action-oriented programming technique. This technique enables the first and the second phase of the decision-making proces to be executed simultaneously.

This has some advantages :

- the question delivered is sensitive to previous answers
- the direct processing of the answer allows the presentation of intermediate results
- the direct processing of the answer allows the presentation of intermediate results
- hierarchical reasoning is applied, so that by enlarging the prototype the system can be made "seaside resort-sensitive"

A common remark during the analysis and the design phase of the system was ' Every resort is specific or distinct' or 'You need different rules for different resorts, because their characteristics are not the same'. These remarks are true but you can counter them by starting from general objects and applying on these objects the general rules. If you are going in detail you will construct more detailed objects. The number of rules will grow very fast and your knowledge will become very heavy to maintain. Fortunately, expert systems have a technique called 'message passing' to solve this kind of problems. Message passing lets you hide procedures about an object's unique behaviour within the object, rather than writing it elsewhere in the knowledge base. By sending a message to the object, you can trigger a procedure. Message passing is best used when your objects have diverse ways of accomplishing the same task.

Suppose you had to check seaside resort periodically to see if they are quiet. Certainly, you could do this using rules. For example, the three following rules could be used to apply the appropriate formulas to compute the quietness of a seaside resort or accommodation.

Rule 1

IF place = Blankenberge AND period = september AND temperature < 21°

THEN quietness = true

Rule 2

IF place = Bredene AND accommodation = hotel

THEN quietness = true

Rule 3

IF place = Oostende AND period = weekend AND temperature > 25°

THEN quietness = false

Unfortunately these rules would clutter the knowledge base. If there were 50 seaside resorts, you might need hundreds of corresponding rules to check quietness. It would be better to store each formula within the object to which it applies. You could then send the object a message whenever you need to check the quietness. The actual formula would be hidden inside the object and would be revealed only if you choose to inspect an object in detail.

So when your rules begin to include too much procedural code, they become unreadable and difficult to debug. Message passing solves this problem with encapsulation. It keeps the details of a frame's implementation neatly inside the frame,rather than strewn about the knowledge base. This is especially important in large systems, where encapsulation helps to keep the knowledge base comprehensible.

The reader interested in this subject is referred to the literature (HAR 89, WOL 88, VAN 92). So, with this expert system technology you don't need to build a structure that is valid for every problem occurrence.

Neither needs the knowledge contained either in the data structure or in the knowledge base to be fixed in time. So ad hoc revision, enlarging and reshaping of the structures according to changing conditions is always possible.

5. Conclusions

The students tested the system. The advice system mostly favoured a few seaside resorts. Although the students knew the knowledge and data base the results were sometimes surprising. For applying the system in travel agencies the system should be enlarged to the specific characteristics of the holiday resorts and to the accommodations types they usually deal with. So the system could give advice on place and specific accommodation. Weak points of the system are the knowledge rules and sometimes the obtained information (correctness of the values of attributes). However, you can use the system also as a feedback tool. Every time a compliment or a complaint comes in, you can check and update your data and knowledge base. So after some time you will have a rich knowledge base, so that the weak point will become a strong point of your organisation.

6. References

1 HAR 89 Paul HARMON & Brian Sawyer, "Creating expert systems for business and Industry", John Wiley, 1989.

2 SIM 60 SIMON.H.A., "The new scienoo of management decision", Harper and Brothers, New York, 1960.

3 VAN 92 Koen VANHOOF & Joël JEURIS & Frank NOTEN, "Analyzing expert system technology", Research paper BEDR/1992/02, Limburg University Centre Belgium.

4 WAL 88 John Walters & Norman Nielsen, "Crafting knowledge based systems", John Wiley, 1988.

5 WES 1988-1989, WES, Reeks Toeristisch Onderzoek, "Reisgedrag en -opinies van de Belgen 1989", 1989.

CaBaTa: CASE-BASED REASONING FOR HOLIDAY PLANNING

Mario Lenz
Paul-Schwenk-Str. 6, 12685 Berlin, Germany

Department of Computer Science, Humboldt-University Berlin,
e-mail: lenz@first.gmd.de

Abstract

Case-based reasoning has caught growing attention during the last few years. However, it is widely accepted today that pure CBR does not lead to satisfactory results. This paper deals with a mixed paradigm approach which has been applied to the domain of holiday selection in a travel agency. An architecture is presented which allows both usage of ***experience*** — stored as cases — and integration of rules guiding the search.

I. Introduction

Case-based reasoning (CBR) has caught growing attention during the last few years. In general, the case-based reasoning paradigm is motivated by the attempt to simulate ***experience*** of experts.

Very briefly, a ***case*** can be seen as a triple {P, C, R}, where P is a problem description (e.g. a list of attribute-value pairs), C is the classification or diagnosis of the case, and R is an explanation for the chosen classification.

Now the inference heavily depends on previously observed and stored problems and their solutions: Given the current problem description, the most similar of these cases is chosen and its solution adapted to be used as a solution for the current problem, too. To understand how **CaBaTa** works, this explanation should be sufficient — for an excellent introduction to the CBR paradigm see [14].

However, it is widely accepted today that pure CBR does not lead to satisfactory results: Since in pure CBR domain-specific knowledge (rules, constraints etc.) is not used to infer a solution to a given problem, the restriction to previously encountered cases may lead to inefficient inference or even unacceptable results, e.g. when no similar case is stored within the case database. A hybrid architecture is supposed to be of great advantage first of all when parts of the domain may be modelled satisfactory*.

Currently, two directions of research dominate:

- Firstly, so called ***hybrid architectures*** may be used to integrate domain-specific knowledge within classical CBR methods.
- Secondly, using ***mixed paradigm architectures***, the combination of CBR with other inference strategies is investigated.

This paper deals with the first attempt and shows how rules, constraints and other knowledge about the domain may be integrated within a CBR system thus taking advantage of both paradigms, the case-based and the model based one. The simulation of holiday selection in a travel agency is used to demonstrate the power of this architecture.

The key features of the **CaBaTa** system are

- integration of user-defined rules guiding the inference within the CBR-like inference engine,
- dynamic similarity assessment of feature values via user-given context graphs,
- opportunity of iterative approximation to a solution,
- simulation of access to a relational database.

The outline of the paper is as follows: Section II gives a short introduction to the domain chosen to serve as an example to demonstrate the hybrid architecture. Section III describes the way domain-specific rules can be defined and are used within the **CaBaTa** system. Section IV sketches the usage of context graphs to assess similarity values between symbolic feature values. After an example session in section VI, section VII briefly discusses the **CaBaTa** system in relation to important work in the the literature (VII.1, VI.2) and lists some of the

* However, in the context of hybrid CBR the model describing domain knowledge needs not necessarily to be complete or correct.

reserach topics (VII.3) within the **CABATA** system in the near future.

CABATA has been implemented using C++. Currently, it runs on a PC 386 or 486 and requires Microsoft Windows© 3.1.

II. The chosen domain

The simulation of a travel agency was chosen to serve as an example to demonstrate the **CABATA** architecture** . Whilst at the beginning this decision was made more or less accidentally, it offers now a great advantage over other systems dealing with, for instance, technical diagnosis: Due to the vague expressions used to describe the domain it is not possible to restrict the inference to hierarchical structures expressing causal or structural knowledge. Mention e.g. the different opportunities to spend a ***recreation*** holiday: While some people like pure bathing and beaching, others want to enjoy sports or even go on adventure trips. And, of course, nobody would be satisfied if he was integrated within the wrong group.

The task of **CABATA** is to choose one of its stored cases describing past holiday trips as a suggestion for a new trip satisfying user-specified conditions. These conditions are given as case descriptions and include features such as

- the ***type*** of holiday (e.g. recreation, active, language etc.),
- the chosen ***region*** (both general descriptions such as mountains or sea, and particular countries, cities or areas),
- the wanted means of ***transport*** (e.g. coach, car, train or plane),
- the ***season*** of the holiday trip,
- the estimated ***price***,
- ...

While some features are numerical ones, others may take symbolic values. This will be of particular importance in section IV.

The process of selecting the best applicable case from memory is designed to be an incremental one, i.e. after a suggestion has been made by the system, the user may modify the set of conditions to adapt the solution.

In comparison to other systems, **CABATA** has not been designed for

- any kind of booking activities
- queries about vacancies etc.

III. Integration of domain-specific rules

As already mentioned in the introduction, it is highly appreciated to have the opportunity to encode domain specific knowledge to be used when searching for an appropriate comparative case. This may be done in **CABATA** by defining rules guiding the inference: These rules have the form

```
IF   <feature1> <rel1> <value1>
THEN <feature2> <rel2> [<value2>].
```

where

`feature1` contains the attribute of the case description that — when satisfying the given condition — implies a certain modification of the inference.

`rel1` describes the relation between `feature1` and `value1`. This may be one of the ordinary arithmetic relations (=, ≠, <, > etc.), or a relation named `isA` to express if the value belongs to a certain type hierarchy, i.e. is a sub-type of `value1`.

`value1` is the value to which `feature1` is compared using `rel1`.

`feature2` contains the attribute of the case description for which a certain condition must hold.

`rel2` states the relation to `value2` that must hold for `feature2`. Here two types are possible: Firstly, as above it may be one of the ordinary arithmetic relations or the `isA` relation. Secondly, it may be a statement indicating the importance of `feature2` when comparing two cases (reaching from *not important* to *most important*). In the latter case `value2` cannot be selected.

`value2` gives the value to which `feature2` is compared using `rel2`.

On the basis of this scheme, rules may firstly be used to increase or decrease the influence of particular features if certain condition hold, e.g.

```
IF HOLIDAY_TYPE = CITY
THEN SEASON IS OF LESS INTEREST.
```

stating that, when planning to visit a particular city, the season is less important than in the usual case.

** However, all parts of the inference engine have been implemented independently of the domain under consideration (except for the graphical user interface).

Secondly, these rules may serve as restrictions (constraints) when demanding that a particular feature be of a certain value, for example

```
IF REGION isA SEA
THEN REGION MUST NOT BELONG TO MOUNTAINS.
```

helps to avoid anomalies caused by the propagation of similarity values through the context graphs(see section IV) such as:

- The Alps have something in common with Italy.
- Italy has something in common with the Mediterranean Sea.
- Thus: The Alps have something in common with the Mediterranean Sea.

Note: To *have something in common* expresses that the similarity value between the mentioned feature values is different from 0, the actual value is of no importance here.

Another useful constraint should be

```
IF HOLIDAY_TYPE = BATHING
THEN REGION MUST BELONG TO SEA.
```

Thus, in combination with the similarity graphs described in section IV, the integrated rules allow for a similarity assessment which depends on the context of the comparison of the attribute values.

IV. Usage of Context graphs

For every symbolic feature being part of the case description a context graph is constructed containing information about

- generalisation and specialisation
- similarities
- semantic relations

between all values of an attribute. These graphs have to be defined via binary relations between particular feature values (the edges of the graph). Similarities and semantic relations between arbitrary values are propagated through the graph. However, a tool has been constructed to serve as an aid during this process, first of all to allow larger parts of the graphs to be displayed and edited. Thus the risk of local acceptable changes leading to global inconsistency (see the example in section III) is less likely.

The similarity itself is expressed using a number of measures ranging from *nothing in common* via *similar* to *identical* thus giving reasonable flexibility to describe domain knowledge.

V. On finding the solution efficiently

As already mentioned in the introduction, the inference process in CBR systems consists of finding the most similar case stored in a database. The main problems now are: How is *similarity* measured, and how can an efficient memory management be realised ?

The first question was partly answered in the preceding paragraphs — the following example session (section VI) will help to clarify the way similarity is determined in **CABATA**. Due to space limitations a more detailed explanation of that problem is not possible here.

The second problem is most often solved by applying *indexing strategies* to the case database — as is known from traditional databases. In **CABATA**, too, a kind of indexing can be used: Options available are

- A rule-based indexing strategy which makes extensive use of the user-defined rules already when extracting stored cases from the database. This ensures that cases which definitely are not applicable due to the violation of constraints (see section III) will not be extracted from the database and thus the expensive comparison of the current problem case to that case will not be performed.
- A similarity-based indexing which ensures that the values of all attributes of the cases to be compared are within a previously defined similarity interval. This can be interpreted as restricting the search through the context graphs (section IV) to a certain neighbourhood of the according attribute value of the current problem case. This strategy can be used in a similar way as the rule-based one.

Since currently **CABATA** does not actually use a database (but keeps all data in main memory), these indexing mechanisms lead only to mediocre improvements concerning the performance of the systems. However, already now a SQL query is generated which can easily be used within the interface to a real database.

Summarising, the following instructions roughly describe the behaviour of **CABATA**:

1. **Pre-process** the current problem case: Extract as much information as possible from the given problem to enable the system to efficiently retrieve cases from the database.
2. **Extract** the potentially appropriate cases from memory.
3. **Classify** the current problem case, i.e. compare it with every extracted case yielding a similarity value.

4. Supply these **classification results** (ordered according to the similarity) to the user; and, if asked for, supply detailed information about comparisons of cases.
5. Follow further instructions (i.e. re-classify, modify domain-specific knowledge etc.).

VI. An Example Session

Assume the following description of a planned holiday:

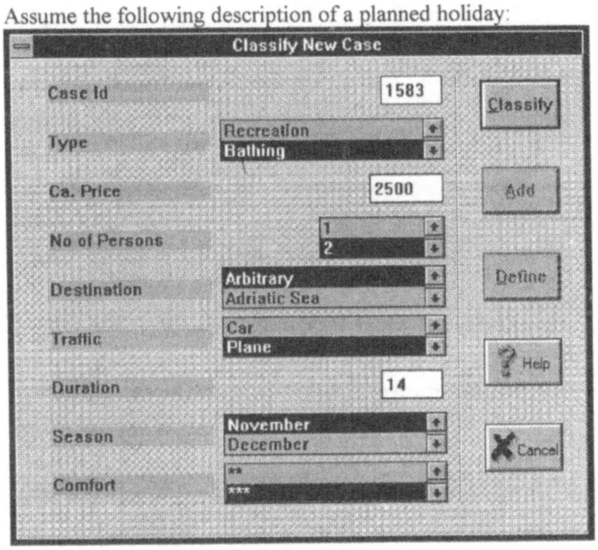

Fig. 1: Definition of a new case: The user wants to go on a bathing holiday in November but does not know where to go to.

Due to space limitations both the underlying model-based domain knowledge and the integrated rule table are not shown here. Currently the first consist of about 500 binary relations while the latter contains approximately 20 rules of the form shown in section III.
The above newly defined case is pre-processed and classified using a case database of currently approximately 1500 cases.

Using both, rule-based and similarity based indexing, the following query to the database is generated:

```
SELECT *
FROM CASE_DB
WHERE HOL_TYPE IN (BATHING)
AND    REGION IN (Adriatic Sea, Algarve,
       Atlantic, Barbados,Cote d'Azur, ...)
AND    TRAFFIC NOT IN (CAR)
AND    SEASON IN (October, November, December)
AND    COMFORT NOT IN (Hol_Flat)
ORDER BY No;
```

The case shown in Fig. 2 is found as a very good solution while Fig. 3 presents a case that violates a constraint (namely that BATHING requires tthat the region be a kind of SEA) and is therefore not applicable.

VII. Discussion

VII.1 Relation to other work

As a basic introduction to CBR served [14]. Here the main ideas are introduced including the MOPs suggesting a general memory structure for CBR. Moreover, some applications are demonstrated.

BARLETTA and MARK [8] suggest *Explanation Based Indexing* as a method to use domain-specific knowledge for an efficient memory management. This could be of use in future work on **CABATA**. However, it has to be extended to be more flexible and context-sensitive.

Of particular importance for the development of **CABATA** was the work of PUPPE and GOOS ([11,12]). The idea of using rules to modify the importance of case attributes was taken from the CCC+ system. However, since the domain is not technical diagnosis, an adaptation of the way rules are integrated was necessary.

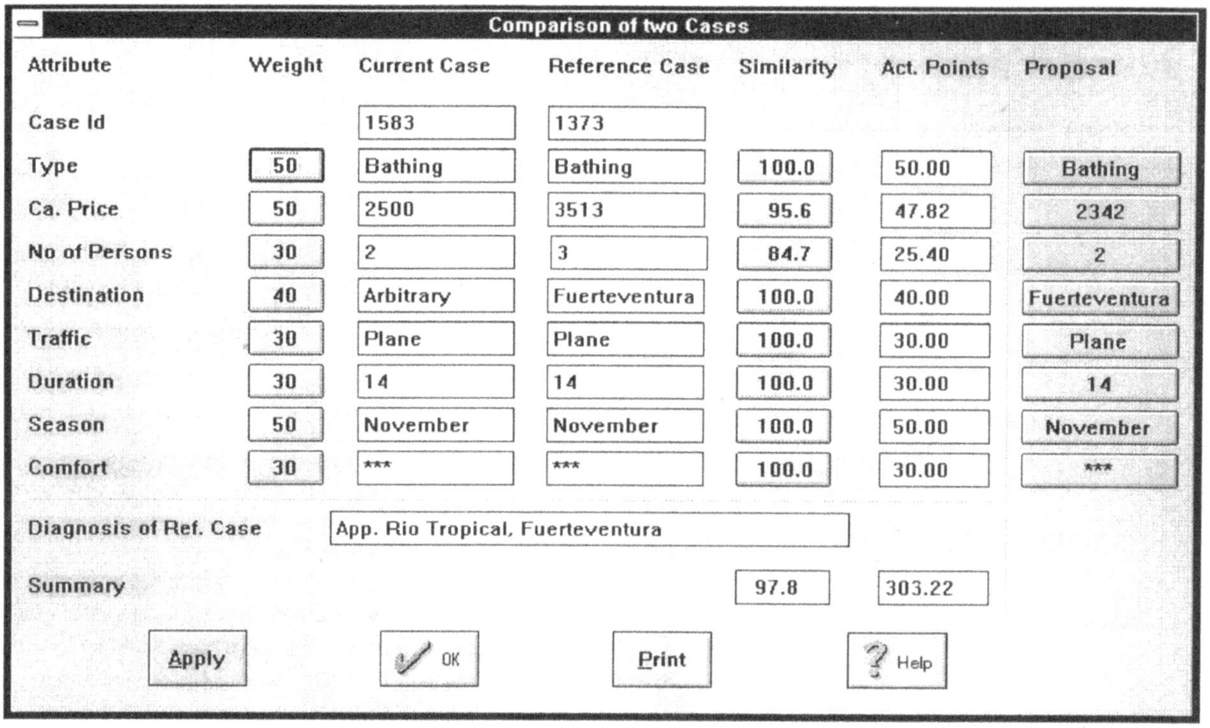

Comparison of two Cases

Attribute	Weight	Current Case	Reference Case	Similarity	Act. Points	Proposal
Case Id		1583	1373			
Type	50	Bathing	Bathing	100.0	50.00	Bathing
Ca. Price	50	2500	3513	95.6	47.82	2342
No of Persons	30	2	3	84.7	25.40	2
Destination	40	Arbitrary	Fuerteventura	100.0	40.00	Fuerteventura
Traffic	30	Plane	Plane	100.0	30.00	Plane
Duration	30	14	14	100.0	30.00	14
Season	50	November	November	100.0	50.00	November
Comfort	30	***	***	100.0	30.00	***
Diagnosis of Ref. Case		App. Rio Tropical, Fuerteventura				
Summary				97.8	303.22	

Apply | OK | Print | Help

Fig. 2: Best case found as a solution for the current problem.

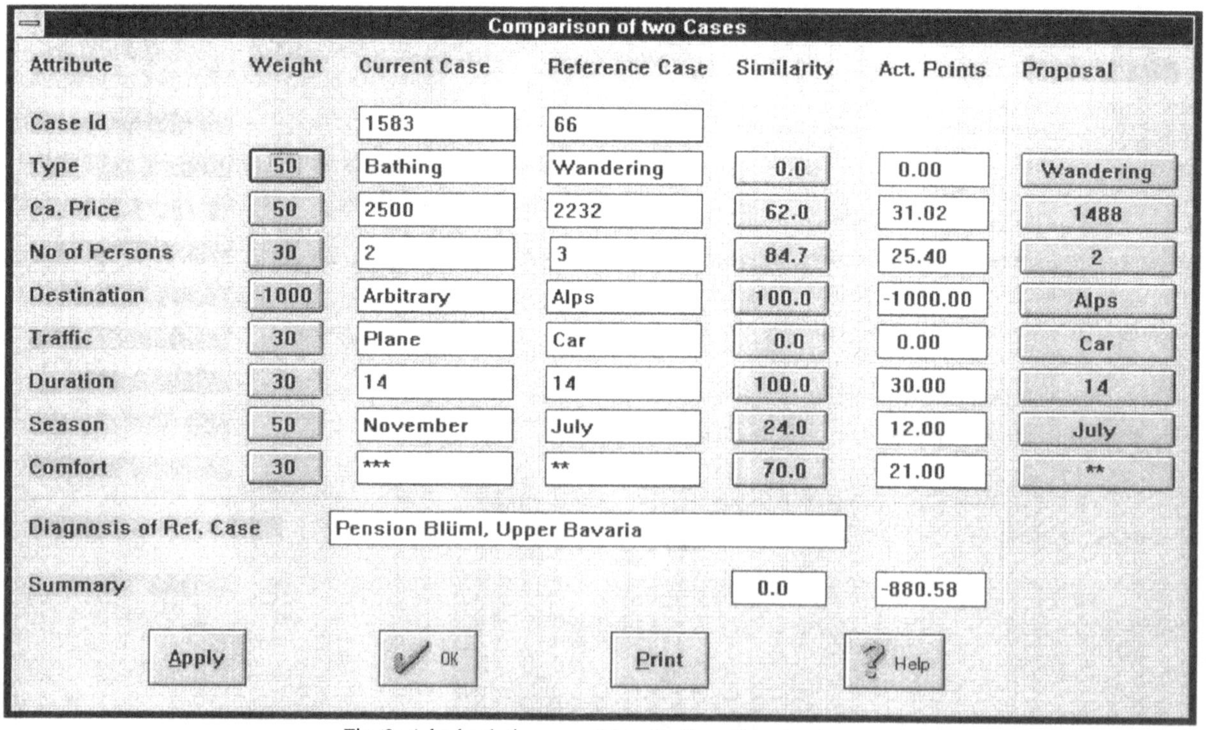

Comparison of two Cases

Attribute	Weight	Current Case	Reference Case	Similarity	Act. Points	Proposal
Case Id		1583	66			
Type	50	Bathing	Wandering	0.0	0.00	Wandering
Ca. Price	50	2500	2232	62.0	31.02	1488
No of Persons	30	2	3	84.7	25.40	2
Destination	-1000	Arbitrary	Alps	100.0	-1000.00	Alps
Traffic	30	Plane	Car	0.0	0.00	Car
Duration	30	14	14	100.0	30.00	14
Season	50	November	July	24.0	12.00	July
Comfort	30	***	**	70.0	21.00	**
Diagnosis of Ref. Case		Pension Blüml, Upper Bavaria				
Summary				0.0	-880.58	

Apply | OK | Print | Help

Fig. 3: A bad solution case. Note the line of destination.

Another project dealing with technical diagnosis is the **MOLTKE** workbench ([3,4,5,6,7,13]). Here, too, context graphs are used to represent experience knowledge and an attempt is made to combine various sources of knowledge and inference strategies. However, it is not clear, whether all results can be simply adapted to other domains (e.g. the decomposition of tasks). As mentioned in the introduction, technical diagnosis is more restricted than other domains: Causal principals used to construct technical devices should enable the user to build a satisfactory model.

AHA, KIBLER and ALBERT ([1,2]) demonstrate how *Machine Learning* techniques can be used within the CBR context. In particular, the investigations on the power of the described *EB*n algorithms may help in extending CBR systems.

VII.2 Why Case-Based ?

In comparison to traditional (e.g. rule based) expert system techniques, CBR offers some major advantages:

- The CBR approach is psychologically motivated, i.e. an employee in a travel agency does not follow strict rules when serving a customer. Rather, he or she will probably have some kind of experience — knowledge of human nature — that will suggest the one or other type of holiday.
- In particular in domains where huge databases of previously encountered problems and their solutions exist, the CBR approach takes advantage of this (implicit) knowledge. Thus the system will ***develop*** when being used over a longer period of time. Rule based systems, on the other hand, remain very often static, i.e. if not modified by the programmer they may pretty well repeat the same mistakes.
- A CBR system does not give a definite answer to a problem, rather it suggests a list of solutions ordered according to their likely appropriateness. Moreover, reasoning by cases is not necessarily ***correct,*** as the logicians say. While in some areas, such as technical diagnosis or theorem proving, this may cause hard problems, these two points are regarded very useful for all topics dealing with social and psychological problems — human behaviour does not follow rules of correctness.
- Traditional reasoning systems will fail in ***weak-theory domains***, i.e. in domains where the underlying model is not tractable, is too expensive to acquire, or does not even exist. These domains don't cause problems to the CBR approach.

Both, PAGE's GALILEO [10]and OLIVER's SABRE [9] are computer-based distributions and reservation systems. Their purpose is to serve as an aid concerning the questions of vacancies and reservations. In these systems it is assumed that the user already knows about the main details (destination, means of transport etc.) of his holiday trip.

WERTHNER's TIS [15], on the other hand, does not deal with these organisational aspects of holiday planning. Rather, TIS is designed to supply a connection between

- those participants offering particular tourism services (e.g. private owners of hotels, local authorities) and
- those using these services (the private end-user as well as commercial travel agencies selling these services).

The main objective of TIS is to provide information about the available services in **Tyrol**. This restriction allows for a much more detailed presentation of the services, including exact descriptions of particular hotels etc. **CABATA**, on the contrary, is able to operate world-wide — it completely depends on the *experience* of the system: the stored cases.
Furthermore, the aim of **CABATA** was not to provide a commercially usable product, but rather to investigate the application of CBR to weak-theory domains. Thus the underlying data — though taken from catalogues — is currently much too weak for the system to be used commercially. However, an extension of the database should not cause any principal problems.

VII.3 Future work

Future work on the **CABATA** system will include

- improvement of the algorithms used to propagate similarities through context graphs to avoid certain anomalies,
- research about the opportunities to integrate *Machine Learning* techniques to allow learning beyond the storage of cases, i.e. on the level of control or domain knowledge,
- integration of methods for efficient memory organisation and case retrieval (e.g. indexing),
- extension of the integrated model-based knowledge.

References

1. Aha, D.W., Kibler, D., Albert, M.K.: Instance-Based Learning Algorithms. *Machine Learning* (6), 1991
2. Aha, D.W.: Case-Based Learning Algorithms. *Bareiss R (ed): Proceedings 3rd DARPA Workshop on CBR*, 1991
3. Althoff K-D., De la Ossa A., Maurer F., Stadler M., Weß S.: Case-based Reasoning for Real World Applications. *SEKI-Report SR-90-23*, University of Kaiserslautern, 1990
4. Althoff K-D., Maurer F., Rehbold R.: Multiple Knowledge Acquisition Strategies in MOLTKE. *SEKI-Report SR-90-21*, University of Kaiserslautern, 1990
5. Althoff K-D., Maurer F., Traphöner R., Weß S.: Die Lernkomponente der MOLTKE-Werkbank zur Diagnose technischer Systeme. *KI 1/91*, 1991
6. Althoff K-D., Weß S.: Case-Based Knowledge Acquisition, Learning and Problem Solving for Diagnostic Real World Tasks. *SEKI-Report SR-91-07*, 1991
7. Althoff K-D., Weß S.: Case-Based Reasoning and Expert System Development. *SEKI-Report SR-91-16*, University of Kaiserslautern, 1991
8. Barletta R., Mark W.: Explanation-based indexing of cases. *Proceedings AAAI-88*, 1988
9. Oliver J.: Leisure SABRE - A Global means of distribution for tourism products. *Computer Networking and the Public tourism organization*. Perugia, Italy, 1991
10. Page S.: Galileo - A Global Distribution System. *Computer Networking and the Public tourism organization*. Perugia, Italy, 1991
11. Puppe F., Goos K.: Improving Case-based Classification with Expert Knowledge. *Proceedings GWAI-91*, Springer Verlag, 1991
12. Puppe F.: Problemlösungsmethoden in Expertensystemen. Springer Verlag, 1990
13. Richter M, Weß S.: Similarity, Uncertainty and Case-Based Reasoning in PATDEX. *SEKI-Report SR-91-01*, University of Kaiserslautern, 1991
14. Riesbeck C.K., Schank R.C.: Inside Case-Based Reasoning. Lawrence Erlbaum Associates, 1989
15. Werthner H.: Tiroler Tourismus Information System. Wirtschaftsinformatik, 35 (1993) S. 43-50

A GENERAL TRAIN CONNECTIONS GENERATION PROCEDURE

Karl Anton Froeschl

Institut für Statistik, Operations Research und Computerverfahren
Universität Wien
A-1010 Wien, Universitätsstraße 5, Austria
E–Mail: froeschl@smc.univie.ac.at

Summary

A general method of constructing train connections for given train schedule data is presented. The proposed approach – named TIC (Train InterConnect) – derives a subset of possible train connections between two specified train stations of some railway network using basic schedule data as well as precompiled train connection data. In particular, TIC's train connection generating algorithm deals with both linear and circular courses. Although the mathematics involved in the TIC approach is rather simple, it is claimed that TIC provides an encompassing formal model for generating train connections. In principle, the proposed approach is extensible easily to other types of traffic connections as well. The present paper only describes TIC's core procedure deriving course sequences, leaving out the computation of service days and travel times of actual train connections.

1. Introduction

This paper presents a new approach to the generation of train connections as the cardinal building block of a railway passenger information system named TIC (=Train InterConnect). Essentially, the system's purpose is the dynamic construction of train sequences connecting any two specified railway stations of the network (cf. [2]). The TIC system is intended to be *general* in the sense that (i) it can deal with both, linear and circular, courses and (ii) its capabilities are by no means restricted to generating *train* connections; as long as time table information is isomorphic to railway schedules, any type of public traffic connections (e.g., by plane, ship, bus, etc.) is covered as well. In particular, an extension of TIC to include several different (but, of course, interconnected) public traffic systems simultaneously is conceivable quite easily.

The primary source of data for a train consulting system is, apparently, train schedule data as issued by railway corporations. In general, train schedules are published in book format; such railway guides have the train data structured into a series of time tables, each covering a subset of closely related train connections. A train connection running from its origin station through its terminal station is called a *course*. Strictly speaking, each *train* is an instance of some course (thus, in fact, we better use the less appealing term *course connection* instead of the quite familiar term *train connection*). In a sense, a railway guide is a self–contained source of information for some definite period of time (e.g., one year). For the sake of improved readability, time tables are furnished with various cues (such as arrows pointing at other train columns, etc.) which, in fact, do not add any real information but prove valuable in speeding up search. Conversely, in formal terms train schedule data of a railway guide is *not yet sufficient* to create a semantic model of "reasonable" train connections; it just produces a model of running trains.

First, many of the train connections possible theoretically are entirely useless from a practical point of view (such as transfer connections requiring, say, several months of transfer delay at a junction). Hence, what makes a particular train connection a *useful* one must be defined *in addition to* train schedule data. For instance, any transfer connection will have to be ruled out if the transfer delay elapsing at its junction(s) is either below or above some prespecified bounds. In view of trains running daily, it is obviously reasonable to set the upper bound of tolerable transfer delay to 24 hours at most. Similarly, hardly anyone would accept train connections passing the same route more than once.

Second, the typical time table format fails to exhibit direct connections properly in case of *through coaches*, i.e. cars changing trains. From a passenger's view, any through coach realizes a direct connection (although it combines parts of different courses). Merely indicating that a train is carrying through coaches, however, does neither elicit train junctions nor the source or the destination courses of a through coach. For this reason, there must be added either (i) fictitious courses representing (individual) through coaches, or (ii) an *index* of through coaches to the train schedules providing a cross reference to involved courses.

To sum up, the intended set of train connections, i.e. the *semantic connection model*, is obtained only after augmenting pure train schedule data – as provided by time tables – with a particular interpretation which, in general, is defined *intensionally* (and, moreover, typically in implicit terms). Therefore, any effective train connection consulting system must be conceived of as an algorithmic generator of an appropriate semantic train connection model.

In the following paragraphs the pivotal procedure for generating course sequences from schedule data is described whereas the transformation of course sequences to complete train connections (including actual departure and arrival times as well as the indication of service days) is omitted (cf. [2] for a detailed account). In section 2 some formal notation is introduced and the TIC data model is presented, whereupon TIC's main internal data structure, viz. course concatenation data, is discussed. The algorithm for generating course sequences is stated, in mathematical notation, in section 3 including some indications what still needs to be done to obtain complete train connections ready for display. Finally, some remarks concerning reasonable extensions to the core procedure are added.

2. The TIC Data Model

Essentially, TIC embodies a data base of time tables augmented with pre-compiled information about possible *concatenations* of courses. Quite in contrast to other approaches to automated generation of train connections (e.g., [1,4]), TIC does not use time table data in the first place; instead, it tries to string together parts of courses connecting departure and arrival stations irrespective of temporal relations (which, in fact, are considered later on after course sequences have been established already). To facilitate the generation of course sequences, a pool of course concatenation data is prepared ahead of time such that for each pair of courses the set of possible transfer junctions (i.e., where trains can be changed) is retrievable simply from a concatenation table.

The TIC approach is based on one fundamental precondition, viz. *strong course connectedness* of the underlying railway schedule: for any station of the railway network there must be at least one course (each day) either passing through (i.e., having a stop) or originating from it such that – by changing trains appropriately – a complete round tour visting *all* stations of the network can be arranged. This precondition, of course, is fulfilled for any useful railway network. Another – particular – feature of the TIC system is its complete ignorance of geographical relations, i.e. the *connecting logic* relies on course data exclusively. This approach is reasonable since railway courses themselves are already implemented in terms of geographical relations whence peculiar cases are excluded from the beginning. As a consequence, the TIC system does not consider the real distances a trip has to cover during course sequence generation; on the contrary, distances covered by train connections are measured simply as the number of necessary train changes.

Notation and Definitions

The basic tools used in the formal description of TIC are *sets* and *sequences*. Basically, sequences are a kind of lists (cf. [3], ch. 9, for a concise definition). In fact, ordinary sequences represent a subclass of lists albeit with a particular interpretation whereas *labeled* sequences are a bit more specific in that they also carry additional information associated with the operator stringing together a sequence's elements.

As usual, $|\mathrm{E}|$ denotes the cardinality of a finite set E. In addition to the ordinary power set, $\mathcal{P}(\mathrm{E})$, the set of all non–empty subsets of E is referred to as $\mathcal{P}_1(\mathrm{E}) \stackrel{\text{def}}{=} \mathcal{P}(\mathrm{E}) \setminus \{\emptyset\}$. In the sequel, let E be a non–empty set of elements $\{e_i\}$. Now, for any subset $\{e_1, \ldots, e_n\} \subseteq \mathrm{E}$ a term $\ell = e_1 \rightarrow e_2 \rightarrow \cdots \rightarrow e_n$ is called an E–*sequence* (or *sequence*, for short). The set of E–sequences ℓ of length $|\ell| = n$ is denoted as

$\mathcal{L}_{\underline{n}}(E)$. Additionally, for $n > 0$ let $\mathcal{L}_n(E) \stackrel{\text{def}}{=} \bigcup_{q \geq n} \mathcal{L}_{\underline{q}}(E)$. Thus, $\mathcal{L}(E) \stackrel{\text{def}}{=} \mathcal{L}_1(E)$ denotes the *universe of finite sequences* over set E. Note that according to this definition no element is allowed to occur repeatedly in a sequence. Since, occasionally, circular sequences are referred to, these will be denoted by a bar put over the sequence symbol, i.e. if $\ell = e_1 \rightarrow e_2 \rightarrow \cdots \rightarrow e_n \in \mathcal{L}_{\underline{n}}(E)$ then $\bar{\ell} = e_1 \rightarrow e_2 \rightarrow \cdots \rightarrow e_n \rightarrow e_1$ denotes its circular variant.

In case of *labeled* sequences, a label chosen from some distinguished set L is attached to each pair of consecutive elements. In formal terms, $\ell = e_1 \stackrel{l_{12}}{\rightarrow} e_2 \stackrel{l_{23}}{\rightarrow} \cdots \stackrel{l_{n-1,n}}{\rightarrow} e_n$, for $\{l_{12}, l_{23}, \ldots, l_{n-1,n}\} \subseteq L$, is a valid labeled E–sequence. Correspondingly, L–labeled E–sequences with length $n > 0$ are denoted as $\mathcal{L}_{\underline{n}}(E, L)$. Also for labeled sequences, let $\mathcal{L}_n(E,L) \stackrel{\text{def}}{=} \bigcup_{q \geq n} \mathcal{L}_{\underline{q}}(E,L)$ and $\mathcal{L}(E,L) \stackrel{\text{def}}{=} \mathcal{L}_1(E,L)$.

Furthermore, the class of sequences is enlarged to the class of *multi–sequences* which differ from sequences by admitting multiple occurrences of elements (as a consequence, even the set of multi–sequences over a finite set becomes infinite). However, note that labels still must not occur repeatedly in a multi–sequence. Ordinary and labeled multi–sequences will be denoted by $\mathcal{L}^*_{\underline{n}}(E)$ and $\mathcal{L}^*_{\underline{n}}(E, L)$, respectively. In case of multi–sequences allowing also labels to occur repeatedly, the symbol $\mathcal{L}^{**}$ replaces $\mathcal{L}^*$.

Manipulation of (multi-)sequences requires a few elementary operations such as access to different portions of a sequence. Subsequently, the following (total) functions will be used: $\mathbf{ft}(\ell)$ returns the first, $\mathbf{lt}(\ell)$ the last element of sequence ℓ; $\mathbf{rev}(\ell)$ returns the reverse (i.e., the re–directed ordering of elements) of sequence ℓ. Basically, these are the common list processing operations albeit applied to sequences.

Two sequences ℓ' and ℓ'' can be *concatenated*, $\ell' \circ \ell''$, if $\mathbf{lt}(\ell') = \mathbf{ft}(\ell'')$. Evidently, sequence concatenation is associative but not commutative. A sequence $\ell' \in \mathcal{L}_1$ is a *proper subsequence* of $\ell \in \mathcal{L}_2$ if either $\ell_l \in \mathcal{L}_1$ and $\ell_r \in \mathcal{L}_2$ or vice versa such that $\ell = \ell_l \circ \ell' \circ \ell_r$. Sequence concatenation as well as the subsequence relation are defined analogously for multi–sequences.

Each sequence defines a particular ordering of its elements. Hence, it is convenient to have a means of testing precedence relationships between sequence elements. An element e_i precedes element e_j in sequence $\ell \in \mathcal{L}_2$, denoted formally as $e_i \prec_\ell e_j$, if $\ell = e_1 \rightarrow \cdots \rightarrow e_i \rightarrow e_{i+1} \rightarrow \cdots \rightarrow e_{i+p} \rightarrow e_j \rightarrow \cdots \rightarrow e_n$ $(1 \leq i,j \leq n)$ for some $p \geq 0$.

TIC operates on several sets of *basic objects* from which all other sets are derived subsequently. The most important sets of objects are the set **S** of *stations*, the set **C** of *courses*, and the set **P** of *profiles*. The set **S** comprises all objects representing railway stations contained in the entire railway network. Scheduled trains serving sequences of elements of **S** are termed *courses*, i.e. for each $c \in \mathbf{C}$ there is a subset $\{s_1, s_2, \ldots, s_n\} \subseteq \mathbf{S}$ such that $s_1 \rightarrow s_2 \rightarrow \cdots \rightarrow s_n \in \mathcal{L}_2(\mathbf{S})$ and either $s_1 \rightarrow s_2 \rightarrow \cdots \rightarrow s_n$ (linear course) or $s_1 \rightarrow s_2 \rightarrow \cdots \rightarrow s_n \rightarrow s_1$ (circular course) is the stops sequence of c (obviously, n depends on c). A course object c, however, does not only contain its stops sequence but also all specific information related to the course (such as the course's time column, course attributes, etc.).

The set of courses **C** is partitioned into equivalence classes, called *profiles*, w.r.t. stops sequences: whenever two courses $c', c'' \in \mathbf{C}$ have identical stops sequences they belong to the same profile $p \in \mathbf{P}$. Thus, each profile $p \in \mathbf{P}$ represents all trains of the railway network serving the very same sequence of stations.

In order to achieve a coherent description of TIC several formal function symbols are introduced as listed in Tab. 1. For the sake of simplified reading, functions returning single values are denoted by lower case greek letters whereas for set valued functions greek capitals are used throughout. The precise meaning and usage of these functions will be elucidated as appropriate.

Tab. 1: Description of Function Symbols Used

f	Mapping	Description: **f** returns
Σ	$\mathbf{P} \rightarrow \mathcal{P}_2(\mathbf{S})$	a profile's set of stops
σ_o	$\mathbf{P} \rightarrow \mathbf{S}$	origin (station) of a profile
σ_t	$\mathbf{P} \rightarrow \mathbf{S}$	terminal (station) of a profile
λ	$\mathbf{P} \rightarrow \mathcal{L}_2(\mathbf{S})$	a profile's sequence of stops
K	$\mathbf{P} \rightarrow \mathcal{P}_1(\mathbf{C})$	a profile's courses
Π_h	$\mathbf{S} \rightarrow \mathcal{P}(\mathbf{P})$	profiles stopping at a station
Π_o	$\mathbf{S} \rightarrow \mathcal{P}(\mathbf{P})$	–"– originating in a station
Π_t	$\mathbf{S} \rightarrow \mathcal{P}(\mathbf{P})$	–"– terminating in a station
π	$\mathbf{C} \rightarrow \mathbf{P}$	a course's profile membership
X	$\mathbf{P} \times \mathbf{P} \rightarrow \mathcal{P}(\mathbf{S})$	a profile pair's *change set*

Obviously, the formal representation of course information is of fundamental importance to any system generating train connections symbolically. In TIC, course data is divided into *courses* and *profiles*. The notion of "course" is based on the concept of a conveyance serving a specified set of stops *periodically* (typically, trains run once a day at constant times). As an immediate consequence, TIC does not distinguish *through coaches* from ordinary courses since both realize *direct* connections within the served sequence of stops. Thus, both ordinary courses and through coaches are likewise members of set $\mathbf{C}$. Note that TIC accounts for linear as well as circular courses but rules out courses containing *loops*, i.e. stops sequences $s_1 \rightarrow s_2 \rightarrow \cdots \rightarrow s_i \rightarrow \cdots \rightarrow s_i \rightarrow \cdots \rightarrow s_n$ with s_i occurring repeatedly for some i, $1 < i < n$ (in preparation of further processing, the profiles of circular courses $\bar{\ell}$ are, in fact, represented as $\bar{\ell} \circ \bar{\ell}$ where the repetition of $\bar{\ell}$, termed *course continuation*, is not a proper part of the course but used for determining possible transfer junctions).

Course Concatenation Data

The generation of course sequences regards only the courses' stops sequences indicated, for each course $c \in \mathbf{C}$, by the profile membership of the course c, $\pi(c)$. Conversely, *profiles* comprise classes of courses identical w.r.t. their stops sequences. Hence, for each $p \in \mathbf{P}$ there is a pair $\langle \lambda(p), K(p) \rangle$ where $\lambda(p)$ represents the profile's stops sequence and $K(p)$ is the profile's associated set of courses. As courses with identical stops sequences are comprehended to profiles, course changes (or *transfers*) can be captured in terms of changes between profiles. Given a set of profiles, all – pairwise – profile changes can be determined ahead of actual use as described subsequently. For each pair $p', p'' \in \mathbf{P}$, $(p' \neq p'')$ all reasonable junctions used to string together courses of profile p' with courses of profile p'' are collected in a *change set* $X(p', p'')$. Note that, in general, in the reverse direction there will be a different change set $X(p'', p')$. The resulting change sets are arranged in a *course concatenation table*.

W.r.t. changing trains, pairs of profiles are in one of three relations to each other. First, the profiles' stops sequences may be disjoint whence obviously no transfer between profiles is possible. However, if these stops sequences are not disjoint they may share either one stop or many (sometimes even almost all) stops; such pairs of profiles will be called *adjacent* profiles. Typically, we think of adjacent profiles sharing exactly one stop at which transfers will have to take place. Conversely, railway schedules are arranged such that adjacent profiles frequently overlap. Particularly, this happens whenever local trains are "embedded" into the stops sequences of higher order trains (i.e., semi–fast or express trains). Likewise, also national express trains are nested into international trains. A similar situation arises in case of courses serving *almost the same* sequence of stops.

Disregarding a few exceptional cases, each stop shared by different profiles is a possible candidate for changing trains. In spite of this property, the set of reasonable transfer stops between a pair of adjacent profiles can be reduced subject to the (weak) assumption that individual courses do not change their travelling characteristics – primarily, travel speed – intermediately: if two profiles share a common subsequence of stops, it is sufficient to consider only the subsequence's "border" stops as junctions. Evidently, in view of the introduced assumption if two trains differ relevantly at all, one of them will be preferred over the other throughout. Of course, a pair of adjacent profiles may have more than one subsequence of stops in common; in this case all resulting junctions must be collected properly.

Basically, change sets are generated as follows. First, each pair of profiles $p', p'' \in \mathbf{P}$, $p' \neq p''$, is screened for maximal subsequences of stops *shared* by p' and p''. A stops sequence $\ell \in \mathcal{L}_1(\mathbf{S})$, is shared by two profiles if $\lambda(p') = \ell'_l \circ \ell \circ \ell'_r$ and either $\lambda(p'') = \ell''_l \circ \ell \circ \ell''_r$ (*unidirectional* subsequence) or $\lambda(p'') = \ell''_l \circ \mathbf{rev}(\ell) \circ \ell''_r$ (*counterdirectional* subsequence). Directionality, of course, only matters in case of $\ell \in \mathcal{L}_2(\mathbf{S})$. A shared subsequence ℓ^* is *maximal* if there does not exist another shared subsequence ℓ such that ℓ^* is a proper subsequence of ℓ, i.e. $\ell = \ell_l \circ \ell^* \circ \ell_r$ for at least either $\ell_l \in \mathcal{L}_2$ or $\ell_r \in \mathcal{L}_2$.

Now, if two profiles p', p'' share a subsequence at all, each maximal subsequence ℓ^* shared by p', p'' is transformed into a set – termed *change form* – containing only the *first* and *last* possible junctions of ℓ^* (which, in fact, may coincide). Singleton change forms are called *unary*, whereas change forms with two elements are called *binary*. Change forms are built depending on (i) the length, (ii) directionality, and (iii) relative position of the shared subsequence ℓ^* in p' and p'', respectively. Altogether, only three different types of change forms can occur, viz. $f_1 = \{\mathbf{ft}(\ell^*)\}$ (unary), $f_2 = \{\mathbf{ft}(\ell^*), \mathbf{lt}(\ell^*)\}$ (binary), and $f_3 = \{\mathbf{lt}(\ell^*)\}$ (unary). In case of $|\ell^*| = 1$, of course, these types collapse (i.e. $f_1 = f_2 = f_3$) to a unary change form provided that $\sigma_o(p') \neq \mathbf{ft}(\ell^*) = \mathbf{lt}(\ell^*) \neq \sigma_t(p'')$; the change forms resulting for $|\ell^*| > 1$ are summarized in Tab. 2. The different constellations are distinguished by indicating the relative positions of $\mathbf{ft}(\ell^*)$ and $\mathbf{lt}(\ell^*)$ w.r.t. p' (leftmost columns) and p'' (top rows); letting $\tilde{\Sigma}(p) \stackrel{\text{def}}{=} \Sigma(p) \setminus \{\sigma_o(p), \sigma_t(p)\}$, $m'_q \in \tilde{\Sigma}(p')$ and $m''_q \in \tilde{\Sigma}(p'')$ denote (for $q = 1, 2$) intermediary stops such that, throughout, $m'_1 \prec_{\ell^*} m'_2$ and $m''_1 \prec_{\ell^*} m''_2$. The majority of constellations pertains to unidirectional subsequences (left–hand side of Tab. 2). Obviously, counterdirectional subsequences (right–hand side of Tab. 2) *always* result in unary change forms. Note that constellations omitted from Tab. 2 as well as table entries marked as "$\emptyset$" do not imply that $\Sigma(p') \cap \Sigma(p'') = \emptyset$; in these cases, shared subsequences merely do not contain meaningful junctions. Likewise, boundary junctions of shared subsequences have to be stripped off if they coincide with profile origins, or terminals.

Tab. 2: Change Forms for $|\ell^*| > 1$

$\mathbf{ft}(\ell^*)$		$\sigma_o(p'')$ or m''_1		m''_2
	$\mathbf{lt}(\ell^*)$	m''_2	$\sigma_t(p'')$	$\sigma_o(p'')$ or m''_1
$\sigma_o(p')$	m'_2 or $\sigma_t(p')$	f_3	$\emptyset$	$\emptyset$
m'_1	m'_2 or $\sigma_t(p')$	f_2	f_1	f_1

Finally, for each pair of profiles the change set is obtained by taking the set union over (non–empty) change forms. If $\Sigma(p')$ and $\Sigma(p'')$ are disjoint or do not yield at least one non–empty change form, $X(p', p'') = \emptyset$.

3. Generation of Course Sequences

TIC constructs train connections in a two stage procedure. In the first stage, *profiles sequences* are derived. In the second stage, actual courses are substituted into these profiles sequences. In order to obtain concrete train connections eventually, the courses' days of service must also be taken into account (cf. [2]).

A simple two–step algorithm is used by TIC to produce profiles sequences. Initially, a set of profiles sequences is generated which does not take care of the actual feasibility of necessary transfers. Thereupon, each profiles sequence is transformed into a further set of sequences such that to each transfer between profiles a particular junction is assigned. Finally, the resulting set of profiles sequences is scrutinized to determine the subset of elements with *feasible* sequences of junctions for further processing. In all of this, TIC's profiles sequence generating algorithm is based on course concatenation data as defined in the previous section.

Henceforth, a specified pair of departure and arrival stations will be named a *trip*. Furthermore, the departure station of a trip will be denoted as $\mathbf{s}_{\text{in}}$, the arrival station as $\mathbf{s}_{\text{ex}}$ ($\mathbf{s}_{\text{in}}, \mathbf{s}_{\text{ex}} \in \mathbf{S}$). Naturally, $\mathbf{s}_{\text{in}} \neq \mathbf{s}_{\text{ex}}$ is supposed to hold.

As a preliminary step the set $\mathbf{P}$ is augmented temporarily by two artificial profiles $\mathbf{p}_{\text{in}}$ and $\mathbf{p}_{\text{ex}}$. These profiles are added mainly in order to achieve a smooth description of the algorithm. Both profiles contain one station and one fictitious course only, i.e. $\Sigma(\mathbf{p}_{\text{in}}) = \{\mathbf{s}_{\text{in}}\}$, $\Sigma(\mathbf{p}_{\text{ex}}) = \{\mathbf{s}_{\text{ex}}\}$ and $K(\mathbf{p}_{\text{in}}) = \{\mathbf{c}_{\text{in}}\}$, $K(\mathbf{p}_{\text{ex}}) = \{\mathbf{c}_{\text{ex}}\}$. Furthermore, these profiles' change forms are defined uniformly as follows: for each $p \in \Pi_o(\mathbf{s}_{\text{in}}) \cup \Pi_h(\mathbf{s}_{\text{in}})$ a change set $X(\mathbf{p}_{\text{in}}, p) = \{\mathbf{s}_{\text{in}}\}$ is added to the course concatenation table. Likewise, for each $p \in \Pi_h(\mathbf{s}_{\text{ex}}) \cup \Pi_t(\mathbf{s}_{\text{ex}})$ a change set $X(p, \mathbf{p}_{\text{ex}}) = \{\mathbf{s}_{\text{ex}}\}$ is added. Subsequently, two further sets of profiles are referred to, viz. $N^+(p) \stackrel{\text{def}}{=} \{p' : X(p, p') \neq \emptyset\}$ (successor profiles) and $N^-(p) \stackrel{\text{def}}{=} \{p' : X(p', p) \neq \emptyset\}$ (predecessor profiles), resp., of profile p.

Starting with $\mathbf{s}_{\text{in}}$ and $\mathbf{s}_{\text{ex}}$ the sequence generating algorithm considers transitively successor profiles of $\mathbf{p}_{\text{in}}$ and predecessor profiles of $\mathbf{p}_{\text{ex}}$, resp., proceeding step by step in order to find paths connecting $\mathbf{p}_{\text{in}}$ and $\mathbf{p}_{\text{ex}}$. These paths of type $\mathcal{L}_3^{**}(\mathbf{P}, \mathcal{P}_1(\mathbf{S}))$ are gathered in set $E(\mathbf{s}_{\text{in}}, \mathbf{s}_{\text{ex}})$ which, in general, will also contain infeasible elements: the mere existence of a profiles sequence connecting $\mathbf{p}_{\text{in}}$ and $\mathbf{p}_{\text{ex}}$ does not imply automatically that the involved change sets warrant feasibility of *transfer sequences.* In particular, if three or more profiles are strung together, it might happen that a change from the first to the second profile is possible only *after* a change from the second to the third profile. Likewise, it might also happen that individual stations are hit repeatedly, thus causing undesired loops. The set of profiles sequences of type $\mathcal{L}_3^*(\mathbf{P},\mathbf{S})$ connecting $\mathbf{s}_{\text{in}}$ and $\mathbf{s}_{\text{ex}}$ derived from $E(\mathbf{s}_{\text{in}},\mathbf{s}_{\text{ex}})$ by eliminating infeasible members and determining concrete transfer sequences (i.e., junctions to change between profiles) will be denoted $P(\mathbf{s}_{\text{in}},\mathbf{s}_{\text{ex}})$.

Since the sets N^+ and N^- produce a directed *cyclic* structure, the algorithm's sequence expansion loop must be terminated explicitly. This is accomplished by means of a parameter $l_{\max}$; if we let the shortest element of $E(\mathbf{s}_{\text{in}},\mathbf{s}_{\text{ex}})$ have length l_o, sequence expansion stops after having generated all profiles sequences ℓ with $|\ell| \leq l_o + l_{\max}$. For reasons of computational economy, sequence expansion proceeds alternately from both ends. Note that although the sets E_{in} and E_{ex} are singletons initially (step 0), their elements are labeled sequences of type $\mathcal{L}^{**}(\mathbf{P},\mathcal{P}_1(\mathbf{S}))$ throughout.

Step 0: Initialization

$$l := 0; \quad l_o := \infty; \quad \mathrm{E}_{\text{in}} := \{\mathbf{p}_{\text{in}}\}; \quad \mathrm{E}_{\text{ex}} := \{\mathbf{p}_{\text{ex}}\}$$

Step 1: Expanding partial profiles sequences

$$\begin{aligned}
(*)\ \text{IF } & |\mathrm{E}_{\text{in}}| \leq |\mathrm{E}_{\text{ex}}| \\
& \text{THEN } \mathrm{E}_{\text{in}} := \{\ell \circ (\mathbf{lt}(\ell) \overset{X(\mathbf{lt}(\ell),p)}{\rightarrow} p) : \\
& \qquad \ell \in \mathrm{E}_{\text{in}} \wedge p \in N^+(\mathbf{lt}(\ell))\} \\
& \text{ELSE } \mathrm{E}_{\text{ex}} := \{(p \overset{X(p,\mathbf{ft}(\ell))}{\rightarrow} \mathbf{ft}(\ell)) \circ \ell : \\
& \qquad \ell \in \mathrm{E}_{\text{ex}} \wedge p \in N^-(\mathbf{ft}(\ell))\};
\end{aligned}$$

$$E_l(\mathbf{s}_{\text{in}},\mathbf{s}_{\text{ex}}) := \{\ell' \circ \ell'' : \ell' \in \mathrm{E}_{\text{in}},\ \ell'' \in \mathrm{E}_{\text{ex}}\};$$

$$\text{IF } E_l(\mathbf{s}_{\text{in}},\mathbf{s}_{\text{ex}}) \neq \emptyset \text{ THEN } l_o := \min(l_o, l);$$

$$\begin{aligned}
\text{IF } l < l_o + l_{\max} \text{ THEN } & l := l+1; \quad \text{GOTO } (*) \\
\text{ELSE } & E(\mathbf{s}_{\text{in}},\mathbf{s}_{\text{ex}}) := \textstyle\bigcup_{l'=l_o}^{l} E_{l'}(\mathbf{s}_{\text{in}},\mathbf{s}_{\text{ex}});
\end{aligned}$$

Step 2: Factoring out change sets and elimination of infeasible sequences

$$\begin{aligned}
P(\mathbf{s}_{\text{in}},\mathbf{s}_{\text{ex}}) := \{ & p_1 \overset{s_{1,2}}{\rightarrow} p_2 \overset{s_{2,3}}{\rightarrow} \cdots \overset{s_{n-1,n}}{\rightarrow} p_n \in \mathcal{L}_3^*(\mathbf{P},\mathbf{S}) : \\
& p_1 \overset{X(p_1,p_2)}{\rightarrow} p_2 \overset{X(p_2,p_3)}{\rightarrow} \cdots \overset{X(p_{n-1},p_n)}{\rightarrow} p_n \\
& \in E(\mathbf{s}_{\text{in}},\mathbf{s}_{\text{ex}}) \wedge \\
& s_{k,k+1} \in X(p_k,p_{k+1}) \text{ for } 1 \leq k < n \wedge \\
& \eta(p_1 \overset{s_{1,2}}{\rightarrow} p_2 \overset{s_{2,3}}{\rightarrow} \cdots \overset{s_{n-1,n}}{\rightarrow} p_n) \in \mathcal{L}_2(\mathbf{S})\};
\end{aligned}$$

where $\eta(\ell)$ denotes the entire sequence of stops of consecutive profiles in $\ell = p_1 \overset{s_{1,2}}{\rightarrow} p_2 \overset{s_{2,3}}{\rightarrow} \cdots \overset{s_{n-1,n}}{\rightarrow} p_n$, i.e. letting $\ell_k = s_{k-1,k} \rightarrow \cdots \rightarrow s_{k,k+1}$ such that $\lambda(p_k) = \ell'_k \circ \ell_k \circ \ell''_k$ for $1 < k < n$, $\eta(\ell) = \ell_2 \circ \cdots \circ \ell_{n-1}$. Evidently, this also implies $s_{k-1,k} \prec_{\lambda(p_k)} s_{k,k+1}$ $(1 < k < n)$ for feasible sequences.

At this stage, we are left with a set $P(\mathbf{s}_{\text{in}},\mathbf{s}_{\text{ex}})$ of profiles sequences with specified junctions such that any replacement of a profile p by some course $c \in K(p)$ yields a feasible course sequence.

In principle, TIC considers *every* course sequence resulting from a systematic replacement of profiles by individual courses for each profiles sequence in $P(\mathbf{s}_{\text{in}},\mathbf{s}_{\text{ex}})$. These course sequences of type $\mathcal{L}_3^*(\mathbf{C},\mathbf{S})$ are collected in set $\Gamma(\mathbf{s}_{\text{in}},\mathbf{s}_{\text{ex}})$ which is TIC's counterpart of the semantic train connection model's *connecting set* of trips from $\mathbf{s}_{\text{in}}$ to $\mathbf{s}_{\text{ex}}$. Formally, Γ is derived from $P(\mathbf{s}_{\text{in}},\mathbf{s}_{\text{ex}})$ simply as follows:

$$\begin{aligned}
\Gamma(\mathbf{s}_{\text{in}},\mathbf{s}_{\text{ex}}) := \{ & c_1 \overset{s_{1,2}}{\rightarrow} c_2 \overset{s_{2,3}}{\rightarrow} \cdots \overset{s_{n-1,n}}{\rightarrow} c_n : \\
& p_1 \overset{s_{1,2}}{\rightarrow} p_2 \overset{s_{2,3}}{\rightarrow} \cdots \overset{s_{n-1,n}}{\rightarrow} p_n \in P(\mathbf{s}_{\text{in}},\mathbf{s}_{\text{ex}}) \wedge \\
& \langle c_1, c_2, \ldots, c_n \rangle \in \times_{i=1}^{n} K(p_i)\}
\end{aligned}$$

Although Γ now comprises all train connections relevant for a trip from $\mathbf{s}_{\text{in}}$ to $\mathbf{s}_{\text{ex}}$, these train connections' actual days of service are still undetermined. Additionally, transfer connections have to be ruled out if change delays fall out of the admissible range. To this end, arrival and departure times of courses must be combined with the courses' service days in order to model the *real* flow of events.

As a final step, the generated set of train connections is subjected to a formal evaluation procedure. Basically, each course sequence $\ell \in \Gamma(\mathbf{s}_{\text{in}},\mathbf{s}_{\text{ex}})$ is evaluated individually in terms of several *performance measures* of train connections which comprise (i) train features (such as travel speed, departure/arrival times, train comfort, etc.), (ii) connection features (such as number of required train changes, transfer delays, etc.) as well as (iii) explicit and implicit passenger preferences. In fact, any kind of performance measure can be defined provided that basic data are available (cf. [2]). Each of these criteria contributes to a general additive weighted scoring function. Before train connections are displayed, they are ranked according to achieved connection scores.

4. Conclusion

Although the TIC approach has not yet been applied to a comprehensive set of real time tables, non-trivial train connections for many sample trips (based on a subset of schedule data from the Austrian Federal Railways' train schedule) have been derived with satisfactory results. Since the algorithm generates quite a large set of connection candidates before recommended connections are sifted out in the evaluation stage, careful implementation of TIC is necessary to speed up response. To this end, geographical knowledge could be used to cut off many change sets, too.

As a particularly interesting augmentation, TIC can be extended to cover multiple public traffic systems. Basically, this integration requires extra data relating stations of different sub–systems. In fact, additional information associating geographical locations with stations and traffic systems, resp., will become necessary either. Likewise, also minimal change delays for transfers between different traffic systems would have to be known.

References

[1] Dhawan V., Rajput V.S., Asthana R.G.S. (1991) *Intelligent Rail–Air Travel Planner.* Proc. 7th CAIA (IEEE), pp. 412–418.

[2] Froeschl K.A, Fritz R. (1991) *TIC – Automated Generation of Train Connections in a Railway Passenger Consulting System.* Technical Report SMC–105.

[3] Manna Z., Waldinger R. (1985) *The Logical Basis of Computer Programming: Vol. 1 – Deductive Reasoning.* Addison–Wesley, Reading Ma.

[4] Tulp E. (1987) *TRAINS.* Thesis, Dept. of Mathematics and Computer Science, Free Univ. of Amsterdam.

Acknowledgement: *The TIC train connection model has resulted from a close collaboration with Robert Fritz who also has implemented a program prototype of the TIC approach.*

MATOURA: MULTI-AGENT TOURIST ADVISOR

Constantin Halatsis[1], Panagiotis Stamatopoulos[1], Isambo Karali[1], Constantin Mourlas[1], Dimitris Gouscos[1], Dimitris Margaritis[1], Constantin Fouskakis[1], Angelos Kolokouris[2], Panagiotis Xinos[2], Mike Reeve[3], André Véron[3], Kees Schuerman[3], Liang-Liang Li[3]

[1]Univ. of Athens, Dept. of Informatics, Athens, Greece
[2]Expert Systems International, Athens, Greece
[3]ECRC, Munich, Germany

MaTourA is a tourist advisory system about Greece that is being implemented in the parallel constraint logic programming language ElipSys. The purpose of MaTourA is to facilitate the work carried out in travel agencies by providing an interactive way to construct personalized tours, select predefined package tours and handle the underlying touristic information. The system has been designed as a set of high-level interacting agents. In this direction, the ElipSys language was extended with the appropriate features to support the development of multi-agent systems.

Introduction

The introduction of the on-line computer services in the area of tourism has contributed significantly to improving services and sales. The need, however, remains largely unfulfilled, although immediately apparent, for an integrated and friendly access to the relevant data. Thus, tourism informatics as well as other applications of on-line systems need a presentation and usage environment that would make the computer immediately accessible. The necessary element that is missing so far and which is confining the effectiveness of the systems in use is above all the picture.

An effective advising process for the traveler requires the capture of the integrated information material in every possible form from all the sources and services. To be specific, the information from the hotel units must be connected to the relevant updates for cultural activities by the authorities on the exact areas that interest the visitor. Technology and the method utilized to communicate with and inform the tourist must be characterized by a global presentation that includes information in many forms, e.g. text, sound, photograph, and movie clips.

Following the above, a specific application on tourism, called MaTourA (**M**ulti-**a**gent **Tour**ist **A**dvisor) [7, 6] is presented in this paper. MaTourA is currently under development by the University of Athens and Expert Systems International in the context of the ESPRIT 6708 APPLAUSE Project (Application & Assessment of Parallel Programming Using Logic). MaTourA has been designed and is currently being implemented in the ElipSys language [2, 9, 4], a parallel constraint logic programming system developed at the European Computer-Industry Research Centre (ECRC).

APPLAUSE is a three year project that began

in May 1992. The main aim of the project is to assess the advantages (and disadvantages) of the ElipSys language in various application areas, namely planning & scheduling, decision support and multi-agent systems. ElipSys is a pure parallel logic programming system which supports, apart from parallelism, other additional features, such as constraint satisfaction over finite domains, that may be exploited to design and implement applications useful in a real-world environment.

The multi-agent systems approach adopted in the case of MaTourA is a major research area of Distributed Artificial Intelligence (DAI) [3], in which agents of various types and capabilities cooperate in problem solving. MaTourA comprises a set of autonomous agents reflecting the procedures involved in a tourist advisory environment. In order to support the development of MaTourA, ElipSys was extended appropriately with a three-layered socket based communication scheme capable to satisfy the interaction requirements of the MaTourA agents.

MaTourA is the evolution of another application, the single-agent PErsonalized Tourist INformation Advisor (PETINA) [12, 13] developed by the University of Athens in the ElipSys language. PETINA is a prototype with rather shallow knowledge and simplistic form of reasoning. Thus, it was straightforward to implement it as a conventional ElipSys application. However, this is not the case with MaTourA, so a multi-agent architecture seems appropriate and *sine qua non* for the application.

In the following, short overviews of the multi-agent systems technology and the ElipSys language are presented, as well as a brief description of the communication oriented extension of ElipSys. Then, the MaTourA functional and structural specifications are discussed and the agents of the system are described. Finally, the implementation issues concerning the first prototype of the system are presented.

Multi-agent Systems

As it is stated in [3], in the multi-agent systems area of DAI, "*research is concerned with coordinating intelligent behaviour among a collection of (possibly pre-existing) autonomous intelligent agents, how they can coordinate their knowledge, goals, skills and plans jointly to take action or to solve problems*".

The approach that has to be followed for the development of a multi-agent system is to build a separate subsystem for each problem domain and, then, make these susbsystems cooperate. There are many advantages in a procedure like that. Firstly, the modularity achieved reduces the complexity of the whole system, which, in addition, is more reliable, in the sense that it can continue to operate even if part of it fails. Moreover, there might be a speedup in execution, since the subsystems can operate in parallel. Another advantage is that the subsystems are reusable. Finally, the knowledge acquisition procedure is facilitated, since it is easier to find experts in narrower domains.

The cooperation among the agents of a multi-agent system may be achieved in various ways, according to the model employed for this reason. The research in this direction has produced models for cooperation, such as the blackboard [8, 5], the contract net [11] and the actor [1] models. In any case, there are some problems that have to be addressed, such as description, decomposition and allocation of problems among a group of intelligent agents, synthesis of results as well as representation and reasoning by an agent about the actions, plans and knowledge of other agents.

The ElipSys Language

ElipSys is a parallel logic programming language which incorporates various powerful execution mechanisms. The language supports OR-parallelism, AND-parallelism, data-parallelism, a data driven computation rule and constraint satisfaction techniques over finite domains. All these features make the language ideal for stating and describing search-based applications and combinatorial problems.

OR-parallelism aims at the concurrent exploration of the various alternative clauses that define an ElipSys procedure. AND-parallelism results from the concurrent execution of two goals in conjunction. This feature is not provided by the ElipSys execution model, neither it is supported by the run time environment of the language. It resides only at the language level and is actually compiled into OR-parallelism. Data-parallelism is a kind of parallelism arising from the concurrent treatment of the elements of a set of data.

In addition, ElipSys provides a data driven computation rule on top of the usual depth-first left-to-right execution strategy of Prolog. This rule modifies the reduction order of goals according to instantiations of variables by declaring that every goal that refers to a specific predicate has to be delayed, if its arguments are not adequately instantiated. A delayed goal is awakened when the desirable degree of instantiation is achieved. Finally, ElipSys supports constraint satisfaction techniques over finite domains, which lead to a priori pruning of the search space and thus, they result in more optimized execution.

ElipSys has been designed for maximum portability between different parallel platforms. A hybrid scheme is used, based on shared memory and message passing. It is currently available on various machines, namely Sun workstations (in sequential and pseudo-parallel mode), Sequent Symmetry, Sparc based multiprocessors from Sun and ICL and the KSR-1 distributed memory machine. On the latter, the hardware supported shared virtual memory is used.

A Communication Scheme in ElipSys

The features of the ElipSys language that were described earlier aim to support the efficient solution of problems that may be mapped to a search of OR-trees. The parallelism offered may serve as a means for the concurrent exploration of branches of these trees and the constraint satisfaction mechanism, as well as the data driven computation to a lesser extent, may be used to prune the OR-trees and reduce the search space. Unfortunately, this computational environment is not sufficient to support the development of multi-agent systems like MaTourA. The reason is that for such kind of systems, a framework is needed to allow the agents to communicate and exchange information. In any case, the searching facilities provided by ElipSys are indispensable at the intra-agent level, especially if someone wants to have really intelligent agents.

For this reason, an appropriate extension of ElipSys was needed that could be integrated smoothly with the core system and that would be able to support the interaction requirements of MaTourA. A framework such as the one provided by SICStus Prolog [10] would be profitable. What was actually done for the MaTourA case was to enhance ElipSys with SICStus-like communication facilities and to extend them so as to support the transparent interaction among agents. The whole framework may be viewed as a three-layered communication scheme. These layers consist of the following:

Low-level built-ins: These correspond very closely to the actual UNIX system calls used by an ordinary process interface to network entities. They implement all the required primitives to support the communication among processes through stream sockets in the Internet domain. The low-level built-ins were implemented in C and connected to the core language through the ElipSys to C interface.

Medium-level predicates: These can be used to pass arbitrary terms between a blackboard server and various clients. These predicates are functionally similar to those used in SICStus Prolog for communication with a Linda server. This set of predicates was implemented in ElipSys on top of the previous low-level built-ins and supports the upper layer of the communication scheme.

High-level predicates: These predicates were tailored to be used for a virtual point-to-point message passing (through the blackboard) by multi-agent applications. They are the ones that support the development of MaTourA as well as other applications of similar nature. ElipSys processes are able to exchange messages through predicates, such as *send_request/3*, *get_message/3*, *send_answer/3* etc. which were also implemented in ElipSys.

The Functionality of MaTourA

MaTourA is a tourist advisory system whose purpose is to help travel agents satisfy the needs of their customers/tourists. The system has been designed using a multi-agent architecture in a way compatible with DAI principles. More precisely, the different procedures carried out in a travel agency correspond to MaTourA agents. Some of these agents are responsible to handle primitive touristic information, i.e. information related to accommodation, transportation etc. The agents of MaTourA cooperate in order to solve certain problems given to the system. Each agent contributes to the solution by using its knowledge to solve subproblems of the global problem.

The functionality of MaTourA covers the different topics that characterize the work in a travel agency. More precisely, the system handles various types of requests to construct personalized tours that satisfy the tourists' wishes. Certain kinds of requests refer to the selection of precompiled package tours offered by travel agencies. Information retrieval and maintenance is also supported by the system and, finally, training is supported, so as to facilitate the use of the system by travel agents.

The Structure of MaTourA

MaTourA comprises a set of agents each reflecting procedures involved in a tourist advisory environment. Each agent accomplishes a specific functionality and manipulates specific knowledge. These agents may either answer queries on their own or coordinate their knowledge and communicate with each other in case joint action is required.

MaTourA consists of the following agents: Tour Generation Agent, Activity Agent, Event Agent, Site Agent, Accommodation Agent, Transportation Agent, Ticketing Agent, Package Tour Agent, User Interface Agent, Info Retrieval/Maintenance Agent and Training Agent.

Tour Generation Agent: The Tour Generation Agent is responsible for the generation of personalized tours, taking into account user wishes. These tours are time/location schedules providing, for each day, a desirable timetable. The term "locations" refers to the elementary sites maintained by the Site Agent. The Tour Generation Agent constructs the requested personalized tours. In order to carry out this task, it needs information supplied by many agents of the MaTourA system. More precisely, the Activity, Event, Site, Accommodation and Transportation Agents are queried by the Tour Generation Agent. Requests of four types are accepted. These are the following in increasing degree of complexity: i) A full time/location schedule is provided to the agent, e.g. 15 Jul 93 — 19 Jul 93 in Athens, 19 Jul 93 — 25 Jul 93 in Rhodes, 25 Jul 93 — 31 Jul 93 in Heraklion, ii) The visit period of the tour is given, but not the very locations. However, a wider area/division is supplied or, alternatively, a starting location for the tour, e.g. 15 Jul 93 — 5 Aug 93 in Cyclades, iii) Specific locations are given but no information about time, e.g. a tour in Thessaloniki, Edessa, Kavala, Alexandroupoli and iv) Neither specific locations nor information about time is provided, but a tour with a given starting location or in a wider area/division is requested, e.g. a tour starting from Ioannina.

For each type of request, cost criteria as well as interest preferences are given to the agent. Moreover, acceptable transportation means and accommodation constraints are taken into consideration, if requested. Finally, a set of Daily Plan Templates (DPTs) are supplied to the agent. Each DPT corresponds to a typical day that the tourist would like to spend on a specific location. A DPT consists of time/action pairs, e.g. 10:00 — 14:00 swimming, 18:00 — 21:00 sightseeing.

Activity Agent: The Activity Agent holds information about activities and is able to answer related requests coming from other MaTourA agents. Activities are possible tourist's visits to various spots, such as visits to museums, galleries, archaeological sites etc., or even more, beaches for swimming, surfing etc. In general, activities are related with spots that might be of interest to a tourist.

Event Agent: The Event Agent holds information about events and, as is the case with the Activity Agent, it answers requests relevant to this information which come from other MaTourA agents. Events differ from activities in that they are short term shows with rather temporary nature, such as exhibitions, music concerts etc., while the activities are more permanent in time.

Site Agent: This agent deals with the sites of Greece. A site is a geographical entity of the country. The concept of sites is an important one for MaTourA as the whole tour generation facility of the system works considering the sites as a fundamental starting point. In addition, plain site information is vital for any system that deals with tourism. The concept of sites is related with a site inclusion relation. This inclusion considers three levels of sites: i) *elementary sites* which are the cities, towns and villages, ii) *areas* which are the islands and the provinces of Greece and iii) *divisions* which are large islands, island groups, regions and land areas.

Accommodation Agent: This agent handles information about lodgings where a tourist may be accommodated and returns it after the appropriate requests are made. In a real-world tourist advisory system, this agent has to be connected with external reservation systems.

Transportation Agent: The Transportation Agent holds information about connections between elementary sites through different transportation means. Thus, various transportation graphs, each one for a specific transportation means, are coded for all the elementary sites in Greece. As transportation means, *private car*, *bus*, *train*, *boat* and *airplane* are considered, resulting to five different transportation graphs. The Transportation Agent supports plain information retrieval and it is also capable to answer more complicated requests, such as ones that refer to routing problems. Whenever it has to solve a problem that involves ticketing issues, the Ticketing Agent is requested.

Ticketing Agent: The Ticketing Agent has information about the connections that are established between different elementary sites all over Greece by public transportation means. Various information retrieval requests are supported, however the most complicated task that the agent carries out refers to the computation of time schedules for given routes through elementary sites. As is the case with the Accommodation Agent, in a real-world system, the Ticketing Agent has to be connected to external reservation systems.

Package Tour Agent: This agent is responsible for producing package tours that match requirements described in requests which are sent to it. A package tour is a precompiled tour as it has been constructed by a travel agency.

User Interface Agent: This agent is responsible for controlling all user interactions with the MaTourA system. The main theme of the User Interface Agent is to observe, analyze, constrain and guide the user interaction with MaTourA. The model of interaction makes use of advanced dialogue techniques to implement a user friedly and responsive system. During the interaction, the User Interface Agent attempts to extract implicitly as much information of the user as it can capture, before this becomes annoying to the user and a considerable load to the dialogue.

Info Retrieval/Maintenance Agent: This agent satisfies the MaTourA requirement to deal with large in volume, persistent data. The functionality supported by this agent deviates from the common functionality supported by the contemporary commercial RDBMSs in the sense that MaTourA needs to store non-conventional data, such as complex data structures and, to a lesser extent, deductive rules.

Training Agent: The Training Agent stands by the User Interface Agent to assist the user in the use of the tourist advisor. This agent may either be invoked by the user or automatically intervene during a session when the User Interface Agent decides. The users of MaTourA are modelled according to user stereotypes (naive, intermediate and experts). When presenting information to the user, the intelligent help facility formulates the contents, the context and the style of the presented help information to the appropriate level of the type of the individual user.

The First Prototype

A first prototype of the MaTourA system has been already implemented in ElipSys version 0.6 and runs on Sparc-based Sun workstations under SunOS 4.1.2. This prototype covers most of the MaTourA agents, some of them with their full functionality (AcA, EvA, AmA, TkA) and others partially (TGA, StA, TpA). The purpose of the development of the prototype was twofold. Fistly, it aimed at the verification of the correctness of the three-layered communication scheme that was developed as an extension of the ElipSys language and, secondly, it served as an initial demonstrator of the functionality of MaTourA.

Conclusions

MaTourA is a Multi-agent Tourist Advisor, an application which is being implemented in the ElipSys language in the context of the ESPRIT 6708 APPLAUSE Project. ElipSys is a parallel constraint logic programming system that was extended with a socket based communication framework, in order to be able to support the design and development of multi-agent systems, such as MaTourA.

MaTourA major capabilities are to construct tours that satisfy user wishes and to provide information about a variety of entities that present touristic interest. User wishes involve various information that logically and physically refers to different subsystems which, actually, are the system agents. In addition, maintenance of the stored information as well as user training are provided by the system.

MaTourA functionality needs clearly a multi-agent system platform both as a programming tool and as a computational model. The system consists of a set of agents each accomplishing specific functionality and manipulating specified knowledge. These agents may either answer the query that was put to them on their own, or communicate with each other in case supplementary information is needed by an agent.

A prototype version of MaTourA has been implemented in the extended ElipSys language. This version is currently being updated, so as to achieve the full functionality of MaTourA.

Acknowledgments

The APPLAUSE Project is partially funded by the ESPRIT Programme of the Commission of the European Communities as ESPRIT Project 6708.

References

[1] G. Agha and C. Hewitt. Concurrent programming using actors: Exploiting large-scale parallelism. AI Memo 865, Massachusetts Institute of Technology, 1985.

[2] U. Baron, S. Bescos, S. Delgado-Rannauro, P. Heuzé, M. Dorochevsky, M. Ibáñez-Espiga, K. Schuerman, M. Ratcliffe, A. Véron, and J. Xu. The ElipSys logic programming language. Technical Report DPS-81, ECRC, December 1990.

[3] A. Bond and L. Gasser, editors. *Readings in Distributed Artificial Intelligence.* Morgan Kaufmann Publishers, Inc., San Mateo, California, 1988.

[4] *ElipSys User Manual for Release Version* 0.6, April 1993.

[5] R. Engelmore and T. Morgan, editors. *Blackboard Systems.* Addisson-Wesley Publishing Company, Wokingham, England, 1988.

[6] C. Halatsis, P. Stamatopoulos, D. Margaritis, I. Karali, C. Mourlas, D. Gouscos, and C. Fouskakis. Tool assessment. APPLAUSE Deliverable D.WP3.4, University of Athens, May 1993.

[7] C. Halatsis, P. Stamatopoulos, Z. Palaskas, I. Karali, C. Mourlas, D. Gouscos, D. Margaritis, and C. Fouskakis. MaTourA specification. APPLAUSE Deliverable D.WP3.2, University of Athens — Expert Systems International, May 1993.

[8] B. Hayes-Roth. A blackboard architecture for control. *Artificial Intelligence*, 26:251–321, 1985.

[9] S. Prestwich. ElipSys programming tutorial. APPLAUSE Deliverable D.WP4.ECRC.4A, ECRC, November 1992.

[10] *SICStus Prolog User's Manual*, August 1992.

[11] R. Smith. The contract net protocol: High-level communication and control in a distributed problem solver. *IEEE Transactions on Computers*, C-29(12):1104–1113, December 1980.

[12] P. Stamatopoulos, I. Karali, and C. Halatsis. PETINA — Tour generation using the ElipSys inference system. In *Proceedings of the 1992 ACM/SIGAPP Symposium on Applied Computing*, volume 1, pages 320–327, 1992.

[13] P. Stamatopoulos, I. Karali, and C. Halatsis. A tour advisory system using a logic programming approach. *Applied Computing Review*, 1(1):18–25, 1993.

A HYBRID EXPERT SYSTEM FOR AVALANCHE FORECASTING

M.Schweizer[1], P.M.B. Föhn[2], J.Schweizer[2], A. Ultsch[3]

[1]*Institute for Informatics, University of Zürich, Winterthurerstr. 190, CH-8059 Zürich*
[2]*Swiss Federal Institute for Snow and Avalanche Research, CH-7260 Weissfluhjoch/Davos*
[3]*FG Informatik, Philipps University of Marburg, Hans-Mehrwein Str. 22, D-35043 Marburg/Lahn*

Abstract. A new approach to the problem of avalanche forecasting is presented. A hybrid neural expert system will be developed to assess the avalanche danger for a given region. Using snow, weather and snow cover data as input parameters the system evaluates the degree of danger for a given region. It integrates extended symbolic computing from traditional Artificial Intelligence, by generating symbolic rules from subsymbolic data, with unsupervised neural networks. The new approach is compared to present methods of avalanche forecasting.
Keywords: avalanche forecasting, neural networks, Kohonen, self-organization, rule-extraction, hybrid expert systems.

1. Introduction

Snow avalanches represent a typical and frequent hazard in mountainous regions. They are a limiting factor for the tourism in winter time. Access roads, villages and ski resorts may be endangered by avalanches. Hence avalanche protection is essential for the development of winter sport activities like skiing or snow boarding.
Beside constructions (e.g. snow fences) and avalanche zoning the avalanche forecasting is the most efficient way to protect tourists and inhabitants of ski resorts. During winter time the public is informed daily or several times a week about the degree of avalanche danger and according recommendations by the so called "avalanche bulletin" [1].
In Switzerland the Swiss Federal Institute for Snow and Avalanche Research (SFISAR) is in charge of the public avalanche warning for the whole area of the Swiss Alps [2]. On the basis of daily sampled snow, weather and snow cover data the avalanche danger is daily assessed for each region in the Swiss Alps by some experts using their individual knowledge and long term experience. Any tools providing assistance for this difficult task are welcome. It is a field which is excellently appropriate to develop, test and use any kind of expert systems.
Including connectionist components and rule based systems in the new *hybrid expert* system it will be possible to provide a powerful assisting tool.

2. Present approaches to the avalanche forecasting for a region

The avalanche bulletin predicts the avalanche activity for a climatologically uniform region. For the interests of tourism, the avalanche activity is described by the probability of an avalanche situation rather than by individual avalanches. The key questions are: *where, when, which types of avalanches* will occur. In Switzerland the probability of an avalanche situation is given since 1985 as degree of danger (from 1 to 7). This structure which has been confirmed by the international group of avalanche forecast services should also be adopted by any expert system. Since 1993 the new international scale of degrees of danger contains 5 degrees which easily may be adopted from the previous scale of 7 degrees.

The complexity of the problem leads to different methods to assess the avalanche danger [3].
The *deterministic method* tries to model the physical processes in the snow cover and to calculate directly the avalanche release using principles of fracture mechanics. However, existing snow cover models [4] are not detailed enough to achieve this goal. Additionally the single slope result would have to be extrapolated to a whole region.
The *statistical approach* uses daily data over several years. The snow and weather data is correlated statistically to the data of observed avalanches. Present systems give as result the observed avalanches (single events) of the ten nearest neighbouring days [5].
Föhn and Hächler [6] combined the two approaches to develop a deterministic-statistic model which correlates the physical process of snow settling with the avalanche activity. The model is appropriate for heavy snowfall periods.
Existing *expert systems* are partly also based on statistical exploitation of a large database. The input parameters are more elaborated and the given result is partly the degree of danger which is more useful than just single avalanches. However, a prerequisite for this approach is a corresponding data set consisting of the verified degrees of danger for the given region. The *verification* of the avalanche danger which has to be done day by day is as the assessment itself an expert decision [7]. Some of the presently used expert systems are more process oriented or use rules to predict the local danger slope by slope [8].
In the traditional *synoptical approach* a human expert analyses the snow and weather data and assesses the avalanche danger using his long term experience and knowledge about avalanche formation processes. As none of the methods and tools developed in the last years are fully successful, the synoptical method forms still the basis of the decision process supplemented with several systems using the other methods (*supplemented synoptical method*). The connections are presented in Fig. 1.

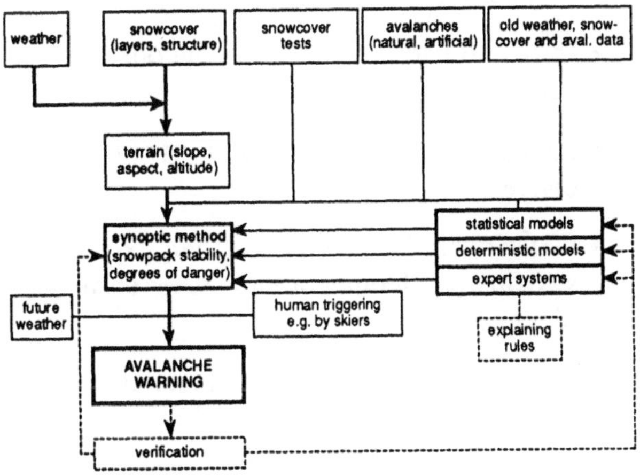

Fig. 1 Forecasting methods, input parameters and their relation

To give an idea about the efficiency of the presently used methods some of the systems are briefly presented. All of them were tested, used and rated in the Davos/north of Grisons area for several years. The statistical system NEX_MOD uses the method of the ten nearest neighbours (days) and evaluates about 50% of the days correct. The expert systems COGENSYS™ DAVOS and COGENSYS™ MODUL (the latter is process oriented and uses partly implicit rules) get a rate of 60% and 70% correct diagnosis respectively [9]. To compare, the avalanche bulletin based on the supplemented synoptical method is correct on about 70% of the days. The weather forecast has an overall performance of about 80 to 85%.
The quality of all present systems varies substantially during winter time. Unfortunately, the most dangerous situations which are however rare, are often insufficiently interpreted.

3. A new approach

To improve and to homogenize the decision process of avalanche forecasting a new system is developed with the following objectives:

- assessment of the degree of avalanche danger on the basis of daily snow and weather data
- ability to use incomplete or inconsistent data
- ability to explain the result (degree of danger)
- better overall performance than existing systems, preferably about 80% correct diagnosis
- better performance in critical situations

As the SFISAR is now located for more than fifty years on the Weissfluhjoch 2670m.a.s.l. a large extensive database exists. It includes not only snow and weather data but also observations about the avalanche activity. Due to many studies on the subject of avalanche forecasting a dataset is available which suggests to use a connectionist system. They are able to *generalize*, to work with *incomplete* or *inconsistent* data. Nevertheless they lack transparency. They are black-box systems like present systems. For example, the rules leading to the avalanche danger can not be explained to a user. This problem can be solved by combining connectionist models and knowledge based systems. By integrating the two approaches it is possible to eliminate the weakness of each single method by exploiting the strength of the other [10,11]. The tools developed to build such a system are used to generate a *hybrid* expert system for avalanche forecasting. They include a symbolic learning algorithm called *sig_m* [12], that is based on statistics and the *U-Matrix* method [13,14] to analyse data by exploring the structure of a Kohonen Map, which is formed by an unsupervised learning self-organizing neural network [15]. So the developed system realizes automatic knowledge acquisition by integrating symbolic learning with neural network learning methods [16]. The case database consists of a thousand days (7 winters) each of them characterized by 18 weather, snow and snow cover parameters from the Davos/north of Grisons area. It is about the same database which is used in the COGENSYS™ expert system and which is supplemented day by day with the verified degree of avalanche danger.

The procedure of the knowledge acquisition is shown in Fig. 2. For each of the classes 1, 4, 5 and 6 (equal to degree of danger, class 7 never occurred) out of the case base there can be

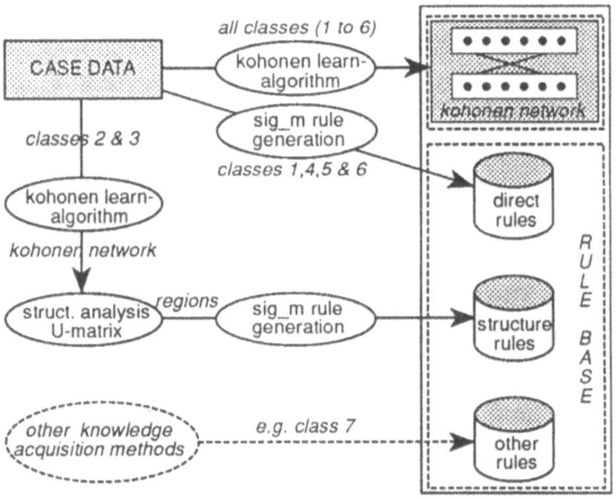

Fig. 2 Tools and procedure in the developement of the hybrid expert system

extracted *direct rules* using the *sig_m* method. The classes 2 and 3 are more difficult to distinguish. This are the cases of classes where the neural Kohonen Network assists in the process. A Kohonen Network can then be used to detect structures in the dataspace of the learned cases using the *U-Matrix* method. This method enables the visualization of clusters in the statespace of the trained data. Using this method, the two classes could be divided into 18 sub-

classes where they are better distinguishable. The *sig_m* method then could be applied to the data cases using the corresponding subclass rather than the original class. The resulting *structure rules* can be used to detect the classes 2 and 3 by using the relation between subclasses and original class. Thus, the problematic cases that were difficult to distinguish could be isolated in two subclasses represented by two corresponding rules. Class 7 never occurred in the database. This class will be described using other knowledge acquisition methods (e.g. expert rules).
The so generated rules are able to make a diagnosis for most of the cases. Some of the diagnosis may be wrong. It is also possible that more than one diagnosis, or even no diagnosis is given for a specific day. These problems can be partially resolved by using a Kohonen Network that was trained with all cases *including* the class value (Fig. 2 top). This leads to a *supervised* learning method. Such a network can *always* give a diagnosis (but no explanation for its assessment).

The architecture of the *hybrid expert system for avalanche forecasting* is shown in Fig. 3. It is build on a **rule-base** (RB)consisting of *direct rules, structure rules* and eventually *other rules* generated by other knowledge acquisition methods (experts etc.) and a **Kohonen Network** (KN). Both, the rule base and the Kohonen Network perform a diagnosis that is combined in a **black board** for a final diagnosis with attributes that are related to the results found by the subsystems. The attribute "singleKN" means that the rule base could not make a diagnosis and therefore the final diagnosis is equal to the diagnosis of the Kohonen Network. "KN/RB" means that both diagnosis of the subsystems are the same and therefore the final result. "KN/RBm" means that there are multiple diagnosis found by the Rule Base one of which is the same found by the Kohonen Network and therefore is the final result. "conflict" finally means that the subsystems found different diagnosis.

In the case where some input values are unknown the Kohonen Network still can perform a diagnosis, whereas the rule base may not work because of the missing parameters. These

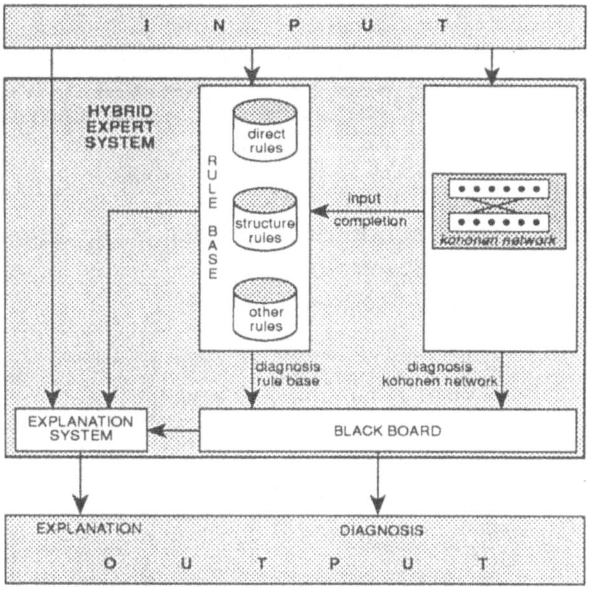

Fig. 3 Architecture of the hybrid expert system

parameters can be filled with *default* values which can be found by the Kohonen Network. That means the network also performs the task of *completion.*
By including a symbolic rule base, the lack of explanation capability of the Kohonen Network can be partially reduced. In cases where the rule base takes part of the diagnosis it can also act as an explanation tool.

The hybrid expert system is **not** intended to perform an extensive evaluation of the avalanche danger by itself. But it is able to support the human experts in the decision process by proposing a diagnosis and by explaining the rules used.

4. Results

The system is not fully implemented yet. So the overall performance of the hybrid system can not be given at this time. The performance of the rule base is given in Table 1. The learn set included 717 cases, whereas the test set included 342 cases.

sets (# cases	% correct	% wrong	% no diag
learn set (717)	74	13	13
test set (342)	72	4	24
both (1059)	73	9	18

TABLE 1. Performance of rule base

The specific performance for each of the different classes (degrees of danger) is given for all cases (learn and test set) in Table 2.

class (# cases)	% correct	% wrong	% no diag
1 (411)	84	6	10
2(384)	68	13	19
3(218)	55	9	36
4(30)	97	0	3
5(11)	100	0	0
6(5)	100	0	0
total(1059)	**73**	**9**	**18**

TABLE 2. Performance of different classes

The overall performance of the hybrid system (rule base and Kohonen Network) will be better than 73% (the performance of the rule base system). Previous studies showed that the Kohonen Network will have a performance of about 80%. Hence about 80% of the cases that could not be evaluated (18%) by the rules will be correctly classified by the Kohonen Network. So the overall performance of the hybrid system is expected to be greater than 80%.

5. Conclusions

The new approach showed to be a powerful method to solve the problem of avalanche forecasting. It will be possible to build a reliable support system for the decision process which evaluates directly the degree of avalanche danger for a given region. The basis forms a reliable database including a verification of the avalanche danger. The new hybrid expert system will have an overall performance greater than 80%. It will be able to deal with incomplete or inconsistent data. In the cases the rule base is involved in the diagnosis process the system is also able to explain the result by showing the rules used. The method is appropriate to transfer the know-how of avalanche forecasting to local experts. Based on the results presented a hybrid expert system for operational use will be developed for regional avalanche forecasters.

Acknowledgments

This research was supported by the "Swiss National Science Foundation" (SNSF) and was partially supported by the "German Department of Research and Technology" (BMFT), project WINA.

References

[1] Föhn, P.: Das Schweizerische Lawinenbulletin. In *Mitteilung Nr. 38 des Eidg. Instituts für Schnee- und Lawinenforschung*, 1985.

[2] Jaccard, C.: Die Rolle des Eidg. Instituts für Schnee- und Lawinenforschung für das Gebirge. In *Schweiz. Z. Forstwes.*, 5:357-365. 141, 1990.

[3] Buser, O., Föhn, P., Good, W., Gubler H.and Salm, B.: Different methods for the assessment of avalanche danger. In *Cold Reg. Sci. Technol.*, 10, 199-218, 1985.

[4] Brun, E., Martin, E., Simon, V., Gendre, C. and Coleou, C: An energy and mass model of snow cover suitable for operational avalanche forecasting. In *J. Glaciol.*, 35 (121), 333-342, 1989.

[5] Buser, O.: Avalanche forecast with the method of nearest neighbours: an interactive approach. In *Cold Reg. Sci. Technol.*, 8, 155-163, 1983.

[6] Föhn, P., Hächler, P.: Prévision des grosses avalanches au moyens d'un modèle deterministe-statistique. ANENA. In *Comptes Rendues du 2e Rencontre Int. sur la Neige et les Avalanches*, Grenoble, 12-14, 151-165, Avril 1978.

[7] Remund, J.: Verifikation der regionalen Lawinengefahrenprognose. *Diplomarbeit am Geographischen Institut der ETH Zürich*, Nr.70.5, 1993.

[8] Bolognesi, R.: Artificial intelligence and local avalanche forecasting: the system AVALOG. In *Proc. of the Int. Emergency Management and Engineering Conf.*, Arlington, 1993.

[9] Schweizer, J., Föhn, P. und Plüss, Ch.: COGENSYS™ Judgment Processor (Paradocs) als Hilfsmittel für die Lawinenwarnung. In *Interner Bericht Nr. 675*, Eidgenössisches Institut für Schnee- und Lawinenforschung, 1992.

[10] Ultsch, A.: Konnektionistische Modelle und ihre Integration mit wissenbasierten Systemen. *Forschungsbericht Nr. 396*, Universität Dortmund, FB Informatik, Feb. 1991.

[11] Palm, G., Ultsch, A., Goser, K., Rückert, U.: Knowledge Processing in Neural Architecture, Delgado-Fraias, J.G., Moore, W.R. (eds) : *VLSI for Neural Networks and Artificial Intelligence*, Plenum Publ., New York 1993.

[12] Ultsch, A., Li, H.: Automatic Acquisition of Symbolic Knowledge from Subsymbolic Neural Networks. To appear in: *Proc. Intl. Conf. on Signal Processing*, Peking 1993.

[13] Ultsch, A., Siemon, H.P.: Kohonen's Self Organizing Feature Maps for Exploratory Data Analysis. In *Proc. Intern. Neural Networks*, 305-308. Kluwer Academic Press, Paris 1990.

[14] Ultsch, A.: Self-Organized Feature Maps for Monitoring and Knowledge Akquisition of a Chemical Process. In *Proc. Intl. Conf. on Artificial Neural Networks*, 864-867, Amsterdam 1993.

[15] Kohonen, T.: Self-Organization and Associative Memory, *Springer Series in Information Sciences*, 1989 (3rd ed.).

[16] Ultsch, A.: Self-Organizing Neural Networks for Knowledge Acquisition. In *Proc. 10th Int. Conf. on AI 92*, ECAI Vienna 92

Distributed Quality Control: A Challenge for Software System Development

Gernot Starke, Oliver Scholz

Lehrstuhl Informatik III, Technical University of Aachen, Ahornstr. 55, D-52074 Aachen, Germany, ☎: (+49) (0)241-8021 311, E-Mail: gernot@rwthi3.informatik.rwth-aachen.de

ABSTRACT

For highly distributed user environments, like they are found in the field of tourism, special measures have to be applied to assure that only software products of *required* quality are produced. By combining established systems analysis methods with a specific quality model, detailed *quality requirements* are detected and can be mapped onto a model of the development process. This results in project specific process models, which can support and improve system development.

INTRODUCTION

System developers in the field of tourism have to face the problem af an unusually wide distribution of their work. Their customers and prospective users are easily spread all over the world:

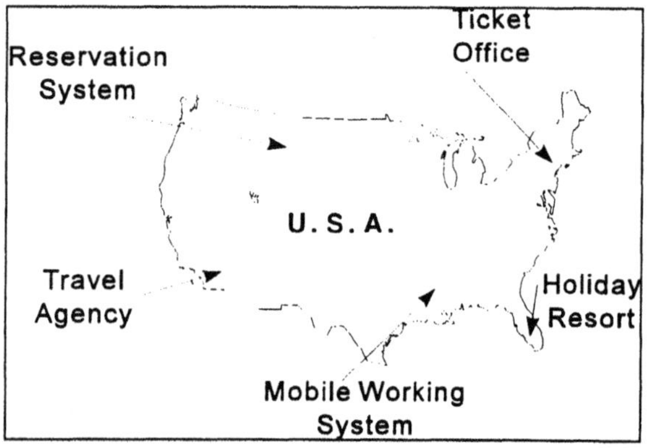

Fig. 1: *Distributed users and developers*

Furthermore the variety of system users is higher than in most other application domains. These aspects add some interesting facets to the requirements of information system development: special models are needed for

- management of *distributed* quality
- development of highly distributed systems with a large variety of users and different quality requirements.

This paper tackles those vital aspects from the viewpoint of the system development process. Focussing on that aspect is necessary, as developers have to conentrate on producing the best possible technical solution instead of wasting effort converging on a common process [Card 90].

Software engineering has supplied development organisations with a variety of methods, techniques and corresponding tools which (at least in principle) allow quality to be engineered. Nevertheless the often mentioned *software crisis* demonstrated that the prime challenge remains the integration of those aspects together with a specialised model of software quality into a project-specific supportive environment.

A well defined model of the development process seems to be the only way to achieve these goals. Within this context a whole new discipline has emerged: Software Process Modelling (e.g. [Curtis+92]).

In this paper we will show how development processes can be modelled and what kind of quality models are neccessary to support the required *distributed quality control*.

The rest of the paper is organised as follows:

The basic concepts of software process engineering are introduced and a brief example of a process model is presented. Afterwards a view-and-product-oriented quality model is presented, together with an example of its usage. These approaches are then combined to achieve the desired *distributed quality control*.

Finally our application experience is described and the further work is outlined.

Software Process Engineering

A well defined model of the development process yields numerous benefits for developers and customers. The model itself must be project-specific and allow for dynamic changes within development (e.g. key developer leaves project or requirements engineering method needs to be changed).

Currently the majority of process models are textual descriptions, which are not supported by tools, not specific to certain projects and nearly impossible to comprehend, resulting in low acceptance. Those *project handbooks* are not capable of handling any kind of dynamic changes, which occur in every procect. Furthermore they are too abstract to guide and support project personnel.

Process Model Terminology

Software process engineering provides a solution out of that unsatisfying situation by means of a sound basic terminology (intuitively depicted in fig. 2) plus a model description language and growing experience on how to construct *better* process models, which is the basis for *Total Quality Management*. Concentration on the development process is a necessety, which other industries have recognized for years[1]

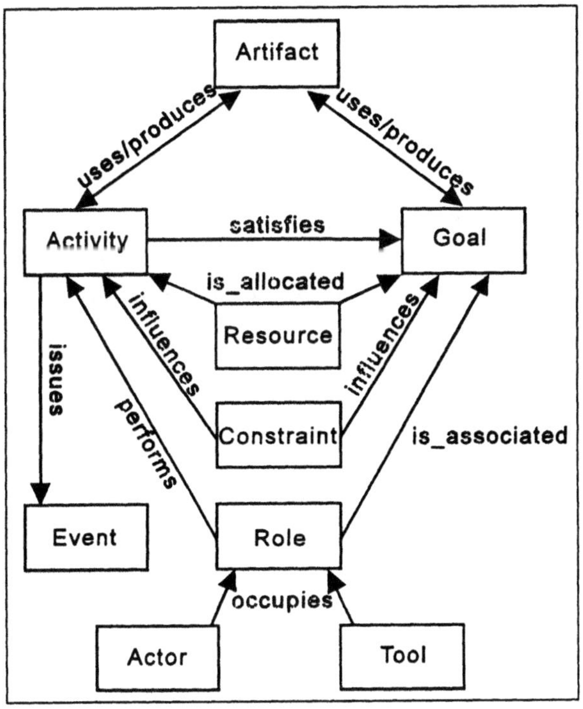

Fig. 2: *Process Modelling Terminology*

Process Modelling Language

Our modelling approach Pro-SA is based on the well known structured analysis method [Yourdon 89], enhanced by a powerful control [Hatley+87] and information model and a corresponding execution mechanism (see [Starke+92, Starke+93] for technical details and further references).

The graphical notation of data and control flow diagrams [Starke+92, Beeck 92] facilitates understanding of the model. A brief example of the notation is given in fig. 3. Together with the hierarchisation capability of structured analysis this results in greater acceptance. The method allows for dynamic changes, which frequently occur during actual process execution.

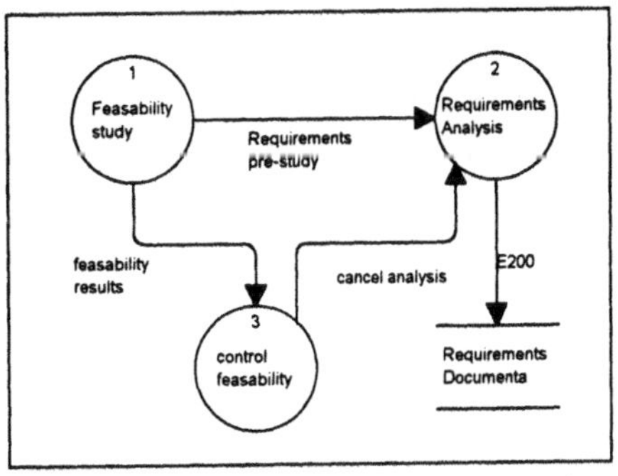

Fig. 3: *Process Model Example (excerpt)*

Types versus Instances

Process models are expressed on a *type* level, indicating activity *templates*. During process execution, those types have to be *instantiated* to yield real development activities. An example is the implementation activity IMP, which follows the design activity DES, depicted in fig. 4. On the left side the appropriate part of the model is drawn, whereas on the right side three implementation-activity-instances are shown. The number of instances together with their parameters can only determined during execution time of the process.

[1]Especially the Japanese manufacturing industries have reached a degree of perfection in optimising their processes which is only dreamed of in other countries. This *Kai'Zen* is regarded as their key success factor.

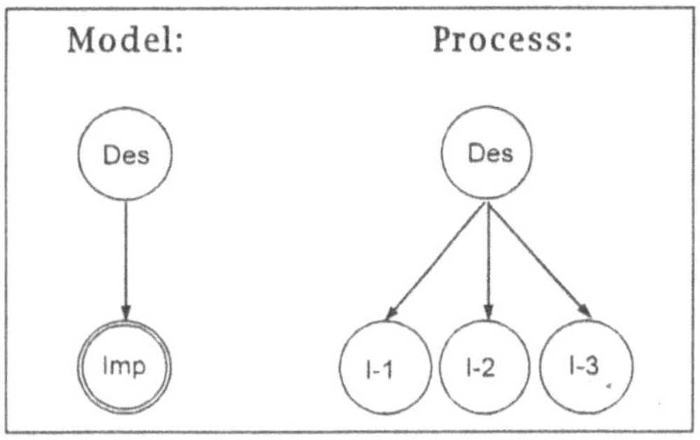

Fig. 4: *Type versus Instance in Pro-SA*

Process Life Cyle: The Meta-Model

Within an enterprise a customized process model has to be build, which suits its overall needs and corresponds to the technical domain in which the organisation is active. For example, developing real-time systems needs a different process model than compiler construction.

For every project this company model is tailored to suit this projects' specific needs (see fig. 5). The quality model, introduced in the next section, is a major component of this tailoring, together with detailed risk analysis and configuration management.

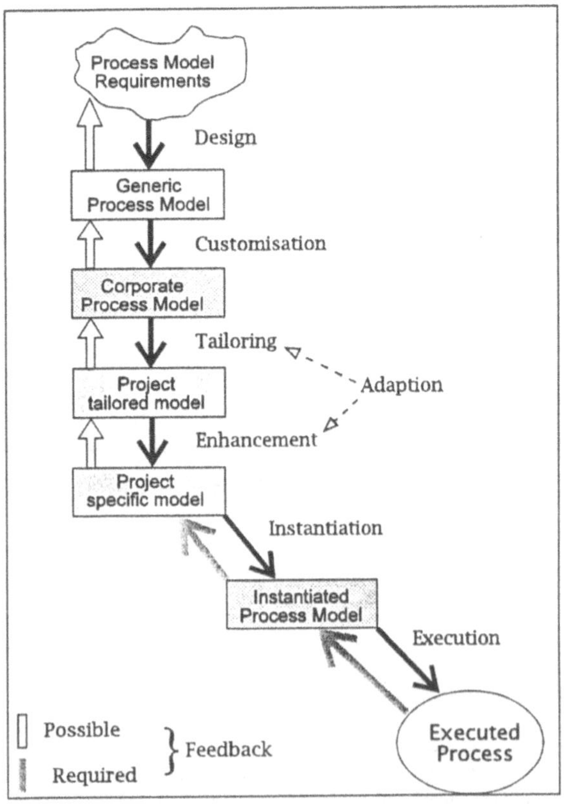

Fig. 5: *Meta Model*

The *generic model* in fig. 5 can be either a process standard (like the proposed ISO standard of *Information Technology Life Cycle Process* or the EuroMethod V-Model, which originated in a German government standard.).

Compared to standard life-cycle models, a detailed and well-defined process has proven to

- be more productive
- be more efficient
- support project execution

Interaction and feedback between the real-world development process and the instantiated process model yield the possibility to support process enaction. It facilitates the integration of project management, resulting in a much more concise process.

Quality Model

The ISO standard definition of quality

> *...totality of features and characteristics of a product, process or service that bear on its ability to satisfy stated or implied needs.* [ISO 8402]

primariliy focusses on the *application* of the product. As the ISO definition lacks a precise description of quality features or attributes which can be quantified, it is not suited for concrete planning and evaluation purposes. Structure and definition of quantifyable features and attributes are added by a quality model. Existing literature models (McCall, Boehm etc.) suffer from a lack of applicability, due to an extensive number of possible attributes.

Our quality model is organised in tree structure, yielding excellent readability and comprehensability, which is vital for acceptance of the model. The upper tree levels are depicted in fig. 6. As the model has been derived from industrial needs, its applicability and acceptance is very high.

Together with the model we deliver an extensive glossary, which is illustrated by several examples to facilitate understanding of the complex terminological distinctions which exist between various quality attributes.

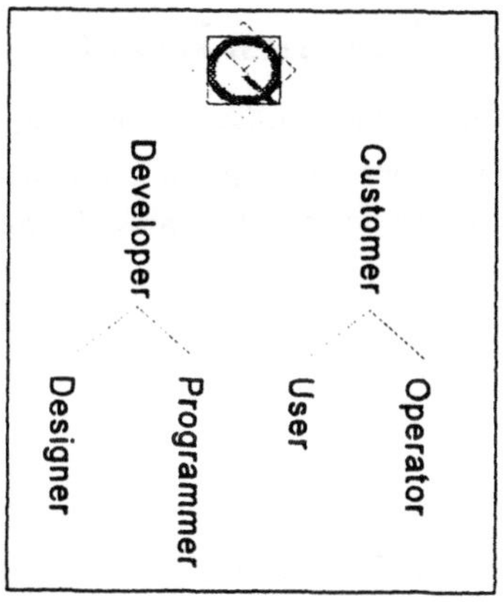

Fig. 6: *Quality Model*

The model can be decomposed further on, which is essential in heterogeneous user or developer structures, a situation which is given in extensively distributed tourism information systems. A possible decomposition within a typical tourism scenario is depicted in fig. 7

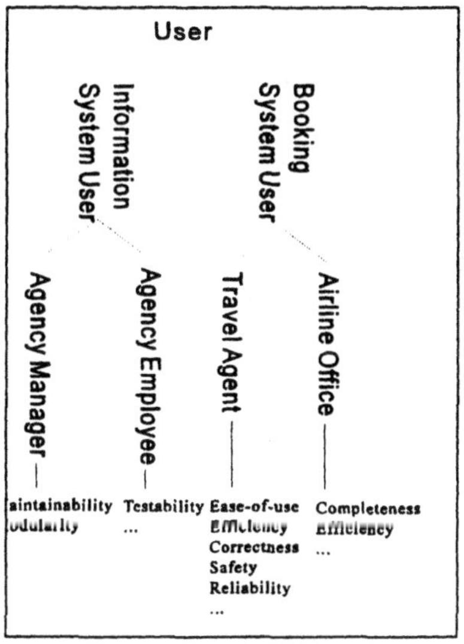

Fig. 7: *Detailed Q-Model for User*

Application of the quality model is as follows:

1. Every customer organisation denotes all its quality requirements by means of a detailed questionnaire, a sample of which is presented in fig. 8. It is most likely that the prospective users and operators of the software will give completely different ratings.
   In the application domain of tourism with its extremely widespread, distributed and heterogeneous users groups, many different quality requirements will occur.
2. Afterwards the development organisation adds its own quality requirements. For example for *reusability* those will vary from the customers' view.
3. In the third step all those different *views* on the desired quality of the system-to-be-developed have to be integrated into a single, consistent and realistic model. The metrics, tests or reviews to quantify the quality attributes have to be established. This third step corresponds to the conventional *Quality handbook*.

Finally the combined quality attributes are mapped onto the model of the corresponding development process, identifiying the activities which are crucial for the desired combination of quality features and attributes.

Quality Attribute	Importance
Functionality	
Completeness	
Consistency	
Useablility	
Learnability	
Efficiency	
Effectiveness	
Simplicity	
....	

Fig. 8: *Quality Requirements Questionnaire (excerpt)*

That *mapping* activity requires a great deal of process experience. Within our experience from several industrial projects, tool support within that crucial task would be very helpful, but it can definitely not replace project and process experience.

Once that *Project Specific Process Model* has been constructed, the actual development process can be started.

Quality Attributes and Features

The complete list of our models' quality features and attributes is shown in the appendix.

DISTRIBUTED QUALITY CONTROL

As mentioned before, the process model is tailored to suit the needs of specific projects and application domains. For geographically extremely distributed systems with a variety of user-classes (as it is the inherent situation in tourism industry) this means, that

- The quality model has to be adapted to the variety of user classes. Essentially this is a problem of detecting the non-functional requirements of different user groups. The quality model presented in the previous section provides a pragmatic and flexible solution.
- Quality control activities *per se* must be decentralized. Responsabilities must be distributed, the concept of *role* has to be enhanced by a *role location*.
- Feedback and quantification mechanisms to report and measure quality have to be decentralized. Different feedback mechanisms might exist at different user sites, the activities to incorporate this feedback should reside centrally.
- A distributed hierarchy of quality control activities has to be established. The usual notion of independent quality control is therefore, like the role concept mentioned before, enhanced by a *location* attribute.

Those mechanisms strongly facilitate quality control and risk analysis in the development of information systems.

EXPERIENCES

The proposed process and quality modelling techniques have been applied to the development of an metereological and aeronautical information system (METAIS), which has been part of the European ESPRIT-II research project COMPLEMENT[2]. Our department successfully developed an overall process [Starke+92] and quality model for the system. The process model was extensively analysed after completion of the project. Several areas of potential process improvement were detected, especially at the interface between different development phases, eg. requirements analysis and design.
The quality model has been verified in several other application domains, (e.g. insurance holding, manufacturing enterprise, consulting firm). In general the acceptance of different views has been excellent.

[2]METAIS has been carried out in 1992 by the COMPLEMENT consortium under ESPRIT-II contract 5409. Partners in the METAIS subproject were 12 organisations from 6 European countries.

FURTHER WORK

Focusing mainly on the practical and pragmatic aspects of process modelling we will apply our approach to model further industrial development processes. A process support environment based on the proposed techniques is currently under development.

APPENDIX: QUALITY MODEL

User view:	
Functionality	Functional coverage
	Functional completeness
	Reliability
	Completeness
Useability	User-friendlyness
	Learnability
	Efficiency
	Effectiveness
	Recognizeability
Operator view	
Behaviour	Feasability
	Efficiency
	Instrumentation
Safety	Integrity
	Robustness
	Access control
Developer view	
Functionality	Completeness
	Correctness
Comprehensability	Simplicity
	Similarity
Maintainability	Correctability
	Adaptability
	Changeability
	Testability
Reuseability	Interfaceability
	Enhanceability
	Portabilty

BIBLIOGRAPHY

[Beeck 92] M. v.d. Beeck. Integration of Structured Analysis and Timed Statecharts for Real-Time and Concurrency Specification. Technical Report 92-26, Technical University of Aachen, December 1992.

[Card 90] D.N. Card. Software Quality Engineering. *Information and Software Technology*, Vol. 32, Nr. 1, January/February 1990, pp. 3-10. Butterworth Publishing.

[Curtis+92] B. Curtis, M. Kellner & J. Oliver. Process Modelling. Communications of the ACM, Vol. 35, Nr. 9, September 1992, pp. 75-90.

[Hatley+87] D. Hatley & I.A. Pirbhai. Strategies for Real-Time System Specification. Dorset House, New York, 1987.

[Starke+92] Gernot Starke & Michael von der Beeck. SA/RT/IM for Software Process Modelling. In: *Proceedings of the European Workshop on Software Process Technology*, September 1992, Trondheim, Norway. Lecture Notes in Computer Science, LNCS, Nr. 635, pp. 18-21, Springer Verlag, Heidelberg, 1992.

[Starke 93] Gernot Starke. *People* and Software Process Models. In J. Gornostaev, editor: Proceedings of the *International Conference on Information Technology and People*, May 1993, Moscow, Russia, pp. II/112-II/120. Published by: International Institute for Scientific and Technical Information (ICSTI).

[Yourdon 89] E. Yourdon. Modern Structured Analysis. Prentice-Hall., 1989.

ACKNOWLEDGEMENTS

The authors would like to thank `uli@sweet.heart.com` and `stefan@qualidata.uucp` for many interesting comments and fruitful discussions on the sofware process.

TOURIST INFORMATIONSYSTEM MÜHLVIERTEL TIM

Mag. Dr. Hubert Roiß
TELEHAUS FREIWALD
A-4240 Freistadt, Zemannstr. 27

Michael Forster
TELEHAUS FREIWALD
A-4240 Freistadt, Zemannstr. 27

Mag. Michael Plakolb
Forschungsinstitut für Anwendungsorientierte Wissensverarbeitung
A-4232 Hagenberg, Softwarepark Hagenberg

Abstract

Since 4th of Juli 1992 the telecottage FREIWALD offers a Tourist Information System, which includes all interesting Tourist data of the Mühlviertel, a region of Upper Austria. The application is called TIM (Tourist-Information System Mühlviertel) and can be used by all 400.000 users of the Austrian viedeotextsystem (BTX) in Austria, Switzerland, Germany and Luxembourg. The Informationsystem TIM covers information on the culture, commerce and life of the region and also include typical products from the craftsmen and from the industry of the region, thus inducing necessary synergetic effects from trade and commerce.

1. Introduction

1.1 Background of the TELEHAUS FREIWALD project

The TELEHAUS FREIWALD pilot project originated in the Freiwald Rural Development Plan drawn up by 6 local authorities in the Mühlviertel region to the north of Freistadt in Upper Austria.

The starting point for this project was that the bypassing of rural areas in the information society can only be halted if it is possible to get access to the information of the innercity areas. The frame work for the setting up of the TELEHAUS FREIWALD was investigated in a basic study in 1990.

This study showed that plans to encourage business to settle in periphal border and mountain regions with weak infrastructures stand no real chance of being successful because of the advantages caused by the concentration of the population of the central areas. On the other hand strategies for the transfer of innovation, marketing and technology can considerably improve the competetiveness of existing businesses.

In particular moves towards European integration and opening of Eastern Europe require specific regional political measures.

The suburban area of the Mühlviertel which lies between the Danube and the Bohemian Forest and along the Linz-Budweis axis been characterised by dynamic growth while the peripheral areas to the north, west and east areas of emmigration.

The TELEHAUS FREIWALD was officially opened in Freistadt in Upper Austria on 14 August 1991 with the support of numerous supporters and partners from commerce and politics.

1.2. Objectives

The TELEHAUS FREIWALD will offer assistance to the disadvantaged areas of the Mühlviertel in the areas of tourism, trade, handicrafts, agriculture and also in community administration and consumer protection.

The TELEHAUS FREIWALD aims to set up practical applications using specific telematic services after the problems have been analysed as pilot projects.

The creation of opportunities for distance working in the rural areas as a way of preventing a further centralisation of commercial and administrative activity will be invastigated through specialised research projects.

The geographical position of the Mühlviertel on the southern border of Czechoslovakia calls for a new direction in crossborder regional politics.

Austria`s potential membership of the European Community demands timely preparation for new commercial and political frame works for this structurally weak region.

1.3. Technical Approach

The telematic communication system VIDEOTEXT (BTX) will be used by the TELEHAUS FREIWALD because it can dissaminate information quickly and economically. All 122 of the local authorities in the Mühlviertel will be connected through this network.

The complete database will be field on the internal videotext computer (MICROVAX) and transferred for national and international forwarding (to Germany, Switzerland and Luxembourg) via the DATEX-P lines at the videotext central office in Salzburg.

The setting up of the FREIWALD TELEHAUS tourist pilot project is taking place in cooperation with and with the approval of the above mentioned regional and national tourist organisations. Particular attention will given to the use of telematic services for farm holidays in order to achieve greater profitability for and to improve the chances of employment in agriculture through an increased capacity to cater for tourism. By including Southern Bohemia it should be possible to lay the basis for a cross border policy on tourism for the Bohemian Forest-Sumava region. As a result of this, assistance in organisation and marketing will be offered for neighbouring Southern Bohemia, a region in Czechoslovakia which has many cultural and natural attractions. It is precisely through the transfer of information that the position of the Mühlviertel and Southern Bohemia, as the "European Forest Park" or the "Green Roof of Europe" could be established as far as "soft tourism" is concerned.

Three points speak of the Tourist Information System:

- ☞ Because of information density an increased supply of the region is produced;
- ☞ The usage of the tourist system is cheap; and
- ☞ The handling for users is very easy;

<u>2.1. The structure of the system</u>

<u>2.1.1. The header page</u> of TIM offers following selections:

Informations about leisure-time
adventure-world Mühlviertel 10
search with a catchword 11

Informations about the regions of the Mühlviertel
all regions of the Mühlviertel 12
region known 13

Informations about the villages of the Mühlviertel
search of a village for summer holidays 14
search of a village for winter holidays 15
village known 16

User Interface (sea next page):

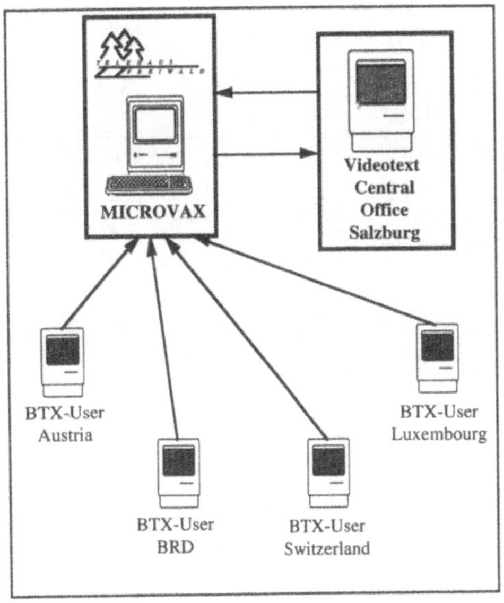

Fig. 1 Computing Facilities

<u>2. TOURIST INFORMATIONSYSTEM MÜHLVIERTEL TIM</u>

<u>2.2. Background</u>

Tourism in the Mühlviertel is extensive (800.000 overnight stays per year). Individual local authorities are, however, unable to offer their guests a comprehensive programme of entertainment and events because accomodation is only available on a small scale and is scattered over a wide geographical area. Even attractive, high quality events only draw small audience because of the lack of information.

☞ The establishment of the Tourist Informationsystem Mühlviertel (TIM) should lead to an increase in the quality of a whole range of tourist attractions.

☞ The establishment of an Events Database should provide motivation for both locals and tourists and the same time lay the foundation for a professional regional tourist policy.

☞ The establishment of a regional Reservation System should create the preconditions for the exploitation of new channels of distribution for small and middle sized concerns.

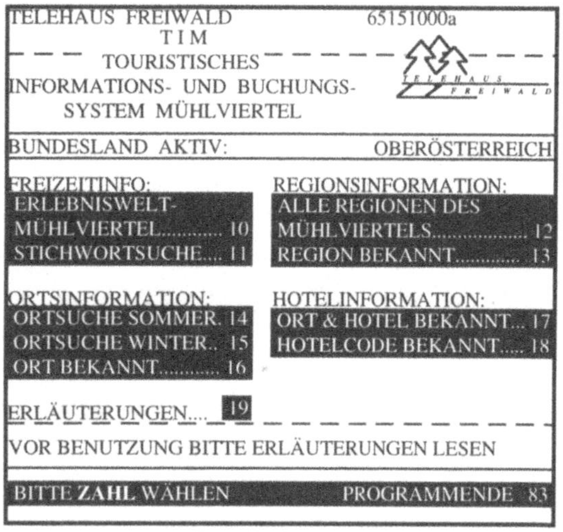

Fig. 2 The header page

2.1.2. Informations about leisure-time: These informations offer a view about the supply of all 122 villages of the Mühlviertel. With choice of figure 10 the BTX users get the data of the "adventure-world Mühlviertel". This includes a list with informationfields and there it is possible to choice the interesting fields by feeding the BTX-terminal with the respective type. The whole informationsystem is set up like a search-tree.

User Interface:

Fig. 3 Screen dump: Leisure Time

With the help of this principle the user gets the detail informations and has also the possibility for exceeding to the respective informations of the village or the event database.

In this application it is also possible for the user to search the interesting possibilities for leisure-time by a catchword (figure 12) such as castle, fishing, etc....

2.1.3. Informations about the regions of the Mühlviertel: With the choice of figure 12 for example the system offers the regions of the Mühlviertel (Freistadt, Rohrbach, Perg and Urfahr/Umgebung). The user has the chance to find an interesting region and then he can demand the special informations of the village. Of course its also possible to choose the village directly or with a catchword.

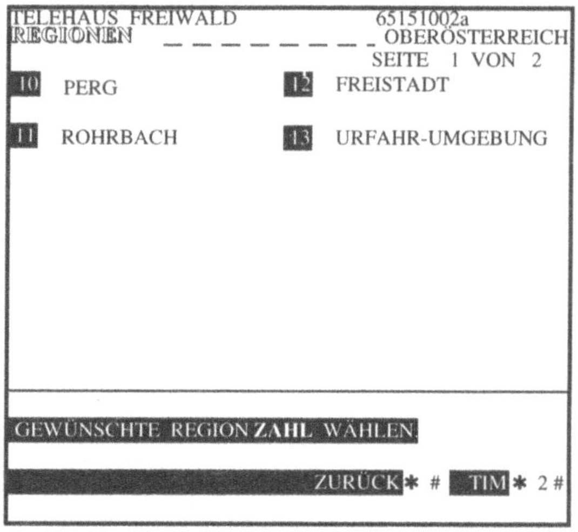

Fig. 4 Screen dump: Regions of the Mühlviertel

In this part of the system the user can order a prospect from the village or the region.

2.1.4. Support by searching a village for summer or winter holidays: The guest has the possibility to search villages for summer (figure 14) or winter (figure 15) holidays by description of some factors he wants to have such as disco, possibilities for fishing, golf, etc........

The user gets all villages of the Mühlviertel, which offers this arrangement.

2.1.5. The Event Database includes the topical events of all 122 villages of the Mühlviertel and of Southern Bohemia.

2.1.6. The Reservation System: This part of the application can be used for booking rooms in hotels and by farmers. The user gets informations about the services and prices of the letters and has the possibilty to book the rooms directly.

3. Dataorganisation and Attendance

The employees of the TELEHAUS FREIWALD control the data and are responsible for the actuality of the data.

THE TIM PROJECT: TOURISM INFORMATION AND MARKETING

cand. real. Erling Maartmann-Moe*, dr. Paul Byerley and M.Sc. Ricardo Guinanco*****

* Norwegian Computing Center, P.O. Box 114, Blindern, 0314 Oslo, Norway, phone: (+47) 22 85 25 80, fax: 22 69 76 60, e-mail erling.maartmann-moe@nr.no

** DeTeBerkom, Technisches Zentrum Berlin, Voltastrassse 5, 1000 Berlin 65, phone: (+49) 30 467 01 214, fax 30 467 01 444

*** Telesystemes, Le Capitole B4, 55 Av. de Champs Pierreux, 92029 Nanterre, France, Phone (+33) 14 61 45 214

1. Introduction

The objectives of TIM[1] are the provision of advanced communication services, linking tourism and travel companies across Europe, in order to support the marketing of tourism and travel products.

The TIM project is supported by the European Commission under the RACE programme, and is currently a 3 year project with a total cost of approximately 12 million ECU. There are 24 project partners from 8 EEC- and EFTA countries. The partners are made up of industrial companies, market research companies, and the TIM "users"; tourist boards, hotel organisations, travel agencies, automobile clubs, and special events organizers.

The project began in April 1992. The project has already delivered extensive analyses of users´ business strategies and operational requirements, and on the basis of these has defined the global functions, and global and local site architectures of TIM. This has then governed both the design of each TIM component and a business case analysis for each user company.

An integration prototype demonstrating the basic functionality of the TIM system was shown at a press conference in Florence in May 1993.

2. The objectives and goals of the TIM system

TIM services can be viewed under two categories, those services which support the business objectives of Point-of-Offer organizations, and those which support the business objectives of Point-of-Sale organizations.

Point-of-Offer Business Objectives

The Point-of-Offer organizations in TIM include tourist boards, destination companies, hotels and sport events (1994 Winter Olympics). Their objectives include; obtaining greater control of product development and marketing, marketing at Point-of-Sale-sites, being able to target their marketing within a segmented market, distributing high quality multimedia marketing information for the description of complex products and product differentiation, and being able to distribute updates and last minutes offers at any time of their choosing.

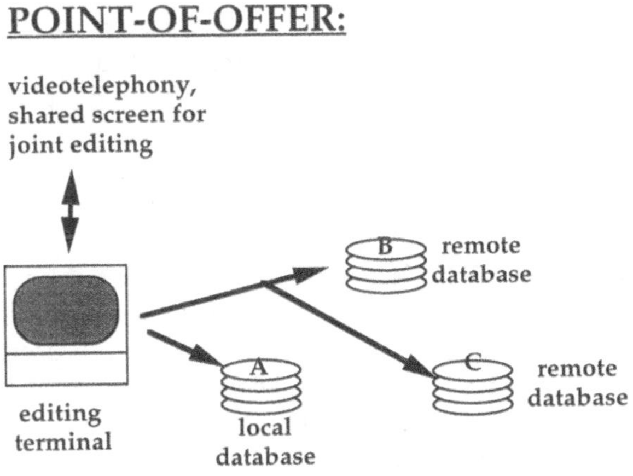

Fig. 1

The TIM services for Point-of-Offer

The TIM system will enable Point-of-Offer organizations to create multimedia marketing material and to place it on the TIM distributed database when they wish. They will be able to decide where it is distributed, in order to minimise the cost of retrieval for their targeted customers. Statistical functions will monitor the use of the material and hence enable refinements in the users´ marketing strategies. Conversational services will be avaliable for collaborative work requiring shared screen facilities etc.

Point-of-Sale Business Objectives

The Point-of-Sale organizations in TIM include travel agencies, a national automobile club for import and export tourism, and tourist boards for import tourism. Their objectives include; obtaining access to to a much larger range of product offers, having access to more appealing and accurate product descriptions, the ability to add more value at Point-of-Sale and thus to extend their own product range, streamlined booking of complex multi vendor products, and the integration of business and leisure markets.

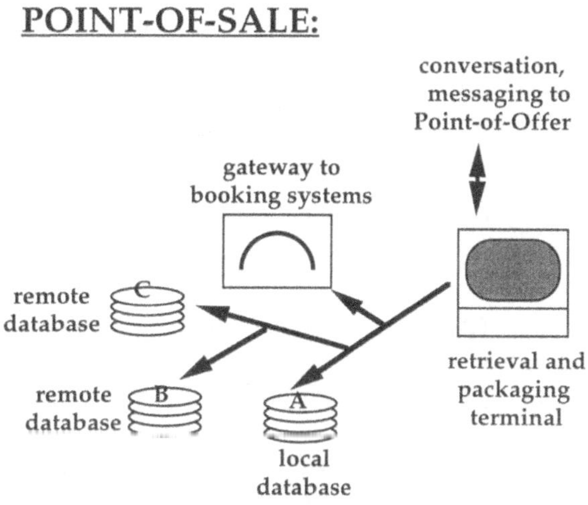

Fig. 2

The TIM services for Point-of-Sale

The TIM system enables a customer or a sales professional to browse the multimedia information located on the distributed database and to use it to create a specific package. The package can contain any number of elements of travel, accomodation, and special events from different vendors. The package can be purchased via a single booking action which is communicated via a gateway to international and local booking systems. These services are integrated with conversational and messaging services to Point-of-Offer for further resolution. In order that the services to Point-of-Sale are compatible with the business objectives of Point-of-Offer the TIM system does not support the distribution of packages, so created, to Point-of-Sale sites other than those which belong to the organization which created the packages.

The TIM system is complex. The sections which follow this is an attempt to show how this complexity has been broken down into manageable units, and the design results so far.

3. The Functionality of TIM

Retrieval

The TIM system will allow hotels, tourist boards etc. who wish to market their travel products to create high quality promotional material and to have this made directly available via telecommunication services to point of sale sites such as travel agencies. At the travel agency this information can be browsed independently by the traveller or it can be used with professional staff to construct a travel/holiday package designed specifically for the traveller, which can then be purchased.

Booking

A customer designed package could have elements from many travel and holiday/event providers from many different locations. The TIM system will enable the purchase of all these separate elements. The TIM system will be connected to the international booking systems and to local booking systems. This will enable both real time transactions and messaging. To the traveller only one purchase needs to be executed, the purchase of the package.

Authoring

In the TIM system, hotels, tourist boards, sports events etc. will design their own marketing information. They will be able to design high quality multimedia information, to update this information easily, and to distribute it to their potential customers, all from the same terminal. The TIM system therefore includes multimedia authoring facilities, for the extraction of information from videotape or disk into the terminal to the integration of the multimedia material into one object.

Conversation

Authors of multimedia material often need to work cooperatively. The TIM system provides for more than one author to be able to view the same material from separate terminals and to discuss it. Conversational services are also important at point of sale for example for a travel agent to discuss an offer with a local or non local holiday provider. These facilities are also provided in TIM with a video telephone integrated into the terminal at the point of sale.

Distribution

The essence of TIM is to enable hotels, tourist boards, sports events etc. to get their marketing information to locations where it will be used in a holiday or travel purchase. Therefore the TIM system provides a database distributed throughout Europe and interconnected via communication services into which an approved author can distribute the multimedia information or updates. The author can target databases near potential customers and ensure that appropriate language versions for text and speech media are available at the correct locations. All information on the database whatever its location is retrievable from every point of sale site and the TIM system will ensure that retrieval will be from the nearest database. In addition the TIM system monitors the use of the marketing material at all the point of sale sites and authors will be able to retrieve this statistical information to help them improve their marketing strategies.

4. The TIM Architecture

The TIM architecture (see fig. 3 next page) is designed to meet the needs of a very complex and diverse usage context, linking a large number of users in different countries together. The main components of the architecture – the database, the gateway system, the terminal, and the telecommunications and network services – respond to specific requirements from each user site, and will at the same time provide an integrated system that is able to develop with technological evolution, especially with respect to networks and telecomunication services.
The objective of the architecture is to provide a Global Architecture of the TIM system, and a customized architecture for each TIM user site.

The Global Architecture as illustrated in the figure above, shows how the TIM system is built on the basis of national TIM databases connected to each user site. These databases are complete with respect to the country they represent. This means that all data, including multimedia data types like video, images and sound, are stored locally, and accessible on-line. The national databases are connected by the international telecommunications network, and a TIM Global Supervising node. The role of this node is to act as a mailbox, to provide gateways, and to provide multimedia data from non-local databases that are not accessible in real time. This way the local user sites may configure their databases to contain external multimedia data of particular interest to their markets. TIM users connected to a broadband island will have the option of real-time acces to all TIM multimedia data. The supervising node will become less

The following figure illustrates the TIM Global Architecture.

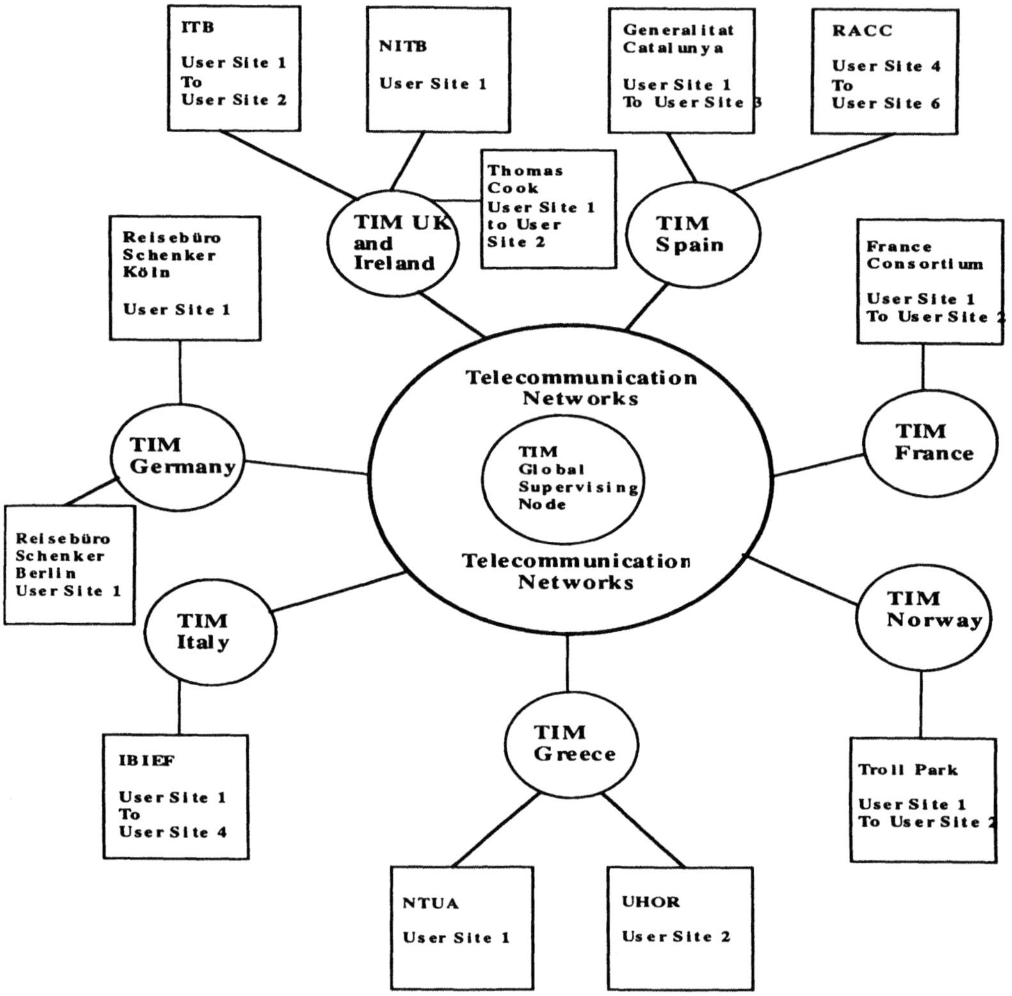

Fig.3

central to the architecture as broadband networks become more cost-effective for the TIM users. The motivations behind this architecture is characterized by the following main principles:

Flexibility

The TIM architecture has taken into account the varying needs of all its user organisations, representing both sales organisations like travel agencies, and holiday providers in six countries. The TIM terminal may act as a stand-alone unit connected to the TIM system, as well as a terminal integrated in a LAN in a travel agency. It is also designed to interface to a wide variety of existing local and centralized reservation systems via the TIM gateway.

Evolution

TIM is an application pilot developed in close cooperation with its user organizations. Consequently, TIM is restricted to propose architectures that are cost effective for the users. TIM is currently mainly based on ISDN communication. N-ISDN will provide all the low data rate network needs for TIM. At the same time the TIM architecture already incorporates broadband subsystems for selected user sites, and is designed to be able to include such technologies as like ATM and B-ISDN as they become available and more cost-effective.

Integration

The TIM Terminal is designed as a general terminal able to integrate with existing environments in travel agencies. With the prospect of TIM cooperation with CRSes like Galileo, Sabre and Amadeus as well as the local systems already participating in TIM, the TIM terminal will technically integrate into an environment today consisting of more than 100.000 terminals.

Standards

The TIM system is based on acknowledged, stable technologies and upon etablished ISO and industry standards.
The TIM Terminal will be based on WINDOWS NT. It is widely recognized that NT will be one of the most important operating environments for networked, client-server applications. The development of the TIM system is well aligned in time with the emerging products based on NT.
The TIM Database will be based on well established RDBMS technologies able to support the complex distributed TIM environment.
TIM Telecommunications and networks will be based on ISDN, B-ISDN and industry standards like TCP/IP for communication protocols. The TIM Gateway is compliant with ISO standards with respect to both access language and Remote Database Access. The subsystems are based on TCP/IP and X.25 network protocols.
For multimedia data, TIM will be based on standards like JPEG and MPEG for image storage and exchange, and on H.261 for videotelephony.
The TIM Architecture and its design process takes into account RACE recommendations from RACE projects R1077 Usage Reference Model, and R1044 on Customer Sevice Functions and Reference Configuration Development.

5. The current status of TIM

The first TIM prototype was demonstrated at a press conference in Florence, Italy in April 1993 after the project had been running only one year. This prototype was an integration prototype mainly designed to test the integration of the multimedia extentions and the communication facilities in a PC. It was also a test on some user interface aspects both for point of information and point of sales terminals. At this demonstration, the TIM gateway was also shown functioning connecting the TIM system to the Official Airline Guide in Chicago via Saritels facilities in Rome.

TIM is now developing a full scale prototype based on the architecture and on the user interface specifications made in cooperation with users both at point of offer and point of sale. The full scale prototype is based on Microsoft SQL server running under windows NT on the server side, and clients based on Microsoft Windows based PCs. A net of local databases in each user county will be connected with a global database for the TIM system, situated at the Telesystemes facility in Paris. They will be linked by ISDN connections as the basIs for connectivity, but certain arieas of TIM will also be linked by a broadband communication. One example of broadband in TIM is the connection between Belfast and Dublin in Irland where TIM participates in the Tironet 2 MB experiment.

The full scale prototype is expected to be implemented by the beginning of 1994 and will be tested through 1994 in actual use with both point of sale and point of offer facilities. TIM as a project is currently expanding its basis on the user side, and has recently admitted more travel agencies and local tourist boards as new partners in TIM.

References:

P.F. Byerley, P.K. Barnard, J.May: Computers, Comunication and Usability.

North-Holland studies in Telecommunication Volume 19, 1993.

[1] The TIM consortium includes: DeTeBerkom, Alcatel-SEL, IFC Research, Alcatel-TITN, Alcatel-Espace, Alcatel-FYCSA, Télésystèmes, Saritel, Alitalia, MARI, Institut Cerdà, IDATE, Norsk Regnesentral, NTU Athens, IBIEF, Northern Ireland Tourist Board, Bord Failte, Gulliver, Generalitat Catalunya, RACC, Département de L'Hérault, Ministère du Tourisme, MediaPark Köln, Reisebüro Schenker, Troll Park-Lillehammer Olympic Development Association, Thomas Cook

INFORMATION SYSTEMS AND THE GOALS AND TARGETS OF THE ORGANIZATION: FIT OR MISFIT

G. John van der Pijl
Tilburg University

P.O.B. 90153
5000 LE Tilburg, The Netherlands
e-mail: PIJL@KUB.NL

Although organizations have invested a lot in information systems not all of these investments return what is expected of them. In this paper an approach is presented to assess whether the systems available to an organization actually support it in reaching its goals and targets. The approach is positioned in the context of a more general model for studying the quality of information in an organization.

1. Introduction

Information systems play an important role in the tourist industry. The more dependent on information systems organizations become, the more important it is to assess from time to time that the information provided still serves the purposes of the organization. In this paper an approach for such an assessment is presented.

In literature and in practice we find a lot of different approaches to the problem of assessing the quality of information. The quality model presented in Figure 1 shows that there are essentially two ways of looking at the quality of information in an organization. The first is to look at the subject from the angle of the organizational goals that have to be served by the information in question. This approach is called the 'teleological' point of view. The second approach is to look at the quality of information as the result of the process by which the information has been provided to the organization. This approach is called the 'causal' point of view.

The teleological point of view links the framework to the literature on information planning (e.g. [PARK88]). From the teleological point of view the quality of information can be judged in terms of its contribution to the organization's goals and targets. Strassman[STRA88] gives an example of relating goals and targets to information systems. In the quality model of figure 1 several types of goals and targets are distinguished. First, we have the goals on the level of the organisation as a whole. These describe the activities the organization wishes to undertake and the returns it expects from doing so. Profit, continuity and employment are well known goals at this level. Most organizations design implicit or explicit strategies in order to reach these goals. Second, we have targets at the level of the business processes in which the activities are organized. These will be more concrete like minimizing costs of a production process or maximizing the volume of sales. But not only task related types of goals and targets influence peoples opinions on the quality of information. An important role is played by personal interests like earning an income, getting a powerful position in the organization or feeling respected.Finally the model distinguishes between user targets and provider targets. The quality of information systems can not only be judged from the point of view of the user of information but also of that of the provider. Providers of information will try to influence the behaviour of those they provide information to. In their quality judgement they will check whether the behaviour that is induced by the information is actually as

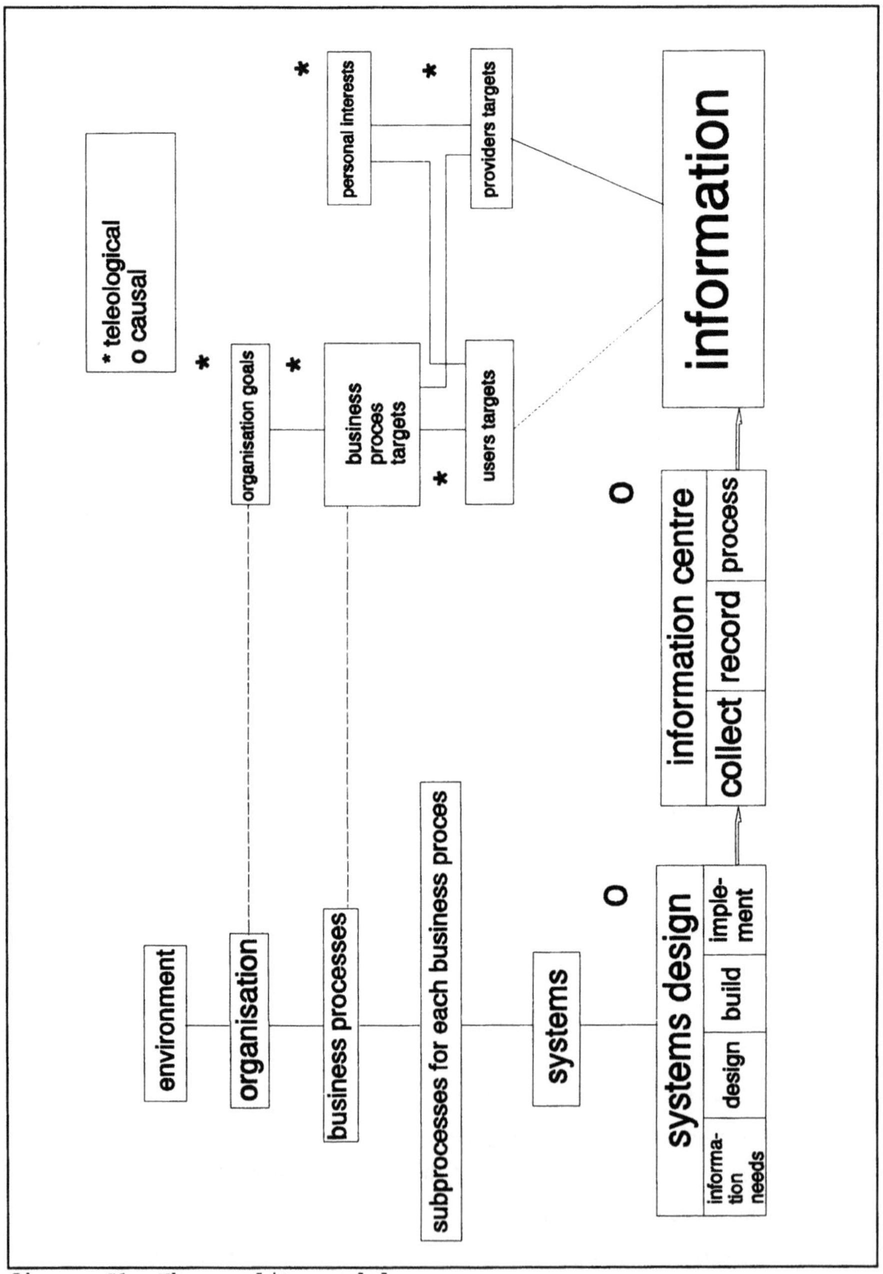

figure S1: The quality model

planned. For example: a tourist board will provide information about its region. The information will serve its purpose if it attracts the right number of tourists. Only if this effect is reach the information will, in the eyes of the tourist board, be of good quality.

From the causal point of view, quality aspects of information have to be translated into quality aspects of the process during which the information is produced. This process, that is represented at the bottom of figure 1, consists of a number of steps. The first one is to translate the needs of the organization into information needs and to design, build and implement these systems. The second step is to exploit the systems of the first step in some form of centralized or decentralized information centre and to use them for collecting, recording, processing and presenting data. Quality demands with regard to information have to be translated into quality demands for each of these steps. The causal point of view corresponds with the approach chosen by ISO-9000, which in turn is strongly influenced by the work of Deming[DEMI82] and Juran[JURA74]. The norm ISO 9000-3 is especially aimed at the systems design step. For the information itself and for the information centre processes from which it arises quality features and characteristics have been formulated by, among others, Mollema and Rijsenbrij. A more elaborate description of the quality model and its background is given in [EGTE92] and in [PIJL93].

2. An approach for assessing the teleological aspects of quality

In literature several methods are described to look at the causal aspects of the quality of information (e.g.ISO-87). There also are methods for judging systems in the light of low level user targets e.g. the measurement of user satisfaction). There are however no generally applicable methods for assessing the quality of information systems or the complete information architecture of an organization in the light of the higher level organization goals and process targets. Therefor, starting from the model above, an approach was designed for judging the teleological, i.e. strategy- and goal-related, aspects of quality. In this approach the organization's environment, its goals and targets, its structure and its culture are described first. From those the need for information and the types of information systems required are deduced. In other words, the "SOLL position" is established. Next the existing information architecture is described: the "IST position". Finally the quality assessment can be made by comparing the required and the available information and the required and the actually installed information systems. In the remainder of this text each of the elements of the approach will be discussed.

environment

An analysis of the opportunities offered and the threats posed by the environment, makes it possible to draw conclusions with respect to the information needs of the organization. Porter[PORT80] presents a framework for analyzing an organizations environment. The framework distinguishes suppliers, buyers, potential entrants and substitutes as important forces in the environment. Information systems can strengthen or weaken the position of the organization viz a viz each of these forces. For a regional tourist board, for example, the big tour operators are important buyers that will have to be provided with timely and adequate information. Other (new) tourist regions may be new entrants in the market. They may take our position in the market if we don't answer to the needs of the tour operators. Thus in our quality assessment we check wether the possibilities of information systems are used for this purpose as much as possible. We could for example try to establish a closed user group network for communication with the tour operators. This would seriously hamper the possibilities of others for entering the market.
Therefore in our analysis of the environment we carefully study the relationship to each of the market forces and systematically look for the possibilities of information

technology. The description of these possibilities forms the "soll position" that can be compared to reality.

Another element of the analysis of the environment is to establish its diversity. The reason for this is that different parts of an organization will probably deal with different parts of the environment. Lawrence and Lorsch[LAWR73] demonstrated that departments of an organization tune their behaviour to those parts of the environment with which they are communicating most intensively. Therefore, the bigger the differences between partial environments are, the bigger the differences between the departments dealing with them will be and the less likely it will be to find a strictly hierarchical and unequivocal structure of goals and targets in the organization. We can, for example, imagine that hotel staff selling rooms to tour operators stress goals for formal capacity planning methods and ask for information systems that support the planning process. On the other hand personal dealing with visitors directly will stress the need for flexibility in order to accommodate to the visitors wishes. They may ask for information systems that help to look for creative solutions for their day to day problems.

Thus if we find that the environment of an organization is very diverse, we won't be surprised to find a great diversity of goals and targets for different levels and groups in the organization in the next steps of the analyses.

<u>organizational goals</u>

In the teleological approach to the quality of information we look for the contribution of information systems to the goals and targets of the organization. Therefor describing the relation between systems and goals is the heart of the method. We try to assess as explicitly as possible how important the information systems are for reaching each of the organizations goals. For the important systems we then check whether they are functioning well.

In order to do so we have to start with describing the goals of the organization as a whole. From the literature on organizational goals it is clear that it is impossible to formulate a normative set of goals that each organization has to pursue. Therefore one has to find out the specific set of goals of a specific organization by analyzing its written statements on this topic and by interviewing the relevant stakeholders.

The literature gives however some hints what type of goals to look for. Ansoff[ANSO65] shows that both long and short term goals are relevant. Rhenman[RHEN73] points out the relevance of both internal and external goals: for some organizations, like for example local or regional tourist boards, the goals will partly be set by external parties.Bahlman and Meesters[BAHL88] demonstrate that variety in goals and targets (that may arise when parts of the organization have to do with very different parts of the organization) can improve the chances of survival for organizations. Simon[SIMO60] argues that maximization of goals is hardly ever realistic. This means that we have to look for a set of goals from different parties which can be satisfied instead of optimized at the same time.

Organizational goals will be translated into strategies or strategic actions. From these we try to derive some elements of the "SOLL position" for information systems. For drawing conclusions with respect to the information needs from strategies directed at *economic* goals, we find a number of instruments in the literature. Useful approaches are those of Porter[Port85] and Wiseman[WISE85]. According to Porter an organization has a choice between four market strategies. It can try to be the cheapest seller on it's market or it can try to add specific qualities to its products that attract specific types of customers. Thus a touristic region could choose to aim at a large capacity of low priced facilities or it might aim at a very specific type of facilities at a somewhat higher price. Both of these strategies can be followed on a market as a whole (e.g. the tourist market as a whole) or on a segment of the market (e.g. the market of elderly tourists). Wiseman adds a greater variety of possibilities to Porters strategies and demonstrates that strategies can be directed at the organization itself but also at the behaviour of the competition. Both authors demonstrate that making the strategies explicit facilitates formulating the features and characteristic of the information infrastructure that is needed to support the strategies. For other strategies than those serving economic goals no instruments have been found. In those cases it is recommended to make the strategies as concrete and explicit as possible and to systematically evaluate all goals and strategies for possible consequences for information systems.

Finally we can compare the features of the "SOLL position" with the features of the actual "IST-position" in order to arrive at a quality judgement for the information systems.

Within organizations there always will be several levels of goals, ranging from very broad mission statements to concrete targets for business processes or parts thereof. In exceptional situations it is possible that goals formulated on different levels and by different persons fit together nicely, but generally there will be discrepancies. In the context of judging the quality of information in an organization these differences have to be made explicit and translated into consequences for the quality-judgement.

<u>the process-targets</u>

In order to reach its goals an organization will arrange its activities as business processes. Davenport[DAVE93] defines a business process as a structured, measured set of activities designed to produce a specified output for a particular customer or market. The organizations goals are, more or less accurately, translated in targets for the business processes. Information systems can be used to reach these process targets. This can be done by automating parts of the business process, using information systems for managing the business, incorporating information technology in the product, or using the communications possibilities of IT-infrastructure.

In order to assess the teleological aspects of the quality of information in an organization we start out to describe the business processes with there process targets and the information systems supporting them.

For describing the business processes we can use one of the many techniques available in literature and even in automated form. For production organization Porters "Value Chain" can be used as a starting point. The description has to be at such a level of detail that the link between information systems and the (sub)processes they support can clearly be established. For each (sub)process the targets are established by reading documentation and by interviewing people in the organization. Especially if different opinions on the process targets are expected a wide range of people have to be interview. The effects of different views on the process targets on the evaluation of the quality of information systems has to be made explicit.

The description of each information system consists of a number of items:

- a brief description of the functionality of the system. In earlier research the subdivision into automating parts of the business, management information, IT in the product and communication is used;
- the relationship of the system to the business processes: to which targets of which processes does the system contribute;
- the users and providers of the information. This item is particularly relevant for the management information systems;
- a global indication of the user-satisfaction, based on global questions in the interviews.

On the basis of the descriptions of the business processes and the information systems we have to find out how important the contribution of information systems is for reaching the business process targets and through those for the goals of the organization. For this analyses an adapted form of a method proposed by Bedell[BEDE85] is used. The adapted form of analyses consist of 12 steps which are briefly described now.

The first ten steps determine the importance of one specific system for the organization.

> step 1: determine to which (sub)process the system under consideration contributes.
>
> step 2: determine which targets of that process are supported by the system.
>
> step 3: determine how important the system is for reaching each of these targets.
>
> step 4: determine the relative importance of each of the targets supported.
>
> step 5: determine the importance of the system for the process by combining the results of steps 3 and 4.
>
> step 6: determine which goals of the organization are served by the process to which the system relates.
>
> step 7: determine the relative importance of the process for reaching those goals.
>
> step 8: determine the relative importance of each of the organizational goals served.
>
> step 9: determine the importance of the process for the organization by combining the results of steps 6, 7 and 8.
>
> step 10: determine the importance of the information system for the organization by combining results of steps 5 and 9.

If we want to get an impression of the importance of the total information infrastructure for the organization as a whole we can add two additional steps:

> step 11: determine the importance of the support delivered by all information systems related to a (sub)process by repeating steps 2 to 6 for each system and adding up the results.
>
> step 12: determine the importance of the information infrastructure for the organization as a whole by repeating step 11 for all process and combining the results.

It will be clear that the analysis described in these twelve steps has to done in cooperation between a researcher and the members of the organization. The method becomes difficult to handle if the diversity in opinions on goals and targets becomes very big. In that case one might decide to limit the analysis to certain sets of goals and targets.

The analysis can be done in a strictly quantitative but also in a more qualitative way. In the first case for each of the steps 3, 4, 7 and 8 quantitative scales can be used. In the first applications of the method global indications of the importance of systems, targets and processes were used. These could be translated into qualitative judgements on the quality of information in the organizations under consideration. In several try outs with quantitative scales respondents found it hard to give the exact answers that this type of questioning requires.

organizational structure

The structure of the organization is an important determinant of the amount of communication that is needed to coordinate

the activities of an organization. When we look at factors influencing the information needs of an organization we therefor also look at its structure.
Again the first step is to describe the structure of the organization. This is done by describing the hierarchy of decision making in the organization and by classifying the organization in terms of Mintzbe.g's typology. than deduce
The organizational structure is described in terms of its hierarchy and in terms of the typology of Mintzberg. Thus the organization is classified as a simple structure, a machine bureaucracy, a professional bureaucracy, a divisionalized form or an adhocracy.

From the degree of centralization/decentralization and from the classification according to Mintzberg [MINT83] we try to derive aspects of the "SOLL position" in terms of features and characteristics of the information systems. The only author hypothesizing a strict relationship between organizational structure and the information needs of the organization is Leifer [LEIF88]. He uses a typology of organizational structure based on Mintzberg. Leifer's ideas, however, have not been tested in practice. In this study we use Leifer's and Mintzberg's ideas to support our common sense when we look at the demands for information infrastructure generated by the organizational structure.

Finally we compare the "IST situation" with the "SOLL situation" to arrive at a judgement of the structure related aspects of the quality of information.

<u>organizational culture</u>
It seems reasonable to suppose that there is a relationship between organizational culture and the role of information in the organization. There is however no literature describing any explicit relationship. In this study we tried to describe culture by determining the position of the organization and its parts on a set of scales representing different aspects of culture. The scales are borrowed from Hofstede [HOFS88]. Then again common sense is used to derive aspects of the organizations information needs. Comparing these needs with the actual situation leads to the judgement on the culture related aspects of quality.

The first tests of the method proved that the aspects of culture as distinguished by Hofstede were not easy to understand for respondents in the organization. Furthermore it was not easy to draw clear conclusions related to information systems from this kind of description of the organization. On the hand members of the organization had there one vision on cultural differences between parts of the organization. From these differences some conclusions on information systems could be drawn. There it may be wise in future applications of the method to look for the ideas on culture that circulate among the members of the organization.

3. Conclusions

It is possible to construct a model for looking at the quality of information in an organization that brings together several approaches to the subject that are found in literature. From this framework we can derive an approach for assessing the strategy and goal related aspects of quality of information in an organization. The approach concentrates on revealing the goal and target structure of the organization and assessing if information systems support these goals and targets. Besides the goal and target structure also the environment of the organization, it's structure and it's culture should be taken into consideration. This approach has up to now been tried out in two organizations. In both cases it proved helpful in structuring the management's thoughts about the role of information in there organization. Moreover, the conclusions of the evaluations proved to be good starting point for formulating the future information policy of the organizations.

References

[ANSO65] X,, H., 1965, *Corporate strategy, an analytic approach to business policy for growth and expansion,* McGraw-Hill Book Company, New York.

[BAHL88] Bahlman, J.P. en B.A.C. Meesters, 1988, *Denken & doen, een studie naar de ontwikkeling en strategische heroriëntatie van zes Nederlandse ondernemingen*, Tilburg.

[BEDE85] Bedell, E.F., 1985, *The computer solution; strategies for success in the information age*, Dow Jones-Irwin, Homewood, Illinois.

[DAVE93] Davenport, T.H., 1993, Proces Innovation; reengineering work through information technology,
H.B.S.Press.

[DEMI82] Deming, W.E., 1982, *Quality, productivity and competitive position*, MIT, Centre for advanced engineering study.

[EGTE92] Egten, C.A. van and G.J. van der Pijl, 1972, *Kwaliteit van informatie*, Limperg INstituut, Amsterdam.

[HOFS88] Hofstede, G. e.a., 1988, *Organizational cultures-beyond the fad; a qualitative/quantitative study across twenty cases,* manuscript, RUL.

[ISO-87] ISO-9000 to 9004 quality standards, 1987.

[JURA74] Juran, J.M., 1974, *Quality control handbook,* McGraw-Hill, New York.

[LAWR73] Lawrencew, P.R. and J.W. Lorsch, 1973, *Organization and environment; managing differentiation and integration*, Irwin, Homewood.

[LEIF88] Leifer, R.L., 1988, Maching computer-based information systems with organizational structures, in: *MIS Quaterly*, March, p. 63-73.

[MINT83] Mintzberg, H., 1983, *Structure in fives; designing effective organisations*, Prentice-Hall International, Englewood Cliffs.

[PARK88] Parker, M.M. en R.J. Benson, 1988, *Information economics; linking business performance to information technology*, Prentice-Hall International, Englewood Cliffs.

[PIJL93] Pijl, G.J. van der, 1993, *Kwaliteit van informatie in theorie en praktijk*, PhD thesis, Limperg Instituut, Amsterdam.

[PORT80] Porter, M.E., 1980, *Competitive strategy: techniques for analyzing industries and competitors*,The Free Press, New York.

[PORT85] Porter, M.E., 1985, *Competitive advantage:creating and sustaining superior performance*, The Free Press, New York.

[RHEN73] Rhenman, E., 1973, *Organization theory for long range planning*, New York.

[WISE85] Wiseman, C., 1985, *Strategy and computers: Information systems as competitive weapons* , Dow Jones-Irwin, Homewood.

STRATEGIES FOR BALANCING THE COMPETENCE-GAP

Kai A. Simon, BSc

Univ. of Gothenburg / Chalmers Univ. of Technology

Abstract

Information Systems are invading our lives and our society with an accelerating speed. Many times the needs for rationality motivate investments in sophisticated technical solutions, developed by experts, without any consideration to the people that are going to use them. This situation leads to a gap between the existing and the required competence of individuals being part of the information systems. The more sophisticated technical systems we get, the more serious are the requirements for human competence to use them. This report discusses some aspects causing the competence-gap and strategies to balance it, with a special focus on human issues in system development and implementation processes.

Introduction

Very often, computerized information systems are only conceived as being economic resources. This conventional point of view is the main hinder to mobilize human energies in productive and innovative applications of information technology. With the challenges we have to face today the question is, how far these conventional approaches are still convenient. It is therefore important to enlarge the existing economist-toolbox by adding strategies to help the "victims" of new systems, the people, to get more involved in the development and implementation processes that concern them. The individuals being part of the information systems have to be conceived as critical factors for the successful development of the whole organisation. This has to be seen as a very important contribution to the development of a corporate identity and the mobilization of corporate energies in any kind of institution.

The purpose of this paper is to provide some answers to a few critical questions associated with the competence gap created by the accelerated investments in information technology, namely:

- Which factors are responsible for the competence-gap?
- Which strategies can be used to balance it in a successful way?
- How can system analysts and organizational members contribute to the success of system development processes?

According to my opinion, these questions gain high priority in the debate on information technology due to the fact that it influences all areas of our society. Information technology provides many opportunities for the development of enterprise systems. It can - if used in an appropriate way - increase a companys competetive-power, improve working-life, reduce production- and coordination-costs etc.

An aspect that has not been considered with the same intensity as technology itself is the human competence required to employ technology.

The fact is, that information systems should not be decoupled from the other elements of the organisation, especially the individuals. The development of information systems, organisation, technology and human competence must be seen as an inseparate critical process.

Which factors cause the competence-gap?

Almost all kind of organisations have implemented information technology - at an increasing pace - during the last years. The expected results such as increased productivity, cost-reduction, improved decision-making and an enhanced ability to respond to environmental changes etc. depend on the ability and motivation of the people using information technology in their daily activities (3). Looking at the results of current research, one may conclude, that information systems and information technology often fail to satisfy the expectations mentioned above. A study of 2,000 US companies revealed that about 40% of the implemented systems did not achieve the expected results (11). It is important to point out that more than 90% of the failures were related to low human competence as well as organizational complexity. E. Levinson summarizes:
"While the 1960s were the era of hardware failures, and the 1970s of software deficiencies, the issues for system failure in the 1980s have become organizational and managerial."(12)
Unfortunately, there are no indications, that this period has come to an end.

For achieving success in information system implementation a large number of aspects concerning individuals have to be taken care of, as there are user-training and -support, job-design and -specification, performance-measuring and issues like health and ergonomics (2). Current research proves, that human issues do not receive the attention they deserve.
As a matter of fact, a lot of system development is still performed without user participation. Some of the arguments for excluding them are:

- Users do not know what they want.
- Users will use the systems being provided with anyway.
- Users are no system experts, so leave them outside the development process.

This points of view, still very common among system specialists has in many organisations led to a situation, that the human competence is not regarded as a critical success factor, neither for the development of new systems, nor for the reorganization of existing ones. This causes the problem that the individuals competence is not developed towards the new technological opportunities.

That depends on the fact, that either organizational members seldom are involved in system development processes at a stage that allows them to achieve real influence or they do not get a chance to get involved at all. Their real role was most often restricted to react on problems emerging after the implementation.
Often the technical specialists have to take all the blame for the negative consequences, but even the organizational members themselves are not totally innocent due to the fact that their attempts to be involved in system development were not hard enough. The management of organisations has to take its part of the responsibility as well, because they have been delegating the critical decisions concerning system development and implementation to technical specialists.
The main argument for this form of delegation is based on the belief that the systems to be developed have a technical nature more than a social.
According to my opinion, an appropriate strategy for design and implementation of information systems must be based on the active development of human competence and abilities as well as on the adaption of the technological possibilities to human skills and limitations. Thereby we can improve both the quality of life and the realization of a company´s expectations.
Konosuke Matsushita of the Matsushita Corporation has been critical to the traditional approaches on system development and implementation and states that:
"The intelligence of a handful of technocrats ... is no longer enough to take up (the new technological and economic) challenges with a real chance of success." (2)

Which Strategies can be used to balance the Gap successfully?

I have found that there are three strategies which can be used in order to obtain a successful balance between required and existing human competence. These are:

- standard-strategies to adapt individuals to the systems requirements
- system-strategies aiming to decrease the complexity of the information systems
- system-strategies aiming to increase organizational capacities to manage the issues of information

It is important to point out, that the strategies above should not be used totally independent from each other. Instead i propose that the most appropriate way for achieving a successful system development and implementation process is to provide an adequate combination between them.

Standard Strategies to adapt individuals to the systems requirements

The standard strategies, mainly developed during the 1960s and 1970s, were aimed to adapt the individuals to the systems requirements because the systems themselves were conceived as static elements. The standard strategies includes aspects like recruitment, changes in the categories of work and their structure, education and skills training as well as standardization of work and technology. In order to use the capabilities of a system in the best possible way, several types of training and education have to be used.

Today this education is often restricted to the so called "type A"-learning (13), which means that the system users are educated only in the technical use of the systems. The need of knowledge about the relation between technology, organisation and individuals is frequently neglected. The education and training concerns all categories of organizational members such as managers, supervisors and clerical workers.

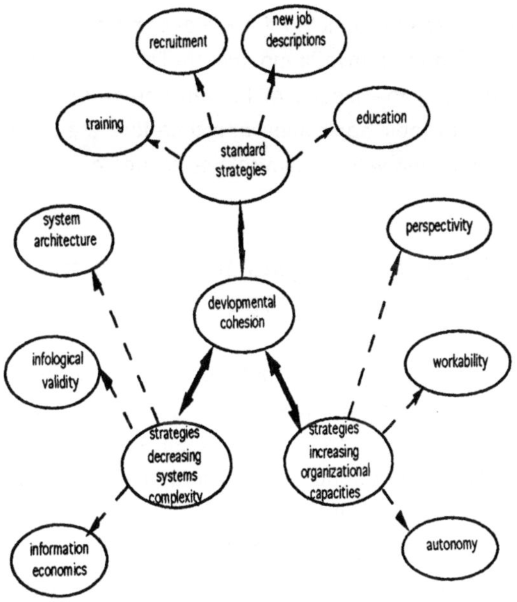

Fig. 1: Strategies to balance the competence-gap

The elaboration of these standard strategies may be solve a number of competence-problems, but not all of them. There will always be a lot of new questions which may be seen unanswerable. For instance, introducing information technology in organisation increases the complexity of tasks, diffuses responsibities and increases the amount of social conflicts. None of these issues can be managed in a satisfying way by traditional approaches.

Another critical issue is that the roles and tasks of organizational members may change dramatically. The belief that only training and education increases motivation and innovation is not true. Therefore these changes will always lead to undesirable consequences. Some of the critical questions are:

- Why should technology influence the roles and tasks of individuals?
- How can individuals with their limitations face the accelerating technical developments?
- Who decides the form, function and content of training?

These and other questions are posed and a lot of research will have to be done and a lot of failures will be made before these questions are answered.

It may even be doubted if it will ever be possible to answer them. I have found, that traditional strategies concerning the issues of human competence are limited in their application and therefore they must be completed with system-related strategies.

System Strategies to balance the Competence-Gap

System strategies do not conceive information systems as static. Instead they are conceived as flexible and aiming to support an ever changing human environment. System strategies are based on a few critical assumptions concerning the interdependencies between the human activity system and the information systems. Human activity systems and information systems are mutually dependent from each other. Therefore their development can not be considered in isolation. Changes in human activity systems must be followed in the information systems and changes in information systems must be followed by changes in the human activity systems. There is no way to avoid this mutual dependency, but with help of system strategies we can balance the effects of changes.

System-Strategies to decrease Information Systems Complexity

The first kind of systems strategies aims to decrease the complexity of information systems. This can be obtained by the following actions:

- choose the appropriate system architecture
- increase the infological validity
- consider the issues of information economics

System architecture
The architecture of information systems has to be chosen from a perspective that integrates individuals, organisation, information and the technology used in this context. The system architecture will support the balance of individual autonomy and the needs for coordinated action. The information system architecture must provide a harmonious integration among systems in order to support cooperation and to satisfy individual needs at the same time.

Infological validity
The information systems designed to support individual needs must be characterized by a high degree of infological validity. Issues of consistency, completeness, relevance, information load, presentation forms, etc. must be defined in terms that matches the cognitive capacities of individuals. This means that information systems should be designed with respect to local languages, working styles, world views and norms. The implementation of infological validity presumes an appropriate system architecture, the right level of autonomy and the differentiation of information support.

Information economics
Information economics reflects the needs for differentiation of information in global respectively local information (16). Not all information is relevant to the needs of cooperation and coordination of human activities. According to current research 80% of the information flowing within an organisation is of local nature. Only a few percent of the rest is conceived as valuable for the cooperation of human activities and must be globalized. This means that a well designed information system must provide "the correct information at the right place at the right time in the right form and amount". I call this the informations "just in time concept".

System-Strategies to increase organizational capacities

The actions mentioned above can decrease the complexity of information systems by adapting them to individual and collective needs. But these actions can only provide a limited effect. Therefore organisations must be designed in a way that improves their capacities to handle the issues of information. The following actions aim to provide some directions toward this objectives.

• ensure perspectivity

• provide appropriate level of autonomy

• obtain workability

Perspectivity

Organisations are incomprehensive systems. The ever changing organizational environment, the technologies employed in production and administration, the heterogenous needs of markets, the differentiated interests of organizational members as well as the size of organisations are typical factors reflecting the comprehensibility of organizations. In order to provide a base for management one must reduce the organizational incomprehensibility. Systems thinking may be seen as a proper strategy in this direction if it is based on a human perspective. This means that areas of responsibility as well as decisions taken within these areas must be in correspondence to the cognitive capacities of individuals. Furthermore, perspectivity means a better understanding of how information and information systemis are related to human work. Systems thinking provides an adequate platform firstly to develop information systems that support local needs without losing the overall perspective on cooperation and coordination of human actions and secondly to design organisations capable to manage the usage of information.

Autonomy

Usually comprehensibility presumes a high level of autonomy. Otherwise the bureaucratical hierarchy can hinder the effects of systems thinking. Delays, information overload, social conflicts and competition, as well as misunderstanding can be conceived as consequences of dismatching between system structure and management philosophy. With a high level of autonomy individuals are even responsible for the development, implementation and use of their own systems. In this sense, the systems under concern are designed to satisfy the individual needs. This ensures that the system implementation can not fail because of a large motivation potential'of people to improve their working environment and efficiency.

Workability

While autonomy is a necessary factor to mobilize individuals within an organisation, workability reflects the needs for a harmonous cooperation between individuals. Workability is based on firstly mutual agreement on the objectives to be achieved by cooperation as well as on the role of the information systems and information systems architecture within this context. Secondly, workability implies reciprocity. In other words mutual contributions to the expectations of the involved participants. Workability is the result a political process including negotiations and compromises in order to establish a common image of reality.

Struggling with Developmental Cohesion

Developmental cohesion reflects the need to conceive organisations, their information systems, the people working in them as well as the technologies employed as an indivisible system. The expression of this need can be seen as a paradigm for the development of organizations in the 1990s. Developmental cohesion means, that the development of information systems always has to be integrated and coordinated with the development of organisations as well as with the development of individuals cognitive capacities.

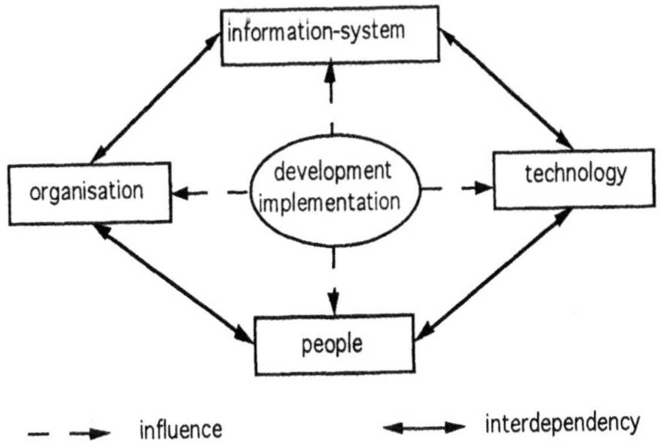

Fig. 2: Developmental cohesion

Furthermore, developmental cohesion means that these processes are controlled by those who are responsible for the enterprise activities. Any form of delegation to experts implies risks, conflicts and Mis-information systems. By this way, individuals are motivated to improve their competence in order to be in control of the changes that influences the success of their enterprises.

The Role of Organizational Members

Organizational members can influence the developmental cohesion in three different ways, as there are

- the reactive way
- the supportive way
- the proactive way

When playing a reactive role organizational members get involved at a very late stage, after the implementation is completed. That restricts them to react on emerging problems like dissatisfaction and low performance rates. The effects of such a delay may be given in terms of personal conflicts, increased personnel turnover, complaints etc.
All these factors reflect a low developmental cohesion which can be given by inappropriate implementation procedures and organizational policies. Changes in organisations, people, technology and information systems are often treated in an "ad hoc" manner, resulting in inefficiency, ineffectiveness and inhuman working environments.

In the supportive role the organizational members get involved in the development process. It is expected that they create alternative scenarios about possible problems related to the implementation and how these problems may be solved. This may include the design of training programs, support in the solution of social conflicts and development of new policies for competence development. In such an environment it is expected that developmental cohesion has a moderate level.

The proactive role of organizational members is doubtless the most demanding and successful one. They are expected to be involved in the development process at the earliest stage and will thereby be able to point out and avoid potential problems from the very beginning. Their goal is to improve their working environment. This is done by designing an "ideal system", that is far from potential social problems and threats. This environment is expected to mobilize both the technical and the non-technical resources in a cooperative and successful process for satisfying mutual expectations. In this sense it is expected that developmental cohesion has a high value.

The Role of the System Analysts of the Future

The most important point is, that the system analysts of the future have to learn how to manage the issues related to the developmental cohesion of organisations. This means that he or she must learn to think in system terms in order to understand the interdependencies between information systems and human activity systems. Information systems are designed to support human activities. But the effectiveness and efficiency of this support depends the competence and the cognitive capacities of the organizational members to manage the issues of information.

According to my opinion, the acceptance of such a framework implies critical changes in the work structure of system specialists. The future expects a closer cooperation between organizational members and system analysts, system developers, system operators etc.

Furthermore it is expected that the system analyst of the future is able choose appropriate methods in order satisfy the analytical needs of developmental cohesion. This means that current methodologies are limited and unappropriate to satisfy the futural requirements of organizational analysis, architectural analysis, system analysis aso.

Lastly, system analysts of the future must be able to support both the strategical and operational environments of an organisation. In the first case it is expected that scenarios or strategies are developed. These strategies refer to all factors involved in my conception of developmental cohesion. In the second case the analyst must be able to support the needs of local or indiviual working environments. The potentialities of information technology can be utilized for the successful achievements of human expectations.

Sources/References

(1) *Information Technology as a Competative Burden,* Timothy N. Warner, in Computers in the Human Context, ed. Tom Forester, MIT press, 1989

(2) *Human Factors in Computer-integrated Manufacturing,* John Bessant and Alec Chisholm, in Computers in the Human Context, ed. Tom Forester, MIT press, 1989

(3) *Human Issues in New Office Technology,* Richard J. Long, in Computers in the Human Context, ed. Tom Forester, MIT press, 1989

(4) *Information Technology in Banks: Taylorization or Human-centered Systems?,* Steve Smith, in Computers in the Human Context, ed. Tom Forester, MIT press, 1989

(5) *Computerization and the Transformation of Work,* Charles Dunlop and Rob Kling, in Computerization and Controversy, ed. Charles Dunlop & Rob Kling, Academic Press, 1991

(6) *The Mechanization of Office Work,* Vincent E. Giuliano, in Computerization and Controversy, ed. Charles Dunlop & Rob Kling, Academic Press, 1991

(7) *Computerization, Office Routines, and Changes in Clerical Work,* Susan Iacono and Rob Kling, in Computerization and Controversy, ed. Charles Dunlop & Rob Kling, Academic Press, 1991

(8) *Intellectual Assembly Lines: The Rationalization of Managerial, Professional and Technical Work,* Judith A. Perolle, in Computerization and Controversy, ed. Charles Dunlop & Rob Kling, Academic Press, 1991

(9) *The Third Wave,* Alvin Toffler, Bantam Books, New York, 1981

(10) *Den nya tekniken - förändring eller anpassning,* Svante Leijon, Flemming Norrgren, Sigvard Rubenowitz, Bengt Rundblad, Axel Targama, ISBN 91-7246-069-5

(11) *Implementation of Office Automation,* T.K. Bikson and B. Gutek, Rand Corp., Santa Monica, CA, 1984

(12) *Implementation Path Analysis: A Method for Studying Implementation of Information Technology,* E. Levinson, Office: Technology and People, vol. 2, 1985, pp. 287-304

(13) *Word Processing: First Step to the Office of the Future,* K.F. Curley, Praeger Publishers, New York, 1983

(14) *New Information Technology: Organizational problem or opportunity,* R.E. Walton and W. Vittori, Office: Technology and People, vol. 1, 1983

(16) *System för företagsstyrning,* Börje Langefors, Studentlitteratur, Lund, Sweden

(17) *Management Misinformation Systems,* Russell Ackoff

SCENARIOS FOR CSCW APPLICATIONS IN TOURISM

Mag. Ronald Maier
Institute of Business Informatics
The Koblenz School of Corporate Management
Burgplatz 2, D-56179 Vallendar
Telefon: ++49/261/6509-172, Telefax: -179
E-Mail: maier@wi.whu-koblenz.de

Mag. Jürgen Galler
Institute of Information Systems (IWi)
Universität des Saarlandes
Im Stadtwald, D-66123 Saarbrücken
Telefon: ++49/681/302-2190, Telefax: -3696
E-Mail: galler@iwi.uni-sb.de

Abstract

This paper discusses the possible use of Computer Supported Cooperative Work (CSCW) technologies in the field of tourism. Cooperative work processes in tourism are investigated and important factors are identified which influence the implementation of CSCW systems in tourism. To give some impressions of what future tourist CSCW systems could look like scenarios are developed. These scenarios might stimulate future research work to improve the use of information technologies in the field of tourism.

1. Motivation

It is only recently that applications supporting people who work together are being developed. Nevertheless, the research and practical experiences gained in the field of Computer Supported Cooperative Work (CSCW) have made quite a few CSCW systems available. In the field of tourism many different partners (e.g. organizations, enterprises, associations) have to cooperate to fulfill different tasks concerning the services expected by their customers: usually the products or services provided by a single tourist organization are only a part of the complex "product" holiday. This is an important difference between tourist organizations and the traditional consumer goods industry or services.

Today the situation concerning the application of information and communication technologies in tourism is as follows: the information systems installed in tourist organizations are designed to support a single persons work or a single organizations work respectively. It is remarkable that the developers of information systems in tourism pay little attention to the fact that people and even organizations work together. This is a drawback for the development of highly integrated forms of cooperation between tourist organizations. The authors believe that the application of CSCW technologies can change the way organizations cooperate and improve quality and efficiency of these cooperations. These new forms of cooperation lead to a more holistic approach to the production of tourist goods and services. The aims of this paper are

- to analyze the situation concerning cooperative work processes in tourism that are suitable for being supported by CSCW technologies;
- to examine the potentials of the application of these technologies;
- to develop scenarios that outline CSCW information systems which support these processes.

2. Cooperative work processes in tourism - important factors

The CSCW technologies were chosen as follows: Electronic Mail Systems, Electronic Black Board Systems [see 12,19], Workflow Automation Systems [see 11, 7], Electronic Meeting Systems [see 2], Group Decision Support Systems (GDSS) [see 1, 13], Video Conferencing Systems [see 4, 6], Asynchronous Conferencing Systems [see 5],

Collaborative Authoring Systems [see 21], Screen-Sharing Software [see 9,23]. For all these technologies numerous commercial products or at least research prototypes exist.

The authors took into account a wide variety of tourist organizations like accomodation companies, camping sites, cultural organizations, leisure associations, restaurants, tourist centres, travel agencies, travel insurances, travel organizers and transport organizations.

Considering the possible application of the listed technologies in these organizations the authors found a number of factors which influence the use of CSCW technologies in tourism and lead to a first differentiation of technologies into those fruitful for tourist organizations and those less important in this field. The factors are as follows:

Organization types

Almost eighty percent of the tourist organizations are small companies which have no complicated cooperative work processes within one organization. Therefore it is not possible to apply the traditional knowledge about CSCW systems gained from applications in consumer and investment goods industry.

Cooperation forms

Tourist organizations have to cooperate with many different organizations located in different places. Therefore in tourism inter-organizational cooperations are basic strategic factors for prosperity. There is a need for systems that support inter-organizational cooperation.

Impact on services and products

The capabilities of CSCW technologies in tourism lie in their direct impact on the services tourist organizations offer. In the traditional application fields of CSCW technologies work processes between persons are supported, but there is no influence on the products or services themselves.

Technical infrastructure

A possible problem can be seen in the infrastructure needed for CSCW technologies: communication infrastructure, central databases, and a central coordinating organization. Currently CSCW systems are mainly implemented inside companies using the existing infrastructure. This is not the case for CSCW systems in tourism. Even if the global, international communication infrastructure (like "information highways" [10] in the USA) improves, the need for the integration of small tourist organizations still exists.

3. Potentials of CSCW technologies in tourism

Figure 1 shows a classification of cooperative work processes and CSCW technologies respectively. The cooperative work processes the authors found in the field of tourism are of all types, I, II, III and IV processes.

place	synchronous (time)	asynchronous (time)
different place	II	IV
same place	I	III

Figure 1: The Time/Place-Matrix to classify technologies supporting group work [Source: Krcmar 1992]

However, most of the cooperative work processes are type III and IV processes. The reason might be that the most important cooperative work processes in tourism are not limited to the boundaries of one organization. Today there seems to be no need to synchronize these inter-organizational work processes. Quite a few CSCW technologies like Workflow Automation, Co-Authoring Systems, Electronic Blackbord Systems or simply E-Mail could be applied to support these asynchronous processes.

Type I and II processes are not very common. The application of CSCW technologies which support people working together at the same time in the same place like Electronic Meeting Systems (EMS) or Group Decision Support Systems (GDSS) seems less justified regarding the cooperative work processes of tourist organizations.

The technologies supporting people working in different places at the same time (like Video Conferencing, Screen Sharing) may be applied in very special situations, but again there seem to be less possibilities of applying these technologies in every day work of tourist organizations.

Nevertheless, the last two technology classes (supporting type I and II processes) can be used to support business tourists. These people travel to take part in meetings, work together and communicate with one another. The tourist organizations whose main target group consists of business people (e.g. congress and seminar hotels) need to take a close look at technologies focusing on people working together at the same time. In that case both types of work processes, type I and II, are of particular interest.

4. Scenarios

To show the wide variety of possible application fields the authors chose two scenarios that are completely different: the first scenario concentrates on tourist holidays and the second on business travelling. The first scenario, the Interactive Leisure Management System, deals with type IV cooperative work processes. The second scenario, the Interhotel Electronic Meeting Rooms, deals with type I and II cooperative work processes.

The following two sections are divided into five parts. First the **assumptions** are stated which form the basis of the construction of the scenarios. These assumptions are supposed to outline situations where the scenarios work effectively. Then the **organizations** which should take part in implementing the CSCW systems and which should take advantage of the new technologies for their work are identified. In a next step the **functionality** is presented which gives some impressions of what basic functions are needed. An **example** is given to illustrate what the future utilization of the information systems by the tourists could look like. In the end some of the supposed **benefits** for the tourist organizations are presented.

5. Scenario 1: Interactive Leisure Management System

5.1 Assumptions

1: The easier it is for tourists to get information the more they will inform themselves.

2: The more tourists know about the facilities provided by the tourist organizations the more they will use these facilities.

3: The trend to short term holidays continues. Therefore tourists prefer not to plan their holidays in advance but to get "fast information" on their holiday resort.

4: The more tourists can satisfy their holiday needs by using the provided facilities the more likely it is that they are contented with their holidays.

5.2 Cooperating Organizations

Figure 2 shows the numerous tourist organizations that are supposed to cooperate on the Interactive Leisure Management System. The central position of the tourist centre illustrates the key role of this organization in the coordination process. The Interactive Leisure Management System can be seen as the integrating platform which the various cooperations should be based on.

Figure 2: Cooperating organizations of the Interactive Leisure Management System

5.3 Functionality

The functions considered in this scenario can be divided into three groups:

Cooperation functions: coordination of the various events and facilities offered by the tourist organizations; a platform that supports the standardization process for data communication between the tourist organizations.

Information functions: a platform that standardizes the data flow from the tourist organizations to the tourists. Therefore it is much easier for the tourists to compare offers and to combine services from different tourist organizations (e.g. theatre, restaurant and transport companies); daily actual multimedia information about activities, facilities, things to do in the surroundings.

Communication functions: video and audio communication with all cooperating organizations; reservation; booking; credit-card paying for the booked facilities; feedback; cross-selling: the system proposes additional activities or facilities depending on what kind of activity the tourist is interested in.

5.4 Example

Figure 3 shows the process of finding the right combination of services supported by a dialogue with the Interactive Leisure Management System.

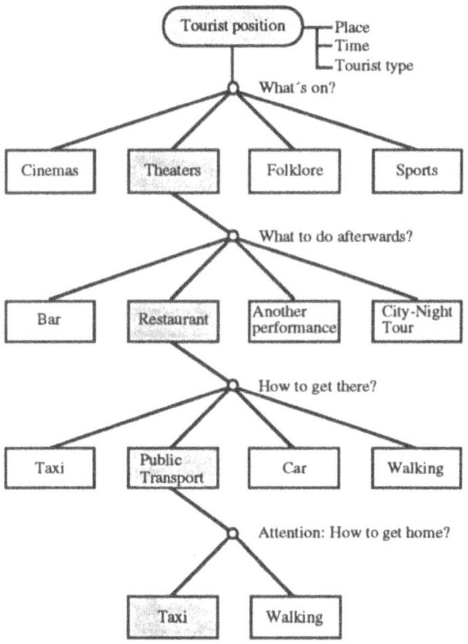

Figure 3: The selection process as a dialogue with the Interactive Leisure Management System

It is already late afternoon of the first day of his short-term holiday in Innsbruck and Mr. User does not know exactly what to do this evening. He decides to use the Interactive Leisure Management System to get some ideas of what is on in Innsbruck. Mr. User is a sporty culture-lover who is also interested in typical tyrolean traditions. The system makes some proposals of evening activities and Mr. User chooses the theatre. He browses through a short abstract of the play and he gets some impressions of what the theatre looks like. He books a seat and chooses to pay with his credit card.

After booking the system makes some proposals of possible activities after the performance. Have a drink in a fancy bar nearby or a full-scale dinner in a restaurant offering "Greek week" right now? Mr. User decides to try the restaurant and the system makes a reservation for half an hour after the end of the performance. In a next step the system wants to know if Mr. User needs some help concerning the transport to and from the theatre and the restaurant. Mr. User chooses the public transport and he gets a small map of the next station, which bus line to take and the departure and arrival times. Then the system proposes to take a taxi from the restaurant back to his hotel because there is no bus after 10 p.m. in that sector and Mr. User receives the phone number of a taxi company operating round the clock.

The system eases the process of finding missing links in the service chain. The consequent utilization of this system helps to improve not only the information of the tourists but also the coordination of the services and products. That is why the described approach to cooperation is far more than only an information system.

5.5 Benefits

The main benefits can be divided into two groups: it is easier for the tourists to get individual and up-to-date information and there is a better chance for organizations to sell their services. Beside these main benefits there are the following advantages:

- the organizations can check if their services match the services of other organizations;
- the tourist centre as the coordinator of this system has a better overview over its region;
- the system can be used for a market research by evaluating the user behavior (information requested and the services booked);
- the media changes in communication (from electronical data to paper and vice-versa) either between organizations or between organizations and tourists are reduced;
- it is easier to identify which services are used often and in which combination.

6. Scenario 2: Interhotel Electronic Meeting Rooms

6.1 Assumptions

1: The demand for information and communication technologies which support meetings and seminars held by business tourists will increase.

2: Managers of international companies spend a lot of time travelling to and from meetings. It will be more and more important to avoid this unproductive time and to gain managerial capacities.

3: Managers will take more advantage of information and communication technologies.

6.2 Cooperating Organizations

The group of cooperating organizations in this scenario consists of hotels, consultants, supervisors (moderators, experts in the field of group dynamics), experts in the field of information and communication technologies, information brokers, companies providing databases on specific subjects, multi-national companies.

6.3 Functionality

Considering the following list of functions it is important to guarantee a high level of data security inside the meeting room and especially when using international networks.The functions of this scenario are divided into three phases:

Before the meeting: The business people that want to book an electronic meeting room get information about the hotel itself and the facilities of the meeting room, proposals for experts to supervise the meetings or to handle the equipment, guidelines to check the compatibility with their own information technologies or data interfaces to handle the converting processes and ciphering methods or programs respectively.

During the meeting: Connections to databases of the home companies of the users; connections to public databases worldwide via all important networks; access to information brokers; group decision support system functions, such as CATeam functions [see 17, 20]; video conferencing with international experts or absent colleagues especially those located in foreign countries; communication with hotel facilities and employees (e.g. information systems specialist, receptionist, restaurant); electronic flip chart to support automatic documentation of hand-drawn drafts and outlines; video camera and recorder for documentation of the meeting; still-video to digitize pictures from the video camera; multi-functional screen (as a consistent platform for video-conferencing, data projection, GDSS chauffeur screen, video monitor).

After the meeting: Automatically generated reports concerning the following subjects: starting point of the meeting (consisting of documents provided before the meeting by the participants); meeting process; contents of the meeting; feedback; results of GDSS brainstormings and anonymous votings; results of data base queries.

6.4 Example

Figure 4 shows the structure of the CSCW technologies used in the Interhotel Electronic Meeting Rooms in this example.

The managers of the European headquarters of the multi-national company (MNC) have to discuss some aspects of their marketing strategy for the next five years. Because of the importance of the European market for MNC this task has to be performed together with the top management in the USA. For this reason the European managers decide to meet at the Open International Hotel (OIH) which provides electronic meeting rooms all over the world. They use the GDSS facilities to support the brainstorming process in which all the managers (European and American) take part. Via vi-

sual phone they consult a marketing information broker located in Russia who is specialised in marketing for Eastern European countries.

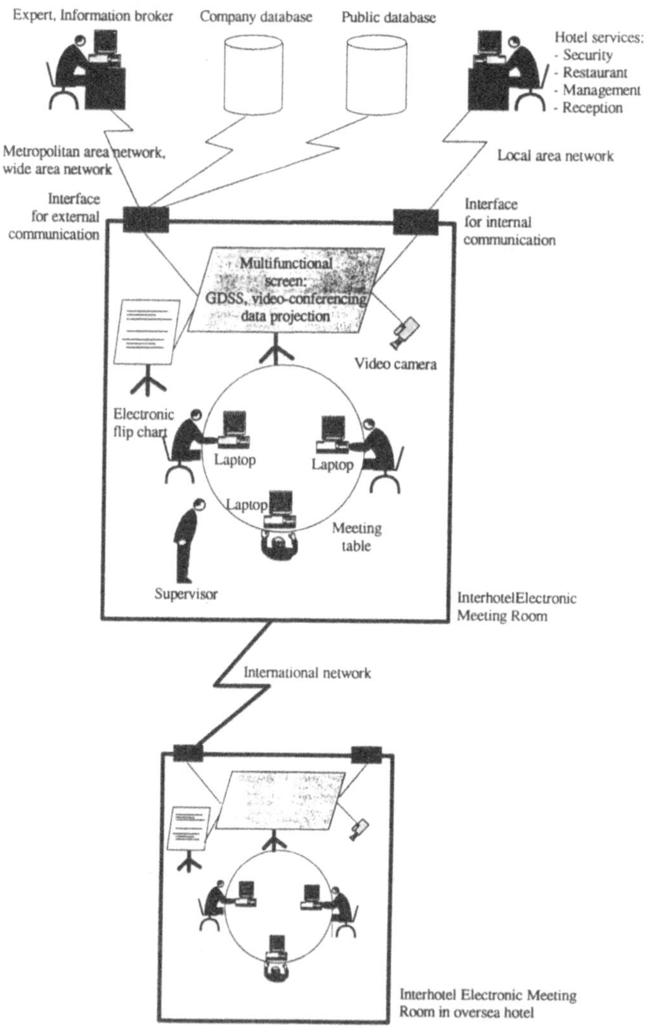

Figure 4: Example of the application of an electronic meeting room in tourism

With the help of the information broker they access some external databases to increase their knowledge about marketing in Eastern Europe. They use data connections to the MNC branches in Poland and Hungary to get the latest sales figures. The European managers discuss their proposals for a new strategy with the top management in the USA via video conferencing. The top management has access to all the data provided by the participants and to the new data worked out during the meeting.

They agree on a new marketing strategy and all the participants immediately get an electronic report containing specific data of the process and results of the meeting.

6.5 Benefits

The installation of Interhotel Electronic Meeting Rooms guarantees longterm benefits to each of the cooperating partners. Together they can offer a service which they could not offer on their own.

- The services hotel-chains can provide with this electronic equipment can be seen as competitive advantages over accomodation organizations which cannot offer this service;
- The experts have the benefit of being part of an integrated service and get a new target group;
- The companies taking advantage of an integrated service of high technologies, experts and accomodation benefit from reduced costs for business travels, time savings for managerial activities and an improved quality of decision making [see 17, 20].

7. Prospects

With this paper the authors wanted to give some impressions on future CSCW systems in tourism. Future research work should take a closer look at the stepwise procedure that leads to the implementation of CSCW systems in tourism. It will be crucial for tourist organizations to develop consistent informatic strategies [see 15, 16]. The coordinated development of tourist information systems is essential to face the new challenges.

It will be also of great importance that the tourist organizations base their applications on open systems to guarantee easy and free communication with their cooperation partners [for the problems concerning migration to open systems see 18]. The increasing number of information systems in tourism shows the need for specific reference models and systems integration concepts like the ones developed for industry [see 22].

The authors are convinced that it could be of help for tourist organizations and technology providers not only to consider CSCW technologies, but also other technologies like expert systems, multimedia, client-server or objectoriented programming.

Bibliography

[1] Applegate, L., Konsynski, B., Nunamaker, J.: A group decision support system for idea generation and issue analysis in organizational planning, in: Proceedings of the Conference on Computer Supported Cooperative Work, pp. 16-34, ACM Press, Austin, Texas, 1986

[2] Austin, L., Liker, J., McLeod, P.: Determinants and patterns of control over technology in a computerized meeting room, in: Proceedings of the Conference on Computer Supported Cooperative Work (CSCW '90), pp. 39-52, ACM Press, Los Angeles, California, 1990

[3] Biervert B., Dierkes, M. (ed.): Informations- und Kommunikationstechniken im Dienstleistungssektor, published by Gabler Verlag, Wiesbaden, 1989

[4] Bulick, S., Abel, M., Corey, D., Schmidt, J., Coffin, S.: The US West Advanced Technologies prototype multimedia communication system, in: Proceedings of the IEEE Global Telecommunications Conference (Globe Com), pp. 1221-1226, 1989

[5] Caldwell, R., Van Nest, W., Tynan, A., Leach, R.: Conferencing selection and implementation: University of Arizona case history, in: The Second Guelph Symposium on Computer Conferencing, pp. 209-222, University of Guelph, Guelph, Ontario, Canada, 1987

[6] Egido, C.: Video conferencing as a technology to support group work: A review of its failures, in: Proceedings of the Conference on Computer-Supported Cooperative Work (CSCW '88), pp. 13-24, ACM Press, Portland, Oregon, 1988

[7] Erdl, G., Schönecker, H.: Vorgangssteuerungssysteme im Überblick - Herkunft, Voraussetzungen, Einsatzschwerpunkte, Ausblick, in: Office Management, pp. 13-21, 3/1993

[8] Freyer, W.: Tourismus - Einführung in die Fremdenverkehrsökonomie, published by R. Oldenbourg Verlag, München, Wien, 1988

[9] Greenberg, S.: Sharing views and interactions with single-user applications, in: Proceedings of the ACM/IEEE Conference on Office Information Systems, pp. 227-237, Cambridge, Massachusets, 1990

[10] Grunenberg, N.: Von Pioniergeist keine Spur, in: Die Zeit No. 45, November 5th, pp. 3-4, 1993

[11] Hasenkamp, U., Syring, M.: Workflow-Management - Beispiele Zeitschriftenproduktion, in: Office Management, pp. 32-36, 6/1993

[12] Hayes-Roth, B. : Blackboard systems, in: Encyclopedia of Artificial Intelligence, Vol. 1, New York et al. 1987, S. 73-80

[13] Kraemer, K., Pinsonneault, A.: Technology and groups: Assessments of the empirical research, in: Galegher, J., Kraut, R., Egido, C. (eds.), Intellectual Teamwork: Social Foundations of Cooperative Work, pp. 373-404, Lawrence Erlbaum Associates, Hillsdale, New Jersey, 1990

[14] Krcmar, H.: WI - State of the Art: Computerunterstützung für die Gruppenarbeit - Zum Stand der Computer Supported Cooperative Work Forschung, in: Wirtschaftsinformatik, Vol. 34, No. 4, pp. 425-437, 1992

[15] Lehner, F.: Informatik-Strategien - Entwicklung, Einsatz und Erfahrungen, published by C. Hanser Verlag, München, Wien, 1993

[16] Lehner, F.: Entwicklung von Informatik-Strategien - Koordination und Anpassung zwischen Unternehmenszielen und Informationstechnologien, in: Scheer, A.W. (ed.) : M&C - Management & Computer, Vol. 1, No. 3, pp. 165-174, 1993

[17] Lewe, H., Krcmar, H.: Computer Aided Team with Group Systems: experiences in practical use, in: Wirtschaftsinformatik, Vol. 34, No. 2, pp. 111-119, 1993

[18] Maier, R.: Ein Vorgehensmodell für die Migration zu offenen Systemen, in: PIK - Praxis der Informationsverarbeitung und Kommunikation, Vol. 16, No. 3, pp. 151-156, 1993

[19] McDonnell, D. , Raymond, J.: Integration of the electronic blackboard and the electronic overhead projector, in: The Second Guelph Symposium on Computer Conferencing, pp. 193-197, University of Guelph, Guelph, Ontario, Canada, 1987

[20] Petrovic, O., Krickl, O.: Traditionally moderated versus computer supported brainstorming - a comparative study, in: Wirtschaftsinformatik, Vol. 34, No. 2, p. 120-128, 1993

[21] Sarples, M.: Computer Supported Collaborative Writing, published by Springer Verlag, London et al., 1993

[22] Scheer, A.-W.: Wirtschaftsinformatik, 4th edition, published by Springer Verlag, London et al., 1994, in preparation.

[23] Srinivas, K., Reddy, R., Babadi, A., Kamana, S., Kumar, V., Dai, Z.: MONET: A Multimedia System for Conferencing and Application Sharing in Distributed Systems, CERC-TR-RN-91-009, West Virginia University, Morgantown, 1992

GENERAL ASPECTS OF AN INFORMATION SYSTEM (IS) FOR FINANCIAL JUSTIFICATION OF INVESTMENTS IN TOURISM MARKETING INFORMATION SYSTEMS (TMIS's) DEVELOPMENT

Dr. George Emmanuel Haramis

University of Macedonia
156 Egnatia Ave., P.O. Box 1591
GR-54006 Thessaloniki, Greece

Abstract

The general aspects and the flow chart of an IS for financial justification of TMIS's Development are proposed by this paper.

The System will support decisions for investments on TMIS's Development and will be based on the method of net present value and/or the method of internal rate of return and risk consideration.

The paper contains:
- General aspects of what is a TMIS
- Financial Justification of a TMIS Development
- The proposed IS for Financial Justification of TMIS Development.

1. What is a Tourism Marketing Information System

A *System* can be defined as a series of interrelated elements that perform some activity function, or operation.

More specifically an *Information System* (IS) is considered to be an organized unit of people, machines and various means which has defined targets and always consists of 3 sections: Input - Processing - Output.

Furthermore, a System of relative and essential information for the programming, control and operation of a company can be considered a Management Information System (MIS).

The term *Marketing* describes the functions whose objective is the creation of customers and the offer of a firm's products or services to them. It has actually become very popular and has become widely accepted as a substitute for the term *sales*, which has been reduced to indicating a subset of the functions of Marketing. The reasoning behind this substitution is based on the perception that *selling* to a customer is a secondary target, compared to the *marketing* of a firm's products or services.

The term *Tourism* refers to the temporary traver to and residence in another country (or another region of the same country) for leisure and/or cultural and/or benificial purposes. The word *tourism* is derived from the French word "tour" and the ending -ismus, -isme, -ism. Its origin is the Latin tornus, which - even today - is found unchanged in the Greek word tornos (τόρνος). Initially, this meant the woodworkers' compass; later it came to indicate the known machine.

A *Tourism Marketing Information System* (TMIS) is the I.S. used by a company in managing its tourism marketing activities.

The objectives of a TMIS (systems requirements) or the value that the system will provide to users during its lifetime cover:
- Organisational arrangements.
- Position responsibilities.
- Planning and control procedures for effecting tourism marketing operations.
- Procedures and operations for the acquisition, processing, retrieval, and dissemination of tourism market research information.
- Procedures for the analysis of information, which will be used in the management of tourism marketing decisions.

2. Financial Justification of a TMIS Development

Capital investment decisions require the review and evaluation of many factors. During the evaluation of an investment for the development of a new TMIS (or any IS), it is essential that the following four statements be considered:

- The development and operation of a system has a high cost.
- Usually it is very difficult to identify and measure the benefits of a system.
- Systems are not for ever; so it is important to estimate their life.
- Systems require maintenance.

On the other hand, it is well-known that other factors, apart from the financial ones, such as EDP Users satisfaction, market conditions, back-up requirements, company organization, company competition influence a decision for the development of a TMIS.
However, it is recommended that management be aware of the financial factors before making a decision that may be influenced by other non financial factors.

It is proposed in this text that the investment decision for systems development be based on the method of Net Present Value (NPV) and/or the method of Internal Rate of Return (IRR).

Due to interest or cost of money, a monetary unit received in future has a different value than a monetary unit received today. Thus, in order to consider the value of benefits received in the future, it is necessary for these benefits (cash flows) to be discounted to their present value, based on specified discount rate.
Furthermore, the difference between the present values of inflows (benefits) and outflows (total development cost), gives the NPV.

Generally, if the NPV of discounted cash flows is positive, the investment is worthile and the system must be developed; if negative, the investment will not be financially beneficial to the company and the decision for the development of the system must be based on other non financial factors.

The NPV is the most important method in the event of the analysis of only one investment. However, when there are two or more investments, it then becomes more difficult to analyse them, as it is not correct to select the one having the higher NPV, because it may need more investment than the others to obtain it. So, the calculation of the IRR of each investment, as well as their comparison, becomes essential.

By IRR we mean the discount rate which gives the amount of all the discounted cash flows a net present value equal to zero.

In accordance with this definition, we accept that the IRR indicates how high an interest rate one can afford to pay to borrow money and still break even on the investment.

After having calculated and compared the IRR's (of all the investments), the highest rate shows the best investment, and the system must be developed, under the presupposition that this rate of return is greater than the cost of capital, i.e. the interest the company has to pay to borrow money.

It is well known that the planning of investments is based on an estimation of future conditions and, hence, includes the element of uncertainty; uncertainty, irrespective of its origins, always embraces risks. Thus, a certain degree of risk is included in every investment that should be considered during decision making for systems development.

We can say that the risk of unacceptable result always exists during investment planning, as it is based on predictions concerning time and cost of systems development, and systems life.

Given the existence of risks, traditional criteria for the evaluation of systems are no longer reliable; for example, an analysis based on the methods of net present value and internal rate of return, indicates to what degree the system will have an acceptable return; it is quite possible that such an analysis shall fail, since it does not make any provision for a possible associated risk, which may be as high as 50%, and which will lead the investment to fail.

In order that the risk during the planning of investments for TMIS's be limited, it is essential that the following actions be taken:

- Each system having a high uncertainty degree must be divided into two or more systems to be developed, (but these systems are to operate as sub-systems of one integrated system).
- Review points and revision of the plan for each investment, must be determined in a clear cut and precise manner.

A hypothetical example (result) of Risk Analysis in the development of two IS's is depicted graphically in "Fig. 1".

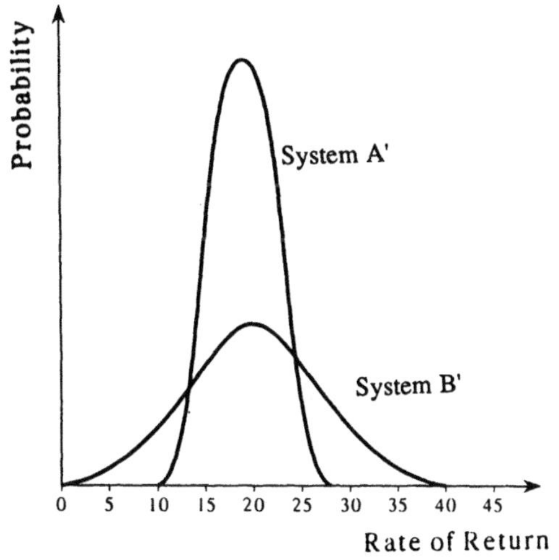

"Fig. 1" *Graphical depiction of a hypothetical result of Risk Analysis in the development of Systems A' and B'.*

In this, the probability function of the rate of return of the investment in each one of the systems, shows that the investment in System A' could equally achieve the highest, as well as the lowest rate or return, and that the investment in System B' is unlikely to achieve a return higher than 25% or less than 10%. From this, we can see the influencing by Risk Analysis of the person who shall decide on the investments, in his undertaking to choose between differing investments for systems development.

Risk is generally expressed in terms of probability that a given event will occur. It is true that the quality of a prediction is higer when the probability results from the processing of historical data of similar past events. However, historical data usually does not exist and the probabilities are based on subjective opinions.

Business managers are frequently characterized by adjectives which refer to their capacity for decision making on planning and their leadership; there does not exist, however, one word which characterizes their capability regarding their outlook on risk, and the application of the appropriate policies needed to confront it. It is a fact that the more the experience of managers or analysts increases, the more the degree of uncertainty and risk from the investments decreases.

It is thus very important how experienced the users and the systems analysts are, when giving their estimates for each cash flow showing its values in the worst, most likely, and best cases. However, it is not so easy to estimate these values, as they usually have to quantify such elements as the life of the system, the costs to develop and run the system, the benefits, and so on. This problem can be overcome using the Simulation Technique.

The Technique of Simulation under Risk permits systems analysts to specify a range and the nature of the frequency distribution for each cash flow.

Values for each cash flow will be selected at random from that cash flow's estimated frequency distribution and used in calculating a total value of the investment (system).

The Triangular Probability Distribution that can be used for the selection of sample values for each "cash flow" (values of x) on which the Simulation shall be based, is graphed in "Fig. 2".

This figure depicts the distribution of the various values; the "sum" of all the associated probabilities is equal to 1.00 (100%); therefore, the area of the triangle must equal 1.00.

As an illustrative example, we take values of x for the worst, most probable, and best cases, i.e. values of 0, 2, and 4 respectively.

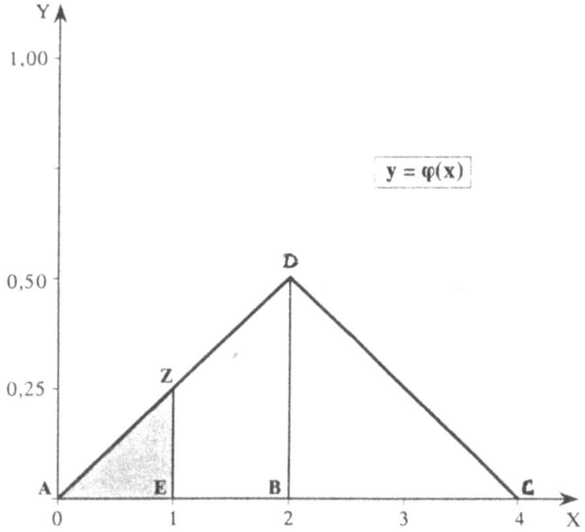

"Fig. 2" *Triangular Probability Distribution for x=0 (worst case), x=2 (most probable case) and x=4 (best case).*

Since the area of the triangle ACD equals 1, AB=2, AE=1, BC=2, AC=4, etc. (Fig. 2), we can easily calculate BD.

$$(ACD) = \frac{(AB)\cdot(BD)}{2} + \frac{(BC)\cdot(BD)}{2} = 1$$

$$\frac{2\cdot(BD)}{2} + \frac{2\cdot(BD)}{2} = 1$$

and (BD) = 0.5

Knowing BD, it is easy to calculate EZ, using the known relation:

$$\frac{AE}{AB} = \frac{EZ}{BD}$$

from which we get

$$(EZ) = \frac{(AE)\cdot(BD)}{AB}$$

where the area of triangle AEZ is

$$(AEZ) = \frac{(AE)\cdot(EZ)}{2} = \frac{(AE)^2\cdot(BD)}{2(AB)} = \frac{1^2 \bullet 0.5}{2\bullet 2} = 0.125$$

This section of the area of triangle ACD in the left-hand side of the perpendicular EZ (triangle AEZ), projected along the base AC, after the relevant calculations, is depicted in "Fig. 3".

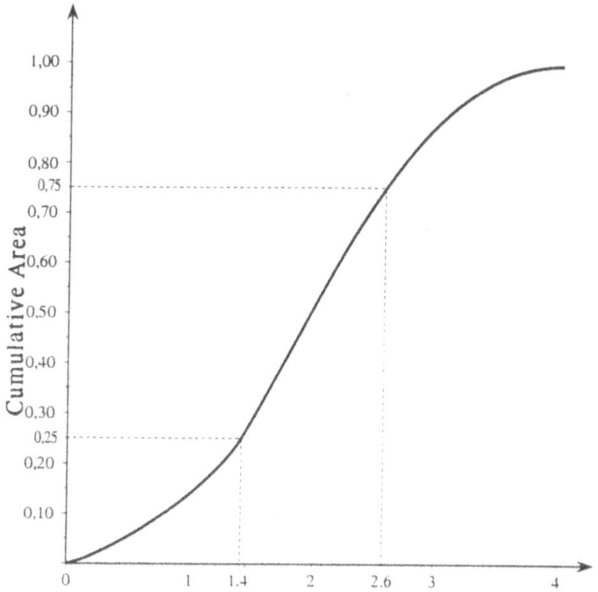

"Fig. 3" *Cumulative area for all values of x from 0 to 4, inclusive ($0 \leq x \leq 4$).*

In this, one can observe that 50% of the total area (from 0.25 up to 0.75 of the cumulative area) corresponds to values of x from approximately 1.4 to 2.6. The span of 1.2 between these values, is approximately 30% of the area of probable values of x.

In every case where a sample value of "cash flow" is chosen, a random* number is generated between 0.000 and 1000. This number is used as a "cumulative area" and, at the same time, leads to the determination of the apporapriate value of x.

In the previous example, if we suppose that the random number 0.250 has been "generated", then (approximaterly) 1.4 should be chosen as a value for x.

3. The Proposed IS for Financial Justification of TMIS Development

Considering all the above, an IS is proposed and its

* Random numbers are generated in such a fashion, so that each one of them has the same probability of "coinciding" with any number between 0.000 and 1000, and are converted to "cash flow" values by the appropriate probability distribution.

general aspects and flow chart are presented hereunder:

The procedure of this system with regard to consideration of risk operates as follows:

- The system accepts values for the worst, most likely, and best cases.
- Systems analyst selects sample values (sample cash flows table creation) ranging between the worst and the best cases, with an emphasis on values closest to the most likely case.
- As the sum of all probalities is equal to 1 or 100%, a random number between 0 and 1 is selected, by a program of the system, for each sample cash flow value and gives its corresponding probability (cumulative area figure).

This procedure is repeated as many times as the systems analyst considers sufficient.

Because the consideration of risk takes place after the calculations of the IRR's, it is certain that the error of discounting the same things again is avoided.

Basically, the proposed IS will have as **Input** (per system/investment) information on the possible values of cash flow (benefits, costs), will calculate the NPV (Routine R3 of the Flow Chart) and/or the IRR (Routine R4) and will use the simulation technique (Routine R5) for the consideration of risk. The system will have as **Output** listings with the NPV's and IRR's, together with the corresponding probabilities for the attainment of any defined level.

Finally, the System will advise the consideration of some non financial criteria (Routine R9), in case an investment (system) is financially not worthwhile.

3.1 IS Flow Chart

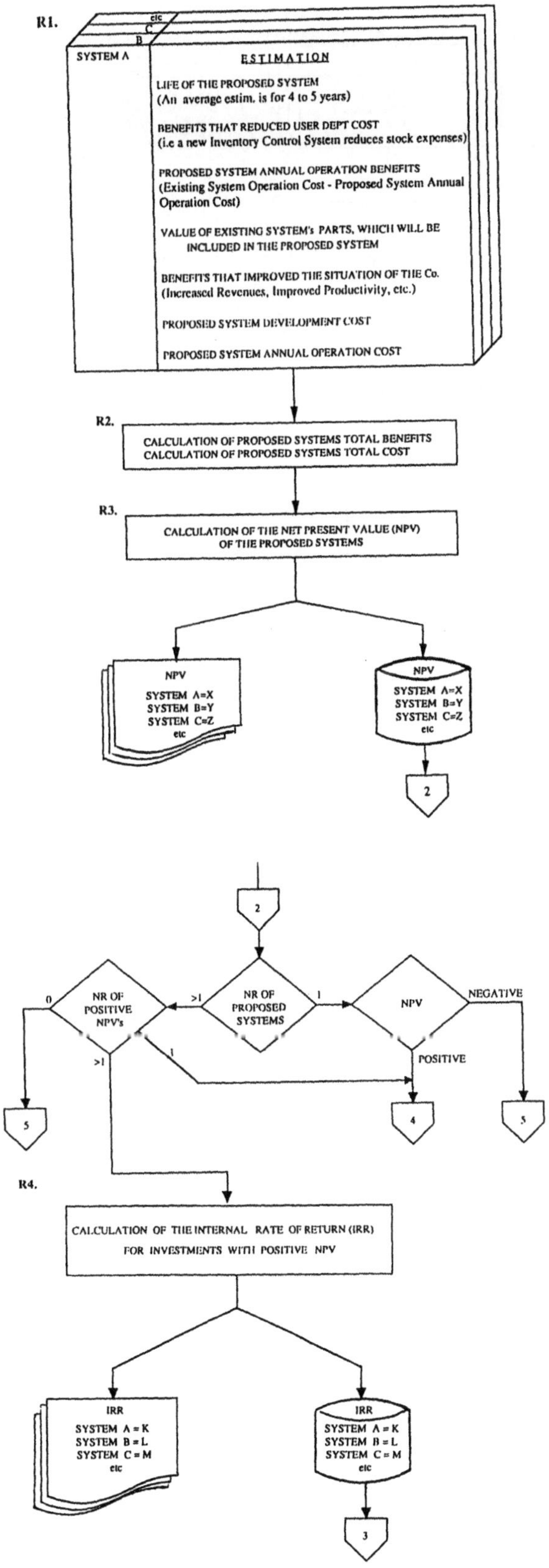

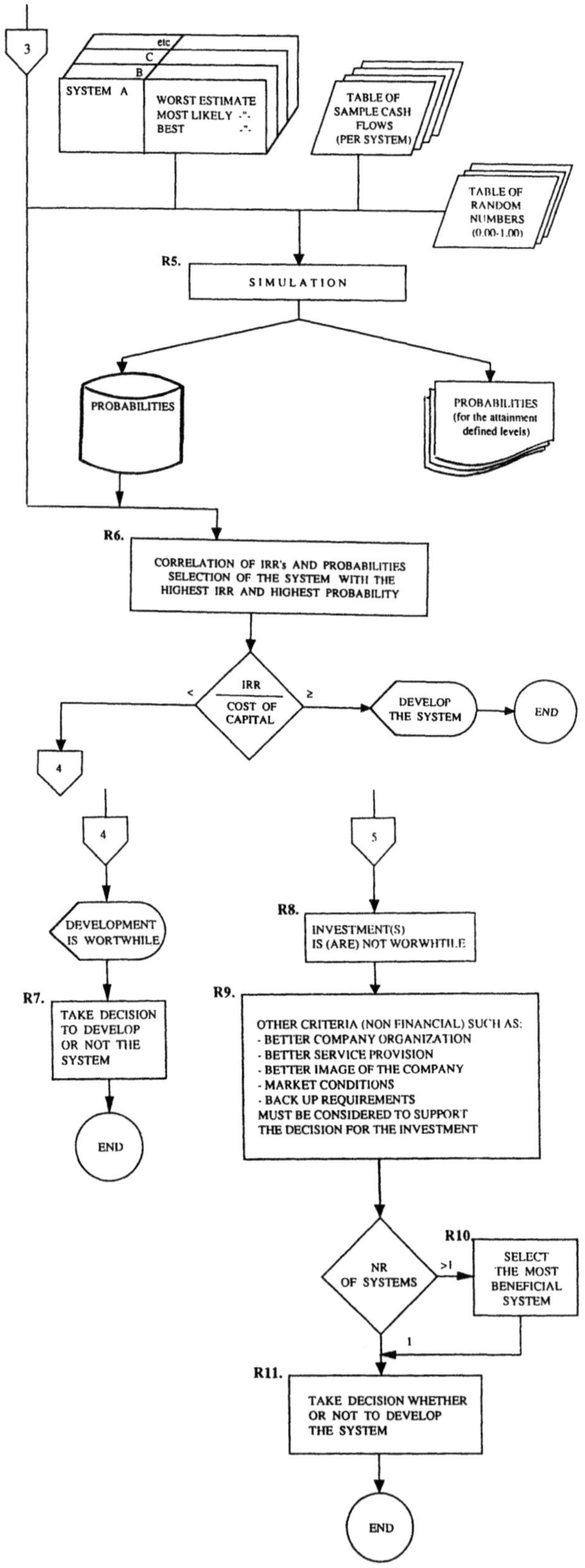

<u>References</u>

1. Burke, J.F., Computerized management of tourism marketing information : Tourism Management, 12/1989, 279 (1989).
2. Crouch, G.I., Expert Computer Systems in Tourism / Emerging Possibilities : Journal of Travel Research, 2 / winter 1991, 3 (1991).
3. Buzzel, R., Cox, D., Brown, R. : Marketing Research and Information Systems. New York - St. Louis - San Francisco - London - Sydney - Toronto - Mexico - Panama : Mcgraw-Hill Book Company 1969.
4. Gillenson, M., Goldberg, R. : Strategic Planning, Systems Analysis & Database Design. New York- Chichester - Brisbane - Toronto - Singapore : John Wiley & Son 1984.
5. Handscombe, R. Norman, P. : Strategic Leadership. London - New York : McGraw-Hill Book Company 1989.
6. Howard, K. : Quantitative Analysis for Planning Decisions : Macdonald & Evans Ltd 1975.
7. MacFarlan, F.W., Mckenney, J.L. : Corporate Information Systems Management / The Issues Facing Senior Executives. Homewood, Illinois : Richard D. Irwin, Inc. 1983.

STRATEGIC PLANNING TOOLS INSIDE THE MARKETING-INFORMATION-SYSTEM IN USE BY THE AUSTRIAN NATIONAL TOURIST OFFICE

Karl W. Wöber

Institute of Tourism and Leisure Studies
Vienna University of Economics and Business Administration, Austria

Abstract

In the 1980s national and regional tourist offices experienced profound changes in their environment. The complexity of business has increased with the growth of the number of products and services produced in multiplying markets. Competition and pressures from other suppliers have intensified. It is not surprising that these factors have brought changes in the information demands of organizations. This paper describes a framework for understanding the role of information and executive information systems in national tourist offices which has proved useful in research and consultation.

Introduction

We are familiar with the phenomenon of private and public research institutions publishing one study after another while tourism managers still tend to base their decisions on rough estimates, without the backing of reliable and solid data. This exposes a lack of collaboration between tourism researchers and those in the field. In other words, the problem is not so much a lack of data as a lack of easy and fast information retrieval.

Most countries in the world have used the enormous advances in computing to create systems that more or less extensively record tourism data. Nevertheless, some countries have encountered difficulties in efficiently using this data for advertising purposes or to plan their marketing strategies in conjunction with various decision support techniques.

During the past two decades, the processing of a growing volume of information has become a major problem, and this is a difficulty that is not only being faced by the international tourist trade. For this reason alone, it has become essential to create a database that gives users efficient access to all the future-oriented opportunities that computer technology can offer us. In other words, we need a database that gives untrained personnel access to simple-to-operate, user-friendly functions.

Outline of the project

The destination organization sector of the tourism industry comprises the various tourist offices and tourist associations [1]. At the country level we have national tourist offices (NTOs); these are government-funded organizations and most of their operations are performed on a non-commercial basis. NTOs are supplemented at a lower level by regional and local tourist offices. The marketing function of an NTO includes advertising the country internationally and nationally as a tourist destination (this is the "product" of the company), which aims to emphasize the various general attractions that the country offers to tourists. Further marketing activities undertaken by NTOs include the provision of appropriate marketing research studies and the maintenance of information centres.

Since 1984, Austria's NTO has been using a decision support instrument called TourMIS. TourMIS was fundamentally updated at the beginning of 1990, and an extensive database is now available to tourism managers on national and regional level. This PC-aided decision support system was set up by the Austrian Society of Applied Research in Tourism (ASART) together with the Institute of Tourism and Leisure Studies at Vienna's University of Economics and Business Administration. The project was realized in close collaboration with the Market Research Department of the National Tourist Office.

After a two-year trial period, TourMIS was installed at six other branches in Austria. Three companies run TourMIS in a local area network, thus giving more than 50 users access to the tourism data. This success has encouraged the author to continually update the system. Step by step, new planning tools to the system's retrieval functions have been added. These analytical tools help users deal with complex and poorly structured administrative and strategic management problems. The manager uses TourMIS to learn about the tourism environment and take action with respect to it. Currently TourMIS consists of three components (see Fig. 1):

1. A retrieval system for storage and access to key marketing variables by a user friendly interface,
2. several procedures for basic statistical operations (divided into a formulation and a calculation part), and
3. a methods and models interface containing several planning and decision making tools like portfolio presentation, analytic hierarchy processing and budget optimization.

1. The retrieval system

The first and in many ways the most critical element in a decision support system is the user interface. The manager and his stuff must communicate with the system. The new design of the software allows rapid retrieval of data and comfortable production of print-outs of tables

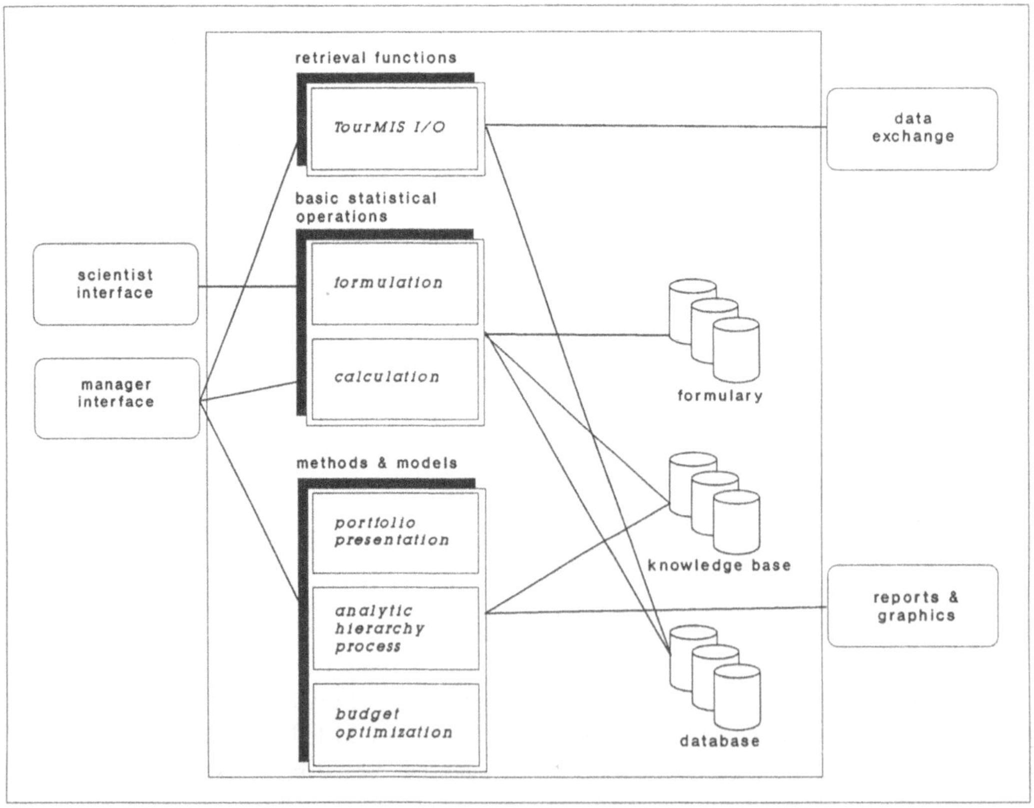

Fig. 1. TourMIS system design
State of development

and graphs, even if the operator is inexperienced.

TourMIS stores data of international travel statistics, the results of travel and guest surveys and selected economic indicators for the countries of origin. It gives tourism managers access to a large number of information sources that were previously unknown or inaccessible to them via a PC. The program provides access to a total of 10,000 time series (which corresponds to about 15 MByte of storage). Depending on the complexity of the data, enquiries are processed in just 2 to 10 seconds.

The data are maintained centrally by the Institute of Tourism to ensure that different sources with different ways of surveying destination countries deliver comparable data. The Institute of Tourism carefully rectifies distorted and incomplete data. In general, all data are updated annually. However, more crucial time series are recorded monthly. The maintenance of demographic data is carried out as soon as the data have been published.

2. Statistical Operations

Statistical operations range from simple (addition, subtraction, etc.) to the most sophisticated multivariate techniques (factor analysis, non-linear parameter estimations, etc.). As simpler statistical functions are frequently the most useful, they are part of the TourMIS program. Simple statistical functions include adding (making significant figures from many smaller), taking ratios, making comparisons, plotting relationships, identifying exceptional cases, and the like.

Even untrained operators are able to use TourMIS to calculate all needed ratios such as market volume and its growth rate, absolute and relative market share and guest-mix ratios of important generating countries. Although the formulae used for calculations are laid down by tourism experts (in the "formulation" part of the program), the actual calculations are carried out simply by pressing a button (in the "calculation" part of the program).

3. The methods and models interface

Strategic decisions in the tourism industry include issues such as which markets are most attractive (e.g. have highest visitor expenditure potential); in which markets are a specific country's "products" most competitive; how promotional budgets should be allocated for greatest effectiveness; and what the promotional message should convey [2]. The most widely used methods of strategic planning techniques are portfolio models, where a company is viewed as a portfolio of individual businesses or products and brands. The simplest model is the growth-share matrix which was developed by the Boston Consulting Group (BCG) and consists of three assessment criteria for products:[3],[4]

- market growth rate (attractiveness)
- relative market share (performance), and
- contribution to overall sales (importance).

In this approach the company classifies all of its strategic business units (SBUs) in the business portfolio matrix. The assessment criteria are portrayed along the vertical axis representing growth rate, the horizontal axis representing relative share, and through the diameter of circles representing the importance value for each major generating country. A practical example of the growth share matrix applied to tourist receiving countries give also Mazanec and Calantone [5]. TourMIS uses this kind of portfolio presentation as its communication interface.

Each quadrant represents a distinct type of success situation (stars are high-growth, high-share SBUs; cash cows are low-growth, high-share SBUs; question marks are low-share, high-growth SBUs; and dogs are low-share, low-growth SBUs). Recommended decisions and strategies for products and markets in the various quadrants of the matrix are only suggestive, and not prescriptive. Additional insights into the desirability of pursuing these suggestions can be gained through four additional kinds of analysis:[3]

- share momentum analysis
- product portfolio trajectory analysis
- analysis of major competitors' portfolio

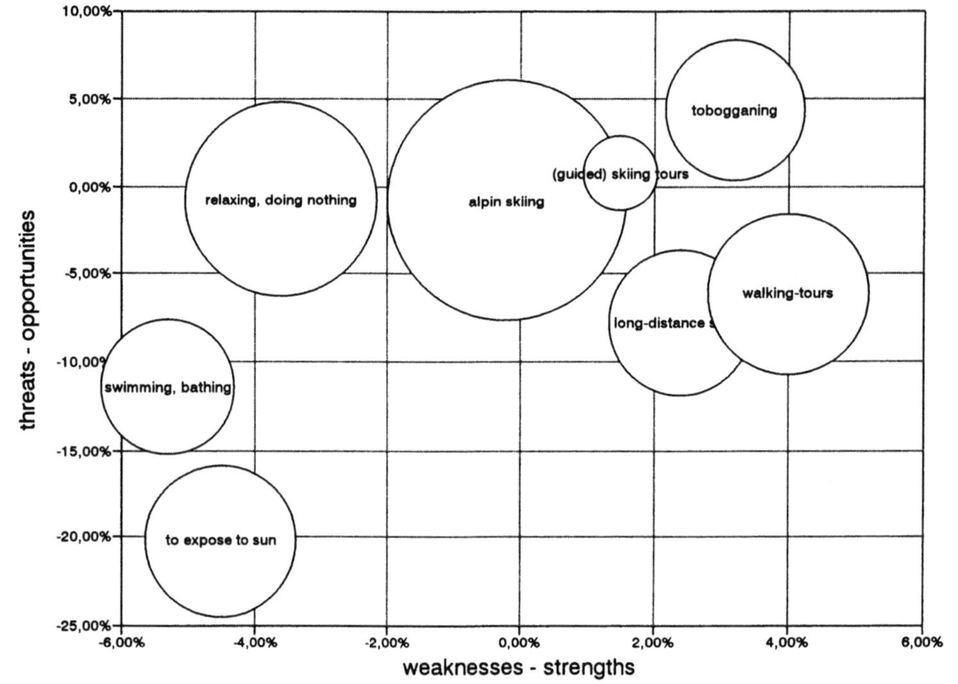

Fig. 2. Share momentum analysis
German guests tend to more alternative winter sports - results from the Austrian guest survey (Gästebefragung Österreich (GBÖ), winter 1989 and 1992)

Share momentum analysis

Share momentum analysis examines the relationship between the growth rate of a strategic business unit and its served market. Three possibilities exist: share growth, share maintenance and share erosion. Figure 2 shows a comparison of the Austrian guest survey 1989 and 1992 where the German guests tend to more alternative winter sports. During the last winter seasons tobogganing and tour-skiing are the new passions of German guests in Austria. For an individual country like Tyrol which has its strengths in exactly these sort of activities strong promotional effort will be very effective.

Product portfolio trajectory analysis

Analysis of a firm's portfolio at a given point in time provides only a static perspective. Development of portfolio matrices for previous time periods using historical data to track the portfolio trajectory (the progression or movement of SBUs over a period of time) may be warranted to analyze trends and gain a dynamic perspective. Portfolio matrix scenarios can be developed for future years on the basis of projected market growth rates and tentative decisions regarding the market share strategies for the various SBUs. Tracing the trajectory of individual SBUs in years past and for future years could provide insights into past successful and disastrous paths taken by SBUs, prospects for maintaining a balanced portfolio in future years, and the need to develop new SBUs to overcome present imbalances and the likelihood of future portfolio imbalances. With TourMIS the success or failure of marketing measures can be evaluated with deviation analysis based on the sequential presentation of portfolio diagrams or by comparing competitors' product portfolios. Figure 3, for example, shows the development of Austria's growth/share matrix from 1981 to 1999 for selected generating countries.

Analysis of portfolio imbalances

Firms strive for a balanced portfolio of SBUs under the BCG approach. In respect to the field of tourism we are all common with fair-share and guest-mix problems. The presence of a fair number of SBUs in the "star" and "cash cow" quadrants is a sign of a healthy and balanced portfolio. Assuming a large number of SBUs in the "cash cow" quadrant, but very few in the "star" quadrant could be an indication that a tourist region is having a glorious present, but an uncertain future. As the market evolves over time, declining market growth rates would shrink the size of the market for today's "cash cows". As high-growth markets become mature low-growth markets over time, a region currently without SBUs in the "star" quadrant will find itself without "cash cows" in the future.

Analysis of major competitors' portfolios

A firm should not base its market share strategy decisions solely on its portfolio of businesses. Every attempt should be made to develop similar matrices for major competitors. Imbalances in the portfolios of some competitors and strengths in the portfolios of others may provide insights into the strategies they are likely to pursue.

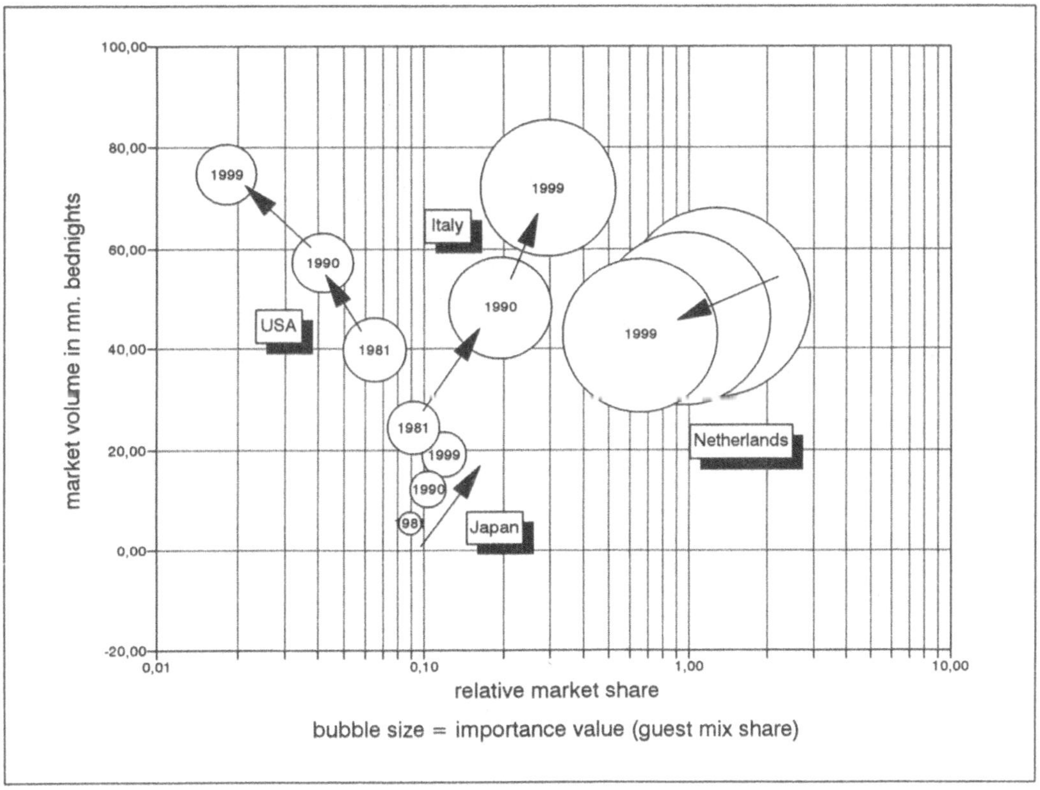

Fig. 3. Product portfolio trajectory analysis
The development of Austria's growth/share matrix for selected generating countries
(1981 - 1999)

For important SBUs additional gain and loss analysis can be necessary. In TourMIS period performance and destination preferences of 20 different generating countries are constantly monitored on the basis of bednights sold. For Austria's NTO the comparison with 9 major European receiving countries gives a proxy for relative profit performance. The system also offers this new approach for monitoring the competitive success and failure of regional tourism planning (see Fig. 4).

Analytic Hierarchy Processing

There is considerable disagreement concerning the adequacy of the growth-share matrix approach using single factors as indicators of industry attractiveness and a firm's competitive position [6]. Multifactor portfolio matrix models like the General Electric/McKinsey business screen portfolio matrix, the Arthur D. Little life cycle portfolio matrix or the Shell directional policy matrix (for a brief introduction see [3] and [7]) reveal differences in perspective, methodology, assumptions, data, conclusions and implications. However, all of these approaches allow for two or more assessment criteria to be condensed into each of the two dimensions named market attractiveness and business or competitive position.

Clearly, the factors employed to determine market attractiveness or business position are not of equal importance and have to be weighted. In this context multi-criteria decision making (MCDM) has been widely studied in Management Science/Operations Research (see [8], [9], [10], [11] and [12] as examples of the very large MCDM literature) and the resulting theories and methods have been applied in several fields, such as marketing, group decision support and computer assisted negotiation (for the role of MCDM inside of executive information systems

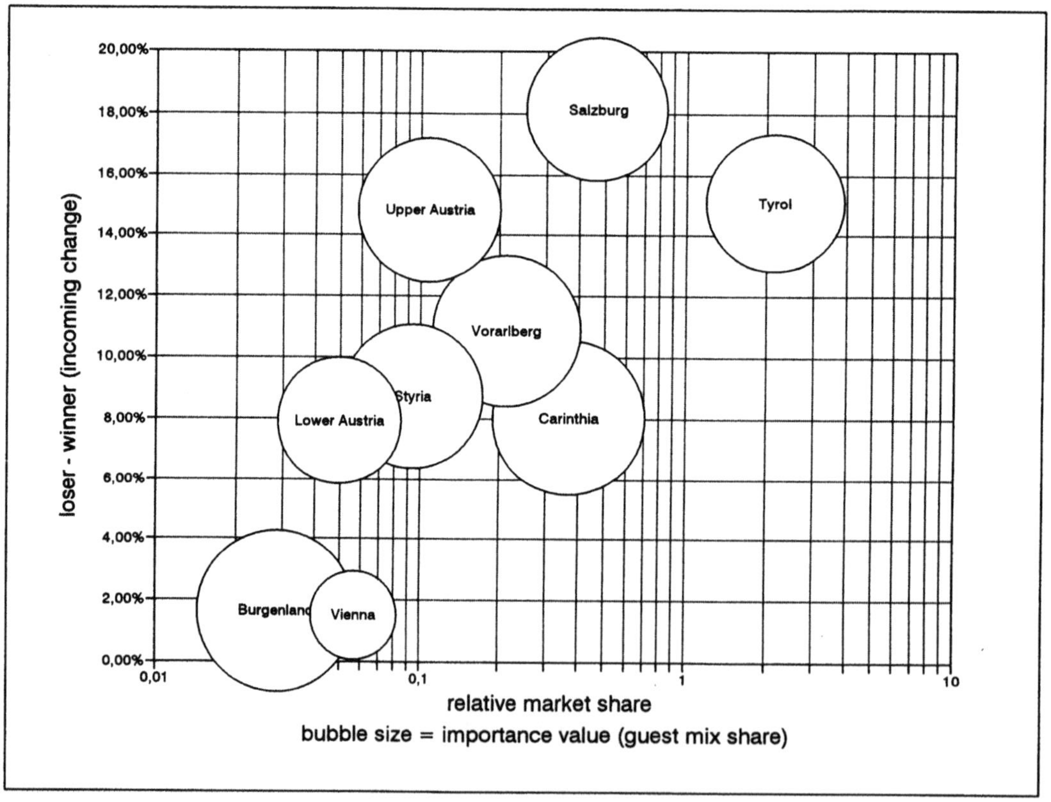

Fig. 4. Analysis of major competitor's portfolio
Nine Austrian regions competing for the
German's outgoing 1988-1989 measured by nights in all accommodations

see also French and Angehrn in [13]).

This rating task, of course, needs some PC assistance. In TourMIS an analytical hierarchical model (AHP) permits the strategic assessment of alternative possibilities. The procedures for the individual estimation of the necessary weightings are elicited by pair-wise comparison followed by transformation into a cardinal scale (see [11] and [14]).

The quality of the weight estimations fully depends on the managers making the judgments, on their competence, experience, and willingness to cooperate. For this purpose the implemented procedure (for the algorithmic details of the eigenvector method see [8]) includes a measure to check the internal consistency of the managerial judgments. Only consistent judgments are stored in the database for later use and revision. Finally, in addition to the above mentioned traditional portfolio approaches, multifactor models are generated with the system. Therefore all the judgments can be combined with data from the TourMIS database. Most of the weights and data estimated for establishing the multifactor portfolios are also available for other major decision making processes. This instrument, for example, is used by the Austrian National Tourist Office for an optimization task when dividing up its annual advertising budget between its branch offices and tourism-generating countries (see [15] and [16]). Calantone and di Benedetto also demonstrate the use of the AHP-method in a tourism application. This application involves the assessment of alternative redevelopment scenarios at a state park. The article provides an example of the application of this technique and also the outcome of the decision process (see [17]; also [18] and [19]).

The PC-aided interactive support of multi-criteria decision making allows the decision maker to evaluate visually the impact of different criteria on a "rational" ranking (weighting scores) of the alternatives. Equally important is that the decision maker is not obliged to accept the rankings proposed by the system. The major aim of using a mathematical method for generating such a ranking is not to deliver "optimal solutions". The method here rather plays the role of a "rational myth" which stimulates the user to understand and express their preferences (in this context see also Little's idea of a "decision calculus" [20]).

Summary

For a national or regional tourist office operating in a changing environment, management is required to assess how forces in the environment and within their own organizations will effect future prospects. Therefore, information technologies have significant impact on business success. Most countries in the world have used the enormous advances in computing to create information systems that more or less extensively record tourism data. The two principal functions of information systems are processing information and then communicating it. The world of communication is changing faster than the processing world and the changes within the next ten years will be even more crucial.

Experience has shown that it is not possible to create a turnkey decision support system for the top-level management of a tourist office. A willingness to combine management science with practice is necessary before one can be sure of a necessary minimum of acceptance of such an application. As anticipated in the introductory section, the alternative support perspective and the design guidelines proposed in TourMIS lead to a different kind of decision support system. The paramount characteristics of this system are

- the high level of human-computer interaction achieved during a decision making process, and
- the object to support user in a better understanding and communication of their decisions rather than to "solve" them.

The real benefit is centered in the process which requires hard, strategic thinking by all those involved. Discussions between managers open up new possibilities for future options and a richer set of strategic choices emerge after the work is done. Moreover, the simple visual format of output offered in TourMIS is relatively easy to grasp and, in itself, stimulates more useful thinking.

References

1. Witt, S.F., Brooke, M.Z., Buckley, R.J.: The Management of international tourism, London: Unwin Hyman 1991.
2. Henshall, B.D., Roberts, R.: Annals of Tourism Research, 12(2), 219 (1985)
3. Day, G.S.: Journal of Marketing, 41 (April), 29 (1977)
4. Wind, Y., Mahajan, V.: Harvard Business Review, Jan-Feb, 155 (1981)
5. Calantone, R.J., Mazanec, J.A.: Annals of Tourism Research, 18(1), 101 (1991)
6. Wind, Y., Mahajan, V., Swire, D.J.: Journal of Marketing, 47 (2), 89 (1983)
7. Kerin, R.A.: Mahajan, V., Varadarajan, P.R., Contemporary perspectives on strategic market planning, Boston: Allyn and Bacon 1990.
8. Hwang, Ch.-L., Yoon, Kw.: Multiple Attribute Decision Making, Methods and Applications, A State-of-the-Art Survey, Berlin-Heidelberg-New York: Springer 1981.
9. Roy, B.: The outranking approach and the foundations of ELECTRE methods, in: Bana e Costa, Carlos A. (Ed.): Reading in multiple criteria decision aid, Berlin-Heidelberg-New York: Springer 1990.
10. Hansen, P.: Essays and surveys on multiple criteria decision making, Proceedings, Mons. Berlin-Heidelberg-New York: Springer 1982.
11. Saaty, T.L.: The Analytic Hierarchy Process. New York/London/Toronto: McGraw-Hill 1980.
12. Vincke, P.: Multicriteria decision-aid, Chichester: Wiley 1992.
13. Holtham, C (Ed.).: Executive Information Systems and Decision Support. London: Chapman & Hall 1992.
14. Dyer, R.F., Forman, E.H.: An analytic approach to marketing decisions, Englewood Cliffs: Prentice-Hall 1991.
15. Mazanec, J.: International Journal of Research in Marketing, 13, 609 (1986)
16. Mazanec, J.A.: Annals of Tourism Research, 13(4), 609 (1986)
17. Calantone, R.J., di Benedetto, C.A.: Annals of Tourism Research, 18(2), 202 (1991)
18. Mazanec, J.: How to evaluate a travel market, econometric modeling vs. multiattribute decision making with management estimates, Aix-en-Provence: Les Cahiers du Tourisme (Centre des Hautes Etudes Touristiques) 1986.
19. Wind, Y., Saaty, T.L.: Management Science, 26 (July), 641 (1980)
20. Little, J.D.C.: Management Science, 16 (April), 466 (1970)

INTEGRATING TOURISM SERVICES VIA GATEWAYS

Gregorio Lella, Gianluca Lo Reto

SARITEL S.p.A. Sarin Telematica
S.S. 148 Pontina Km. 29,100 00040 Pomezia Italy

The objective of the RACE TIM project is the provision of a European wide network of services which will support the direct marketing of tourism products.

In order to be able to provide customers with reliable and timely information, available through all tourism sources the TIM Gateway will complete the available options connecting to information sources, and will permit the reservation process linking the relevant CRSs.

The multiplication of on-line information and CRS services, has made it impossible for an average user to cope with the large number of command languages, operational modes, communication protocols or simply with the diversity of available services.

The TIM Gateway is aimed to minimise this kind of obstacle, providing a uniform interface and a seamless access to information/reservation services.

Introduction

TIM[1] challenge is to develop a system that meets the needs of tourism markets, by the provision of a European wide network of services which will support the direct marketing of tourism products [1][2].

To succeed in it, besides using new multimedia techniques for information services (distributed on ISDN and IBC networks), the users require the integration with existing information & reservation services.

For the overall TIM system it is a major user requirement to integrate the multimedia tools used to identify the products to sell, with the tools for formalizing the sales. The TIM gateway will permit a reservation process linking each point-of-sale to the relevant CRSs (Computerized Reservation Systems) and will complete the available options connecting to external information sources.

The multiplication of on-line information and CRS services, has made it difficult for an average user to cope with the large number of command languages, operational modes, communication protocols or simply with the diversity of available services offered by each CRS.

This situation is made worse by the lack of agreed standards.

The TIM gateway is aimed at minimizing these kinds of obstacle, providing a uniform interface and a seamless access to information/reservation services.

It will permit thus, an integration of the user environment with the external world, bringing a more efficient tool for travel management.

In particular, TIM Gateway will provide the users with many benefits:

- One Access Point: the user will not deal with multiple connection cable, network management, etc., but just with a single TIM connection. The TIM Gateway will manage the other connections on request;
- Better service: an efficient and effective tool for travel management. Using all the TIM functionalities, the user will easily select a tourist offer and then formalise this, automatically performing all the needed reservations;
- Integration: a unique query/reservation language is used to access every CRS;
- Better dissemination of information: using the TIM Gateway, it will be possible both to export and to import every kind of information;

---

[1]TIM (Tourism Information and Marketing) is a project supported by the European Communities, under the RACE program. The TIM consortium includes: DeTeBerkom, Alcatel-SEL, IFC Research, Alcatel-TITN, Alcatel-Espace, Alcatel-FYCSA, Télésystèmes, Saritel, Alitalia, MARI, Institut Cerdà, IDATE, Norsk Regnesentral, NTU Athens, IBIEF, Northern Ireland Tourist Board, Bord Failte, RACC, Generalitat Catalunya, Thomas Cook, Département de L'Herault, Ministère du Tourisme, MediaPark Köln, Reisebüro Schenker, Troll Park, Lillehammer Olympic Development Association

- Increased productivity;
- Possibility to bridge the gap between the developed and less developed areas of tourism services;
- Commitment to strengthening the reservation areas coverage by adding new CRS connections when needed.

Gateway Functionalities

In the first phase of the project we have obtained an agreement on the most important tasks performed by twelve TIM point-of-sale user companies i.e. travel agencies, tourism boards for import tourism, etc. Their objectives include: obtaining access to a much larger range of product offers, having access to more appealing and accurate product descriptions, and streamlined booking of complex multi-vendor products.

In [3] the following generic tasks for gateways have been identified:

- remote booking using a text based system:

  it involves a tour operator or travel agent booking e.g. a hotel, via a remote database. Occupancy information is sought at the same time in order that a booking can be made. The type of information used is data only;
- remote booking, usually of a hotel, using a multimedia based system:

  this task is the same as above, except that it involves a wide range of information types;
- booking confirmation sent:

  the CRS sends the booking confirmation and communicates with the human entity via a printer or local terminal;
- communication between databases:

  information is sent from one database (typically a multimedia database) to a CRS. The information is mainly data.

The functionalities that the TIM Gateway must then support will include:

- recognising that the resource being accessed doesn't belong to the local system:

  the Gateway identifies that the local TIM system is making a request to access a remote host;
- translating the access request under the rules required by the remote service;
- translating the answer received from the remote service into the format required by the local TIM system.

The requests made to the remote services will mainly be:

- make an enquiry:

  the human entity makes an enquiry of the remote service tc check availability;
- perform booking:

  the human entity requests that a booking of the required service is made;
- make payment:

  the payment for the confirmed booking is made, which should allow for credit card authorisation (a further investigation is needed on this topic).

The messages from the remote services will include:

- confirmation of the requested booking:

  this will typically be a confirmation slip printed at the local printer.

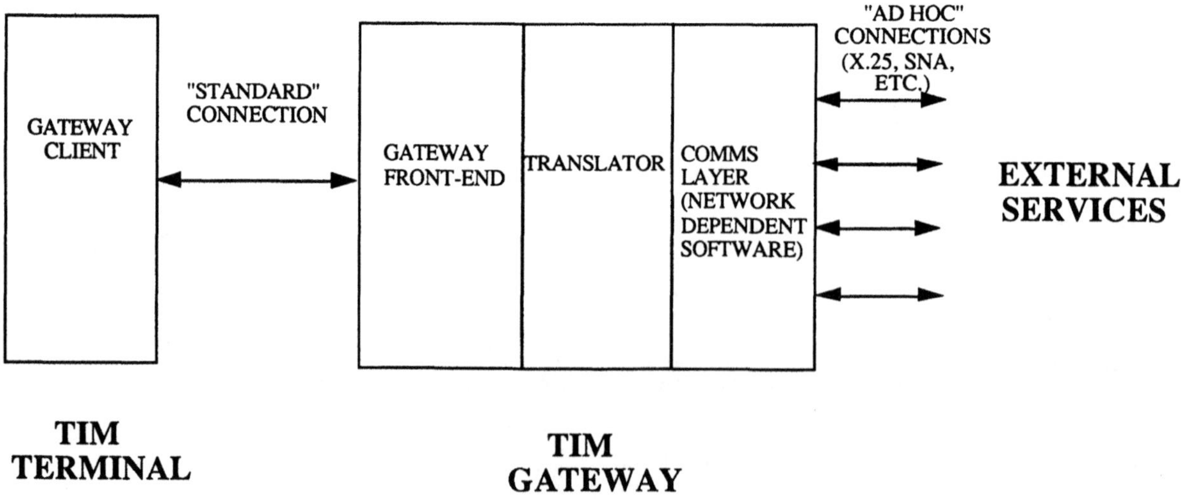

Fig. 1

Issues

There are two types of problems to be faced when implementing a Gateway.

The first ones are those connected with the heterogeneity of the target remote service (different user interfaces, command languages, communications, etc.). In TIM, using the experience gained by some partners in the project TOOTSI[2], we are implementing a tailored interface that will remove those limits. [4]

Furthermore, thanks to the deep commitment to the project of real users, enhancements are foreseen to meet the complexity of tomorrows market.

The second type of problems is peculiar when interfacing CRSs: a traditional gateway approach is not sufficient in this case, and TIM will have to adapt to these new requirements, by improving its telecommunication and operational abilities.

Our current understanding of the overall scenario and of the problems when connecting commercial information and transaction services, has permitted to highlight since now, another set of vital issues (such as security, code of conduct, ticketing, etc.), that must be carefully and thoroughly examined in order to ensure the project success.

Consequently to this awareness, the common TIM architecture and the overall approaches to be adopted in the Gateway, will be designed to allow some flexibility, since it is apparent that dealing with all the different possible constraints will lead to different implementation scenarios.

Technical options

From a technical point of view a Client-Server approach has been chosen that is the most suitable architecture capable for flexibility, scalability and distribution.

Taking into account the description of the existing relevant international standards and industrial trends, the more suitable choice for implementing a Client-Server system able to accept queries formulated in a uniform language and to return it to the user, is the ISO 9579 Remote Database Access.

Furthermore, the project uses the EDIFACT standards (UN Reservation Message and UN Supplier Response) for the definition of the standard message to be exchanged among user applications.

For the "translation phase", that is the passage between the uniform command language and the particular remote service command language, a toolset is being implemented for translation using high level tools based on the result of the ESPRIT project P2109 TOOTSI. [5][6]

In the same way, the "formatting phase", that is the passage between the raw output of the particular CRS to a uniform data model, is supported by high level tools.

Finally, the TIM Gateway also will support many different communication links: ISDN and X.25 for the Client-Server communication, and SNA, X.25, DECNET for the communication between the Gateway Server and the CRSs.

These different communication links will be totally transparent for the user.

In fig. 1, the whole process and the various modules are shown.

- The Client Software running on the TIM Terminal is in charge to accept request from the End-User application, to transform it in transmittable formats and send it to the Server. Furthermore, it accepts the answer from the Server (data or error indications) and returns it to the End-User application;
- The Server Front-End manages the dialogue possibly with multiple Terminals, receiving commands and sending results from/to the line;
- When a command is received it is translated in a command (or a sequence of commands) for the specific remote service. The results obtained are then processed and formatted following a standard definition;
- The dialogue with the specific remote service is managed by the Communication Layer that hides all the different communication links.

Current Development

The implementation work for the TIM Gateway is supported by a workpackage for negotiation with the CRSs used by the TIM user companies.

The current negotiation phase is focused on the following services:

- AMADEUS;
- GALILEO;
- SABRE: the US market leader of the CRS reservation. It is owned by AMR, the parent company of American Airlines;
- IRIS: this is the Reservation system of the Winter'94 Olympics;
- GULLIVER: Reservation system of Irish and Northern Ireland Tourist Boards;
- TELTOUR: Reservation system of the Herault Department in the south of France.

---

[2] TOOTSI (Telematic Object Oriented Tools for Service Interfaces) is an ESPRIT II project, in which some TIM partners are heavily involved

A research agreement has been signed by Galileo, and exchange of technical data has begun with Amadeus, and a research agreement has been proposed to Sabre following initial technical meetings.

A first release of the Gateway environment was used inside the first TIM prototype presented in Florence in late spring '93 which demonstrated a connection to the OAG -Official Airline Guide database based in Illinois USA.

At the end of July '93, after a first set of negotiation meetings, a TIM terminal was connected to Galileo.

We have established a SNA link connection (SDLC) on switched lines between the central Gateway (based in Pomezia Italy) and the Galileo mainframes in Swindon (UK).

A TIM terminal, connecting to the TIM Gateway can now login (password protected) to Galileo test system.

The TIM Gateway toolset is implemented on the UNIX operating system with a SPARC hardware platform, but the software can be executed upon a large variety of hardware platforms, in particular NT-Windows when fully available.

The final implementations will foreseen both specialized gateways at the user sites and a central comprehensive TIM Gateway for international services.

An example

In fig. 2 an actual example of how the TIM Gateway system manages the interaction with the Galileo CRS is presented.

We point out that the Gateway Server navigates through the multiple 3270 terminal screens of the GALILEO user interface (screens 1-7) without affecting the user.

Terminal Client		Server Front-End	Translator	Comm. Layer		GALILEO CRS
Connect(Galileo) OK	X.25	Connect(Galileo) OK	Connect(Galileo) logon XXXX son/YYYY ZZZZZZ sb/ag OK	StartSNA(Galileo) logon XXXX son/YYYY ZZZZZZ sb/ag	SNA	Screen 1 Screen 2 Screen 3 Screen 4 Screen 5

Flight
(depCity=Par and
arrCity=Rom and
date=25Dec and
time=1700)
<record in transmittable format>
		Flight
		(depCity=Par and
		arrCity=Rom and
		date=25Dec and
		time=1700)
		<record in transmittable format>
			A25decparrom
			A.1700
			Flight_List fl =
			{
			Item_Number=1;
			Value=
			{
			ArrCity=ROM
			Avail=CA MA
			DepCity=PAR
			date=25dec
			time=1550
			code=AF638
			desc=NULL
			}
			0x...
			}
				A25decparrom
				A.1700
						Screen 6
						Screen 7

Fig. 2

Acknowledgement

The authors wishes to thank all partners of the RACE TIM project for discussions and comments, most notably Telesystemes team, who has contributed to all significant development of the first prototypes of the TIM Gateways to OAG and Galileo.

We want furthermore to thank Alitalia team for the liaison work currently in progress with the most important CRSs.

References

1. Maartmann-Moe, E., Byerley, P.F., Connell, S., Kvam, P.: Marketing Tourism Products via Advanced Communication Systems: Initial results from the TIM project. Enter Conference Insbruck. (1994).

2. TIM Consortium: TIM Technical Annex. Internal document (1992)

3. Byerley, P.F., Connell, S., et al: Operational Requirements for Marketing Service Creation and Marketing Service Delivery document, TIM Internal document (1992).

4. TIM Consortium: Definition of Data Exchange Formats and Network Interfaces, Internal document (1992)

5. Mahon, B., Meinkohn, F., Lella, G.: TOOTSI: creating a toolkit for building user interfaces to business information services, ONLINE Review 1990, vol 14, n.6

6. Della Vigna R., Lella G., Lo Reto G., Maino D., Mercalli, F.: Issues in mapping on-line service interfaces to an object-oriented data model, Open Systems in a Single Market: Proceedings of the Autumn 1992 OpenForum Business & Strategy Conference: Springer 1992, pag. 127.

IMPROVING SERVICE IN THE FIELD OF TOURISM BY OPEN DISTRIBUTED PROCESSING

Hans Czap

University of Trier, P.O.Box 3825, D 54296 Trier, Germany
+49/651/201-2859, Fax +49/651/201-3959, e-mail:cz@wiinfo.uni-trier.de

Abstract

Open Distributed Processing (ODP) offers interesting capabilities for electronic markets, especially in all those cases where advanced services are offered or sophisticated requests should be met and time is a critical factor of success.
The paper adresses the benefits of ODP against conventional techniques like centralized systems, videotex, or distributed databases, concentrating on economical arguments. In order to show the advantages of this new technology, advanced services are identified which are not supported by the known information- and booking-systems. These deficits serve to introduce the ultimate idea of ODP and to show the most appealing concepts of ODP, namely the trading mechanism, the definition of policies and the integration of ODP-software with existing application-systems.

Keywords

Open Distributed Processing, ODP, Open Systems, Trader, Broker, Policy, Legacy-Applications

1. Electronic Media in the Field of Tourism

Electronic market activities in the field of tourism still suffer from insufficient standardization, thus hindering information flow across different systems. The variety of software systems, i.e the internally used information categories, their names, formats and user interfaces respectively communication interfaces, effectively establishes a market segmentation. The reservation systems in use today only offer a selection of the total market possibilites. Therefore, still the print medium is the only way for customers to gain an overall view of market.

Deficits of the print medium are well known. It does not allow for last minute offers or any additionals installed after printing. Because of shortage of room catalogues are not suited to present any details, for example non-standard services or special quality of an offer. But most important, as an offline nature the print medium does not allow to apply automated selection mechanisms, booking, confirmation, cancellation etc.

Besides the obvious advantages of electronic media, for example running hypermedia-shows to introduce the customer to lodging and surrounding, an online booking system could as well apply special selection policies and accounting routines before confirmation will take place. For example, there might be some priority to regular customers or a check of creditworthy. An other policy could be to select exclusively families with small children or only elderly people and so on.

The possibility to install special policies and to change these policies as one likes, is a key factor in the following.

2. Open Systems as the Ultimate Idea of ODP

In this paper, the term ′open system′ is understood as has been introduced by Hewitt and de Jong (1986). Characteristics of this definition are the lack of a closed user community and the incremental nature of the system. Thus, like the telephone-system, because of a lack of a central controlling instance at any point in time one never knows which connections are in use and which one will be in use next moment. The travel example given by Hewitt and de Jong (1986, p. 150 f) possibly best illustrates, what is meant by the term ′open system′:

"Now assume that the traveler wants to take a vacation in Europe. The traveler′s desire to travel to Europe must be communicated to the travel agent. The process of communication would have to go on at different levels in a dialogue in order to negotiate a European trip. The travel agent must book flights, ground transportation, and hotels. This requires the interfacing with multiple computer systems and conceptual models. The traveler must arrange financing. This might require a negotiating process with the banker or with multiple bankers in order to get the best loan rate. At any step in the problem-solving activity, a problem might arise that would require an approach different from the one corrently being pursued. If the traveler has a limit of $ 4000, and the current trip plan is $ 5000, an adjustment must be made. Perhaps some four star hotels can be replaced by two star hotels. A festival in one country be missed, which would allow a train trip to be substituted for an airplane trip"

Consequently, as characteristical features of ′open systems′ the following might be noted:

(1) Distributed timecritical processing

As the example shows time is a critical factor in these negotiating processes as far as an immediate reply to a request is necessary. In addition, reservation data must be stored at the local computer sites in order to support local information processing. As a consequence, any request for a travelling arrangement, must ask different service providers to send suited offers. To put it in more computational terms: Any request entered in the network by some user in general will generate at different computer-nodes processes for answering. A simple file transfer which is the common technology of Local Area Networks (LAN) today will not suffice. At least a concept like 'Remote Procedure Call' (RPC) is needed, augmented by globale consistency mechanisms like global transactions and recovery.

(2) Openess and incremental nature

Clearly, an advanced service only will be given, if the system is open to any service provider not only with respect to travelling but also with respect to financing, sporting activites, health services and so on. If the situation requires it, these service providers enter into the market and disapear again. Thus, the network has to adapt to these changes, i.e. it must be of incremental nature.

(3) Transparency with respect to heterogenous hardware- and software-systems

As an absolute necessity an open distributed processing application must run on top of existing hardware and operating systems. These systems are owned by different people serving quite different purposes. Thus one has to take heterogeneity into account.

On the other hand, any application based on an open system wouldn't be used, if the user has to become acquainted with different hardware, operating software, storage-systems or user interfaces. Therefore, any ODP-application has to support transparency of place and system.

(4) Interoperability

Performance of selecting and updating procedures as well as the necessity to keep the stored data consistent with reality favors the storage of booking data at the local sites. Thus, local booking-systems must respond to data and messages of the global reservation system (interoperability).

(5) Local Autonomy and Abstract Data Type (ADT)

Interoperability and transparency can only be achieved, if the system in question does not need any knowledge of local specialites of any computer-node in the network. Thus, any local data or information which is needed globally or elswhere must be provided by the local system itself, reacting to specific requests. In other words, viewing the local systems from outside, they have to behave in parts or as a whole like Abstract Data Types (ADTs).

Any ADT is characterized by its interface consisting of a set of procedures and an internal data structure the procedures are acting on. The access to the internal structure is done solely by the procedures of the externally known interface, this way encapsulating the knowledge how the access is implemented. Information flow between different parts of the system can be controlled by messages.

(6) Privacy and Security

Clearly, opening a computer system to unknown users resp. processes, requires enhanced means to guarantee system security.

At any local site, **internal security measurements** could keep track of any request or message passing the system interface to the network and check these events against local security policy. The mentioned ADT-concept supports a local security-policy, since no direct access to data overpassing the interface-procedures is possible.

As an example of a security measurement which might be applied locally, one can consider the concept of confidentiality. Confidentiality is to ensure that only properly authorized individuals or processes can create, use or delete information. In order to guarantee this concept one needs some identification and authentification facilities.

In addition, **global security measurements** are necessary to identify objects as trustworthy and to maintain their integrity, flowing through the network. As an example, consider a reservation-request transmitted, i.e. a data-object which should be imported to change local state. Clearly, there must be some measurements to ensure that there had been no possibilities to change the original state of the object "reservation-request".

3. Architectural Issues of ODP

Since the term "open system" has been used by many different organizations with quite different meanings, the term "open distributed processing" ODP is more suited to emphasize that specific architectural principles will be found in existing systems based on the above ideas.

3.1 Trading

As in the field of tourism, if the provider of a service and it's potential requester don't know about each other, they will need some intermediary agent, like the travel-agency in tourism, to do the matching of service looked for and service offered. This matching of offers and requests is the task of the 'trader' as it is called by APM (Architecture Projects Management Ltd) respectively the 'broker', as it is called by the Object Management Group (OMG).

Any service providers will advertise its services to one ore more (local) traders. Any of these traders itself is a provider of some service, namely the trading service. Announcing this service to other traders will establish a network of interconnected traders and service providers.

Any service-request generated by some user or process will be sent to the trader responsible for this user. In order to match request and offer, the trader searches his repository of service providers (and other traders), selecting all possible providers respectively passing the request on to those traders who are expected to contribute suited providers.

Finally, if a suited offer matching the request is found, an agent is instantiated by the trader binding service provider and requester each other.

3.2 Policies

The process of trading essentially consists of two phases. First, the finding of a set of suited service providers and second, the selecting of one service provider out of the found set. During the first phase, the system is looking for all offers to satisfy the given request, whereas the selection process of the second phase is controlled by applying given policies.
Let's take the example of a traveller looking for a hotel room for one night. In response to the request 'hotel room for a definite night' a list of all hotels having still some vacancy is provided. Besides the desire to sleep, the traveller has some goals regarding price, hotel category, location, room category, services and so on.
On the other hand, the hotel managers themselves run different policies. Some have agreements with special institutions and associations offering price reductions to their members. Some offer special rates to families with children, some won't rent the room for one night only, some forbid animals and so on.
In general, a policy in ODP consists of a goal, a collection of means suited to achieve the goal and a set of constraints controlling selection and application of the means.
As we have seen, both parties, service providers and service requester have their own policies. During phase two of the trading, these policies are used as selecting mechanism.
Policies are not only related to offers and requests. Essentially, they control transactions within and between organizations. Thus, the trading process to bind a service requester to a service provider only will take place, if there is a guiding policy of trading, i.e. some agreement which controls the interaction.

3.3 Architecture

As an illustration of this principal architecture consider the diagram of next page.
Three layers are distinguished. At the back-end, the system side, any database or file system can be used to store data at the local sites. Any request of data generated by the user at the front-end is tranfered to the trader, resp. broker, as a message. After interpretation, the trader transforms this to a sequence of database transactions, thus achieving transparency of storage-systems as well as transparency of location. Details of the front-end are separated from the trader. This concept allows the trader to interact with different terminals and user interfaces. The application programs, like reservation systems etc. consist of different procedures (objects) which are stored as services in application libraries, the so called middleware. The logic of arranging these procedures to meet a specific user request is stored in the policies mentioned before. Policies are user dependent, procedures are not. This way, procedures can be used by very different users, essentially reducing the effort of writing programmes.

3.4 Legacy Applications

ODP-software cannot substitue existing business applications, which are the basis of daily information processing. Rather ODP has to support the exchange of data of the distributed system with these local applications. The integration of existing applicational software and basic services may be done on different levels.

First, the existing applicational system may be viewed as one large dimensioned object (abstract data type ADT), which cooperates with its environment by exchanging messages.

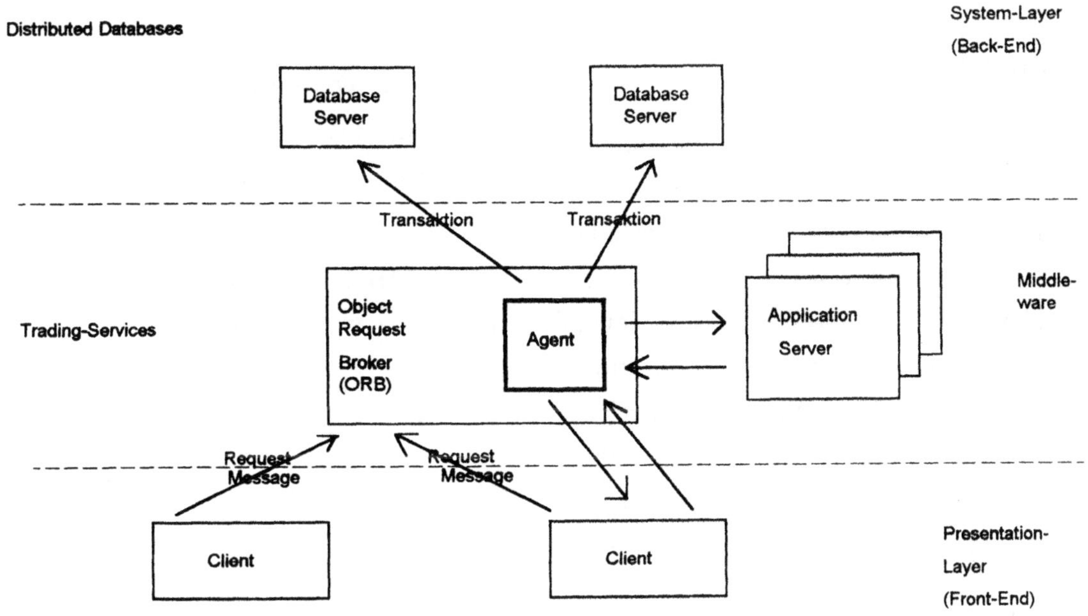

Better adjusted are the situations where the old applicational system can be called in a parametrized way or where user exits are available. The best way to do the integration of old software systems is by the use of application programming interfaces (APIs), as far as they are available.

4. Problems

The opportunites of ODP in different sectors of business and administration, not only in tourism, indeed are overhelming and, sooner or later, these opportunities will change use and application of information technology drastically. But besides these obvious advantages, there are some specific problems which must be met.

First, to participate in an open environment users have to open their computers to an unknown community. Alien processes and possibly alien users will consume expensive computer ressources like processor power, working storage etc. Special care and special measurements have to be installed in order to hinder unauthorized use and any damage of data. This holds with special emphasis to the laws to proctect sensitive or personal data against abuse. Thus, high sophisticated security measurements will be of paramount importance.

Second, there is some need to install a distributed management system in order to keep control of system activities, to record and bill services used by clients and to keep track of contracts established by automated processes, i.e. reservations etc. Especially, the last aspect will become very important, if the existence of a contract is denied by one of the business-partners.

5. Summary

Alltogether, one has to realize on one side the opportunities and enhanced services offered by the technical development of ODP. On the other side, so far management does not know of these opportunities. It still sticks to the classical view of decision maing bounded by the organizational limits of the firm. Any interorganizational decision calculus or decision support system de facto does not exist. Still, the framework of administrative and legal conditions of ODP must be devleoped.

Literature

ARCHITECTURE PROJECTS MANAGEMENT Limited (Hrsg.) (1991): A Systems Designer's Introduction to the Architecture, Cambridge 1991.

ARCHITECTURE PROJECTS MANAGEMENT Limited (Hrsg) (1989): ANSA Reference Manual, Volume A, Cambridge 1989.

BODENDORF, F.; SCHULZ, A.: Globale elektronische Märkte. In: Globalisierung der Wirtschaft. Einwirkungen auf die Betriebswirtschaftslehre, Haller, M. et al. (eds), Bern, Stuttgart, Wien 1993, p.111-125.

CZAP, H. (1993): Communication in Distributed Heterogenous Systems. Preprint, send in to: Bock, H.H.; Lenski, W.; Richter, M.M. (eds): Information systems and data analysis. Studies in Classification, Data Analysis and Knowledge Organization, Vol. 4, Heidelberg 1993.

DIGITAL EQUIPMENT COMPANY 3-4/93: Legacy-Applications: Common Object Request Broker Architecture (CORBA) und Application Control Architecture (ACA).

HEWITT, C.; de JONG, P. (1986): Open Systems. In: On Conceptual Modelling, ed. M.L. Brodie; J. Mylopoulos; J.W. Schmidt; New York u. a. Second Printing 1986, p.147-164.

IBM (1990a): Mit AMADEUS um die Welt, IBM-Nachrichten 40 (1990) Special I, S. 50-55.

IBM (1990b): Wie ein Regal im Supermarkt, IBM-Nachrichten 40 (1990) Special I, S. 56-57.

ISCHEBECK, W. (1989): Betriebsübergreifende Informationssysteme. Information Management, 1/89, S. 2-6.

A FRAMEWORK TO SIMULATE DIFFERENT CONFIGURATIONS OF A DISTRIBUTED TOURISM INFORMATION SYSTEM

Felsinger Peter   Sommerer Wolfgang   Strapetz Wilhelm-Wolfgang   Untergrabner Stephan

Institut für Statistik, Operations Research und Computerverfahren
Universität Wien,
Universitätsstr. 5/9, A-1010 Vienna, Austria

Abstract - Minimizing communication cost is a major goal when designing distributed information systems built on top of a wide area network. We present a framework which is used to model and implement different configurations of a distributed tourism information system. This approach makes building of simulations to estimate the communication cost involved in each considered alternative easy. As an example, we describe the simulation of three different configurations of such a system and discuss the results.

Introduction

The tourism information system TIS, implemented in the Austrian Region of the Tyrol, helps to satisfy the different informational needs of various parties involved in the field of tourism [1]. These parties can be information suppliers, information producers and/or information consumers.

We will present a simple framework and three different server - client configurations which allow the modelling as well as the simulation of current and future architectures of the system, thus to estimate the behaviour of the system in advance. The framework defines the communication model to be used between the different servers and clients [2]. The sample configurations represent different topologies which might be used for real systems. Since we force every configuration to use the same communication model, costs are estimated in a homogenous fashion.

The Model

The first configuration consists of a server which polls it's clients in a cyclic fashion. We assume that the server is equiped with a database system which stores the complete information handled by the system. The clients duplicate (part of) the information stored on the server in a local database system and are allowed to change some part of this information.

These redundant database systems are kept consistent by an update cycle, which is run in fixed time intervals. During the first phase of the update cycle (information gathering phase) the server contacts every (information producing) client in a sequential order and requests the delta information (i.e. the infomation changed by the client during the current time interval). After completing this phase the server database is up to date.

In the second phase, the server distributes the accumulated delta information to all clients. After

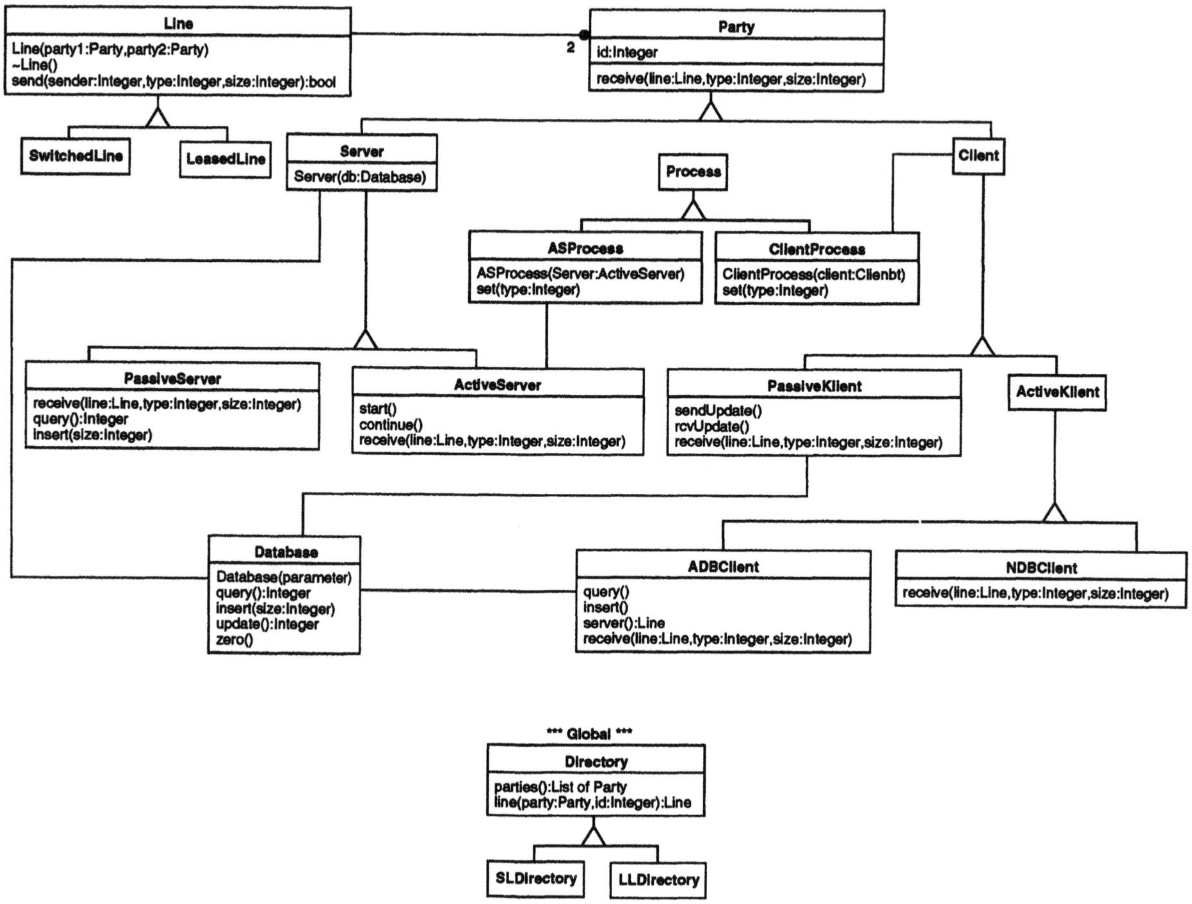

Figure 1: Object Model

finishing this phase all the nodes in the system have consistent information.

The second configuration differs from the first in that the clients do not store any data locally. This implies that clients must have online access to the server for reading and writing. Of course, since there is only one database, it is always consistent.

In the third configuration, the clients are connected to a local database which will be consulted for information retrieval. If the information is not stored locally the client will access the server which supplies the information. Every write access of a client must be done in the local database system as well as in the server database.

We used an object oriented approach in designing our framework. The analysis and design phase was accomplished using Rumbaugh's OMT Notation [3]. Fig. 1 shows the Object Model of the framework. Solid lines without special symbols on either end represent one to one associations. Filled circles at the end of a line represent one to many or many to many relationships depending on the number of circles shown. Inheritance is displayed using triangles.

The basic abstraction of this model consists of the classes Party and Line. These two classes define the communication protocol. It is important to note that we focus on connection oriented communication protocols. This implies that every line

object connects exactly two parties.
Lines can be created using the line method of the only instance allowed of class Directory. This instance is globally accessible to all objects. After a line has been created the two parties can communicate via the send and receive methods. Since the message format is not defined by this abstraction, both participating parties must agree on it.
Class Server and class Client are specializations of class Party. We assumed that a server object is always connected to a database system. We identified two important groups of server objects. Active servers are objects which must conform to a given operational schedule. This operational schedule is controled by the associated ASProcess (Active Server Process) object. This process is launched by the ActiveServer object during its creation and after the operational schedule (which was started by the process) has been completed. The time for the next activation of the ASProcess object is determined by the server. This collaboration between the ActiveServer object and the ASProcess object models the behaviour of the server described in configuration 1.
Passive servers only react to incoming requests. This type of server is typically used in configuration 2 and 3.
Clients are divided into active and passive clients as well. Passive clients reply to incoming server requests. In contrast to passive servers this type of clients has an associated ClientProcess. This is necessary because we assume that the cost produced by the communication is in any case drawn on the clients account. Since the Line object used for communication charges the originator of the communication link, the link for the data transfer has to be created by the client. To model this callback mechanism, the client creates a ClientProcess object, which will be immediatly activated after the client has finished its handling of the server request. Using this abstraction, the only cost drawn on the servers account is just for the establishment of a connection and and for transmiting a request.
Objects of class ActiveClient have to model the behaviour of autonomous entities. This means that they have to produce requests in a somewhat arbitrary fashion. To control this behaviour every ActiveClient object has some statistical parameters attached. It uses this parameter set to launch its associated ClientProcess object, which in turn will control the activity of the client after the time interval, as determined by the launching client, has elapsed.
Objects of class NDBClient (No DataBase Client) differ from objects of class ADBClient (Active DataBase Client) in that they have no local database attached. Obviously, NDBClients forward every request to the server. In case of a read request, ADBClients have to consult the local database first. If they have to perform a write operation it must be done locally as well as on the server.
Table 1 shows the different configurations in terms of client/server class usage.

Table 1: Example Configurations

	PassiveClient	NDBClient	ADBClient
ActiveServer	Configuration 1		
PassiveServer		Configuration 2	Configuration 3

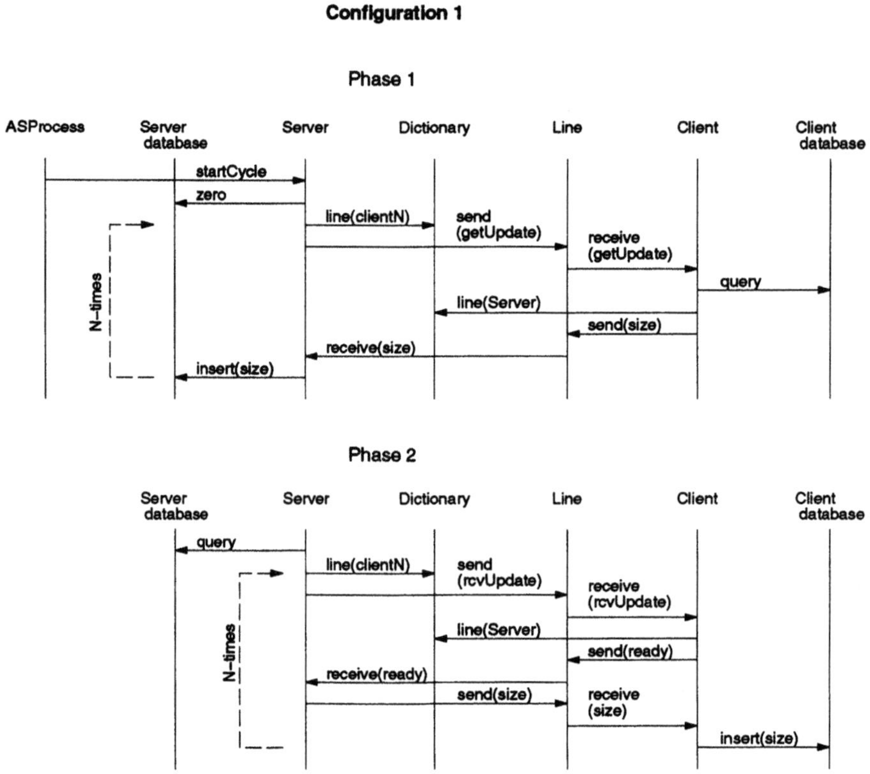

Figure 2 : Scenario for Configuration 1

Objects of class Database are used as data stores as well as information producers. This different behaviour can be controled by parameters, which have to be supplied during the construction of the database object. In configuration 1, client database objects will be used as data producers. In other words it is the responsibility of the database object to determine the size of the update produced by the client since the last information transfer.

In contrast, server database objects are used as data stores in configuration 1. They accumulate all updates received during the first phase of the update cycle. At the beginning of phase 2 of the update cycle, the server consults the database to determine the size of the update to be sent to every client. Fig. 2 shows a typical interobject communication scenario for configuration 1. Time has to be thought along the vertical axis.

In configuration 2, only the server has a database attached. It is used by the server to determine the size of read requests. The size of the write requests has to be determined by the NDBClient object itself. A typical communication trace for this configuration is shown in Fig. 3.

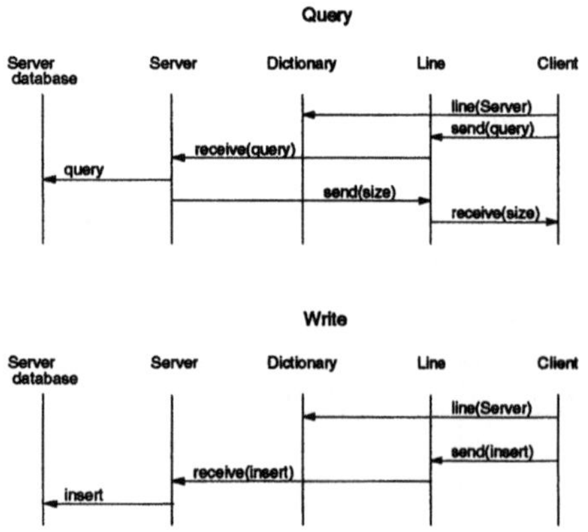

Figure 3: Scenario for Configuration 2

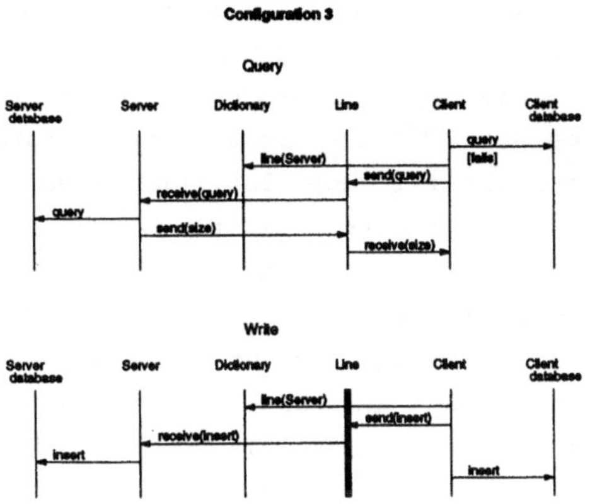

Figure 4: Scenario for Configuration 3

In configuration 3 both sides are equipped with a local database system. The client tries to satisfy read requests by consulting the local database first. It is the responsibility of the database to determine if the request can be satisfied and, if yes, the size of the resulting information. If the request is not satisfied by the database system (query returns zero) the client consults the server, which in turn uses the database to determine the size of the resulting piece of information. Thus, both sides are using the database as an information producer. The size of write requests must be determined by the client itself. The client has to update both the local as well as the remote database. Since we are only interested in communication costs the local update is optional. The corresponding scenario is presented in Fig. 4.

Since all the client - server communication has to be done via a Line object, we can easily accumulate the communication cost produced during a simulation run. In addition, fixed costs

Table 2: Parameter set

Parameter Name	Configuration		
	1	2	3
Number of clients	80	80	80
Baudrate	4875	4875	4875
Timeout (sec)	120	120	120
Number of retries	16	16	16
Category "1" clients (%)	60	60	60
Avg. number of writes	10	10	10
Avg. number of bytes transmitted	3750	3750	3750
Category "2" clients (%)	40	40	40
Avg. number of writes	5	5	5
Avg. number of bytes transmitted	1875	1875	1875
Failurerate (%)	15	15	15
Time to establish connection (sec)	30	0	0
Number of connection establishment retries	2-10	2-10	2-10
Communication cost "1" per minute (ATS)	0,67	-	-
Communication cost "2" per minute (ATS)	2,67	-	-
Communication cost "3" per minute (ATS)	4	-	-
Number of clients with cost "1"	3	-	-
Number of clients with cost "2"	60	-	-
Number of clients with cost "3"	17	-	-
Communication cost per MB (ATS)	-	200	200
Number of successful local reads (%)	-	-	10

like link creation and destruction can be handled in the construction process of Line objects as well.
Since our model falls into the category of discrete event simulation models [4], we have implemented it using the Simula language [5,6]. This language has an outstanding environment for this type of simulation.

The Simulation

Table 2 shows the parameters we used in simulating the three example configurations. The timeout and retry values are used in case that problems arise during data transmision. The rate at which these errors occur is determined by the paramer Failurerate.
Category "1" clients differ from category "2" clients in their activity level. Category "1" clients are twice as active in terms of information production (i.e. volume and frequency) as their counterparts. All clients read about five times as much data as they write. But the average volume transfered in one reading operation is only about 60% of a typical write operation.
Since there are three different pricing categories for telephon calls in Austria, it is necessary to group clients according to this structure. Prices in category "1" are for clients located in the same city as the server. Category "2" is valid for clients within 100 km distance to the server. Category "3" applies to all other clients.

For configuration 2 and 3 we assumed that every client and the server are connected to wide area network (WAN) such as the Internet [7]. Due to a lack of information regarding the cost for configuration 2 and 3 we decided to use the fee of the local Internet provider EUnet EDV Dienstleistungs-Gesellschaft m.b.H* . It is also important to note, that the fixed costs, such as base fees, have not been included in our simulation. Of course, when applying our work to produce information for a specific implementation decision, all costs have to be considered.
Since clients in configuration 3 only access the server for reading if the information is not stored locally, we had to introduce a parameter which controls this characteristic. In our simulation runs we estimated that this would be the case in 10% of all attempts.
For configuration 2 and 3 every system was simulated for ten hours of operation. Simulation runs for configuration 1 performed one complete update cycle. Since these choices represent one operational day for each of the configurations, results are directly comparable.

The Results

Table 3 lists the simulation results we achieved. Since the information is tranfered all at once in configuration 1, the number of reading and writing

* Schottenring 33, A-1010 Vienna, Austria

Table 3: Simulation results

Result	Configuration		
	1	2	3
Number of reading operations	-	2238	2022
Number of update/writing operations	-	725	722
Total volume transfered (KB)	-	527	496
Total cost (ATS)	1326	103	97

operations are not of interest in this case. In addition, we didn't include a value of the total volume transfered in configuration 1 because it can't be compared with the results of the other configurations. When comparing the costs of the different configurations, it is obvious that configuration 2 as well as configuration 3 perform an order of magnitude better than configuration 1. The main reason for this behaviour is the number of clients. In configuration 1, a complete update is distributed to all clients whereas in the other two configurations, only the information needed by the clients is transfered. Of course, the growth rate of the volume transfered in configuration 1 is $O(n^2)$ where n is the number of clients. In configuration 2 and 3 this rate is only $O(n)$.

We included the number of reading and writing operations in table 3 because these numbers erstimate the transaction count. Even if these values are not of interest in terms of communication cost, they are crucial for defining the type, size and performance of the server system.

Conclusion

We presented a framework for simulating the communicational aspects of distributed information systems. Using an object oriented approach, it was easily accomplished to model and implement different configurations of such a system. As an example we introduced three specific configurations of a distributed tourism information system.

Simulating these configurations, we showed that configurations with centeralized information storage outperformed configurations with distributed storage in terms of communication cost. Of course, the parameters used in the simulation influence the results. In other word, the examples presented can not be generalized. However, we showed that simulating different design alternatives of a distributed system can help to identify the most effincient implementation.

References

1. Werthner, H.: TIS - Tiroler Tourismus Informationssystem. Wirtschaftsinformatik 35, 43, (1993)

2. Tanenbaum, A. S. : Computer Networks. Englewood Cliffs: Prentice-Hall 1989

3. Rumbaugh, J., Blaha, M., Premerlani, W., Eddy, F., Lorensen, W. : Object-Oriented Modeling and Design. Englewood Cliffs: Prentice-Hall 1991

4. Cassandras, C. G. : Discrete Event Systems. Boston: Richard D. Irwin, Inc. 1993

5. Dahl, W. J., Nyhrhaug, B., Nygaard, U. : Simula 67. Common Base Language. Oslo: Norwegian Computing Center 1967

6. Birtwistle, G. M. : Discrete Event Modelling on SIMULA. London: The MacMillanPress 1979

7. Comer, D. : Internetworking with TCP/IP. Englewood Cliffs: Prentice-Hall 1988

INFORMATION TECHNOLOGIES AND TOURISM MARKETS

Matthias Ernst and Dirk Walpuski

EcoTel Research Group, Department of Economics, University of Würzburg

The potential changes of electronic information systems and upstream information markets in the tourism sector is almost of revolutionary character. Proceeding from the particularities of this branch, this article reveals its basic patterns of development and summarizes the experiences so far.

I. The Market for Tourist Services

For the valuation of the effects of information and communication technologies it is necessary to give a systematic survey about tourism markets, which are spread worldwide [1]. Tourism markets consist, like all other markets, of three elements: suppliers, consumers, and goods. The goods traded on tourism markets contain in general three kinds of services. Besides pure transport services (airlines, passenger shipping, railways, business, and public passenger road transportation) there is the group of accomodation services (hotel, guest-houses, private lodging) and other services like entertainment programs, for example events, sightseeing tours, car rentals, insurances [2], [1], [3].

The actors on the supply side are the producers of the services, the traders and travel agencies as well as private and business costumers on the demand side. Apart from the producers of single services, transport, accomodation, entertainment program, also the traders belong to the suppliers. These tour operators buy on their own account hotel and transport capacities in advance from the producers and sell them separately or in a set [4].

Then the brokers (travel agencies, bureaus of airlines) supply these tourist services by order to the costumers and handle all the transactions like issuing and payment of tickets. Since the end of the eighties these brokers are responsible for 80% of the revenues in passenger air transportation [5].

II. Information Problems on Tourism Markets

The listed goods distinguish themselves by the fact, that they are only regionally supplied and that they are neither transportable nor storable [1]. So they can be compared with fast perishable products. Due to the worldwide distribution of the suppliers and consumers information and transaction costs are crucial variables. This is true not only for the circulation of price and quality information but also for the handling of the reservations. Clear examples are high business expenses, a low market transparency and a relatively high uncertainty of quality of the costumers. A journey is a typical experience or confidence good, that is to say the quality is not observable before the purchase. The sum of value for the single consumer (tourist), is compared with the available monthly income partly very considerably and the frequency of transactions is relatively small, so that you cannot learn from further experiences. If the services should have any means for the costumer, they must be purchased in a set that is equivalent in space and time.

This can be illustrated with a little example:

An individual traveller T wants to go from A to C via B. But he does not know, whether he will be able to go from B to C respectively whether he can spend the night in B and get a transfer from B to C (e.g. by ship, plane or train). In this case the information costs are extremly high. T needs accomodation twice, three times a transportation service and entertainment programs twice. All together he needs seven separate transactions which must be coordinated spatial and temporal.

The uncertainty of realizing a useful temporal sequence of the separate transactions (transfer - accomodation - entertainment program -...) could be that great, that the demand of such a journey will be dropped.

To cope with these information problems upstream information markets had been installed. These markets reduce information and transaction costs as well as uncertainties of price and/or quality on the subordinated tourism market. Besides the traders especially the travel agencies, which are the connection between supplier and costumer, are part of these markets. Further elements on these informations markets are testing journals, travel journals, hotel and travel guides, but also plane und train schedules etc. Often they are connected to material information carriers and therefore they cannot be distributed and actualized as easy as electronic information carriers.

III. Development of Electronic Information Markets

1.) From internal booking Systems...

The distribution and processing of information and the guarantee of the up- and downstream information flows (like printing and distributing of travel brochures, price lists, reservations, printing of tickets) causes high costs. In the course of high error rates, frequently rebookings respectevly dead positions, the large airlines in the USA developed in the sixties internal EDV based booking systems [6], [7]. After the attempt of the development of one standardized reservation system had failed (1961 DELTAMATIC by Delta, 1961 PANAMAC by Pan Am), the two American companies American Airlines and United Airlines extended independently of each other their internal reservation system to the first functionable and marketable computer reservation systems (CRS). United Airlines entered the market in 1976 with APOLLO as the first [6]. American Airlines followed a short time later with SABRE (Semi Automatic Business Research). Travel agencies which are connected with these systems are able to get available real time informations concerning the flight from the mainframe of the airline via online connections. Using this systems the agencies could furthermore handle and confirm bookings within a second. In the course of cost saving and raised safety of booking linked with an automatic issuing of tickets, the methodes of flight booking were almost revolutionized. The advantages were enormous. Besides the effect of rationalisation, due to the elemination of staff, the extension of offers and the reduction of transaction costs and transaction time, the systems could also be used for marketing strategies of the airlines, like pricing, optimisation of revenue, customer information, ratio of passengers to seats etc. [8], [9].

2.) ...upon the Computer Reservation System (CRS)...

The success of external and internal reservation systems encouraged the competitors to develope their own systems. PARS (Programmed Airline Reservation System), developed in 1965, was installed in 1968 by the airlines United, TWA, and Eastern. A number of systems followed, but these systems, due to the underestimation of the complexity, the linked development costs and the overestimation of the technical possibilities, existed only a short time [6].

The development expenses supposedly summed up to US $ 1 billion for APOLLO and about US $ 3 billions for SABRE [10].

The extension of airways, planes, flightrelations and flight passengers in the second half of the seventies lead to the final breakthrough of CRS, which became a dominant instrument for the handling of flight bookings. Only for the inneramerican passenger flight transportation 95 % of all bookings are running over one of the five biggest CRS, in which the share of the market leaders SABRE and APOLLO adds up to 75 % (SABRE 43%, APOLLO 32%, PARS 10%, Texas Air respectively Eastern Air und nowadays Continental Airlines with SYSTEM ONE 10%, Delta Airlines with DATAS II 5%) [11]. The two airlines United Airlines and American Airlines themselves serve only 30% of these flights [12]. Today SABRE is the biggest non-governmental computer network in the world with more than 70,000 terminals and more than 15,000 travel brokers und reservation companies in 45 countries [13].

The mainframe of the SABRE Travel Information Network with 1,800 employees takes into account up to 45 million prices respectively booking possibilities and manages all together up to 2,000 simultanous transactions per second, 500,000 reservations per day and 40 million changes per month from 650 airlines [14].

Because of the extremly high system costs and the increasing competition of the international air transportation due to wide deregulation on the air traffic the airlines were forced to use all possibilities to reduce costs.

The structure of production and by that the structure of costs of the system suppliers gives, because of the economies of scale, incentives to extend the use of the system possibilities until the barrier of capacity [15].

Therefore the CRS operators either joined together or tried to get a higher operating rate of their system [14].

Table 1: Actors on Tourism Markets

Suppliers

- Service Suppliers
  - Producers:
    - Transport
    - Accomodation
    - Entertainment Programs
  - Trader:
    - Tour Promoters
    - Package Tour Promoters
- System Suppliers
  - Reservation
  - Independent Comparison of Offers
  - Ticketing
  - Additional Services
- Service Brokers
  - Travel Agencies
  - Agencies of the Airlines
  - Bureaus of acceptance of the Tour Promoters

Consumers

- Holiday Travelers
- Private Travelers
- Business Travelers

© Research Group *EcoTel*, University of Würzburg, 1993

So the three airlines TWA, Northwest Airlines and Delta Airlines decided in 1989 to unite their systems DATAS II and PARS. This new system is offered since 1992 under the name WORLDSPAN [16]. This opening of the systems for more suppliers on the tourist markets was not only the consequence of cost analysis. The CRS helped their operators to get a monopolistic position on parts of the air transportation markets. For smaller airlines it is nearly impossible to sell flights without using a CRS and therefore without a notice to their competitors. These dominance of the CRS operators and the implicite preferential treatment of the partnership airlines, e.g. via software controlled priorities of certain suppliers or via special contracts with connected travel agencies, lead in the USA to a charge at the Supreme Court because of a violation against the Anti Trust Law. While the discriminating representation on monitors is prohibited since 1984, the case was nevertheless dismissed of the Supreme Court in April 1992. The operators are still able to charge the inclusion of foreign offers into their own CRS [19]. These charge receipts have turned remarkably to a basic income and profit source of those CRS operators, who are airlines at the same hand. Already in 1986 American Airlines generated, with the biggest reservations system in America, SABRE, US $ 140 million in profits - after deduction of the fees for using competitive systems and the costs for their own CRS, compared to a total turnover of US $ 360 million [10]. The cause of this evolution, which could be noticed in similar ways at the other important CRS operators, is the margin between the requested price per booking and the real costs per booking. Following a study from the U. S. General Accounting Office the costs for one SABRE booking were US $ 0.79, taking into account an interest rate of 15 % for the capital employed, the requested charge was US $ 1.84. The competitor APOLLO had costs of US $ 0.96 per booking and asked a charge of US $ 1.85. [11] In addition to the charge for foreign flight reservations the CRS operators ask from the connected travel agencies a yearly lump sum for using, sometimes even minimum quotas and furthermore user charges for other connected suppliers of services. These methods should not only cover revenues and guarantee high rates of capacity utilization, but should also lead to a certain booking behavior of the travel agencies.

3.) ...to Global Distributing Systems (GDS) with Regional Marketing Systems

Especially this extension of the reservation systems and the impulse to cost savings led to the installation of global distributing systems (GDS). In addition to the electronic reservation of pure transport services, these systems also include accomodation and entertainment programs from the offers of the services suppliers (producers, traders and travel agencies) like theater visits, car rentals, money exchange.
Besides the possibility of the use, the operators of CRS try to break even by leasing personal computers. For the travel agencies this rent is often too high, so that this source of revenue begins to run dry. The economic success of a CRS depends on a large number of participants, therefore the licences for the use are offered without a rent for the terminals. Furthermore the travel agencies receive a bonus for every booking via a CRS. The service carriers should participate in the costs for the use of a CRS. But in this case the pricing is not that easy. For many suppliers the striking price of about DM 500,000 for an interface licence with GALILEO and the linked development expenses are too high [20].

Worldwide there are today three big suppliers of those international GDS. Besides SABRE of AMR, the parent company of American Airlines, there exist COVIA/APOLLO of United Airlines and a number of European airlines and nowadays WORLDSPAN of Delta Airlines and TWA. These GDS are constructed as multi accesss systems. That means that many different service carriers enter their offer in an own system.* The future however belongs to direct access, that is to say you can get access to other (national, regional, local) suppliers in foreign systems with one system using the same language as in your own system. This solution is obvious, especially in Europe, where simultanously different GDS are installed. These GDS do not strictly refer to (flight)business, but they should integrate from the beginning the whole national tourism markets [7]. The most popular competitors within the "European" GDS are the systems GALILEO and AMADEUS. While AMADEUS (start in 1987/88) is a me-too-product (following the American SYSTEM ONE) of Lufthansa, Iberia, Air France and SAS, the system GALILEO, which is carried by Alitalia, British Airlines, KLM and USAIR, is running under a system partnership with the American COVIA/APOLLO of United Airlines. Connected with it are national travel broker systems like the german START (Studiengesellschaft zur Automatisierung für Reise und Touristik) [21], installed in 1979 and connected with AMADEUS, or the systems TRAVI-SWISS, TRAVICOM, TRAVI-AUSTRIA, connected with GALILEO. The linkage of worldwide CRS and european GDS with national and regional travel brokers (even local suppliers und tourism bureaus etc.) is the last stadium of the revolution of booking and reservation feasibilities on spatial distributed tourism markets so far. The increased network effects for the suppliers due to the connection of the systems and the competition of the system suppliers lead to decreasing connecting costs. Nevertheless the price promotors have to pay for connection with the promoter independant system association START/AMADEUS is nowadays DM 100,000 plus additional DM 100,000 (inclusive 10,000 bookings) for every further year of operation [22].

IV. Potential Changes and Economic Implications

1.) Electronic Information Markets

Meanwhile the suppliers do not only work on a faster distribution and cost reduction of these information and transaction systems, but also the market for information carriers on tourism markets is caught by the information and communication technologies. Up to now this sector was dependent on the technological improvements in the printing industry and helped themselves by a separate distribution of brochures and price lists as a helping hand for travel agencies and consumers. This kind of information processing and information transmission is, however, very cost intensive and is subject to temporal restrictions.

An average travel agency stores up to 250 topical brochures for the costumers [23].

Besides this cost burden for the "big" suppliers, this "duty of brochure" is a real barrier to entry for "small" service suppliers and travel promoters [4].

Table 2: System Suppliers

	System Suppliers				
International (Worldwide)	APOLLO/ COVIA	SYSTEM ONE	SABRE	WORLDSPAN	CRS
International (Europe)	GALILEO	AMADEUS			GDS
National	TRAVI-SWISS TRAVI-AUSTRIA	START			Travel Broker Systems
Local and regional suppliers					

© Research Group *EcoTel*, University of Würzburg, 1993

The European project EUROTOP deals with the development and testing of an electronic travel brochure. Digital graphics and informations should be directly retrievable for the travel agencies via ISDN-cables and IBM computer technolgies. A pilot phase with the integration of the EUROTOP terminal into the START-AMADEUS-association (with 70 travel promoters and airlines) at 7 travel promoters and 60 travel agencies in France, Great Britain and Germany so far, should provide first realizations about costs and utility of this innovation [23].

2.) Competition on Tourism Markets

a) Market Structure. By using the new information and communication technologies, the relevant market space expanded. The relevant market space sets the maximum distance, in which competition remains still effective. The extension of the scope of competition reaches not only the spatial expansion, but refers also to temporal, technical, institutional and legal barriers. In all meanings the CRS raise the scope of competition [24].

Due to the use of the CRS the number and the size of the market participants changed too. The number of obtainable

* In the Federal Republic of Germany there is e. g. since 1986 the MARS (Multi Acces Reservation and Information System). Via a Btx computer network you can get access to the reservation systems of British Airways, Pan Am and TWA and via the network of the french Telelut you can reach 18 more Airlines. About 1000 french and 1400 german mostly small travel agencies without an IATA agency use this system.[24].

producers of the transport services, accomodation and entertainment increased and their distribution systems changed, e. g. direct booking. The number of the travel agencies did not shrink anyway, it also increased extremly. So the running costs for a travel agency reduced dramatically due to the use of CRS, and the demand for tourist services rose in the last twenty years. The enormous rise of the service suppliers, the linked specialization and the need of consultation pushed the number of travel brokers, e. g. in the USA in the period between 1976 and 1985 from 12,000 to 27,000 [25] (1986: 7200 principle and about 15,000 auxiliary travel agencies in the FRG) [1].

But as soon as the final consumers would be able to get a direct access to the "electronic travel agencies" using VANS-suppliers via Btx respectively Datex-J-services, for the travel agencies would only remain the part of a distributer of travel documents and the function of a collecting agency. If the service suppliers and the consumers get in contact with each other, the function of the tour promoters would need a new consideration [9].
In connection with this another important aspect of the CRS has to be mentioned. The rise in product diversity on the partial markets let the traditional deliminations of the partial segments of the tourism markets more and more merge into each other. Numerous special tour promotors and special tour brokers (e. g. adventure, bicycle, climbing, club, diving, language, senior, single, surf or trekking tours) arise and the trend to individualized package tours is unmistakeable a result of the higher possibilities of chosing and differentiating, as well as of the competition of quality on markets with CRS aided tour bookings [24].
Besides their advisor function the travel agencies are more and more forced back by the system suppliers into the role of pure terminal operators. Because of the already emerging extension of the GDS in the FRG via Btx-services on the Datex-network of the DBP Telekom, the elimination of a whole trading level has to be feared. At least a crucial shift of function at the travel agencies will appear.

The higher product diversity on all levels and the linked formation of product lines at the travel agencies made the market transparency for prospective travelers more difficult. But anyway, the use of modern information and communication systems could improve this transparency.

On the other hand there are economies of scale for the system suppliers and, as far as the connected service suppliers and service brokers are concerned, high moving costs emerge (costs to switch the system supplier) [26] from these so called network externalities [27], [28]. Therefore a system supplier will be able to build up respectively to increase barriers to entry and to act inbetween certain limits like a monopolist [29], [30]. Considerable profit possibilities appear, which, in connection with a dominant market position on downstream tourism markets, could cut back competition. Especially for small suppliers this could be a problem [10]. Consequently the same economic laws for the operators of CRS are in force as for the technical running on the hardware and software side [20].
As far as the travel agencies are concerned the dependence on one or few tour promoters respectively one single CRS decreased, because, due to the pressure towards standardisation and compatibility of systems, the technical pressure of a booking system did no longer lead to vertical integration.

In spite of the effects on competition respectively market structure, which are shown so far, the vertical integration (the joining of up- and downstream stages of production or distribution) on tourism markets was hardly affected by the use of automatic booking systems. In principle a vertical integration will always take place, when the transaction costs on the market are higher than the transaction costs within a firm. Because of the decreased information and transaction costs a market coordination seems to be more efficient than an in-company coordination. Although transaction costs could be reduced through new information and communication technologies in the company as well, the communication flow between the input and the output market, which works better and better, seems to decrease the advantages of vertical integration.

b) Market Behaviour. The CRS increased the flexibility of prices on tourism markets. By evaluating the single queries in the booking system, the service suppliers and system operators are able to recognize without time lags the quality profiles of certain consumer groups as well as the changes in preferences and trends, so that they can react in their pricing and product design. The time lags between changes in demand respectively in preferences and the supply reaction is reduced.

In addition with the product diversity there appear also various price and tarif modifications. In the USA for example the number of flight tarifs on the US markets rose since the seventies from 400,000 to 7 millions [31]. This is the result of an extension of the kinds of tarifs, which is again the result of product diversity and higher market transparency, due to more intensive price competition. At the one hand you can argue, that higher price flexibility leads to more market transparency, but on the other hand market transparency is a consistent result of functionable price competition. Numerous service and system suppliers use the increased temporal ability of the system to react to price competition and to attain optimal capacity utilisation. Nevertheless this price flexibility does not count for all service suppliers, some of them are liable to price commitments (e. g. public enterprises). For these participants only a ristricted possibility of price flexibility exist [24]. Under aspects of market competition policy, this is an important necessity, which needs a far-sighted deregulation.

On the other hand you can see, that meanwhile the forced price competition, which in the beginning took place only on international and inneramerican flight routes, is not that intensive anymore. The understanding of the suppliers that price reduction leads to an advantage only in the short run, since all competitors react at once due to the market transparency, let prices wars become more seldom. So far the transparent "electronic" market could receive the charakter of an implicit cartel. Especially in this context we have to mention, that on the German tourism market a gentleman agreement about the task assignement on the market exists. There are hardly any European airlines that have their own tour promoter [24]. A forced competition on this sector will take place not before the integration into the single European domestic market.

c) Market Result. On the first view all participants have advantages from the use and the distribution of CRS and GDS. The service suppliers are able to advertise with lower costs and to react faster to changes in demand. The barriers to entry [4] for competitors can be reduced as far as the access to a system is possible.

Because of the new information and communication technologies the barriers to entry for the participants on tourism markets decreased. Barriers to entry are mostly connected with sunk costs. Newcomers have higher costs than established competitors. After all this means higher profits for the latter and a barrier to entry for the first. On electronic tourism markets you can see this fact twice: first for the market of the system suppliers (CRS) and second for the service suppliers, which want to join the system.

Meanwhile even the smallest service supplier is able to open up an enormous market potential by participating in a reservation system. Beside the service "booking possibility" e. g. for small hotels, the reservation systems exercise the function of quality control. So by using the CRS the travel agencies have the certainty to get their finder's fees even from small anonymous and seldom frequented service suppliers. The reservation system therefore exercises a positiv selection and, linked with this, a more rapide and efficient selection of "black sheep" than the markets traditionally could provide [24]. The traditional quality signals (e. g. stars) are used on tourism markets extremly efficient and they are permanently cotrolled through the market.

An imminent market failure, due to asymmetric information (the so called Akerlof-process), which could be a problem especially on tourism markets, is largely avoided. The information and communication technologies reduce the information and transactions costs on downstream tourism markets. This is very significant for the group of travel brokers and travel agencies. Their activities require large numbers of staff. The personnel costs of the travel agencies in 1988 were about 60 % of their running costs [24]. By using modern CRS the labor productivity almost doubled. Thus travel agencies are able to halve the time they need to dispatch an average consumer order in the IATA-business via the German START-system. But this rise in productivity can not be used directly for manpower reduction (and costs reduction), for the reduction of expedients (and tour dealers) is not possible because of the relatively small plant size of the travel agencies. Therefore the rise in productivity is used for a better and more intensive quality competition and costumer service [24].

The participation in CRS has cost advantages especially for small travel agencies in sparsely populated regions. By joining the START-system, communication costs depending on time and distance (telephone, Datex-P, teletext, telefax) can be reduced and become more estimatable. A questionaire of travel agencies connected to START yields an average reduction in telephone and telefax costs of about 22 % after the implementation of START (1979/1981). This reduction could cover 40 % of the terminal rent. In the same period the average sales increased about 17 % [24].

Through the ubiquity of supply information the market transparency and the intensity of competition increase. Because of the higher speed of reaction of the suppliers, even short running changes in demand and supply (e. g. special bargains of capacities that become suddenly vacant, last minute flights) can be taken into account. Therefore the subsisting capacities are more utilized (with the result of booking time dependant price dispersion among the consumers) [32]. With the help of these spot markets even individual bundles of services (e. g. an individual world trip) can be redevided into the single services (transport, accomodation, entertainment program) and can be reselled piecemeal. The external sign for this is e. g. a prolonged right to rescind the contract of tour and fast resale.

The additional sale of services, which would not have been sold without CRS and GDS, is already positive in an economic sense, due to additional income. The increased possibilities of choice and the rationalisation, due to reduced transaction costs lead, via a more intensive competition, to price reductions of tourism services. This fact alone has already a positive effect on welfare.

As a résumé the electronic information markets increase the efficiency of allocation on the downstream tourism markets. Devision of labor, competition and linked with this, supply of needs causing minimum costs can be realized. The CRS aided tourism markets use a given tourist infrastructure in a flexible and efficient way with a minimum use of ressources. The power of the free market's mechanism of coordination to discover, receives through the installation of electronic markets a totally new and real dimension, that was up to now only imaginable in economic theory.

References

[1] Freyer, Walter : Tourismus: Einführung in die Fremdenverkehrsökonomie, 4. Edition., München u.a. 1993.

[2] Feketekuty, Geza: About Trade in Tourism Services, in: Giarini, Orio (Editor): The Emerging Service Economy, Oxford u.a. 1987, pp. 245- 251.[2] Feketekuty, Geza: About Trade in Tourism Services, in: Giarini, Orio (Editor): The Emerging Service Economy, Oxford u.a. 1987, pp. 245- 251.

[3] Richter, Christine: Tourism Services, in: Giarini, Orio (Editor): The Emerging Service Economy, Oxford u.a. 1987, pp. 213- 244.

[4] Hochreiter, Rolf: Tourismusindustrie, in: Oberender, Peter (Hrsg.): Marktstruktur und Wettbewerb in der Bundesrepublik Deutschland, Branchenstudien zur deutschen Volkswirtschaft, München, pp. 629-657.

[5] N.N.: Die internationalen Fluglinien auf dem Weg zum "Mega-Carrier", in: Frankfurter Allgemeine Zeitung, 30.09.1989.

[6] Copeland, Duncan G./McKenney, James L.: Airline Reservations Systems: Lessons From History, in: MIS Quarterly, 1988, pp. 353-370.

[7] Ellis, Martin A.: Elektronische Reservationssysteme, in: EM (Elektronische Märkte)-Newsletter, Nr. 3, St. Gallen 1992, pp. 1-2.

[8] Ernst, Matthias: Neue Informations- und Kommunikationstechnologien und marktwirtschaftliche Allokation. Eine informations- und transaktionskostentheoretische Analyse, München 1991.

[9] Ritz, Daniel: Elektronische Märkte verändern die Tourismusbranche, in: io Management Zeitschrift, Jg. 61, 1992, pp. 77-81.

[10] Katz, Ronald: The Impact of Computer Reservation Systems on Air Transport Competition, in: OECD (Hrsg.): Deregulation and Airline Competition, Paris 1988, pp. 85-101.

[11] U.S. General Accounting Office (Hrsg.): Competition in the Airline Computerized Reservation System Industry, Washington, D.C., 14.09.1988, (GAO/T-RCED-88-62).

[12] Pümpin, Cuno/Steinbach, Klaus: Auswirkungen neuer Informationstechniken auf die strategische Unternehmensführung, in: Altenpohl, Dieter G./Hofman, Jürgen H.O.(Editor): Informatisierung - Wachstum der Grenzen, Zürich 1989, pp.94-101.

[13] Barth, Helmut: Von Platzbuchungssystemen in Verkehrsbetrieben zu globalen Reisevertriebssystemen, in: Kurbel, Karl/ Strunz, Horst (Hrsg.): Handbuch der Wirtschaftsinformatik, Stuttgart 1990, pp. 163-177.

[14] Hopper, Max D.: Rattling SABRE - new ways to compete on information, in: Harvard Business Review, Jg. 68, 1990, pp. 118-125.

[15] U.S. Department of Transportation, Office of the Secretary of Transportation (Hrsg.): Study of Airline Computer Reservation Systems, Washington, D.C., (DOT-P-37-88-2).

[16] N.N.: Deregulierung: Der Himmel ist - fast - ausverkauft, in: Reisebüro Bulletin 8-9, 24.02.1989.

[19] N.N.: Buchungssysteme der Marktführer nicht illegal, in: Handelsblatt, 08.04.1992.

[20] Haldemann, Samuel: Galileo und Amadeus teilen sich den Himmel, in: Computerworld Schweiz, Nr. 4, 1990, pp. 11-15.

[21] Gölz, Stefan: Die Lufthansa AG im START-System, in: WiSt, Wirtschaftswissenschaftliches Studium, Jg. 17, 1988, pp. 312-313.

[22] Weinhold, Marisa, D.: Der Markt für Veranstalterreisen in der Bundesrepublik Deutschland , Frankfurt a.o., 1992.

[23] Lüttich, Karl-Heinz: EUROTOP - Ein europäisches Projekt zur Entwicklung und Erprobung des elektronischen Reisekatalogs, in: EM (Elektronische Märkte)-Newsletter, Nr. 3, St. Gallen 1992, p. 4.

[24] von Bornstaedt, Falk: Telematik in der Tourismuswirtschaft, München 1992.

[25] U.S. General Accounting Office (Hrsg.): Airline Competition: Impact of Computerized Reservation Systems. Report to Congressional Requesters. Washington, D.C., 1988, (GAO/T-RCED-86-74).

[26] Klemperer, Paul: The competitivenes of markets with switching costs, in: The RAND Journal of Economics, Vol. 18, 1987, pp. 138-150.

[27] Katz, Michael L./Shapiro, Carl: Network Externalities, Competition, and Compatibility, in: The American Economic Review, Vol. 75, 1985, pp. 424-440.

[28] Farrell, Joseph/Shapiro, Carl: Dynamic competition with switching costs, in: The RAND Journal of Economics, Vol. 19, 1988, pp. 123-137.

[29] Riordan, Michael H.: Monopolistic competition with experience goods, in: The Quarterly Journal of Economics, Vol. 36, 1986, pp. 265-279.

[30] Salop, Steven C.: Information and Monopolistic Competition, in: The American Economic Review (papers and proceedings), Vol. 66, 1976, pp. 240-245.

[31] Claasen, Werner: Drehscheiben: Schwungrad der Airlines. Was die US-Deregulation brachte: 16 Knotenpunkte und sieben Millionen Tarife, in: USA special, touristik aktuell 16, 1985, 22, p. VII.

[32] von Weizsäcker, Carl Christian: Volkswirtschaftliche Aspekte neuer Medien, unpublished manuscript 1981, 13 pages.

TYPES OF ELECTRONIC AUCTIONS

Martin Reck

Hochschule St.Gallen

Abstract

Auctions as social processes and special types of markets have process rules that determine price determination. These rules allow to distinguish auctions and other markets as well as to classify auction types. Formal specifications of electronic auctions which mimic their classical counterparts can be given by use of trace specifications. For system implementations, e.g. systems in the tourist industry, these specifications can be used as starting points for system developments.

1. Introducing Electronic Auctions

Computer systems are widespread in natural, technical or socio economic environments. They have found widespread use in combination with mechanical or electronic components to form technical system which are often complex in overall structure and behaviour, e.g. traffic systems, production lines, robots, aircrafts, consumer products. Now, to a growing extent, computers are also embedded into social and economic processes. In these cases user communities form the application context and interact in cooperative or competitive processes (e.g. working groups, organizations or markets) via the system.

This paper focusses on a special kind of computer and communication systems in market environments, so called "electronic auctions". The term will be used here to denote

> a computer / communication system that allows a community of market participants to interact in a competitive bidding by submitting bids and offers, causing the system to compute all constituent parts of trades.

The term "bid" ("offer") denotes

> the commitment of a market participant to buy (sell) a certain item under the conditions he or she indicates.

"Competitive bidding" stands for

> a centralized procedure for the exposure of market participants' bids and offers to other participants' orders, so that trades result out of this interaction according to predefined rules.

The electronic auction definition above covers numerous systems, especially trade execution systems [2]. To illustrate the definitions given above, an auction example, that of a continuous auction, is going to be presented now.

2. An Electronic Auction Example

2.1 Introduction

The main function of an electronic auction is to receive buy and sell orders from market participants and to transform them into trades, using an algorithm executing the match. This matching takes place under certain rules that assign execution priorities to orders entered into the system. Other rules determine prices and quantities of trades.

This section presents the example of a continuous electronic auction. It explicates the underlying mechanism for trade determination and is thus closely related to implementations of matching systems running today [3].

2.2 System Functionality

The function of the continuous auction system is to take a sequence of buy and sell orders, each at a certain price and quantity for some type of contract, and to transform it into a sequence of trades, thereby following a predefined set of informally stated execution rules. The rules the system follows are those of price and time priority. With a slight modification, the following rules are those described in [3].

1. Order eligibility: A new order is eligible to be matched with a standing order, and a trade will result, whenever the following conditions occur:

1.1. One order is a buy and the other is a sell order.

1.2. The two orders are for the same item.

1.3. The price of the buy order is greater than or equal to the price of the sell order.

2. Trade price: If an order match is possible according to the criteria of the Rule 1, then the trade will take place at the price of the standing order.

3. Trade quantity: If an order match is possible according to Rule 1, then the trade will take place for a quantity equal to the smaller of the

3.1. remaining quantity of the new order;

3.2. remaining quantity of the standing order.

4. Maximization of total trade size: If there are multiple standing orders eligible for matching with a new order, then matching will be considered in priority sequence until one of the following conditions is attained:

4.1 the new order is completely filled;

4.2 all eligible standing orders have been considered.

5. Standing order priority:

5.1 Price: for buy orders, higher price is higher priority; for sell orders, lower price is higher priority.

5.2 Time: Within the same price type, older orders have higher priority.

For giving a better understanding, a trading example, showing the application of these rules, will be developed now.

2.3 Trading Example

Consider the sequence of buy and sell orders for one specific type of item in Table 1. It will now be shown how the system will react on this sequence of input orders received.

order	time	buy/sell	price	quantity
1	9:01:12	b	42.75	4
2	9:01:55	b	42.77	2
3	9:02:13	b	42.77	2
4	9:03:33	s	42.79	3
5	9:04:67	b	42.73	1
6	9:05:05	s	42.79	5
7	9:06:34	s	42.77	5
...	...	...	...	...

Table 1: Input Orders

The first three orders are buy orders. The first of them at a price of 42.75 and a quantity of 4. The following two orders are at the price of 42.77 and each at a quantity of 2. According to rule 1.1 no match can happen up to now because only orders of the same kind have been entered. The first three buy orders are now standing orders, waiting to be matched with some incoming sell order.

The fourth order is a sell order, conditions 1.1 and 1.2 hold but 1.3 does not hold, because the sell order is at price of 42.79, it is higher than that of the standing buy orders. Now there are three standing buy orders and one standing sell order. The fifth order again is a buy order. According to 1.3 this buy order is not eligible to be matched against the standing sell order. The sixth order is a sell order at 42.79, it can not be matched with a standing buy because rule 1.3 is violated.

For the seventh order conditions 1.1, 1.2 and 1.3 are fulfilled, it is eligible to be matched with a standing buy order. According to the rules of 5, the standing buy order with the highest priority is number 2, the numbers 3, 1 and 5 are following. Now the price and the quantity has to be determined at which the match of the new sell order with the first standing buy will be executed. According to rule 2 the price for the match will be that of the standing order, in this cases it is 42.77. The quantity at which order 7 is to be matched with order 2 is 2 according to 3.2. The first match of the scenario is completed now, the system will output a data item for this trade - the two orders matched are order 2 and 7 at a price of 42.77 and a quantity of 2.

For the remaining quantity (=3) of order 7 according to rule 4 a further match is tried now. The buy order eligible to be matched with the rest of the sell order 7 is the order with number 3. The price of the match is at 42.77 and a quantity of 2. The system will produce the second output data item. There is a rest quantity of order 7 at 1. But no further match is possible at the moment because there is no eligible standing buy order. Order 1 is at the price 42.75, the remaining quantity of order 7 is at the price of 42.77 so that condition 1.3 is not fulfilled. The rest of order 7 is now the standing sell order with the highest priority for matches with new buy orders.

3. Types of Electronic Auctions

3.1 Auction Characteristics

Traditional auctions are carried out with participants present at a single location and often at the same point of time. Electronic auctions change this situation. They allow buyers and sellers to participate in the auction process from spatially distributed places. What I assume to remain unchanged with electronic auctions are the procedural rules that govern the process. They define the

- group of participants (e.g. liquidity requirements, members),
- opening condition,
- the number of bid and offers on each market side
- the form of bids and offers (e.g. closed, open; oral and written),
- allowed sequence of bids and offers (simultaneous; ascending or descending),
- conditions under which a trade occurs (i.e. bids and offers match) and
- the formation of trades (determination of trade constituents).

3.2 Types of Auctions

We distinguish the following auction types by combining some of the characteristics mentioned above:

- *Closed Auction*: Bids are made privately in written or oral form with no special order during a predefined time interval. The bids are opened and published at a certain point of time, then the highest bidder wins [2].

- *English Auction*: The auctioneer seeks an initial bid made publicly from one of the attendant participants. He expects that those bidders interested in the item offered for sale will bid against one another until all but the highest bidder are eliminated. The form of making bids is oral [2].

- *Dutch Auction*: An auction which follows the descending price pattern. The auctioneer starts with a high offer price. He then calls hypothetical prices on a downward scale at predetermined intervals. The expectation is that a would-be buyer will bid the item in before the price declines too far. This scheme can be implemented either by voice or electronically by the so-called Dutch clock. It is the task of the auctioneer to open at an adequate price level. The price must be high enough to permit the bidder with the highest demand price to enter his bid at a maximum. If the auctioneer starts at a price too high, speed of the auction will slow down because it takes longer to decline to the price level of demand. It is the potential speed of the Dutch auction that allows to sell numerous items in a short time interval - an aspect of relevance if goods sold are perishable [2].

- *Japanese Auction*: The bidding starts as soon as the auctioneer gives a signal. As in the sealed bid auction, bids are made simultaneously. They are made publicly by voice or hand sign so that other bidders can adjust their own bids. Bidders make their adjustments very quickly since only a relatively short period is allowed for bidding. At a certain moment the auctioneer spots the highest bid and takes it. This moment is difficult to foresee, in most cases the auctioneer is looking for a particular bid that he will take as soon as it is signaled. The Japanese auction is used in auctioning series of similar goods, each sale is quickly followed by another [2].

- *Double Auction*: Buyers and sellers make bids and offers for the exchange of a single item at a time. New bids and offers entered are required to improve conditions provided by the best standing bid (the highest bid to buy the current item) resp. offer (the lowest offer to sell the unit). Does a buyer accept the standing offer or does a seller accept the standing bid, the unit is transacted. After completion of a transaction, the bidding for a new item starts. The whole auction ends at a predefined point of time [6].

- *Call Auction*: Buyers and sellers make bids and offers which are collected in an order book administered by an auctioneer. The order book is open for bids and offers for a specified time span. After closing the book the auctioneer calculates the price at which the transaction volume is maximal and reveals that price to the market. If he can't find a price at which the market demand- and supply side exactly balance, he can adjust the indicated market price in order to let further orders come in. He then chooses a transaction price at which the market imbalance is minimal. Orders which can't be transacted remain in the order book up to the next "call", or the auctioneer buys or sells for his own account, i.e. acts as a counterpart for trades [8].

- *Continuous Auction*: (cf. 2.)

- *Double English Auction*: The Double English Auction uses two English clocks, a buyer clock set low which is favourable to buyers and a seller clock set high which is favourable to sellers. The buyer clock ascends, the seller clock descends. During their movements, both clocks are becoming less favourable. Before the clocks start, buyers (sellers) are requested to enter privately the maximum quantity of items they are willing to buy (sell) at the initial prices. When these initial quantities are set by each participant, the sum of quantities on the sell and buy side of the market are published to everybody. The clock on the excess side (supply or demand) is started, in case of a balance between both sides, the buyer clock starts. Each buyer (seller) is allowed to stop the buy (sell) clock at a price to indicate, that he is only willing to buy (sell) one unit less at a price worse than the currently displayed price on the buyer (seller) clock. This item is reduced from the buy (sell) side of the market and the clock of the market side with an excess - the demand or supply side - is started. Clocks restart at the price they have previously been stopped.This allows multiple items to be withdrawn from the market at the same price. The process stops when both clocks cross. Those items are exchanged which have not been redrawn [6].

- *Double Dutch Auction*: Two Dutch clocks are in use, a buyer clock that shows the current buy price and a sell clock that shows the current sell price.The buy clock starts high and descends, the sell clock starts low and ascends. The auction ends when the two clocks cross, the market price for transacting items is set at the crossing price. By stopping a clock a buyer (seller) indicates his wish to buy (sell) at the price currently displayed on the buy (sell) clock. His wish is recorded and one of the two clocks is started at the price it was stopped with. This allows the registration of multiple bids to buy (offers to sell) at one price. Clocks don't move simultaneously - only one clock moves at the same time. After a stop, in case of an excess supply the buyer clock is started, in case of an excess demand the seller clock continues to move. If the market is balanced after registration of a sell or buy quote, the clock which moved last proceeds. The process starts with the Dutch buy clock to move [6].

- *English-Dutch Auction*: The English Dutch auction uses one clock initialized high. It is a Dutch Clock from the buyers' perspective and an English clock from the sellers' perspective. Before the clock starts, sellers enter the quantity of items they are offering at the starting price. The total sum of supply is published and the clock begins to move. Both, sellers and buyers are allowed to stop the clock at any time in any order. When a seller stops the clock, he indicates his will to buy an item at the current price. By halting the clock's movement, a seller conversely indicates his intention to sell one item less below or at the current price. This is a difference to the Double-English Auction were a clock stop indicates the unwillingness to sell at a price less favourable than the current price. Has the clock been stopped, it is restarted at the same price. The process ends, when the supply and the demand side of the market are in balance. The market price then is set equal to the price at which the balance occured.

The auction types introduced build a typology as follows:

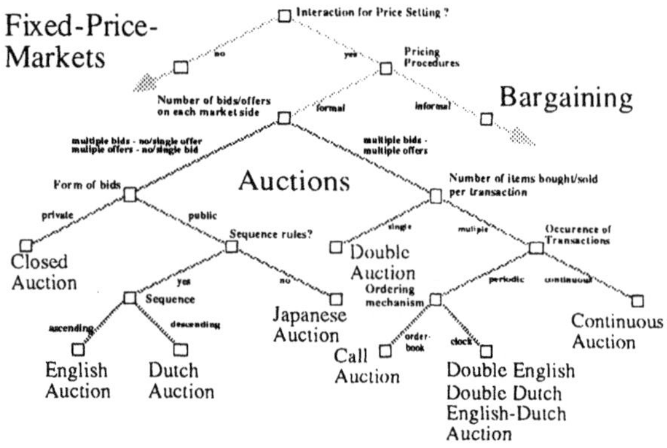

Figure 1: Types of Auctions [7]

Auctions are one type of market allocation mechanism. Figure 1 above suggest to distinguish them from other types of markets by the mode of interaction that takes place between market participants for setting prices in a market. If no interaction takes place, a "take it or leave it" situation is given, that means, the transaction price is set on one market side and has to be accepted by a counterpart of the other side. When going shopping buyers are normally confronted with such a market situation. Also reservation systems are examples for this type of market.

If interaction for price determination between participants of the market's supply- and demand side takes place, processes that are dominated by formal as well as informal rules have to be distinguished. Bargaining is based on social rules which informally determine the price finding process. Auctions are social processes as well [2] but are dominated by formal rules of pricing. The different auction types introduced in this section are arranged in Figure 1 to form a typology. Attributes according to which auction types are differentiated are the number of bids and offers on each market side, the form of bids, the number of items bought and sold per transaction, sequencing rules, the ordering mechanism and the mode of transaction occurrence.

3.3 From Auctions to Electronic Auctions

If we take an auction as it is performed in a traditional way today on one side, and its electronic counterpart on the other, we see, that both are defined by the same procedural rules, we can say that the electronic version 'mimics' the original system [8]. That means, participants of electronic auctions, in principle, face the same process as in a classical auction process, what changes is the way how this process is physically realized. In this sense does Figure 1 show a typology of auctions and of electronic auctions as well.

The remaining part of this paper now addresses the question of how to describe different auction processes adequately, if they are going to be implemented electronically.

4. The Specification of Electronic Auctions

It is assumed, that the behavior of a system, some type of auction in our case, is observable by an external observer as a finite or infinite sequence of actions (traces):

"Imagine there is an observer with a notebook who watches the process and writes down the name of each event as it occurs. We can validly ignore the possibility that two events occur simultaneously; for if they did, the observer would still have to record one of them first and then the other, and the order in which he records them would not matter." [5]

The fundamental structure underlying traces is that of streams (cf. [1]). Given a set of items S the set of ***streams over S*** is denoted by S^{ω}. It is defined as the union of the finite and infinite sequences over S:

$$S^{\omega} = S^{*} \cup S^{\infty}.$$

The basic operations and relations defined on streams are the following. Let s, t, u be streams and a, b, c be items,

- ε denotes the empty stream.
- $\langle s_1,\ldots,s_n \rangle$ denotes the stream that contains the elements $s_1,\ldots,s_n$.
- ft (s) returns the first element of s, if s is not empty; ft (ε) delivers ⊥ (undefined).
- rt (s) returns the stream in which the first element of s is deleted.
- a & s denotes the stream where a is prefixed to s. If a is defined, i.e. a ≠ ⊥, ft (a & s) = a and rt (a & s) = s.
- s • t denotes the concatenation of the streams s and t. If s is an infinite stream, s • t is equal to s. Frequently a • s is written instead of a & s, and a • b is written for a & b & ε, thus using items as streams of length 1.
- $s \sqsubseteq t$ denotes that s is a prefix of t, i.e. ∃u : s • u = t.
- a in s yields true if a occurs in s.
- #s delivers the length of s, ∞ if s is infinite.
- a © s, a filter operation, results in a substream of s that only consists of a-elements, e.g. a © ⟨a • c • b • b • c • a⟩ = ⟨a • a⟩. The operation may be extended so that the first operand is a set of items.

Formally, traces over an action set Act can now be regarded as a streams over Act. It is denoted by $Act^{\omega} = Act^{*} \cup Act^{\infty}$, where Act^{*} denotes the set of finite traces, Act^{∞} the set of infinite traces. Time is modelled in traces by the action √ representing the "ticking of a clock". Infinite traces over set Act containing clock ticks are denoted by $Act_{\surd}^{\infty}$.

Since traces are streams of actions, in a system specification first a set of actions is to be defined. The elements of this set of actions may then be used for building action streams (traces). Obviously not every combination of actions in a stream represents a reasonable system run. Thus, one has to distinguish the reasonable traces from the rest. This is done by means of a predicate that characterizes the allowed runs. Every trace satisfying this predicate is an allowed run of the system.

5. Example: Specifying the Closed Auction System

5.1 The Definition of Basic Data Types

Datasets Price, Item and Participant are elementary in consisting of elements that denote possible prices, objects as well as participants in an auction system. The datatype PRICE is equivalent to the datatype of natural numbers specified by NAT The specifications of datatypes BID, OFFER and TRADE are all built as instantiations of the datatype scheme N-TUP as follows:

> **type** BID = Bid, item, buyer, price:
> **include** 3-Tup (Item, Participant, Price, =, =, =) **as**
> (Bid, item, buyer, price)
> **endoftype**.

Bids are defined as 3-tuples [i, b, p] with a component i that denotes the item to be bought, an element p which represents the price a buyer identified by b is willing to pay. Operations item, price and buyer are selectors that return the component values i ∈ Item, p ∈ Price, b ∈ Buyer if applied to an element [i, b, p] ∈ Bid.

The datatype OFFER with dataset Offer and operations item, price and participant is defined as

> **type** OFFER = Offer, item, seller, price:
> **include** 3-Tup (Item, Participant, Price, =, =, =) **as**
> (Offer, item, seller, price)
> **endoftype**.

Offer denotes the data set of offers, each standing for an offer as it may appear in the closed auction system. item, price and seller applied to an element [i, s, p] ∈ Offer deliver the identifier i ∈ Item for the item to be sold, the reserve price p ∈ Price requested and the market participant s ∈ Participant willing to sell.

A trade t ∈ Trade is specified as a 4-tuple consisting of an identifier for the item exchanged and the buyer and seller involved into the trade. The fourth component indicates the price at which the trade occurs. Formally, this can be expressed by

type TRADE = Trade, item, buyer, seller, price: **include**
4-Tup (Item, Participant, Participant, Price =, =, =, =) **as**
(Trade, item, buyer, seller, price)
endoftype.

Now the specifications above allow to define the action set relevant for the closed auction system definition.

5.2 The Specification of Action Sets

The trace specification following is based on an action set consisting of four elements. For functions bid: Bid → Act, offer: Offer → Act, publish: Offer → Act and trade: Trade → Act this set is defined as

$$Act = \{bid.b, offer.f, publish.f, trade.d \mid b \in Bid, f \in Offer, d \in Trade\}$$

The four actions have the following interpretation: bid.b denotes the input of a bid b ∈ Bid. The complementary action on the supply side of the market is the action offer.f with f ∈ Offer. By publish.f it is made public to the auction participants that an offer f has been entered. The action trade.d signals the occurrence of a trade d ∈ Trade.

Subset

$$Bids = \{bid.b \mid b \in Bid\}$$

is used as an auxiliary construct.

5.3 Specifying the System Behaviour

The closed auction (CA)

i) eventually starts with an offer,

ii) the offer is immediately published and

iii) a bidding for the item to be exchanged starts.

These requirements formally translate to the predicate CA_{Start}: $Act^{*}\surd^{\infty} \to \{true, false\}$ being defined as

$$CA_{Start}.t \equiv \exists f \in Offer;\ s \in Bids\surd^{*}: \surd^{*} \bullet offer.f \bullet publish.f \bullet s \sqsubseteq t \wedge CA_{Bidding}(s,f)$$

For biddings the following properties must hold:

iv) bids refer to the item offered for sale,

v) the same bid only appears once,

vi) the process ends after maximally N time steps, and

vii) bid prices are equal to or above the indicated reserve price.

Predicate

$$CA_{Bids}: Bids \times Offer \to \{true, false\}$$

captures properties iv) and v)

$$CA_{Bids}(t, f) \equiv \forall b \in Bid: bid.b \text{ in } t \Rightarrow item.b = item.f \wedge \#(bid.b © t) \le 1$$

Requirement vi) is expressed through predicate

$$CA_{\surd}: Bids\surd^{*} \to \{true, false\}$$

being defined by the formula

$$CA_{\surd}.t \equiv \#(\surd © t) \le N$$

Finally, predicate

$$CA_{Limit}: Act\surd^{\infty} \times Offer \to \{true, false\}$$

captures requirement vii) through

$$CA_{Limit}(t, f) \equiv \forall b \in Bid, s \in Bids\surd^{*}: s \sqsubseteq t \Rightarrow (bid.b \text{ in } s \Rightarrow price.b \ge price.f)$$

Requirements iv) - vii) taken together translate to predicate

$$CA_{Bidding}: Bids\surd^{*} \times Offer \to \{true, false\}$$

defined as

$$CA_{Bidding}(t, f) \equiv CA_{Bids}(t, f) \wedge CA_{\surd}.t \wedge CA_{Limit}(t, f)$$

The closed auction progresses with the occurrence of a

viii) trade followed by no further actions except clock ticks, if at least one bid has been entered during the closed bidding.

ix) Supposing that no bids arrived, no further actions except clock ticks follow the closed bidding.

These requirements translate to the predicate

$$CA_{Trading}: Act\surd^{\infty} \to \{true, false\}$$

defined by

$$
\begin{aligned}
&CA_{Trading}.t \equiv \forall f \in Offer; s \in Bids\surd^{*}: \\
&\surd^{*} \bullet offer.f \bullet publish.f \bullet s \sqsubseteq t \wedge CA_{Bidding}(s, f) \Rightarrow \\
&(Bids © s \neq \varepsilon \Rightarrow \exists d \in Trade: \\
&\quad \surd^{*} \bullet offer.f \bullet publish.f \bullet s \bullet trade.d \bullet \surd^{\infty} \sqsubseteq t) \wedge \\
&(Bids © s = \varepsilon \Rightarrow : \surd^{*} \bullet offer.f \bullet publish.f \bullet s \bullet \surd^{\infty} \sqsubseteq t)
\end{aligned}
$$

The next predicate CA_{Trade} defines the composition of a trade:

$$
\begin{aligned}
&CA_{Trade}: Act\surd^{\infty} \rightarrow \{true, false\} \\
&CA_{Trade}.t \equiv \forall f \in Offer, d \in Trade, s \in Bids\surd^{*}: \\
&\quad \surd^{*} \bullet offer.f \bullet publish.f \bullet s \bullet trade.d \sqsubseteq t \wedge \\
&CA_{Bidding}(s, f) \Rightarrow \\
&\qquad \exists b \in Bid: CA_{Win}(b, s) \wedge \\
&\qquad item.d = item.f \wedge \\
&\qquad buyer.d = buyer.b \wedge \\
&\qquad seller.d = seller.f \wedge \\
&\qquad price.d = price.b
\end{aligned}
$$

x) A trade is preceded by a closed bidding and one bid of those entered has highest ranking with respect to price and time priority, it is the 'winning bid' (cf. predicate CA_{Win}).

The trade that results in a closed auction is composed of bid and offer data elements as follows:

xi) the item transacted in a trade and

xii) the buyer and seller of a trade are those indicated in the initial offer and the winning bid,

xiii) the price at which the trade occurs is that indicated in the winning bid.

Predicate

$$CA_{Win}: Bid \times Bids\surd^{*} \rightarrow \{true, false\}$$

defines a 'winning bid' in a finite stream of bids by

$$
\begin{aligned}
&CA_{Win}(b, t) \equiv bid.b \text{ in } t \wedge \\
&\quad \forall b' \in Bid: bid.b' \text{ in } t \Rightarrow Price.b' \leq Price.b \\
&\quad bid.b = ft(\{bid.b' \mid Price.b' = Price.b\} © t) \wedge
\end{aligned}
$$

A winning bid

xiv) must be contained in the respective stream, and

xv) it is the only or the first bid at the highest price in that stream.

The overall system behaviour of a closed auction system can now be defined as

$$
\begin{aligned}
&CA: Act\surd^{\infty} \rightarrow \{true, false\} \\
&CA.t \equiv CA_{Start}.t \wedge CA_{Trading}.t \wedge CA_{Trade}.t
\end{aligned}
$$

References

[1] M. Broy: Towards a Design Methodology for Distributed Systems, in: F.L. Bauer, M. Broy, E.W. Dijkstra, C.A.R. Hoare: Constructive Methods in Computing Science, Springer 1989.

[2] C.W. Cassady: Auctions: The Social Construction of Value, Harvester Wheatsheaf, 1989.

[3] I. Domowitz: A Taxonomy of Trade Execution Systems, Dep. of Economics, Northwestern University Evanston (Il), 1992.

[4] K. Garbade: Securities Markets, McGraw Hill Publishing Company, 1982.

[5] C.A.R. Hoare: Communicating Sequential Processes, Prentice Hall, 1985.

[6] K. Mc.Cabe, S. Rassenti, V. Smith: Institutional Design for Electronic Trading, Conference on Global Equity Markets, N.Y. University, Salomon Center, 1992.

[7] M. Reck: The Identification and Formal Specification of Electronic Markets Types, Paper presented at the ICIS Doctoral Consortium, Dallas (TX), 1992.

[8] R.A. Schwartz: Reshaping the Equity Markets - A Guide for the 1990s, Harper Business, 1991.

Principles of reference models and the linking to object oriented systems

Chr. Meijs
Wageningen Agricultural University
Department of Computer Science
Dreijenplein 2, 6703 HB Wageningen
The Netherlands

e-mail: meijs@rcl.wau.nl

Abstract

During the course of an information system planning study, several models are developed. Two kinds of models are distinguished: models for analysis which are utilized to get a clear picture of a problem at hand and models for design. These latter models are more geared towards describing the future organization of support by information systems. If business functions, data and decisions or other aspects can be defined in a stable manner for a given line of business this leads to the definition of so-called reference models. Reference models are created for industries independent of an actual organization. The planning and developement of systems using models, is illustrated for the tourist industry.

Especially for small and medium business the use of reference models appear to advantages. It is often (economic) impossible to carry out a informationplanning study or to develop tailor-made information system for a small organization. The use of reference models stimulates standardization of information technology, for instance the electronic data interchange (EDI).

The reuse of components of reference-models and software packages during an information systems planning and development project, is described in a 10 step approach.

Keywords: information systems planning, object orientation, reference-models, reuse.

1 Introduction

A challenge of major importance for the future is to enable business to master the growing complexity associated with the effective and efficient use of information technology for their information-related activities.

With the rapid evolution of informationtechnology new challenges and exiting new opportunities arise. The tourist industry is an area of enormous potential for applications involving integrating Decision Support System (DSS), Knowledge Based Systems (KBS) and electronic data communication with conventional technologies. In order to avoid the use of models only on a project-to-project basis and a high redundancy factor the use of reference-models is advocated [Scheer92]. It will be argued that improving the practice of information system planning by using reference-informationmodels is very important for the succesful introduction of information systems. An in-depth analysis of the foundations of reference-informationmodel should reveal the fundamental components. The introduction of information-technology has to be accompanied by enough attention paid to the organizational aspects of the businesses and the individual consumer in the tourist industry.

2 Systems planning and development

Prior to conducting an information systems planning project, a preliminary scoping exercise is often undertaken in order to clarify the boundaries of the planningproject. Informationplanning is a decision-making proces, by which management gives direction to the development of the information services. This concerns the formulation of an information strategy and informationplan, the latter containing the strategic planning of information systems [Olle91]. Information systems planning takes place in the context of other forms of planning practised within the business. In practice it is clever to use referencemodels for information systems planning. Models in information planning are usually represented by means of natural language descriptions, charts, matrices and various other diagrams. As is often the case with planning in general, the most critical part of the process is putting the plan to use. To avoid that costly information plans stay on the shelf and gather dust, special attention should be payed to implementation via specific systems development projects [Uijttenbroek92]. The payoff for creating information architectures is in the system development process, but there are still some obstacles for introducing new systems [Hartog91]. Models for understanding can play a crucial role in the effective communication of the participating interest groups. For the user, it is often difficult to specify the information needs correct and complete. Another approach to information requirement determination is, to capture an initial set of requirements and implement this. The system is designed for ease of change. In essence, after an initial set of requirements provide an anchor, additonal requirements are discovered through sytem use.

2.1 Roles of reference-models

The current dramatic changes in information technology increases the importance of standards. To our opinion standards should be consensus-developed, voluntary and available to any vendor or user. The standardization process should provide a stable environment for all users of information technology. Several kinds of reference-models are important for the introduction and standardization of information technology. The following table presents some reference models.

TABLE 1. EXAMPLES OF REFERENCE MODELS

NR.	REFERENCE MODEL	FOCUS ON
1	OPEN SYSTEMS INTERCONNECTION	NETWORK TECHNOLOGY
2	FUNCTIONAL REFERENCE MODEL	BUSINESS FUNCTIONS
3	ENTERPRISE-WIDE DATA MODELS	DATA
4	CIM OPEN SYSTEMS ARCHITECTURE	MANUFACTURING
5	VALUE CHAIN	REENGINEERING LOGISTICS
6	LIFE CYCLES OF PRODUCTS	INNOVATIVE APPLICATIONS
7	LEARNING CYCLE OF KOLB	LEARNING SKILLS
8	OBJECT DATA MANAGEMENT	OBJECT ORIENTED TECHNOLOGY

Planning of information on the branch level can be instrumental in the coordination and stimulation of a well-balanced introduction of information-technology for the involved business. For the resulting models of the planning and development activities we make a distinction between:

- Models for analysis, the purpose of the analysis is to obtain understanding of systems. The informationplanning is based on analysis of problems and opportunities in the current business situation, followed by the identification of changes to business activities. As a consequence of this survey re-engineering the business activities may be necessary and information systems will change in time. The used models are an "improved version" of an organization handbook and can be used to detect bottle-necks in the business processes, to increase the availability and distribution of knowledge of the business itself. Verification of the models is carried out through discussions with projectmembers and other personnel.
- Models for design. The informationplanning is focused on the future organization of information system support. The models contain normative elements, suggesting that in the future new

business functions are required. Design activities are opposite to analysis activities, because they should ultimately describe the full system to be realized. Redesign of an entire organization is rather ambitious, therefore redesign usually means redesign of part of the organization. A typically example of redesign is the reengineering of business processes.

A special kind of reference-model is a *reference-information model.* Common information requirements and decision processes of a class of similar business in a particular sector are modelled, so the perspective of data and functions are emphasized in these models.

Both for planning and development activities, the involved individual projectmembers are subjected to a process of learning and change. The 7th reference model of table 1 may be applied for guiding this learning process. Effective learning means going through the following phases in a number of cyclic iterations: conceptualization, experimentation, action and reflection [Kolb84]. In fig. 1 the main features of the learning cycle are shown. In this cycle, the recurring phases of conceptualization and reflection may be seen as thinking about the system on basis of the accumulated experience, reformulating and revisualizing conclusions and taking action-oriented decisions in a project.

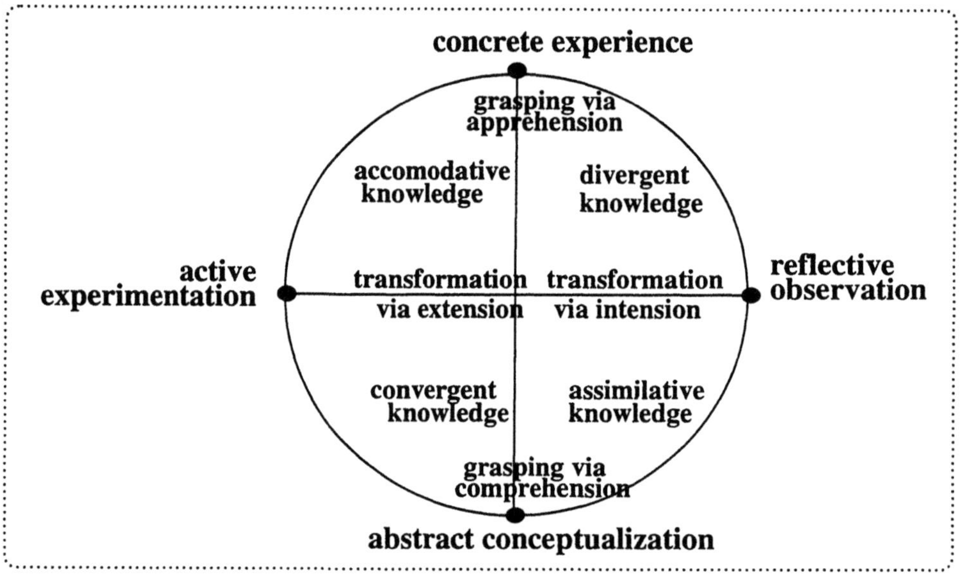

Fig. 1 Learning cycle of Kolb

Practising this model is not limited to the area of information technology, it is also used to set up education and training courses in other area.

2.2 History and background of reference-information models

During the second part of the former decade several reference informationmodels for the agricultural branches as dairy, potplant nursery , poultry and fruit were created in the Netherlands. There are about 100.000 farms in the Netherlands, so each individual farmer can not afford to make tailor-made information models and systems from scratch for his farm. For each type of farm an reference-information model was constructed. The number of farms belonging to a specific branch ranges from the smallest number for Mushroom cultivation farms (750) to the highest for Dairy farms (36000). For the standard farm of a specific branch models of data and processes have been made, using the Information Engineering Methodology. The construction of the models was a joined effort of the branch organizations, agricultural researchers and information engineers. Since the first reference-informationmodels were finished some years ago, evaluation of the use of these models gives us recommendations for the next generation of reference-informationmodels:

- The branch dimension is tentatively a good criterium for grouping the different types of farms, but there also branch crossing components for e.g. the functions strategic planning and financial management.
- The reference-informationmodels are used as a frame of reference for those involved in building management information systems for the agricultural branche. Users from the software industry criticize the models because they notice a gap between the reference-informationmodels and the development of information systems.
- The data definitions of the reference-informationmodels seems to be used most intensive. They are for example important for the introduction of EDI, because it supports the standardization of exchanging data. However, other aspects are lacking in these models, in particular the dynamic components.
- More attention should be paid to the maintenance of reference models. Especially, aspects like the suitability of the applied techniques, support of computer-aided tools, reuse of components and the management of these models are important.

2.3 Metamodel for planning and development

To overcome the mentioned shortcomings of reference-informationmodels and to reduce the drawbacks of current methods for planning and development of information systems [Hartog91], we follow the essentials of the metamethod *Methodology Engineering* [Welke91]. Therefore we elaborate 10 steps for dealing with situations where reference-informationmodels and object oriented technology are suitable, the metamodel of fig. 2 gives an overview of this approach. These steps will be further described, in the first 5 steps of this approach the available reference-models will be adapted, step 6 up to and including step 10 deal with the object oriented system development.
Methodology Engineering results in a meta-activity model, which shows *how* to conduct this approach, and a meta-data model shows *what* products should be delivered. The relation between methods, techniques and tools which are used in favour of an efficient and effective planning and development process, should be maintained carefully. The mapping of the required techniques, products and workbenches is defined as the *method companionship.* For deciding what kind of tool can be used to support the planning and development activities we have to analyse these activities and the corresponding products.

2.3.1 Relevant concepts

Some relevant concepts for this 10 step approach are defined (other can be found in [Olle91], [Otis91] and [Rumbaugh91]). A *business function* is a group of activities which together support one aspect of the business mission. A dominant technique for getting the components of the reference model is via the functional view, where one identifies a hierarchy of functions, completed with the details of data items that flow between them. This is essentially what is called the functional decomposition. In the functional view we specify that data can flow, but not wheter and when it will.
Critical success factors (CSF) are a small number of factors which must go right if the organization wants to achieve its mission and goal. They are not a standard set of measures that can be applied to all organizations within one branch. Some critical success factors arise from the characterics of the industry itself, see for example csf's of the travel industry [Cottrell91]. An organization may have a particular niche within an industry, represented by conditons to be satisfied. The csf's of the business unit manager, must fit and be specialized within the success factors of his organization.
In the context of this study, we use the term *information architecture* to mean a conceptual model for a specific organization. An information architecture is a high level map of the requirements and information needs of this organization and it relates them to specific business functions.
The data classes in this information architecture constitute the major parts for starting the object oriented system development. By organizing objects in class *hierarchies*, lower level objects can receive properties from higher level objects. Objects having generic properties support reusability

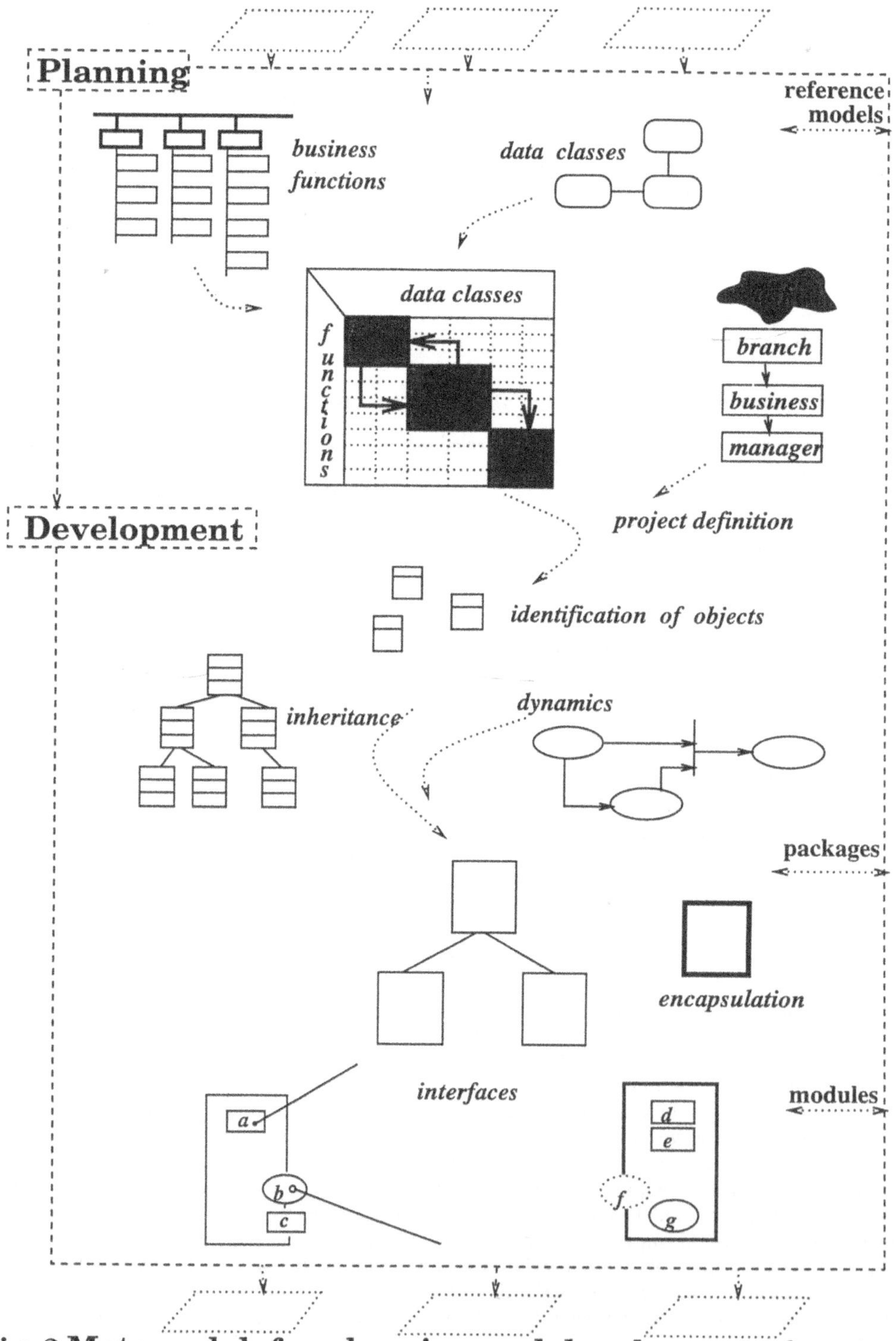

Fig. 2 Metamodel for planning and develoment of systems

by property inheritance from superclass to subclass. Two forms of inheritance may be supported: hiearchical, in which a child object can inherit only from its parent object. Multiple inheritance occurs when an object can inherit properties from several parent objects. Another important concept is ***encapsulation***: objects should hide their internal contents form other system components to improve the maintainability.

2.3.2 Adaptation of reference-models

In the available framework presented in [Olle91] 5 abstraction steps for an information systems planning study are recognized. We have adopted this framework and adjusted it by using a reference-informationmodel in order to reduce the complexity, time and cost of informationplanning sessions.

1. Identify business plan components and information needs.
   The mission and goal statements of the subjected business are used as a starting point. The intention is to focus attention on ways of supporting these goals. The information need to support these is next compared to present business functions, critical succes factors (csf) and data classes of the reference-informationmodel. Typically only 6 to 10 business functions and data classes will initially emerge.

2. Develop business model (from a data perspective).
   Having already identified the major data classes it then becomes possible to identify the matching entity types on a more formal and high level for the business. If it is required that the definitions of functions, csf's and entities are adapted to the local situation.

3. Identify information systems and business areas.
   An initial matrix becomes available after interview sessions in the organization, showing which business functions creates and uses data classes. This matrix can be reordered to illustrate how data classes are shared.

4. Analyse priorities.
   On the basis of recognized critical succes factors and dependencies on other systems it is now possible to decide about the transitions moving from the current systems. A logical list of priorities for information systems in this business is established.

5. Prepare plan.
   A grouping of information systems is carried out, which provide an overview of the systems boundaries and the interfaces. A rolling plan is advocated because in dynamic situations re-planning is often necessary [Uijttenbroek92].

2.3.3 Object orientation

Object-oriented system development claims to improve software design for reliability and maintenance. Further claims are that the development process is made more efficient by reuse. The major part of applied object oriented techniques originates the methodology OMT (Object Modeling Technique) and we adopt concepts from [Otis91]. In specifying objects we distinguish static and dynamic aspects. Static concepts concern the attributes of the objects and the relationships between objects.

6. Build an Object Model.
   Building an object Model starts with identifying objects and classes. Object classes can be refined by using inheritance to organize the class hierarchy. Redundant and vague classes are discarded. A data dictionary is prepared, the object classes are described precisely in this dictionary. The associations, attributes and later on the operations are also described in this dictionary.

7. Develop a Dynamic Model
   Dynamic aspects concern the actions triggered by events and executed by or on objects. Permissible event sequences for each object are stated in a state diagram and we look for stimuli and responses.

8. Functional Model.
   Every class object has associated with it four primary operations: create, delete, amend and retrieve. These correspond to the classic file maintenance operations and are usually left off the diagrams. However, if constraints are attached to these operations then these primary operations should be notated in the diagram. Operations on a more higher level are also included in the model.

9. System design.
   The system may be decomposed in modules. Another important goal of these phase is to identify which objects must be active concurrently and mutually exclusive operations.

10. Object design.
    The tree models from the finished phases are combined and optimized for the implementation of the system. There is a shift in emphasis from object from the real world to computer concepts. For nontrivial operations algorithms are created.

3 A worked example: the tourist industry

In the tourist sector many computerized reservation systems are installed and mostly these systems are conceived as tools for the management and sales of airline and hotel space. These systems have their impact on consumer services and also on the choice of destination.
According the metamodel of fig. 2 and the 10 step approach, several components of reference-models or software packages may be reused. However, special adjustments are often necessary. Therefore we make a distinction between a general and a specific part in the following illustrated steps for the context of the hotel branch and a specific 5 stars hotel.

- Identify business plan components and information needs.

  - Hotel branch general.
    Campaigns in the traditional way of mass marketing in which the consumer is regarded as a passive recipient of enticing messages consequently loses significance [Sahlberg93]. The requirements of consumers can be characterized by greater demands and awareness. Correct, reliable and relevant information about selected destinations will need more attention. An increased exploitation of information technology will facilitate the consumers in their choice of destination and tourist products. Applications shoud be build in modularized way with standardized application dialogues and graphical user interface.
    APARTMENT, CLIENT, EQUIPMENT and FINANCE are important data classes. Some business functions are PLANNING, PERSONNAL MANAGEMENT, MAINTENANCE, and MARKETING, which all are decomposed.

  - Specific for hotel the five stars (*****)

    The definition of the relevant components in the reference-model may be less precise, however they provide a starters set and will be adjusted. Due to reduced interest the laundry, night bar and the babysitter apartment are closed. But new business functions are broached, e.g. *Offering facilities*: included are playing golf, sports equipment for hire and a video corner. A fast food restaurant, sauna, solarium, medicinal bath and a fitness room will be opened next year. For this next future an augmented information architecture is needed. A new data class is added to this information architecture: SPORT.

- Build an Object Model

  - Hotel branch general.

    Some guests of hotels who have less time for traditional eating demand fast food, which services are supported by a catering system. The offering is in the form of a menu, which invites individual selections. Each selection will require specific ingredients. It shall be assumed that a supplier will be involved in the reorder chain of events with a supply of ingredients. The consumer will also pay his/her selection by the tabulation total.

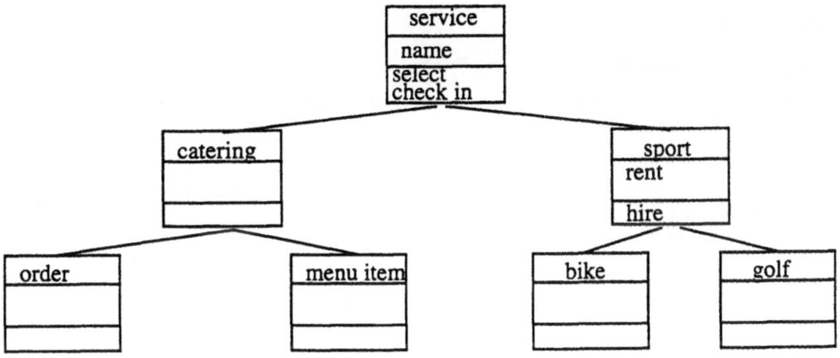

Fig. 3 Object hierarchy

- Specific for hotel the five stars (*****)
  The object model is extended because this business wants to serve also traditional meals (like *erwtensoep*) in the fast food restaurant.

- Develop a Dynamic Model
  - Hotel branch in general.

TABLE 2. EVENT TABLE

NO.	AGENT	EVENT	OBJECT
1	GUEST	SELECTS	SERVICE
2	GUEST	PAYS	BANKACCOUNT
3	EMPLOYEE	REORDER	COMMODITY
4	GUEST	CHECKS IN	SERVICE

Operations responsing to the events are added to the object model.

```
OBJECT Guest SUBCLASS OF Person
creditstatus
OPERATION check in
IF reservation_made
THEN assign SERVICE
ELIF SERVICE IS available
THEN assign SERVICE AND debit BANKACCOUNT.bnr}
ELSE reject
OPERATION credit_worthiness
IF creditstatus IS good
THEN creditworthiness is "sound"

OBJECT Bankaccount
accountname, balance, overdraftlimit
OPERATION credit
balance = balance + amount
OPERATION debit
balance = balance - amount
OPERATION grantoverdraft
IF creditworthiness IS "sound"
THEN overdraflimit = 1000
```

- Specific for hotel the five stars (*****)
  Constraints are attached to these operations.

- Functional Model
  - Hotel branch in general
    Payments of guest are also accepted by electronic transactions, this is shown by the following Data flow diagram:

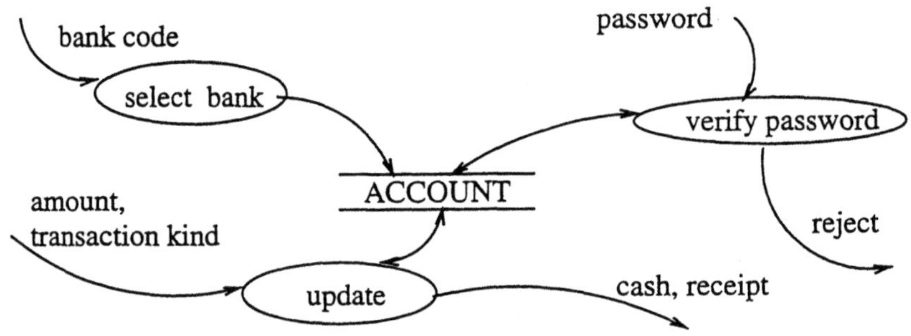

Fig. 4 DFD electronic payment (1st level)

  - Specific for hotel the five stars (*****)
    The system is extended for accepting payments of certain credit-cards where the hotel management succeeded in making special agreements.

4 Discussion

Research has started to optimize the linking between planning and development of information systems. So far, projects in the area of Agriculture, Health Care and Research & Development have been conducted, linking the planning with conventional data modelling techniques. From these projects it is concluded that in practice it is often relevant to focus on more than one perspective, combining the perspectives mentioned in the last column of table 1 is often required. Besides integration of systems in a single business, co-operating networks in the value chain requires external integration. For optimizing the relationships of business in a chain and developing inter-organizational systems we need to focus at least on functions, data and reengineering the logistics. This requires an adjustment of the semantic and pragmatic concepts, which are applied by the involved firms. The concept of integrated systems suggest that interdisciplinary research and development efforts will take on a primary role.
The projects shows us also that it is beneficial to make use of reference models:

- to use already gained experience from other situations or organisations in a structured way
- to improve the communication between firms involved
- to stimulate and standardize systems

The construction of object oriented systems will increase the reuse of components. It has the additional advantage of enlarging the flexibility of business, in order to serve new demands of customers.

References

[Cottrell91] N. Cottrell en K. Rapley; Factors critical to the sucess of executive information systems in British Airways. In: European Journal of Information Systems, vol. 1, nr. 1, 1991.

[Hartog91] R.J.M. Hartog, C.A.J. Meijs; Towards a better understanding of the model concept in the context of information systems development. In: Proc. WC IFIP WG7.6. In Lecture notes in Control and information sciences 174, Springer-verlag, p.84-95, 1992.

[Kolb84] D. Kolb; Experimental learning - Experience as the source of learning and development. Prenctice Hall, Englewood Cliffs, New Jersey 1984.

[Olle91] T. Olle, J. Hagelstein, I. Macdonald, C.Rolland, H. Sol, F. van Assche, A. Verrijn-Stuart. Information system methodologies, a framework for understanding; Addisson Wesley, 2nd edition, New Yersey, 1991.

[Otis91] A. Otis; A reference model for object data management. In: Computer standards & Interfaces 13, 1991, p. 19-32.

[Porter85] M. Porter, V. Millar; How information gives you competitive advantage. In: Harvard business review, pp. 149-160 no. 4 1985.

[Rumbaugh91] J. Rumbaugh, M. Blaha, W. Premerlani, F. Eddy, W. Lorensen; Object-oriented modeling and design. Prentice Hall, Englewood Cliffs, 1991.

[Sahlberg93] Sahlberg; The demand for new information systems in travel and tourism. In: The tourist review, p. 20 -23, no. 2 1993.

[Scheer92] A. Scheer, A. Hars; Extending data modelling to cover the whole enterprise. In: Communications of the ACM vol. 35 no 9 1992.

[Welke91] R. Welke, K. Kumar, H. van Dissel; Methodology Engineering. In: Informatie nr. 5 1991.

[Uijttenbroek92] A. Uijttenbroek, P. Anthonisse, C. Meijs, B. Verdoes; Project management principles; Cap Gemini Publishing. Rijswijk, 1992.

DEVELOPMENT OF ADAPTABLE INFORMATION SYSTEMS IN TOURISM

Vlad Wietrzyk

University of Technology Sydney, Computer Science, P.O Box 123 Broadway
NSW 2007 Australia. **vlad@socs.uts.edu.au**

ABSTRACT

An analysis of existing models and programming languages shows the main problem in requirement engineering: the egreement between a well-defined basic model and a convenient language. One major problem in traditional analysis, design and implementation is the amount of work needed when going from one model to another. This is especially the case in the transformation of the analysis model into the design model. The problem is that the two models have two logically different representations.

The QUELLE project builds on the object-oriented system development paradigm and extends this work in two directions. The first direction is concerned with the utilization of a commercial ODBMS as the underlying data management mechanism. The second direction is concerned with enhancing the paradigm with the explicit modelling of a problem situation providing decision-supporting environment at the application level.

1. INTRODUCTION

Research methodology, from cognitive science and artificial intelligence, is applied to the problem of software representation to support the process of software change.

The QUELLE environment provides knowledge representation and reasoning tools to integrate knowledge about general software design principles, prototypical software architectures, and application domain. Unlike CASE tools and module interconnection languages that represent the structure of a software system without its semantics, the goal of QUELLE is to integrate both the structure and the semantics of software modules and to provide active assistance in the design of systems.

The development of information systems is usually made in an organizational context in which several people co-operate towards the goals of the organization. QUELLE methodology is based on several assumptions which recognise this:

* Communication between users requires that at least some of the concepts are shared at least partially by the involved users see Figure 1.
* Users have their own concepts which they use to comprehend their environment and to interact with it.
* A state of continuous change of the environment effects the organization and the working conditions of users.

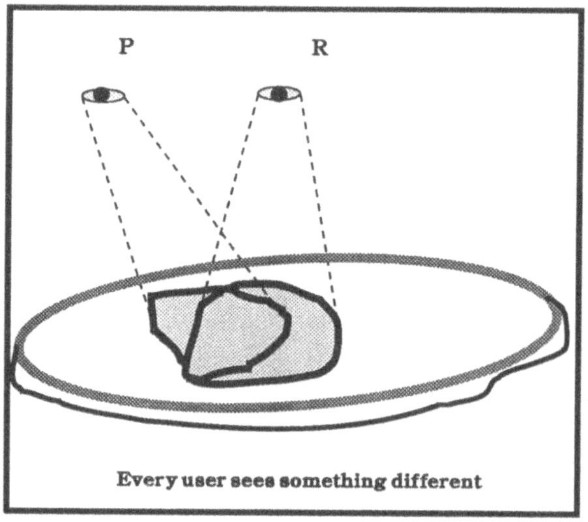

Figure 1.

These assumptions reveal the basic problem in the design of information systems. The knowledge about the universe of discourse must be acquired from users and made shareable within the user community by developing common conceptual model of the community. This knowledge must also be transferred into the information system.

Central in such an approach is the construction of a descriptive model of a problem situation. This empirical model should be object-oriented with specification in a declarative as well as in a procedural mode. Through the process specifications of these objects we can look into the dynamics of decision-making processes and the resulting behaviour.
A data dictionary (a repository) is a definite need here, depicted in Figure 2. The construction of the descriptive model and the process of finding solutions can be facilitated by a design environment, denoted as an inquiry system, in which various kinds of expertise with different knowledge representations have their place.

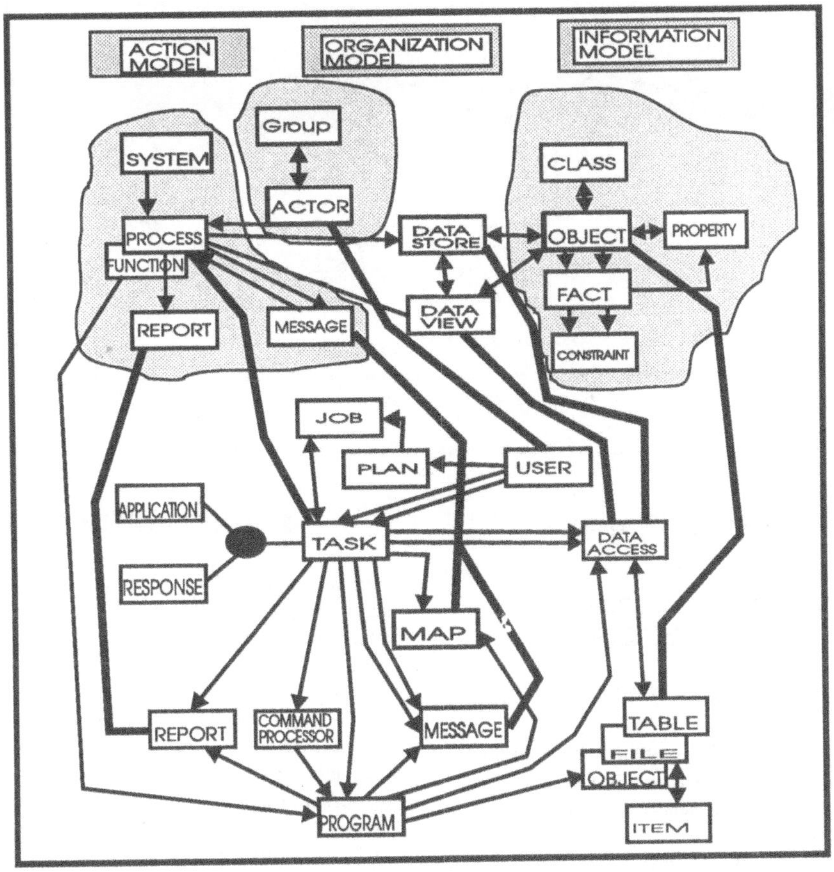

Figure 2.
A data dictionary - the repository image

The work reported in this paper is carried out in part within the framework of the project, whose goal is to build a software engineering environment for developing and maintaining information systems.

2. INTEGRATED FLEXIBLE ENVIRONMENT SUPPORTING DYNAMIC DECISION MODEL BUILDING

We believe that information system in tourism should provide on timely basis - operational speed targeted to real time response, integrated travelling package, tailored to individual needs of travellers (clients - customers). In times of fast economic changes, 'Flexible Travel Agency' to stay competitive needs to provide service affordable to the vast range of members of the population.

Figure 3 illustrates the basic elements of a network decision model using a graphical notation commonly called an *influence diagram*. The decision model formalizes this situation in terms of the decision-theoretic concepts of actions, outcomes, and preferences. Each node in the diagram represents a decision variable, an event variable, or a utility valuation. The rectangular *decision node* ranges over the action alternatives under consideration. The circular *chance nodes* represent the uncertainty in the decision situation. The primary uncertainty in this case is the type of fault. Probabilistic dependencies among events are captured by arcs between their corresponding nodes. For example, the probability of smoke being observed from the engine depends on the type of fault, hence the arc from the node *fault* to the node *smoke*.

The final type of node in the diagram is the *value node*, expressing the decision maker's preferences in the form of a utility function. In this case, the value node captures the trade-off between bus availability and the costs of the replacement and repair procedures.

Given a completely specified model, we can manipulate the network to perform Bayesian probabilistic updating and derive the decision policy maximizing expected utility.

For example, the availibility event in Figure 3 refers to the availibility of particular bus for a particular scheduled excursion.

The parametrized model approach will not suffice, if the nature of a consultation varies from case to case due to structural differences in the decision situation or nonparametric variations in individuals' preferences.

Our approach is to encode general knowledge in an expressive language, then dynamically construct a decision

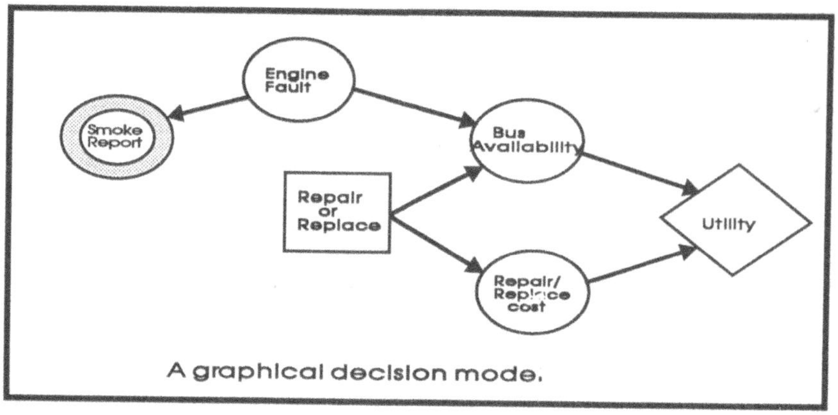

Figure 3.

model for each particular situation or problem instance.

3. QUELLE INTEGRATED KNOWLEDGE ASSISTED SOFTWARE DEVELOPMENT ENVIRONMENT

To solve problems specified by users QUELLE provides the following features:

* - structure and behaviour preserving morphisms from model theory can connect models at different levels of abstraction so that they can be developed to be consistent with each other and can be consistently modified.
* - the transformation of an externally represented problem, into a formalized and system-handable internal representation Figure 4
* - the automatic selection of all methods appropriate for the problem's structure, tailored to the user's personal preferences.
* - the presentation of the internally represented output of the executed method to the user by using visual output.
* - integrated decision support system enabling creation of dynamic models constraint by the needs of individual customer (client)

4. MODEL BASE DEVELOPMENT

The architecture features a model base at the center of its planning, operation, decision-making strategies. In this way, it integrates AI symbolic models and control dynamic models into a coherent system Figure 5.

Autonomous component models for operation, planning, decision-making have been developed in their respective fields so they share many commonalities as well as diffrences in assumptions. In an integrated system, cooperation between them is based on overlapping common functions.

5. A DECISION SUPPORT SUBSYSTEM

Figure 6 depicts a schematic architecture for a decision supporting subsystem based on dynamic, knowledge-based construction of decision models. In contrast to the parameterized decision-model approach, decision supporting system employing knowledge-based model construction do not start with a prespecified structure having the form of a decision model. Instead, the domain is defined by a KB of general facts and relationships. When a particular decision situation is identified through interaction with the user, the DSS subsystem synthesizes a decision model by selecting and deriving concepts and relationships from the KB. DSS subsystem tries to reflect these elements by defining a model.

The model is divided in three basic components Budget Entity, Constraints and Income:

* - BudgetEntity represents an organizational unit which will play a role in budget funding. Travel agencies can (and usually are) geograficaly dispersed. BudgetEntities (units) might be linked together according to rules defined by the organization. Because in general these rules are hierarchical they form the budget model hierarchy.
* - A relation which might exist between any two entities defines constraint. Generic constrain is imposed by amount of money client is willing to spend on customised tour.
* - Profit represents the income expected to be assigned to a specific entity.

Employing an object oriented model, experts explicitly build a semantic network where nodes are budget-oriented entities: (profit, budget-entities, constraint), and links have a budget-oriented semantics.

We can designate three types of links: part-of, has-profit, has-constraint, depicted in Figure 7. These links represent a budget entities.

A method is associated with each type of link for regulating information through the network. Interface hides the semantic network from the financial expert. He only handles a natural budget representation made of "part-of" and "has-profit" links

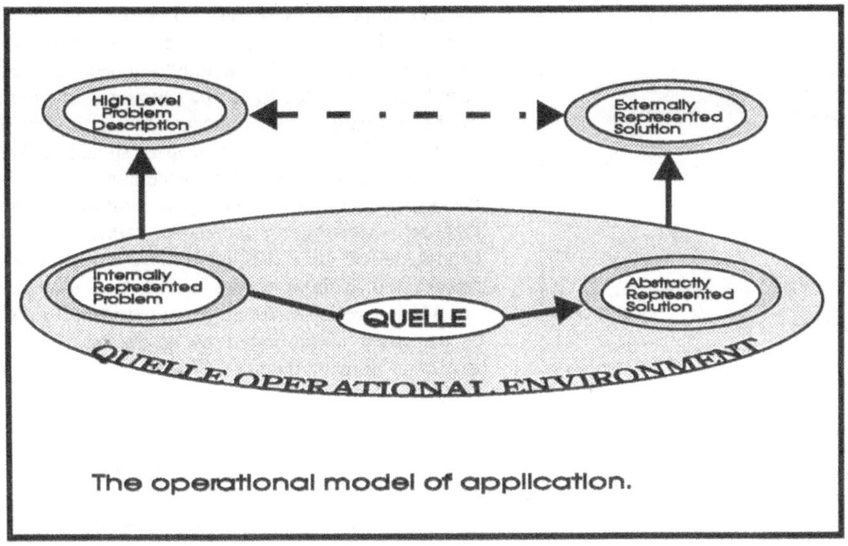

Figure 4.

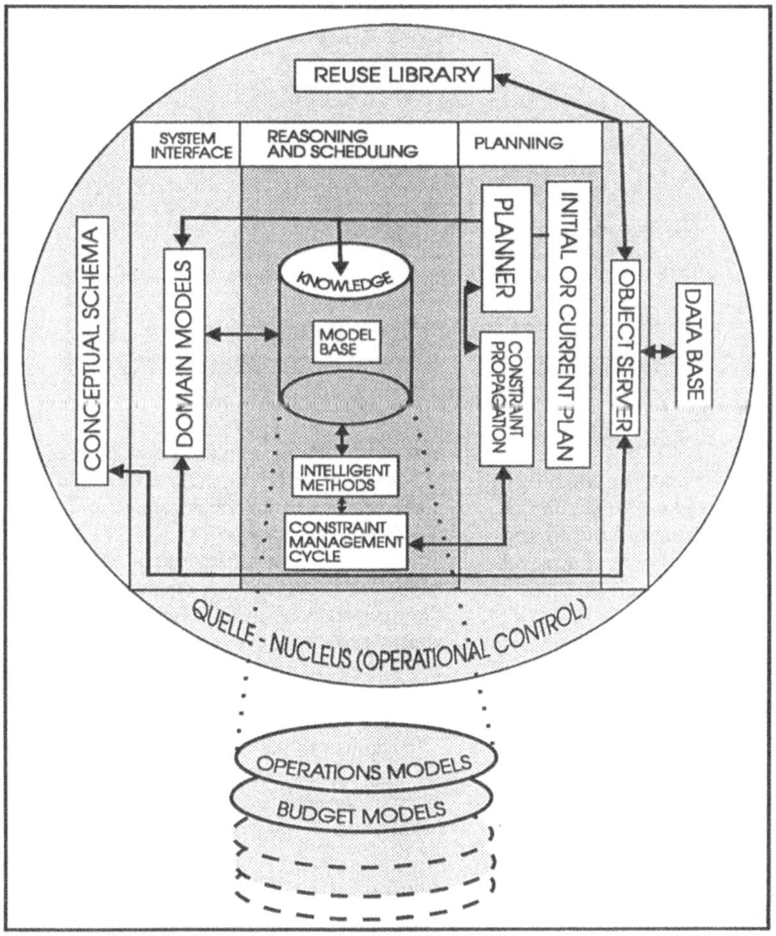

Figure 5.

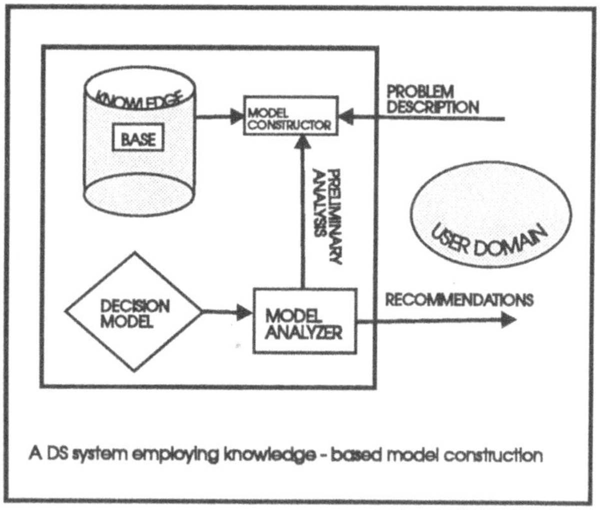

Figure 6.

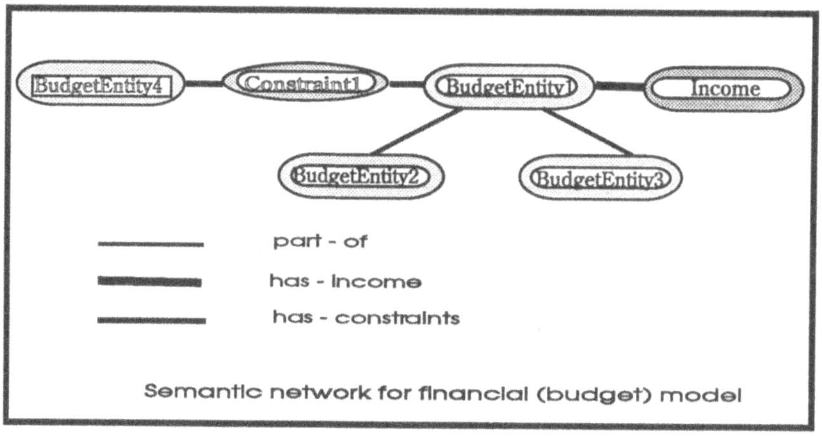

Figure 7.

through a tree-like graphical interface.

The target goal in QUELLE decision support subsystem is to achieve the level of operability, which should enable the user to modify and update the KB in response to changes in the domain or user preferences, without relying on the services of a model construction specialist.

6. METAARCHITECTURE

We can associate with each generic problem a set - preferebly one, generic architectures (metaarchitecture), which can be used to create a system for solving instances of the generic problem. The structure of the metaarchitecture determines the basic solution strategy for solving the problem. The degree of detail in specifying an architecture depends on the generality of the associated problem.

Thus, one could have a very general architecture like, a generic blackboard architecture, which could be used on a large number of problems sharing properties, or one could have a very specific architecture for example, an architecture for designing individually tailored travelling package with specifications related to all the functional modules. The model of the software system representing an instant of a solution defined on the generic problem space should be detailed enough to enable the automatic code generation in the framework of the operational software life cycle. Software maintenance may then be performed on the model rather than on code. The central idea of QUELLE operational environment is to build a correct and accurate model of the total system. In order to provide integrated environment appropriate to the level of the user, system is supported by model/knowledge base which generates domain models relevant to the designer's task at hand.

7. MULTIPLE MODELS

The idea behind the philosophy of QUELLE is that the knowledge-engineering space of choices and tools can to some extend be controlled by the introduction of a number of models. A model reflects, through abstraction of details, selected characteristics of the empirical system in the real world that it stands for [DeMarco, 1982].

Each model emphasizes certain aspects of the system to be build and abstracts from others. In QUELLE we distinguish three separate steps in defining the goals of integrated KB construction, namely: (1) defining the problem that the KB should solve in the organization, (2) defining the function of the system with respect to future users and (3) defining the actual tasks that the KB will have to perform.

In addition to the function of the KB and the problem that it is supposed to solve, the application model specifies the external constraints that are relevant to the development of the application.

8. DOMAIN MODELS

The domain-specific approach to reuse requires an extended

model of software development centered, not on a single project's life cycle, but on a family of programs or systems supporting a particular application area. The domain life cycle is one way to formalize this notion. This approach is depicted in Figure 8.

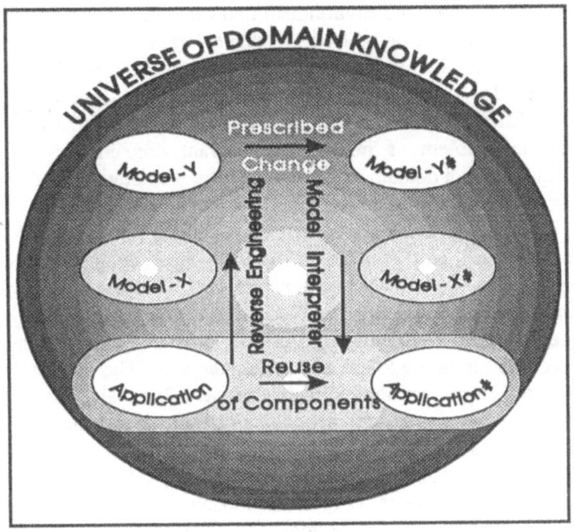

Figure 8.
A generic view of the relationship between models/application and domain life cycle.

The generic idea of reusability is transparent (promoted) through the QUELLE philosophy of design.

9. USING QUELLE FOR THE PRODUCTION OF SOFTWARE

The development process guides the users of QUELLE in systematically constructing specifications which model the problem domain at hand. Output of requirements engineering should be a formal, complete, precisely defined problem specification. With the goal to create conceptual model amenable to formal verification, a specification technique, based on the conceptual task modelling, is introduced. The technique is based on and defined in terms of predicate/transition nets.

We assume that a generic problem that abstracts the *target environment* problem specification and a generic architecture that abstracts a class of blackboard-based architectures have already been encoded in QUELLE. The accompanying software development methodology plays an important role in assisting the user to bridge the gap between informal conceptual model and formal specification.

QUELLE allows users to edit requests intended to be performed by the QUELLE system. A request is then transformed by the dialog-user-interface into an internally represented problem. An internal representation needs to be validated, i.e., it needs to be checked whether the domain was indeed represented in the internal representation. If an internal representation is valid with respect to a problem domain, the domain model is isomorphic to a model (an internal representation) of the problem.

10. OBJECT-ORIENTED PARADIGM WITH QUELLE

The methodology behind QUELLE support the construction of models according to an object-oriented methodology which divides the system in a hierarchy of objects to improve its comprehensibility and to simplify its modification and the reuse of system elements.

The object-oriented software developer works by identifying important abstractions and, for each of them, building a corresponding software module, called a *class*. *Objects* are the **direct instances** of the class.

A refined (validated) internally represented problem is given by the dialog-user-interface to the QUELLE nucleus frame, which creates the internally represented solution of the given problem Figure 5. The QUELLE nucleus uses Object Managers which are integrated part of commercially available object-oriented database systems like ORION, GemStone or Objectivity/DB to handle objects of data and method classes in memory, and also uses an underlying knowledge base which contains knowledge about the location of data and methods, the classification of methods, and the technical details for the communication between an QUELLE-Nucleus and Object Managers.

To solve an internally represented problem as an instance of the generic problems, the system presents the user with a set of different generic architectures associated with the generic problem. The user must select one of these architectures to serve as a starting point for the design. At present, there is only one architecture associated with the information system in tourism problem, and it is automatically selected by the system from the knowledge base.

When a generic architecture is selected, QUELLE creates a customization menu which lists all applicable commands that can be used to refine the architecture. These commands represent methods that can be used to instantiate module parameters.

In this operational setup the endomorphic system concept prevails. Endomorphism refers to the existence of a homomorphism from an object to a sub-object within it, the part (sub-object) then being a model of the whole Figure 9. In order to control an object (design), a system needs a corresponding model(s) of the system to determine the particular action to take.

We propose to illustrate the use of QUELLE through the example of a travel agency application.

Its schema is composed of classes such as Client, City, Monument, Restaurant, and methods associated with each class. Assume we wish to extend the travel agency application by creating a new class, for example, Seaside_resort as a specialization of the class City. To create a new class, we first need to display its immediate superclass. We use the browser by sending to it the *display_class* method (this method is an entry of the standard menu associated to the browser). Then the

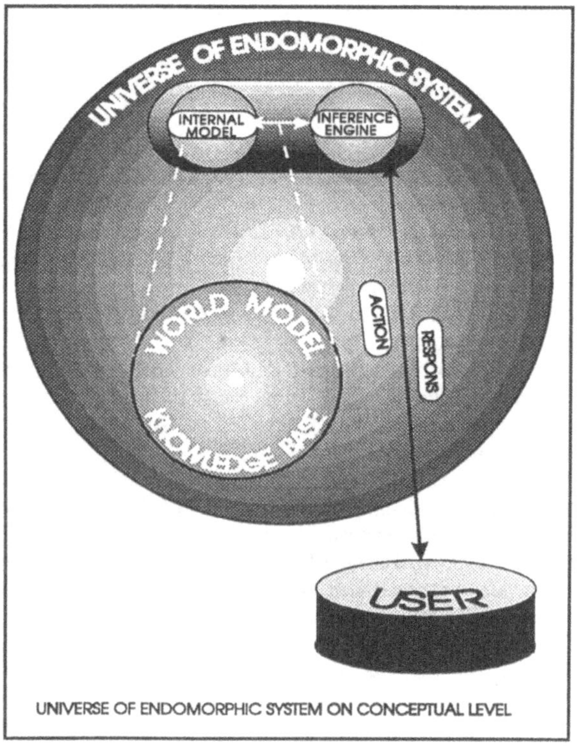

Figure 9.

names of all existing classes appear on the screen. Selecting the *City* item causes the display of the corresponding class. A class is represented by a QUELLE object with the appropriate information.

Now we can call up the standard menu of the class City and select the item *Add_subclass*. A template representing a new class is displayed on the screen. The fields of the template we have to fill are **Name** and **Type**. **Name** is a string; it has to be filled with the string "Seaside_resort". **Type** is a text attribute. It was initialized with the type of the class City as follows:

```
tuple(name: string,
      map: bitmap,
      hotels: set(Hotel))
```

The type of the class Seaside_resort contains all the attributes of its supertype. We add a new one, the **beaches** attribute, which gives:

```
tuple(name: string,
      map: bitmap,
      hotels: set(Hotel),
      beaches: set(tuple(name: string,
                         watching: Boolean,
                         nautic_sports: set(Sport),
                         dog_admitted: Boolean)))
```

The class is compiled by sending the *Compile* method from the standard menu of the class presentation. Then the class is created in the database schema.

11. Summary and Future Directions

The QUELLE system represents our initial attempt in building a prototype environment that can offer varying degrees of assistance to a software designer by employing diverse sources of knowledge in particular in its initial stages knowledge related to information systems in tourism. The QUELLE environment will enable us to explore issues related to the problem of how much relevant domain knowledge contained in a domain model can be reused to develop software environments based on the generic architecture.

QUELLE provides a variety of capabilities to support the process of requirements acquisition and analysis. These capabilities include acquisition, review, evolution support, analysis, and reuse support. These are intended to help analysts satisfy the conflicting goals of software requirements specification in a gradual and systematic way. The system as a whole focuses on the problems of describing systems from different viewpoints, and reconciling different viewpoints.

The architecture of QUELLE features a model base at the center of its planning, operation, decision-making strategies. In this way, it integrates AI symbolic models and control dynamic models into a coherent system. More research is required to ensure that models in the hierarchy have valid abstraction relations to each other. Additionally, although QUELLE employes a reasonable languages for world modelling and conceptual design, methodologies and development assistants for working with these languages, for capturing requirements in a goal-oriented manner and for integrating views - are still unadequate and further research is necessary.

Only in the later phases of the project it became clear that the certain facets of QUELLE software environment can be more effectivelly realized by adopting extended logic programmig approach.

Work on QUELLE aims at building a generic-model oriented environment which will include the representation of data structure and data-manipulation processes, considering specific interdependencies for specific application domains. This poses another demands on a formal modelling language for data and processes (methods), which will constitute a platform for a application domain specific modelling environment - where, the level of abstraction will rise to the application level.

Work on the project is ongoing; some of the capabilities envisioned for the system are already in place, but much work remains to be done.

ACKNOWLEDGEMENTS

We gratefully acknowledge the contributions made by various people who helped with the project.

REFERENCES

[1] [**Booch 86**] G.Booch: Object-Oriented Development. IEEE Trans. Software Eng., vol. SE-12, no. 2, p.211, Feb. 1986.

[2] [**Seidewitz 87**] E. Seidewitz, M. Stark: Towards a General Object-Oriented Software Development Methodology. ACM SIGAAda Ada Letters, vol. 7, no. 4, p. 54, July/Aug. 1987.

[3] [**Wasserman 89**] A.I. Wasserman, P.A. Pircher, R.J Muller: An Object-Oriented Structured Design Method for Code Generation. ACM SIG-Soft Software Eng. Notes, vol. 14, no.1, p. 32, Jan. 1989.

[4] [**Coad 89**] P.Coad, E. Yourdon: Object-Oriented Analysis, Prentice Hall, Englewood Cliffs, New Jersey, 1989.

[5] [**Dusink 89**] L. Dusink & P. Hall: Software Re-use, Utrecht 1989, Springer-Verlag, 1991.

[6] [**T. Biggerstaff & A. Perlis**] T. Biggerstaff & A. J. Perlis: Software Reusability, ACM Press- Frontier Series, New York, 1989.

[7] [**B. Walraet 91**] B. Walraet: A Discipline of Software Engineering, North-Holland, 1991.

[8] [**Madsen 88**] O.L. Madsen, B. Moller-Pedersen: What object-oriented programming may be-and what it does not have to be. In: S.Gjessing, K. Nygaard (eds.): ECOOP'88', Springer Verlag, Aug. 1988.

[9] [**J. Hogger 1990**] CH. J. Hogger: Essentials of Logic Programming, Claredon Press - Oxford, 1990.

[10] [**R. A. Kowalski & M. H. van Emden 76**] R. A. Kowalski & M. H. van Emden: The semantics of predicate logic as a programming language, Journal of thr ACM 23, pp. 733-742, 1976.

[11] [**U. Nilsson & J. Maluszynski 1990**] Ulf Nilsson & Jan Maluszynski: Logic, Programming and Prolog, John Wiley & Sons, Chichester, 1990.

[12] [**F. Lehmann 1992**] F. Lehmann: Semantic Networks in Artificial Intelligence, Pergamon Press, 1992.

[13] [**J. S. Sowa 1983**] J. F. Sowa: Conceptual Structures - Information Processing in Mind and Machine, Addison Wesley,1983.

[14] [**K. Jensen & G. Rozenberg 1991**] K. Jensen & G. Rozenberg: High-Level Petri Nets, Springer-Verlag, 1991.

[15] [**B. W. Boehm 1981**] B. W. Boehm:Software Engineering Economics, Prentice-Hall, 1981.

[16] [**J. Bubenko 1986**] J. Bubenko:Information System Methodologies - A Research View, in 'Information Systems Design Methodologies: Improving the Practice', eds Olle, T. W., Sol, H.G., Verijn-Stuard, A.A., North-Holland.

[17] [**T. DeMarco 1978**] T. DeMarco: Structured Analysis and System Specification, Yourdon Press, 1978.

[18] [**G. Verheijen & van Bekkum 1983**] G. Verheijen & J. van Bekkum: NIAM - An Information Analysis Method, in Olle 1983.

[19] [**M. Jackson 1983**] M. Jackson: System Development, Prentice-Hall, 1983.

[20] [**I. MacDonald 1986**] I. MacDonald: Information Engineering- An improved, automatable methodology for designing data sharing systems, in Olle (1986), pp. 173-224.

[21] [**E. P. Morris 1985**] E. P. Morris: Strengths and Weaknesses in Current Large Scale Data Processing Systems, Alvey/BCS SGES workshop, January 1985.

[22] [**T. W. Olle 1983**] T. W. Olle. et al (eds), CRIS - Information System Design Methodologies: A Comparative Review, North-Holland, 1983.

[23] [**R. Balzer 1983**] R. Balzer & Cheatham: Software Technology in the 1990's: Using a New Paradigm, Computer, November 1983, pp. 39-45.

[24] [**D. L. Parnas & P. C. Clements 1986**] D. L. Parnas & P. C. Clements: A rational design process: How and why to fake it, IEEE Transactions on Software Engineering, 12, 251- 257.

[25] [**R. Balzer, C. Green, and T. Cheatham 1990**] R. Balzer, C. Green, and T. Cheatham: Software technology in the 1990s using a new paradigm IEEE Computer, vol. 16, no. 11, pp. 39-45, November 1983.

[26] [**Olle, T.W. 1986**] Olle, T.W: CRIS3 - Improving the Practice, North-Holland 1986.

[27] [**B. Adelson & E. Soloway 1985**] B. Adelson & E. Soloway: The role of domain experience in software design, IEEE Transaction on Software Engineering, SE-11(11), 1351-1360.

[28] [**M. D. Lubars & M. T. Harandi**] Addressing software reuse through knowledge-based design, in T.J. Biggerstaff & A. J. Perlis (eds), Software Reusability, ACM Press, New York, NY.

[29] [**D. P. Wood & W. G. Wood 1989**] D. P. Wood & W. G. Wood: Comparative Evaluation of Four Specification Methods for Real-Time Technical Report CMU/SEI-89-TR-36, Pittsburgh, Pa.: Software Engineering Institute, Carnegie Mellon University, December 1989.

[30] [**A. Borgida, S. Greenspan, and J. Mylopoulos 1985**] A. Borgida, S. Greenspan, and J. Mylopoulos. "Knowledge representation as the basis for requirements specifications," IEEE Compt., vol. 18, no. 4, pp. 82-91, April 1985.

[31] [**R.M. Burstall and J. Gouguen 1977**] R.M. Burstall and J. Gouguen: "Putting theories together to make specifications," in Proc. 5th Int. Conf. Artificial Intell., Cambridge, MA, pp. 1045-1058, August 1977.

[32] [**S. Fickas 1986**] S. Fickas: "A knowledge-based approach to specification acquisition and construction," Technical Report 86- 1, Computer Science Dept., University of Oregon, Eugene, 1986.

[33] [**Allen, J.F. 1984**] Allen, J.F.: "Toward a General Theory of Action and Time," Artificial Intelligence, Vol. 23, pp. 123- 134, 1984.

[34] [**Y. De Kleer and B.C. Williams 198**] Y. De Kleer and B.C. Williams: "Diagnosing multiple faults", Artificial Intelligence, Vol. 32, pp. 97- 130, 1987.

[35] [**B. Chandrasekaran 1989**] B. Chandrasekaran: A roundtable discussion - Present and Future directions: trends in Artificial Intelligence, OE Reports, SPIE, September, 1989.

COORDINATION MECHANISMS AND SYSTEMS ARCHITECTURES IN ELECTRONIC MARKET SYSTEMS

S. Klein, T.J. Langenohl

Competence Center Electronic Markets, Institute for Information Management,
University of St. Gallen

Abstract

Computerized Travel Reservation Systems (CRS) are next to Computerized Financial Markets one of the most important and prominent applications of electronic market systems.
We want to introduce constitutive elements and concepts of electronic markets as emerging forms of organization and economic coordination. Within electronic markets and interorganizational systems, a wide variety of coordination or trading mechanisms, such as auctions, offer/accept and matching systems, are used. We will present a rough taxonomy of such coordination mechanisms. Aspects of implementing electronic markets will be discussed under the heading of systems architectures namely message passing systems. A particular focus will therefore be set on the comparison of different types of coordination mechanisms and enabling systems architectures. The example of CRS and in particular Galileo is used to illustrate different functional properties of coordination mechanisms and organizational contingencies for their application. Implications and requirements for the systems and application architecture will be discussed.

1. Electronic Markets: An Introduction

The term 'electronic market' has been used in various ways. Many synonyms of electronic markets characterize concrete forms of market transactions, e.g. electronic contracting between participants [17], electronic shopping [14] electronic execution of trading contracts depending on certain inputs of the involved actors. Examples for the application of such transaction forms are: raw material markets [20], travel and transport services [12, 7], commodity markets or financial and trading markets [25].

1.1. Market transactions and market phases

Market transactions between the different players are constitutive elements of a market. They can be coordinated in different ways. *A **market transaction** is a finite sum of interaction processes between members of different roles. The participants try in a certain period of time to settle their interests and expectations amongst themselves. The aim of a market transaction is a trading agreement between supplier and customer and the following settlement of goods and/or services.* In a market transaction, the following actors can be distinguished:

- The supplier and
- the buyer, who want to exchange goods and services. Especially in financial markets, actors frequently act as buyers and sellers.
- In some markets, intermediaries like dealers, brokers or market maker perform supporting functions to improve the efficiency of the transaction process.

The market place provides the (logical) location and infrastructure for the interaction of the market actors. Interaction processes in a market transaction can be combined into classes, so called phases of market transactions. [24]

Phase 1: Information phase

On the input side, information on available products and/or services, their specifications, suppliers and delivery terms are required. On the output side, potential customers have to be identified. In addition some general information on the market situation, branch or technological trends will be useful. This phase results in a list of potential partners in the market and their offer and/or demand.

Phase 2: Trading/matching

As soon as all relevant information has been evaluated, we can proceed to contact potential transaction partners and a matching pair of supply and demand (offer and bid) can be formed. Terms and conditions have to be fixed (terms of payment and delivery, warranties, additional services etc.). The legal basis is established for further transactions.

Phase 3: Settlement

In this phase the deal is settled, goods and services are exchanged for payments. This phase may consist of various derivated transactions that may require a full transaction process. In case of physical goods, possible transactions may be packaging, storage, shipping, insurance, customs clearance, etc. The physical exchange of goods is accompanied by financial and information flows. Now the physical transactions are carried out.

The following schema illustrates the sequence of process during a market transaction.

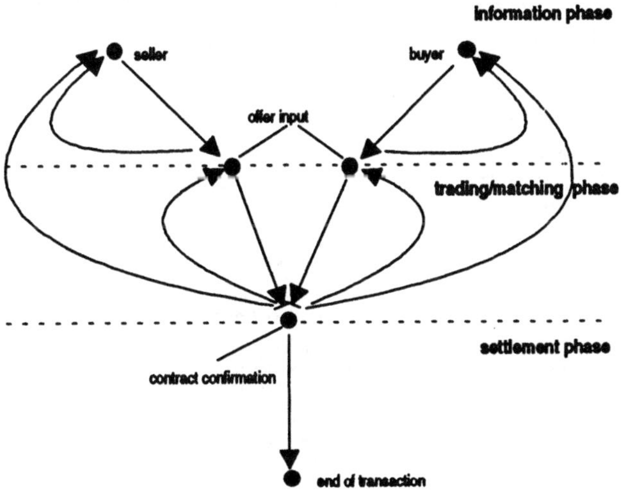

Fig. 1. Phases of a market transaction

1.2. A definition of Electronic Markets and Electronic Market Systems

Still, most existing systems have not realized electronic markets which support all phases of a market transaction. Bakos [1] defines an electronic market system as "an interorganizational system that allows the participating buyers and sellers to exchange information about prices and product offerings". For our purposes, this definition is too broad and unspecified. The exchange of information is only the first phase of a market transaction. Nearly all electronic newspapers and video text based systems would satisfy Bakos´ definition. Electronically contracting between suppliers and customers is more restrictive. Moreover, interorganizational systems are characterized as computerized systems between two or more organizations sharing data or other resources [2], excluding electronic shopping systems because the participants are single persons and not organizations.

Therefore, we define an *electronic market as the totality of exchange relationships between market participants with potentially the same rights. All interaction processes between the actors are supported and automated by an electronic market systems - at least to the completion of the trading/matching phase.*

The term electronic market system represents a more technical point of view [8, 9, 19]. *An electronic market system is an information system, embedded in the context of an electronic market, in order to automate or to support electronically the interaction processes between the actors in a market. The information system consists of a communication network and can be distributed and/or open.* Openness and distribution aspects can be discussed from an organizational or technical point of view.

Electronic markets are hybrid systems, in which people and computers are working together in order to reach certain results. In the near future the vision of a fully automated market in all transaction phases seems not only unrealistic but also not desirable.

Within electronic markets and interorganizational systems, a wide variety of coordination or trading mechanisms are used. We will therefore present a rough taxonomy of such coordination mechanisms. In a separate chapter, aspects of implementing electronic markets will be discussed under the heading of systems architectures namely message passing systems. A particular focus will be set on the comparison of different types of coordination mechanisms and enabling systems architectures.

2. Coordination mechanisms

In electronic market systems, like in traditional markets, various mechanisms of coordination can be employed. They are matching supply and demand, offers and bids respectively. Depending on the degree to which a mechanism automates the allocation process and to the level of centralization, we distinguish three generic mechanisms. They represent ideal types of coordination based on different action patterns of the participants. Most electronic trade systems can be classified according to the coordination mechanisms or a combination of them. The first form, offer/accept (O/A) focuses on the selection of the "buyer", the automated matching (AM) emphasizes the comparison of offers and bids by an intermediary (system). The computerized auction mechanism (CA) represents an active, more or less dynamic process of trading and emphasizes the competition between the bidders and the aspect of price fixing.

2.1. Offer/accept coordination

The O/A mechanism is based on a continuous placement of offers, e.g. available seats, in an electronic order book, usually a database. The buyer can browse the order book and hit suitable offers. Hitting the offer involves a binding acceptance (commit) of offers at displayed conditions (hit and take), for example, a price set by the supplier or market maker. The priority rule is first come-first served.

The offer/accept mechanism can be best compared to the selection from an electronic catalogue. Its main advantage is to provide a high degree of transparency in the information phase of a market transaction. O/A systems provide some assistance for finding suitable offers such as retrieval or sorting algorithms, but in general they rely mainly on an active role of the buyer. CRS systems are among the most well known examples of this type of coordination.

2.2. Automated matching

An automated matching algorithm reduces the complexity of the selection process. Based on a preference profile, the system will scan huge amounts of data and select fitting matches. The function of a matching system is to take a sequence of buy and sell orders and transform it into a sequence of trades according to a predefined set of (informally) stated execution rules [22].

The order book contains orders which are (automatically) executed against incoming bids according to their fit of attributes. Rather than generating trades only based on price or price/time priority, intelligent electronic trading systems provide standards and protocols for extended product descriptions such as grades, qualities, delivery conditions, and, corresponding, the representation of the traders' utilities in terms of preferences and prices [18] The priority of bids and offers is produced through execution rules [10]. Prices are not dynamically adjusted in AM but trades are executed to the predefined price limits.

The traditional example of matching is the real estate market where an intermediary generates matches of buyers and sellers. Nowadays, automated matching gains increasing importance as an intelligent form of trading in commodity markets that require more complex matching than price, volume and time.

2.3. Auction

Auctions are often perceived as the ideal type of a market. Most electronic trading systems for financial or commodity items are based on auction mechanisms that automate the traditional role of a human auctioneer: it books buy and sell orders and matches them based on a price or price/time priority. Auction markets provide centralized procedures for the exposure of buy and sell orders to all market participants simultaneously [11]. Auctions can be distinguished according to variables like sequence (continuous - periodical), transparency of competing bids, or procedure (dynamic trading or submission)[23]. Typical areas of application are financial and commodity items, but also complex, difficult-to-price products like pieces of fine art (social creation of value).

The following list gives an overview of the respective features of the discussed coordination mechanisms:

Features / Mechanism	Matching procedure	Intermediation and activities of the participants	Price discovery mechanism
Offer/ accept	selection from a (filtered) list of offers	electronic catalogue, reservation system, preselection of fitting offers, seller relatively passive, active selection of buyer	not during O/A, price adaptation during feed-back loops based on the scrutiny of buying patterns and competition
Automated matching	(automated) matching of buyer - seller profiles, preferences - product characteristics respectively	distinguished matching function, active role of human intermediary possible, a relatively passive role of buyer and seller (after having defined their respective profiles) possible	matching based on predefined price limits
Auction	matching based on price or price/time priority	market maker, coordination of the auction process; active role of buyer and seller	depending on auction type, for many type price discovery during the auction is a core function

Table 1: Comparison of coordination mechanisms

3. Systems architectures

The term information systems architecture (ISA) is ambiguous and is used in computer science and computer technology in various ways. ISA covers computer, software and network architecture. Computer architecture describes the fundamental organization of a computer. Terms like operating system-, compiler- and database systems architecture focus on construction characteristics of the respective system software category. All terms are a part of the systems architecture, they are connected and interact with each other. Nutt [21] defines systems architecture as: "A system's architecture describes the structure of interconnection of the parts of a system. The architecture specifies component interactions, and ultimately the details of the interface among interoperating components." Systems architecture is the description of the whole system consisting of computer hardware and system software. As electronic markets are open and distributed systems, systems architecture covers also the network architecture. *Systems architecture describes the interior construction, the infrastructure and the functionality of certain system components in open distributed systems. These components are the system software architecture with the underlying computer and the network architecture* (see also figure 2) [16].

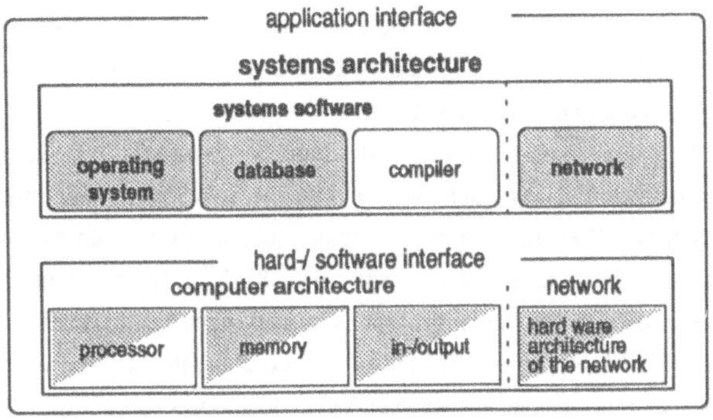

Fig. 2 Areas of systems architecture (the hatched parts of systems software)

In order to build a model of the systems architecture of electronic market systems we distinguish between several design options for market systems based on the information flow. The information flow reveals the connections among the processes in an electronic market system (static aspect). It shows which information a process has and which effects information has on other processes (dynamic aspect) [16]. So in a more abstract way each electronic market system can be described in form of processes and communication links between the processes. Systems which are characterized in such a way are so called message passing systems. Message passing models are used to describe - in distributed environments - the simultaneous execution of sequential processes. Beyond other methods, such as shared variables, message passing is the most important kind of interprocess communication. For the description of distributed systems several models of message passing exist than can be distinguished by the form of interprocess communication. In this paper we are following the work of Lamport and Lynch [15], who classify message passing models by the assumptions made about four separate concerns: network topology, synchrony, failure* , and message buffering. Different models do not necessarily describe different systems, they only represent different points of view of the same system.

* In this paper we make no assumptions about communication and process failures.

3.1. Network topology

The network topology describes which processes can send messages directly to which other processes. The topology is represented by a communication graph whose nodes are the processes, and where a link from process i to process j denotes that i can send a message directly to j. Most models assume an bidirectional graph, where a link joining two processes means that each can send messages to each other. On the other hand one can consider directed graph models in which there can be a link from i to j without one from j to i but not vice versa (unidirectional). In some models each process knows all other processes. In other models, processes have only partial knowledge - usually the identity of its immediate neighbors. The simplest models, embodying the strongest assumptions, are those with a completely connected communication graph, where each non-faulty process knows about and can send messages directly to every other non-faulty process in the graph.
James Martin [4] distinguishes the following six main topologies of communications architectures: mono-central, bicentral, multicentral, horizontal, horizontal-vertical and vertical-vertical structures. The mono-central architecture corresponds to the architecture of a host-system, a system which consists of multiple processes connected to a central host process. The bicentral structure is based on two central processes which other processes can used alternatively. The multi-central architecture is an expansion of the bicentral structure. Between the central processes no direct connection exists. The interconnections do not appear until the horizontal topology has been reached. In this case the processes are on the same level, it is a kind of peer-to-peer connection. The horizontal-vertical architecture is a combination of the mono-central and horizontal structure. In the vertical-vertical structure the central processes are not on the same level, they build a hierarchy of upper and lower processes.

3.2. Synchrony

Synchrony is an aspect to describe the coordination of cooperation and competition between processes. Especially in communication it is the coordination between the exchange of messages among the processes. In an asynchronous model no concept of real time exists. It is assumed that messages eventually delivered and processes eventually respond, but no assumption is made about how long this may take. In other models the concept of time is introduced in the way that upper limits on message transmission time and process response time are known (asynchronous interval concept). If a message is generated in response time to an event at a time t, it arrives at its destination at $t + \delta$, whereas δ is a known constant. The concept of interval response presupposes some form of real-time clock. The simplest type of a clock is a timer, which measures elapsed time; the instantaneous values of different processes' timers are independent of one another. In this configuration it is easy to detect failures as the assumption implies that a failure must have occurred if the reply to a message is not received within 2δ seconds of the sending of that message. Some models make stronger assumptions. The strongest assumptions one can make is a synchronous model in which the entire computation proceeds in a sequence of distinct rounds (synchronous time slices). At each round, every process sends messages based upon the messages that it received in previous rounds. In this model it is easy to simulate the use of synchronized clocks by letting begin each round $\delta + \varepsilon$ seconds after the preceding one.

3.3. Message buffering

In all message passing models, there is a delay between the time when a message is sent and when it is received. Such a delay requires some form of message buffering. In models with message buffering one can distinguish between finite and infinite buffers. Using finite buffering strategies, any link may contain only a maximum number of messages that have been sent over the link but not yet received. With infinite buffers, there may be an arbitrary number of unreceived messages in a link's buffer, and the sender can always send another message over the link. In reality each system has a finite buffer capacity, but this capacity may be large enough to make infinite buffering a reasonable abstraction. In buffering strategies it is possible for messages to be received in a different order than they were sent. Models with first-in-first-out (FIFO) buffering assume that messages received in the same order in which they were sent. In many asynchronous systems, interprocess communication presupposes FIFO buffering. In systems with timers and synchronized clocks a process does not send a message to another process until that the previous message to that process has been delivered, so FIFO buffering is not necessary. At the lowest level, real distributed systems usually provide FIFO buffering.

4. Computerized Reservation Systems as Electronic Markets

After we have introduced definitions and the constitutive elements of electronic markets, we now want to apply these constructs in a concrete application context. We therefore use the example of Galileo, one of the largest CRS in the tourist industry with the main focus on flight reservation. Galileo is a global information system owned by a consortium of airlines. It features global coverage of flights through cooperative arrangements with Covia and Gemini and gateways to other systems. Galileo links 23.000 terminals in 6000 travel agencies and 371 airlines, 62 of them with direct links the rest with an indirect connection via SITA.

CRS are among the most famous examples of inter-organizational systems (IOS) and in particular electronic markets. They have become a major marketing channel for the airlines and are responsible for about 80% of airline bookings [3]. After the systems' growth potentials have been exhausted, the CRS have become a field of intense competition. The product is time critical, relatively homogeneous and the complexity of the product description is low. In sum, it is an information and coordination intensive item [13].

The core functions of CRS are

- flight schedule information,
- reservation and
- booking of flights and special services such as special diets.

Seat assignment at the time of booking so that boarding passes can be issued is available in the US market, not however in most of the European markets.

4.1. Coordination aspects

We use a stylized transaction schema in order to distinguish different coordination aspects in Galileo.

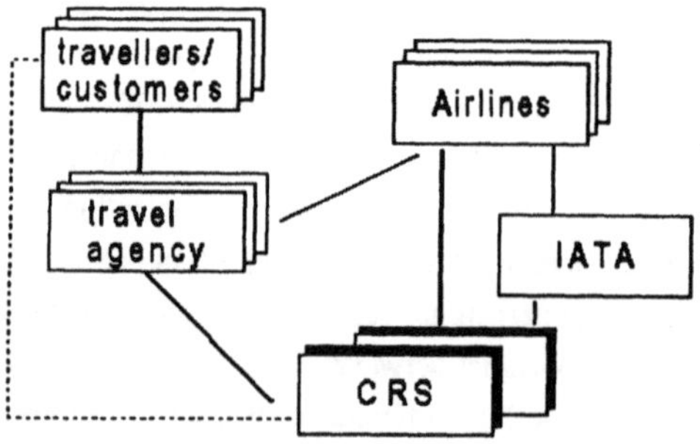

Fig. 3 Actors and transactions in Galileo

(1) Offer/ accept

Basically, Galileo is an O/A system where the customer is usually acting through a travel agent. Based on structured flight information of competing carriers, such as schedule, route, availability of seats and fares, customers select a flight (and seat) according to their preferences.

The CRS features a differentiated *accept*, mainly depending on the business practice concerning the "no show" factor and competitors policies:

- reservation which allows cancellation without costs, and
- booking where customers will be charged for cancellation or modifications in their itinerary.

Depending on the terminal used for booking, Galileo provides differentiated forms of confirmation.

(2) Extended matching: value added by travel agents

While CRS feature only limited retrieval and sorting options, e.g. the flight listings are usually based on departure time instead of costs, large travel agents provide extended matching functions based on detailed flight and customer information. General specifications and preferences about a flight, such as destination, time frame, price, route, number and location of stop overs/ change of aircraft, total time to reach destination, airline, aircraft type etc., and a customer profile, described in terms of class, smoking, seating, dietary preferences, etc. will be matched against available flights. Even business rules can be implemented that link position in hierarchy and conditions of the travel to class and medium of transport etc. The matching process can be automated using specific matching algorithms and customer databases.

In a situation of frequently changing prices and no or low cancellation fees, the automated matching can be extended until immediately before the flight in order to discover even better matches. The Covia-Galileo-Gemini CRS is the basic infrastructure for the Rosenbluth International Alliance (RIA), a global cooperation of travel agents. Several proprietary solutions have been built on the Covia-Galileo-Gemini system, the RIA Global Distribution Network. RIA members can now access client profiles and itineraries directly through Covia-Galileo-Gemini, which is also the backbone for global consolidation of travel information for multinational clients [6].

(3) Adaptation of prices

While O/A and matching refer to the interactions of customer and travel agent with Galileo based on fixed prices, CRSs provide excellent information for the airlines to adapt their prices. In this case, the airlines take a more active role in the market process. Deregulation in the airline industry and the statistical analysis of demand patterns led to a multiplicity of fares particularly in the US market, up to the differentiation of last minute fares depending on the availability of seats. With the results, that during many flights only a few passengers had paid the same fare. Shrinking profits and huge losses*, however, have led to a return to a simple fare system (the fares depend on the time of reservation) with numerous exceptions and short-term adaptation of fares, such as seasonal specials. Recently the US Justice Department filed an antitrust suit that accused the eight largest American airlines of using a CRS to fix air fares. The airlines had used the CRS to signal and negotiate price changes [26].

The analysis of coordination aspects of Galileo has shown that electronic markets often combine several coordination mechanisms, depending on the patterns of interaction and roles of the participants (compare table 1). In the next step, we want to discuss implications for the design of systems architectures of CRS.

4.2. Applications - and systems architecture

CRS are in general on-line transaction processing systems (OLTP) and constructed in form of a client-server model. Nowadays high performance OLTP-systems exist which are able to execute 1.000 transactions per second [5], enough to build global CRS. A transaction T is an atomic unit of an operation, which is controlled by a transaction manager and consists of a finite number of actions ($T=a_1a_2a_3 \dots a_n$). A common database for many users is a core feature of an OLTP-system. Other aspects are a high parallelism in transaction processing and a reliable updating of information. So it is possible for clients to use several resources (servers). The coordination between clients and servers is arranged by a transaction processing manager who controls and routes the accounting services. To realize those systems it is necessary to have a certain (or several) network topology(ies) with restrictions according to infrastructures of those networks.

---

* The airlines that are organized within the IATA face a cumulated loss of 4.8 billion US$ for 1992 alone and a cumulated loss of 11,5 billion US$ since 1990. Neue Zürcher Zeitung Nov. 1 1993, 254.

4.2.1. Topology

In CRS several possibilities exist to construct a network architecture.

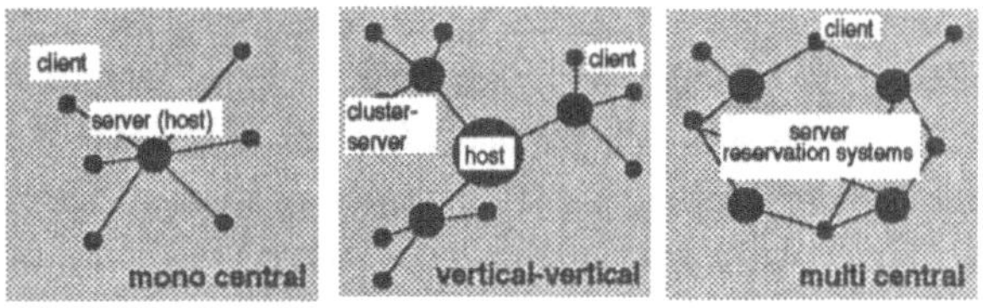

Fig. 4 Possible network topologies for reservation systems

The choice of a certain topology model (static aspect) for an airline reservation system depends on the regional aspects and the individual organization of the reservation system, in detail the structures of the associated travel agencies. The following static, bidirectional structures of a reservation system are possible.

- (1) central host (mono-central topology) and
  - (1a) directly connected diskless terminals, which have only in/output masks,
  - (1b) directly connected workstations, that have their own operating systems and the possibility for data storing and administration,
- (2) cluster wise connected workstations, which are connected with the central host of the CRS over an specially prepared workstation or a special server which is responsible for the cluster (vertical-vertical topology),
- (3) several CRS with the same rights to which customers have access to in form of terminals or workstations (multi-central topology),
- (4) the combination of the above network topologies.

Larger travel agencies in Switzerland, Kuoni and Danzas, have their own (database) host which is connected to the Swissair host. Swissair has a connection to the central host of Galileo in Denver, CO. Smaller agencies send their jobs and bookings directly to the Swissair host and from there to Galileo. These topologies are hierarchically combined configurations of type (2) - cluster wise connected workstations. The configuration of type (3) represents a further development stage of a CRS that offers the customers a connection to a cluster of CRS in a homogeneous way. The typical technical infrastructure of travel agencies in Galileo is a LAN token ring structure using OS/2-Gateway servers. The central system (central host) of Galileo is based on IBM hardware with the TPF-operating system for central booking services. The regional networks of the travel agencies and connections to other central CRS, especially Covia, are placed in a SNA-backbone network.

4.2.2. Dynamic aspects: Information flow

The communication between the supplier(s) and the customers characterize the dynamic aspects of the architecture of a CRS. Therefore, special mechanisms for synchronizing the communication have to be provided and supported by the operating system. The transactions between customers and the system (supplier) can be divided into three market phases: information, trading and settlement phase (see above). In the trading phase, CRS are based on O/A coordination mechanisms, so called fixed price systems. The exclusiveness of the services especially the booking of an aircraft seat makes it necessary to establish a synchronized communication link (in form of synchronous timer or synchronous time slices) between the client and the server, holding the contingent of free aircraft seats. Therefore, the send and receive operations that have to be synchronized are based on blocked communication primitives. Both processes are blocked in their normal execution until the booking is finished. The customer process has to be a so called 'remote invocation send'-process. In this form of communication the receiver (server) confirms per message that the contents of client message, e.g. the booking of a seat, has been executed. Galileo provides different forms of booking functions that are based on these communication primitives: guaranteed booking with buying confirmation, super guaranteed booking with booking reference after finishing of the transaction and secured booking. In the last form the sold seats are directly marked on the seatplan of the airline and the travel agency gets a booking reference. In this case, the travel agent issues a boarding pass with valid seat number. An elder form of booking is called teletype, based on sending a telex to the respective airline. Teletype is a connectionless form of communication. It is an asynchronous message transfer by using mail boxes or ports, special operating system mail boxes.

The buffering of information depends on the way interprocess communication is used and which network typology is available. In a mono-central configuration all customers processes get their information out of a central organized buffer of the supplier. The supplier has only to make sure that the account on information is regulated in an ordinary way (a kind of process synchronization). If customers themselves have the possibility to buffer information (type 1b), message are placed in the buffer of the customers. In this case the supplier must be able to send simultaneous messages to all customers (broadcast) or a certain group of customers (multicast).

Functionalities in the Galileo system which do not require a kind of time critical execution are usually based on a asynchronous interprocess communication (asynchronous interval concept). This guarantees that processes on the server are not blocked through client processes.

In the information phase, customers need information about a flight tariff, date, time, etc. from location *a* to location *b* or they want do know something about special conditions like shortest flight-time, cheapest tariff, special airline etc. All these information is non time-critical. So it seems to be possible to locate these information on a database server of a travel agency and not on the central host of Galileo.

Another aspect in the information phase is the comfort offered by the reservation program to access the necessary information. For the user of such a system, it is important to have effective information retrieval functions that are also based on on-line transaction processing mechanisms. On the level of systems architecture these mechanisms are supported by special database functions and basic functions for resource and file management offered by the operating system.

The comfort of using a CRS depends on efficient and appropriated user interfaces. From the point of view of the customers, user interfaces have to be highly transparent to hide the details of implementation. In general modern user interfaces are graphical interfaces (GUI) with special masks and menus for an easy and comfortable handling of customers requirements to the system. The design and implementation of GUIs is not directly a problem that has to be solved on the application architecture level and supported by certain systems architecture functions. The requirements of the coordination mechanisms with respect to masks and menus are ambiguous. It must be possible to support different forms of information retrieval e.g. in the extending matching mechanism in order to get suitable and temporal acceptable responses on a retrieval for smoking, seating, dietary references etc. Therefore it is necessary to have certain flexibility in adding new functions to and changing functions in an GUI. Portability and extensions in a heterogeneous and open system environments are a prerequisite for a relative independence of systems and network hardware (vendors).

The criteria mentioned in relation to the adaptation of prices (3.2) require several transactions for an adequate updating of price information in (distributed) databases. In this case, data control mechanisms must guarantee integrity and consistency. Problems of redundancy have to be solved and recovery functions for failures in databases have to be provided. The manipulation of data is connected to certain rights. The definition of rules for that manipulation is the task of the database administrator.

The following table relates coordination and architectures aspects:

coordination aspects	systems architectures			application architectures
	topology	synchrony		
		information	matching	
offer/accept	mono-central, vertical-vertical, multi-central	asynchron	synchron	OLTP-systems, (distributed) databases
extended matching			asynchron communication is also possible (RIA)	distributed databases on local servers of travel agencies for a complex information retrieval in the information phase
price policy	-	-	-	special rights for suppliers, price updating and integrity functions

Table 2: Architectural aspects of coordination mechanisms

5. Conclusions

Currently we observe increasing competition among CRSs. Several airlines have joint forces and shared the expenses to built CRS and to provide global coverage. Consequently, system functions and enabling systems architectures become the source of competitive advantages. Innovative designs of IS architectures are prerequisites of additional functions in this context of high performance OLTP. The discussed coordination aspects of CRS reflect crucial development trends for CRS: While initial CRSs provided only limited retrieval options and were biased in their presentation of flights, extended functionalities have been added during recent years. Systems and network architectures provide the technical infrastructure for global coverage and user friendliness.

As the example of RIA shows, travel agents will play a major role as intermediaries for the time being, especially if they succeed to add value for their customers in terms of extended retrieval and accounting functions. The division of labor among CRS and large travel agents has mainly organizational reasons. The complexity at least of parts of the travel business require local presence and know how, combined with access to global information. The usage of the CRS infrastructure for proprietary applications of travel agents is a good example for the trend to increasing cooperation in the industry.

The close scrutiny of business practices of the airlines using CRS by national and international agencies (like the US Justice Department in the case mentioned above) indicates the potential impact of CRS on the market structure. On the one hand, CRS can be used for a strategy of high price flexibility of supply resulting in intense price competition and differentiated prices. Last-minute offers or even auctions could be implemented on CRS and used to increase the load factor. On the other hand, especially large players tend to prefer a more rigid price policy with only limited price competition. CRS thus have become powerful instruments of the respective airlines strategies, however, within the (inter)national regulations.

References

1. Bakos, J.Y.: A strategic analysis of electronic marketplaces, in: MIS Quarterly 15, pp. 295-309, 1991.
2. Barrett, S.: An IS* case: the closed loop scenario, in: Information and Management 10(5), pp. 263-269, 1985.
3. Bradley, C., Smith, D.: Networking Reservations, in: Network World, pp. 22-45, August 22, 1988.
4. Bues, M.: Offene Systeme - Herausforderung an das Informatik-Management. SVD/VDF-Tagung, Zürich, pp. 4-4. March, 1993.
5. Claybrook, B.: OLTP - Online Transaction Processing Systems. John Wiley Verlag, 1992.
6. Clemons, E.K., Row, M.C.,Miller, D.B.: Rosenbluth International Alliance: Information Technology and the Global Virtual Corporation, in: Nunamaker, Jay F., Sprague R.H. (Eds.): Proceedings of the 25th Hawaii International Conference on System Science, Vol. IV: Information Systems, Los Alamitos, Ca., pp. 678-686, 1991
7. Copeland, D.G., McKenney, J.L.: Airline Reservation Systems: Lessons from history, in: MIS Quarterly 12, pp. 353-370, 1988.
8. Dennis, S.G.P.: Automating financial markets, in: Data processing 26(1), Butterworth & Co Ltd, 1984.
9. Dewitz, S.K.: Contracting on a performative network: Using information technology as a legal intermediary, in: Stamper R.K., Kerola R., Lee R., Lyytinen K.J. (Eds.): Collaborative Work, Social Communications and Information Systems. Elsevier Science Publishers B.V. North Holland, 1991.
10. Domowitz, I.: The mechanics of Automated Trade Execution Systems, in: Journal of Financial Intermediation, p. 175f.
11. Garbade, K.: Securities Markets, McGraw Hill, p.426, 1982.
12. Gifford, D., Spector, A.: The TWA Reservation Systems (Case Study), in: Communications of the ACM 27(7), pp. 650-665, 1984.
13. Hooper, M.D.: Rattling Sabre - New Ways to Compete on Information, in HBR, pp. 118-129, May-June 1990.
14. Kimbrough, S.O., Isakowitz, I.: Perspectives in Electronic Shopping: On beyond Automated Order Entry. Center for Research on Information Systems, Leonard Stern School of Business. New York University. Working Paper Series, 1989.
15. Lamport, L., Lynch, N.: Distributed Computing: Models and Methods, Chapter 18, in: Handbook of Theoretical Computer Science. Elsevier Science Publishers B.V. North Holland, 1990.
16. Langenohl, T.J.: Systemarchitekturen elektronischer Märkte (systems architectures of electronic markets), (in print).
17. Lee, R.M.: International Contracting - A formal language approach. Hawaii International Conference on System Sciences. Kona, Hawaii, 1988.
18. Lee, H.G., Lee, R.M.: Intelligent Electronic Trading for Commodity Exchanges, in: EM-Electronic Markets, Vol. 3, No. 9/10, pp. 5-6, 1993.
19. Lee, R.M., Widmeyer, G.: Shopping in the Electronic Marketplace, in: Journal of Management Information Systems 2(4), pp. 21-35, 1986.
20. Lindsey, D., Cheney, P.H., Kasper, G.M., Ives, B.: TELCOT: An Application of Information Technology for Competitive Advantage in the Cotton Industry, in: MIS Quarterly 14. December, 1990.
21. Nutt, G.J.: Open Systems. Prentice Hall Verlag, 1992.
22. Reck, M.: Formally Specifying an Automated Trade Execution System, in: Journal for Systems Software, Vol. 21, pp. 245-252, 1993.
23. Reck, M.: A formal taxonomy of Electronic Auctions, (in print).
24. Schmid, B.; Elektronischer Märkte - Electronic Markets, in: Wirtschaftsinformatik, Vol. 35, No. 5, pp. 465-480, 1993,
25. Siegel, D.R. (Ed.): Innovation and Technology in the Market: A Reordering of the World's Capital Market Systems. Probus Publishing Company, 1990.
26. Tolchin, M.: U.S. Sues 8 Airlines over Fares - Computer Called Price-Fixing Tools, in: NYT, p. D1; D13. December 22, 1992.

GFIRS: A Graphical Fuzzy Information Retrieval System

Stewart N.T. Shen shen@cs.odu.edu
Jin Hu hu_j@cs.odu.edu

CS Department, Old Dominion University, Norfolk, VA 23529, U.S.A.

Abstract

There are several difficulties in information retrieval from database systems for users. One is how users express their intention by using some complex predefined functions or commands provided by a typical system. Another is how to identify the right portions of a database that the users want to base their queries on. Still another is that humans do not always think in exact ways and their ideas may be fuzzy, but most database systems can only handle precise queries. We propose a methodology which combines a graphical database querying model with fuzzy retrieval facilities.

Introduction

From users' point of view, there are several major difficulties in information retrieval from databases. One major difficulty is in using predefined functions or commands of an arbitrary database management system to express their queries. Not the syntax for all the potential queries are easy to understand. This job is even harder for novice users, who often simply can not express what they want in the right way. Another difficulty is that when a database is reasonably large and complex, users can hardly get a clear picture of what are exactly in the database and may not know well enough what in the database are relevant for their intended queries and how and where to begin phrasing their queries. Still another difficulty, in fact the most serious, is that most database management systems do not handle fuzziness, while it is only human to think often in some imprecise way and would like to pose fuzzy queries.

To help alleviate the first difficulty mentioned above, researchers have proposed methods such as using declarative or natural language–like query languages. Unfortunately, systems developed by such efforts were still considered not easy to learn[1]. Thus some researchers went in a different direction and developed two–dimensional query languages such as *Query By Example* (QBE)[2] and *Query by Pictorial Example* (QPE)[3]. QBE provides for user interface frames of tables which are easier to comprehend than other linguistic forms and its query phrasing mechanisms based on these frames are also easier to learn and easier to use. QPE works similarly to QBE except that it deals with two dimensional objects as examples to fill in frames. Such newer development has indeed carried user–friendliness of database systems a giant step forward, and has made database querying not so much a formidable task as before. It is like providing a easy to drive automobile with an automatic transmission.

These query systems are based on the implementation models of different database systems. In other words, in using these systems, a user sees only some forms of records or tables in a given database system. Theses forms do not contain very much semantics and provide only individual local views, with relationships among the records or tables being obscure. Thus even provided with good and easy to learn query mechanisms, a user may still not have a clear picture as to what are exactly in a database, and can hardly decide how to go about to use these excellent mechanisms to phrase queries. It is like given a easy to drive automobile to drive to some new place with no good map or direction. Thus the second main difficulty mentioned earlier still stands in the way for such systems.

To alleviate the second major difficulty, some researchers tried to provide more semantics of a database to users. Some graphical query systems based on semantic database models started to come into being. Most of such systems are based on extended Entity–Relationship (EER) models. PICture Aided Sophisticated Sketch Of database queries (PICASSO)[5] and Eentity–Relationship Query and Update Interface (ERQUI)[6] are two fine examples of such systems. PICASSO is a graphical database query language designed for use with a universal relation database system. The primary objective of PICASSO is ease of use. Graphics are used to provide a simple mechanism for a user to express queries and to provide visual feedback to the user about the system's interpretation of the query. Inexperienced users can use the graphical feedback to aid them in formulating queries whereas experienced users can ignore the feedback. They can pose queries without knowing the details of the underlying database schema and not having to learn a complex formal syntax of SQL–like query language. ERQUI implements an ER query and update interface. The approach is based on utilizing an underlying relational database management system as the major component of an ER system architecture. A user works with the ER model of the database for retrieval or update, and during the process of manipulation of the ER diagrams, the information needed to generate an equivalent SQL retrieval or update statement is accumulated in a specially designed database, which is later used to generate the final executable statement. It provides three groups of operators which are used by users to create ER views, specify queries, and perform updates. Systems like PICASSO and ERQUI may be considered still experimental and they do not attempt to deal with the third type of difficulties mentioned earlier. In these systems, it is somewhat like providing a driver with a nice car as well as a good map or a person who knows how to get to the new place.

However, most database management systems just do not handle the problem of fuzziness, since it is both difficult and inefficient to do so. However, fuzzy queries are just natural and useful thus should not be ignored. Some database systems based on fuzzy theories have been proposed to meet this challenge[7,8,9,10,11,12]. It is like providing a driver with a fourwheel–drive car to drive in the snow, that is extra needed capability is provided. On the other hand, such systems concentrate on dealing with fuzziness but do not take care of the first two types of difficulties. An analogy is that this car is not easy to drive and no good map or direction is given.

This paper proposes an approach that confronts all the three major difficulties discussed above. We propose to combine a graphical query system based on a semantic database model with fuzzy retrieval facilities. Thus it provides ample semantics of a database to users to allow users understand what they are dealing with; it allows them to use convenient query facilities; and when appropriate, it allows users to make fuzzy queries upon crisp databases Since fuzziness is very difficult to deal with, we first introduce the state of the art of how some database systems deal with it.

Some Fuzzy Database Systems

The concept of a fuzzy database system was first introduced by Kunii in DATAPLAN[13]. After his introduction, several fuzzy database systems were proposed by various researchers [7,8,9,10,11,12]. Most of them are based on the relational database and can be divided into two basic categories. One category of fuzzy database systems deal with ambiguous queries on crisp databases. These systems are relatively simple and can handle fuzzy information in some limited ways. Basicly, they provide users with some facilities to express their queries that involve some fuzzy conditions. These fuzzy queries are then converted to precise expressions for retrieval on the underlying crisp databases. The strongest advantage of this method is that one can easily extend one's traditional database system to deal with fuzzy queries without revising the existing database itself. Tahani[7] describes a processing method for fuzzy queries based on the data manipulate language SEQUEL. In addition, modal logic, intuitive logic, and denotational semantics are used in the interpretation of fuzzy queries in his system.

Fuzziness exists not just in queries. The information in a database itself might have some fuzzy properties. In order to let a database management system deal with fuzzy information fully, one must also extend the database model itself into the fuzziness realm. Buckles and Petry[8] introduces fuzziness into the database by means of similarity matrices. This fuzzy database consists of three parts: domain sets, similarity matrices for domain sets, and relations. Similarity matrices are used to deal with the fuzziness and each domain set has a corresponding similarity matrix. In a similarity matrix, every data element of the domain set must be compared to the others and gets its similarity value. Based on that, every operation on this fuzzy database uses similarity to replace traditional equality calculus. Umano[9], on the other hand express the ambiguity in data by means of possibility distributions. A possibility distribution is assigned to each uncertain data element as well as any fuzzy data element.,Queries are proposed accordingly in a declarative form. Results are classified into three sets with respect to the query conditions: clearly satisfy, possibly satisfy, and clearly don't satisfy. Prade and Testemale [10] extended the possibility distribution–relational model by using a special value for null attribute values. Furthermore, relational algebra operations are extended over possibility and necessity measures. The results are obtained as two different fuzzy sets based on possibility and necessity measures. Zemankova–Leech and Kandel [11] proposed another possibility distribution–relational model database. This database consists of three parts: a value database (VDB), a explanatory database (EDB) and conversion rules. The value database is essentially the same as the possibility distribution–relational model mentioned above. The explanatory database is a collection of definitions of named fuzzy sets and fuzzy relations, and can be different for each user. The conversion rules are for processing modifiers and qualifiers.

In summary, these fuzzy database systems are not efficient and not very user–friendly. For example, they do not provide the semantics of a database to users in ways such as ERQUI does. They do not provide easy to use query facilities such as QBE does.

Graphical, Fuzzy Query Information Retrieval System

We propose a system which provides a graphical user–interface that provides full semantics of a database to users; allows users to phrase queries with a easy to understand and convenient to use query facility as QBE; and handles fuzzy queries as some other fuzzy database systems do.

Our system is applicable to underlying crisp databases. One reason for our not dealing with fuzziness in the stored data itself is for efficiency. Another, in fact more important, reason is that there are so many crisp databases of great application values and it would be quite beneficial just to enhance their capabilities in handling fuzzy queries and not to mess them up with any needed reorganization if fuzziness is to be introduced into them.

The Architecture

The overall architecture of the *Graphical Fuzzy Information Retrieval System* is illustrated in Figure 1. The original database and database management system stay intact. A GFIRS user interacts with the system through the *Graphical Fuzzy Information Retrieval Interface* (GFIRI). The sytem provides the user through the *Graphical ER Model Processor* (GERMP) with a graphical representation of the ER model of the external schema that the user requests. The user then navigates through the ER model and selects the interested entities and relationships. The *Query Frame Processor* (QFP) generates the query frames similar to those of the QBE for the user to phrase queries. Limited fuzzy terms are allowed in phrasing the queries, and they are picked up and processed by the *Fuzzy Query Fileter* (FQF). The *Relational Query Processor* (RQP) processes the resulting query as an ordinary QBE–type precise query and calls the database management system to perform the required database information retrieval. The resulting answer is further processed by the Fuzzy Answer Generator to be presented to the user.

The Graphical ER Model for an External Schema

A user requests a specific external schema to perform

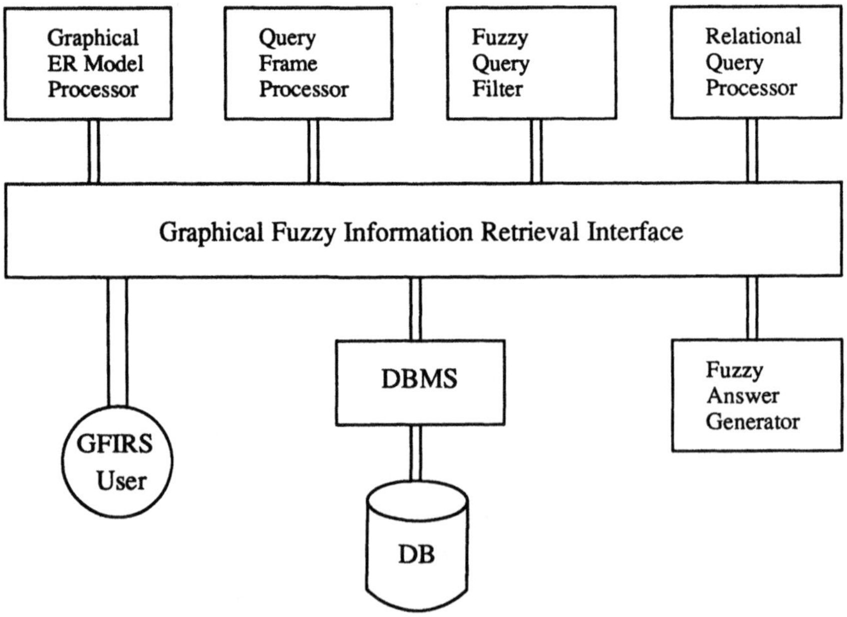

Figure 1. Architecture of the Graphical Fuzzy Information Retrieval System

his information retrieval tasks. The *Graphical ER Model Processor* (GERMP) provides the user with the corresponding graphical representation of the ER model of the external schema. For our purpose of illustration, we use a very simple external schema shown in Figure 2. This external schem coontains entity types STUDENT and COURSE, and a relationship type TAKE. In a typical situation, there will be many more entity types and relationships in an external schema. The attributes of any entity or relationship type are displayed on demand by the user. We have shown the attributes of all the entity and relationship types in the figure.

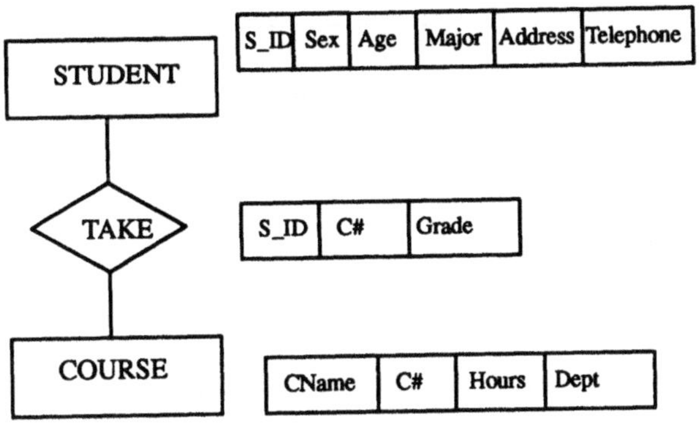

Figure 2. Graphic ER model with attributes

The basic idea in here is that displaying an ER model to a user provides a lot more semantics of the data model to the user. It is like given a map to a driver. Simply giving a set of relations to a user does not give enough information for the user to phrase an appropriate query easily.

Query Frames

After the user selects the desired entity and relationship types for query phrasing, the system generates the query frames for the user to phrase the query. Figure 3 illustrates the query frames generated when STUDENT and TAKE are selected by the use, and also the values given by the user for a query. A query frame contains the name of the underlying relation and the attribute names of the relation. The lower portion of each frame is for the user to give any information to phrase the desired query, as in QBE.

Fuzzy Queries

Phrasing queries in GFRIS is very similar to doing so in QBE. In Figure 3, we illustrate the query "Give the student IDs of any young male students who received some good grades or any CS students who received some good grades". The difference about query phrasing between QBE and here is that we allow fuzzy terms, such as "good" and "young", for certain attributes.

STUDENT	S_ID	Sex	Age	Major	Address	Telephone
	P._x	m	young			
	P._x			CS		

TAKE	S_ID	C#	Grade
	_x		good

Figure 3. Query frames with query conditions

Fuzzy terms are allowed when it can be defined on only a single attribute. In the given example we assume that as far as students are concerned, "young" is determined by Age only and "good" grade is dtermined by Grade only. In other words, if "young" may be determined also on Sex, then we disallow this fuzzy term to be used for Age.

The restriction on fuzzy terms based strictly on a single attribute is very reasonable. Without such a restriction, the fuzzy term processing may become arbitrary complex and inpractical to be implemented for a database system. For example, suppose we have an entity type ANIMAL with attributes Weight, Height, Spieces, and so on. A fuzzy term of "fat" for the attribute Weight is quite inappropriate. Because whether an animal can be considered "fat" depends on at least Weight, Height, and Spieces. With this restriction of limiting to single attributes, we have to also limit fuzzy terms to a given set of candidates for any specific attribute. We studied and later abandoned the idea of letting users define their own fuzzy terms because allowing that could cause users unknowingly violating the restriction.

When more than multiple attributes contain fuzzy terms in a query, it is necessary for the user to specify relative weights for the different attributes. If only a single attribute contains a fuzzy term, then the default weight of 1 is assigned. These weights are used by the Fuzzy Answer Generator in generating the final answers.

The Fuzzy Query Filter picks up the fuzzy terms, checks for validty of the terms, prompts the user for the relative attribute weights if appropriate, and generates correponding precise values. The resulting query is sent to the *Relational Query Processor* to convert to a typical relational language such as relational algebra and SQL. The resulting relational language query is then passed on to the database management system to process and to produce results.

Fuzzy Answer Generation

The results obtained by the underlying database management system are crisp. The *Fuzzy Answer Generator* picks up these answers, uses the attribute weights passed along from the *Fuzzy Query Filter* to convert the answers to a fuzzy form for presentation to the user.

When two or more attributes contain fuzzy terms in a query, the user assigned relative weights are used to modify the membership values which are initially obtained without using the weights. We will discuss this weighting in the next section. The resulting instances are displayed in descending order of their weighted membership values. Figure 4 illustrates the final result of a fuzzy retrieval.

ANSWER

S_ID	mem_fcn_val
12789	1.
21356	.9
31224	.8
24157	.7
12532	.6
32451	.6
32441	.5

Figure 4. Answer to a fuzzy query

Weighting Fuzzy Answers

The weighting algorithm in ranking the answer instances is quite straight forward. To illustrate this algorithm, consider that for the above query "Get the student IDs of any young male students who received some good grades or any CS students who received some good grades". Assume that we first obtain the first intermediate results in Figure 5.

The first group of student IDs are retrieved using the condition "good" and "young" and the second group of student IDs are retrieved using the condition "good" and "CS". The corresponding membership values are given in the table.

ANSWER

S_ID	mfv_good	mfv_young
a	.9	.6
b	.8	.8
c	.7	.7
d	.6	.9
e	.5	.7
a	.9	
c	.7	
f	.8	

Figure 5. First intermediary results

Assume that the user has given relative weights for Grade and Age are 2 and 1, respectively. Then the weighted membership function value for student a is [(0.9 * 2) + (0.6 * 1)]/3 = 0.8 in group one. The students in the second group do not need to have their membership function values weighted, since there is only one fzzy term in the query condition. The weighted intermediary results for the query are shonw in Figure 6.

ANSWER

S_ID	W_mfv
a	.8
b	.8
c	.7
d	.7
e	.57
a	.9
c	.7
f	.8

Figure 6. Weighted intermediary results

ANSWER

S_ID	mem_fcn_val
a	.9
b	.8
f	.8
c	.7
d	.7
e	.57

Figure 7. Final results

Since the query has a disjunction, OR, for the two groups of results, the final weighted membership function values are obtained by getting the maximum values when the same instance apperars in both groups. The final result is shown in Figure 7.

Conclusion

We have discussed various difficulties in information retrieval from databases and the many approaches in trying to overcome these difficulties. We presented our methodology, which combines the advantages of the many different approaches proposed by other researchers. Our methodology allows users to see the semantics of a database with the highest degree of clarity. We provide the most convenient query phrasing facilities. And finally, we allow the use of fuzzy terms in a query to allow query phrasing to be more natural for many applications.

References

[1]. Wong, H.K.T., Kuo, I.: "GUIDE: Graphical User Interfacefor Database Exploration", *Proceedings of International Conference on VLDB*, Mexico City, p.11–21, 1982.

[2]. Zloof, M.M.: "Query–by–Example: a data base language", *IBM system journal*, Vol.16(4), p.324–343, April, 1977.

[3]. Chang, N.S.: "Picture Query Language for Pictorial Database System", *IEEE Computer*, Vol.14(11), p.23–33, November, 1981.

[4]. Rogers, T.R, Cattell, R.G.G.: "Entity–Relationship Database User Interfaces", *Proceedings of 6th International*

Conference on Entity–Relationship Approach, p.323–335, 1987.

[5]. Kim, H.J., Korth, H.F., Silberschatz, A.: "PICASSO: A Graphical Query Language", *Software–Practice and Experience*, Vol. 18(3), p.169–203, March, 1988

[6]. Czejdo, B.: "Design and Implementation of an ER Query and Update Interface", 1991 *Symposium on Applied Computing*, p.325–334, April, 1991.

[7]. Tahani, V.: "A Conceptual Framework for Fuzzy Query Processing — A Step toward Intelligent Database Systems", *Information Processing & Management*, 13, pp.289–303, 1977.

[8]. Buckles, B., Petry, F.: "Query Language for Fuzzy databases", in *Management Decision Support Systems Using Fuzzy Sets and Possibility Theory*, Kacprzyk, J., Yager, R.R. (eds), 1985.

[9]. Umano, M.: "FREEDOM–0: A Fuzzy Database System", in *Fuzzy Information and Decision Processes*, Gupta, M.M., Sanchez, E. (eds.), p.339–347, Amsterdam: North–Holland, 1982

[10]. Prade, H., Testemale, C.: "Generalizing Database Relational Algebra for the Treatment of incomplete or Uncertainty Information and Vague Queries", *Information Sciences*, Vol. 34, p.115–143, 1984.

[11]. Zemankova–Leech, M., Kandel, A.: "Implementation Imprecision in Information Systems." *Information Sciences*, Vol. 37, p. 107–141, 1985.

[12]. Bosc, P., Pivert, O.: "Fuzzy Querying in Conventional Databases", in *Fuzzy Logic for the Management of Uncertainty*, Zadeh, L.A., Kacprzyk, J. (eds), 646, New York: John Wiley & Sons, 1992.

[13] Kunii, T.L.: "DATAPLAN: An Interface Generator for Database Semantics" *Information Sciences*, Vol. 10, p.279–298, 1976.

[14]. Shen. S.N.T., de Mora. C., Liu, L.: "The GKB Methodology as an Intelligent Tutoring System Builder", *Proceedings of International Conference on Intelligent Tutoring Systems*, Montreal, Canada, p.90–96, June, 1988.

A HEURISTIC APPROACH TO DEAL WITH THE SCHEDULING PROBLEM IN THE MO2 DISTRIBUTED MODEL

Boudjema MECIBAH Ammar ATTOUI

Laboratoire d'informatique / Université Clermont-Ferrand II

Abstract

MO2 is an object-oriented model which integrates in the same approach features of DBMS and features of real-time systems. It allows the definition of different kinds of relationships between objects: generalisation / specialisation, aggregation, asssociation. But its principal feature is the ability to distinguish passive objects and active objects. The passive objects react only through the activation of their methods. The active objects can have their own behaviour and can evolve under the sollicitation of various events independently of the activation of their methods. The implementation of the MO2 model on a distributed environnement must take into account the scheduling problem of all types of objects. The crux of our work is to schedule the periodic and aperiodic objects in a dynamic and flexible manner. Our solution is based on a heuristic algorithm.

1: Introduction

Distributed real-time systems are becoming more prevalent in applications such as avionics, process control, and command and control systems. Theses applications have many tasks that have execution deadlines that must be met. In real-time DBMS, Satisfying the timing requirements involves two key issues: First, the degree of concurrence in transaction processing must be increased; second, concurrence control protocols and real-time scheduling algorithms must be integrated. On the other hand, most work on databases focuses on query processing and database consistency, but not on meeting any time-constraints associated with transactions. Consequently, We attempted through the model MO2 [3] to integrate in the same approach classic DBMS features and real-time features in purpose of obtaining a real-time database system. We deal with the scheduling problem of active objects in the purpose of implementation of the MO2 model. The aims of MO2 are : twofold:

modelling the static relationship between objects as in classic DBMS and offering control and cooperative mechanisms as in real-time approaches. In conventional real-time systems, modelling the static relationship between objects as in classic DBMS and offering control and cooperative mechanisms as in real-time approaches. Managing objects with real-time requirements in MO2 presents many problems, the most important one is how objects are scheduled [1]. More current research on scheduling tasks has been restricted to uniprocessor and multiprocessor systems [10]. it is therefore, inappropriate for distributed systems [13]. In addition, many of the proposed algorithms, which assume that all tasks and their characteristics are known in advance, are designed for static scheduling. Our work is directed at developing active object scheduling algorithm for the MO2 model, that achieves flexibility through dynamic scheduling of objects in a distributed, adaptive manner. Our schema for distributed dynamic scheduling requires one scheduler per site. The schedulers interact to determine assignment for a newly arriving object. We assume that the characteristics of periodic objects are known in advance and that such objects must meet their deadlines. The existence of enough processing power at a site for all periodic objects to meet their deadlines is verified at system initialisation time. In addition to the periodic objects, we allows for the arrival of aperiodic objects at any time and attempt to guarantee these objects dynamically.

2. About Distributed and real-time Systems

A distributed system is a Computing system whose behaviour is determined by algorithms explicitly designed to work with multiple loci of control. Examples of such algorithms are those used to control concurrent threads of computation (e.g. concurrence control). We will say that a system is entrusted with distributiveness properties to mean that its design is in accordance with the definition given above [13].
A Real-time system is a computing system where initiation and termination of activities must meet specified timing constraints. Time-dependent value are associated with activity termination's. System behaviour is determined by algorithms designed to maximise a global time-dependent value function [14].

3: A Presentation of the MO2 Model

MO2 is an object-oriented model which integrates both features of DBMS and features of real-time systems. It allows the definitions of different kinds of relationships between objects: generalisation/ specialisation, aggregation, association. But its principal feature is the ability to distinguish passive objects and active objects. An object can be characterised by three parts: the static part (properties), the operation part (methods) and the control part (activity). A class of objects will designate a set of objects which possess the same characteristics (static and dynamic). MO2 distinguishes three types of objects: the passives objects, the actives objects and the actor objects. Passive objects are only information holders by means of the attributes. Therefore, they constitute an element of the system memory and are thus called memory objects. The methods represent the only mean to access and update the attributes (encapsulation Principe). A method may be of an arbitrary complexity and can use methods of other objects. Passive objects are completely described by their properties and their methods.

Active objects constitute the dynamic elements of the system. Each one represent a unit specialised in a precise task. They collaborate for controlling and managing the system according to events which can occur in time. An active object is described by its properties, its methods and its activity. The properties and the methods have the same usage as for passive objects. The activity describes the control and the supervision actions of the active object. An active object participates in the management of the system. It can cooperate with other objects according to precise internal rules depending on external and internal events. External events materialise the interaction of the system with its environment. On the other hand, internal events constitute the basic elements to coordinate the different internal activities of the system. In other words, they constitute the synchronisation tool of the active objects in the absence of a centralised control. Actors are temporary active objects. An actor object is described by its activity. Its behaviour is equivalent to the execution of a program or a transaction in a classic contex. An actor executes the activity actions sequentially and terminates. Figure 1 gives a summary of the three types of objects supported by MO2 and also their utilisation mode.

	passive	active	actor
static part	yes	yes	yes
activity part	no	yes	yes
message reception	yes	yes	no
events emission and reception	no	yes	yes
interruptions interception	no	yes	yes
data persistence	yes	yes	no
activity persistence	no	yes	no
utilization example	E1	E2	E3

E1 = Data storage module E2 = Application module E3 = Transaction

Figure 1: Characteristics of objects

Passive objects can receive messages to which it can reply either by a message or by an exception. An exception is an event recognised by an object. It indicates that the activated method has induced the violation of an assertion (integrity constraint). In MO2, an assertion is a predicate on elements of the static part. Its verification must be guaranteed by the system at different instants or at instants specified by triggers. An actor object cooperates with passive objects only by messages. It can also require the intervention of active object methods on their local data. Finally, it manages events which can be received as well as by other actor objects or by active objects. It's important to note that only active objects and actors can intercept external events (interruptions) from their environment.

The following figure shows the different exchange modes between the different kinds of objects

senders \ receivers	Passive	active	Actor
Passive	messages exceptions	messages exceptions events	exceptions
Active	messages exceptions	messages exceptions events	exceptions events
Actor	messages	messages events	data events

Figure 2: Exchange modes between the different kinds of objects

3.1: Properties

Properties are described in the properties part. In MO2 [4], properties have the semantics of attributes used in certain data models [6]. Attributes are used for two purposes: To characterise objects by intrinsic values and to establish relationship between objects through reference lists. An intrinsic value is specified through a data type, predefined or previously defined by the user. To be general enough, MO2 proposes three types of relationships between objects: the specialisation/generalisation relationship, the aggregation relationship and the user association.

3.2: Methods

The methods are the only available operations which can operate on the static part of the object. No other access means are allowed.

3.3: Read Access Operations

To let user objects access the contents of some object properties, MO2, as in [5], supplies the notion of functions on the properties. Such properties are thus visible from the outside. Nevertheless, the difference takes place in the declaration level of these functions. They are not specified in the properties part, but in the methods part. The major principle of object-oriented approach-separating declaration of attributes from declarations of operations - is thus reinforced. The example below is a definition of such functions which hereafter are called retrieval functions. Attribute names given after the reserved word FUNCTIONS tell the system that functions are read only accesses and that the corresponding attributes are visible from outside.

```
OBJECT CLASS person;
{ Properties:
```

```
        CHAR name[15];
        INT age;
        REFERENCE (1,n) car car-list
                        INVERSE person-list;
        METHODS;
              FUNCTIONS name(), age(), car-list();
};
```

Figure 3: Declaration of retrieval functions on properties

The user can also define, in the methods part, more retrieval functions. These functions can operate on several visible and non-visible attributes. The separation of methods into two different types-retrieval functions and other methods is very important because MO2 parallelism principles are based on this.

3.4: Activity

The activity is a particular method of an object class. Its role is to execute some specific tasks of the class and general tasks which represent the contribution of the class to the control and the supervision of the system. The real-time aspects can be taken into account by means of timing constraints. The coordination between objects is achieved by means of events. There are two types of events: external events (interruptions from the environment) and internal events declared by the users.

3.5: Timing constraints:

In our model, an object is called real-time object if the definition of some of its methods contains timing constraints. A timing constraint concerns either the run time of a method or a block of method, or the periodicity of an object in the ACTIVITY part. This definition is recursive. A class may not contain timing constraints on its own methods. On the other hand, it can require in the body of its methods or in the body of the ACTIVITY part the activation of methods of other classes with timing constraints. Some reserved words are used for the expression of real-time constraints: At, Before, On, Every, Within. To illustrate the declaration of timing constraints, we present the following example.

```
object class control-system
{properties:
      time fire-interval; /* missile interval fire */
      time period;        /* radar period scanning*/
      radar detection-system;/* radar class object*/
      missile cannon;/* fire device*/
      EVENT alert-ev; /* internal alert event*/
            ............................................
methods:
      ..............................................
private
fire-instant-computation(coordinates r, direction d);
{    /*missile fire instant computation according to the
current*/
   /*coordinates         and the direction of the object*/
};
private critical-situation;
{............................};
activity:
      {
      coordinates r;      /*temporary variable*/
      direction d;        /*temporary variable*/
      on alert-ev critical-situation;
      every(me.period)/*scanning loop*/
            {r = me.detection-system.object-position;
            d=me.detection-system.object-direction;
            if (r <> nil)
             { time t;
              t= fire-instant-computation(r,d);
               me.cannon.orientation before(t, alert-
ev);
              at(t) me.cannon.missile-fire
                 within(fire-interval, alert-ev);
               };
            };
      };
```

Figure 4: Declaration of timing constraints

3.6: Distributed computing in MO2

Physical location of an object depends on the nature of the class to which it belongs. Distribution unit for a passive class in the entire class. The objects of this kind of class are located on the same site. This choice results from practical considerations. Nevertheless, duplication of passive objects is possible through a mechanism of snapshot. Snapshots permit also the management of different versions of an object. The objects of an active class may be geographically distant (aircraft control centre, manufacturing system robots). In this case, the system has to manage an additional attribute in the static part to indicate the localisation of the object. This attribute is equal to "nil" for a local object. For a distant object, it contains the identification of the origin site.

3.7: An example

We will use MO2 to model a robot workstation as a component of a manufacturing system, in order to high-light the use of internal events and interruptions to driving and supervising a robot. In first approach, we suppose that the robot is an automat which only offers a set of commands. So, positionnement of the robot for executing a movement is done by a more intelligent object (micro-computer).

A robot is an object whose characteristics depend on its kind (Cylindric, SCARA,...). For each kind of robot, are defined the lenght, the direction of its segments. Also, to each robot, is associated a set of methods to drive and to manipulate it. We note that a "logical robot" object is associated to a "physical robot" object. The activity of the "logical robot" amounts to the supervision of the robot. The manipulation of the robot is done by the associated methods. The activity method of the robot class is prefixed by the attribut "P" which indicates a "fine granularity". This notation imposes that the activity method have to be inherited by each object of the class. By default, its scope is the whole class. In this section we give the description of a flexible manufacturing shop which is composed of a certain number of workstations (robots), a convoyer equiped with pallets and switching devices, a shopfloor control and a database.

```
OBJECT CLASS robot
 {PROPERTIES:
        INT nb-segments;
        LIST segmentRobot segments;
        LIST robotCarrier carries;
        /* mechanic links between the segments*/
        controlSpace      operationalSpace;
        /* operational field of the robot*/
        time      scrutationPeriod
        EVENT spaceViolation;
        ................................
 METHODS:
        move(angularPosition p);
        {/* moves the terminal part of the robot to */
        /* a position in the work space        */
 };
        stop();   {/* cause the robot to stop*/};
        ..................................................
 PRIVATE compute-angularPosition(angularPosition *t)
        { /*  computes the angular position of the */
         /* different segments of the robot*/};
 PRIVATE BOOLEAN controlposition(angularposition
p);
        (/* verify that the different segments of the*/
        /*robot are within the safety space*/};
        ..................................................
 ACTIVITY(P)
        { EVERY(me.scrutationPeriod)
                { angularPosition P:;
                compute-angularPosition(p);
                If not(controPosition(p))
                {stop; SIGNAL(spaceViolation);};
                };
        };
 };
```

Figure 5: Description of a robot class

When a part is introduced in the production line by the input station, it is identified during its presence in the line by the pallet which support it. The shop can produce several kinds of parts. Each kind corresponds to a manufacturing routing (a set of operations to be realised in a determined order). Each operation necessites a certain time. In figure, the reserved word ON EVENT CASE permits the specification of events expected by an object and to associate to each of them specific processing. Finally, the event "partFinish" is set by a robot, when the event "workStationExit" is set by the output station of the shop.

```
robot CLASS workstation;
        {PROPERTIES:
          STRING number;
          switchDevice inputSwitch;
          switchDevice outoutSwich;
        ........};
  OBJECT CLASS part;
        {PROPERTIES:
          STRING number;
          STRING designation;
REFERENCE(1,n) operation
manufactRouting;
    ....................

  METHODS:
    FUNCTIONS manufactRouting(), designation;
        ..................................
  };
  OBJECT CLASS operation;
  {PROPERTIES:
        STRING Number;
        TIME duration;
        kindOperation      Toperation
                .................
                METHODS
                .................
  };
  OBJECT CLASS palett;
     (PROPERTIES
        STRING number;
        part current part;
        STRING nextStation;
        operation nextOperation;
        ........................
        METHODS:
          FUNCTIONS  part, nextStaion;...;
        setNextStation(STRING s);
           {  me.nextStation = s;.....};
          PRIVATE switch-InterruptHandler();
            { if (me.nextStation=workStation number)
                  {WorkStation.inputSwitch.open;
                     workStation.nextOperation;};
                  };

        ACTIVITY
          { ON switchDevice INTERRUPT:
             DO switch-InterruptHandler;};
          );
 OBJECT CLASS productLine;
   (PROPERTIES:
        INCLUDE(1,n) palett pallets;
        INCLUDE(1,n) workstation workstations;
        REFERENCE(1,n) part produce;
        INCLUDE pannelDevice;
        time period;
        .........................
 EVENT workstationExit, failure, operator, partFinished,...;
 METHODS:   ....................

 ACTIVITY:
        (ON EVENT CASE
                workStationExit: DO
            {/* affectation of the next station to the part*/};
                  falure: DO
            {/* updation the configuration of the line*/};
                  operator:DO
            {/* execution of the operator order*/};
 partFinished: DO
 {/* affectation of the outputLineStation as nextStation*/};
 ...............;
 ..........................;
            EVERY(period)
            {pannelDevice.lineStateDisplay;
 /* computes the next station for each current part*/...};
            } };
```

Figure 6: Description of a flexible manufacturing shop

4: Problem Position of Distributed scheduling

Scheduling for distributed systems is significantly more complex than for single-processor system. It is a control problem which in an absence of a common memory, can be solved by the cooperation of communicant objects on each active site. As MO2 is a general-purpose distributed system, our distributed scheduling policy can be divided into two components [7]: a local scheduling discipline determines how the CPU resource at a single site is allocated among its resident objects, while a load distributing strategy distributes the system workload among the sites through process migration. The following figure illustrate our scheduling policy:

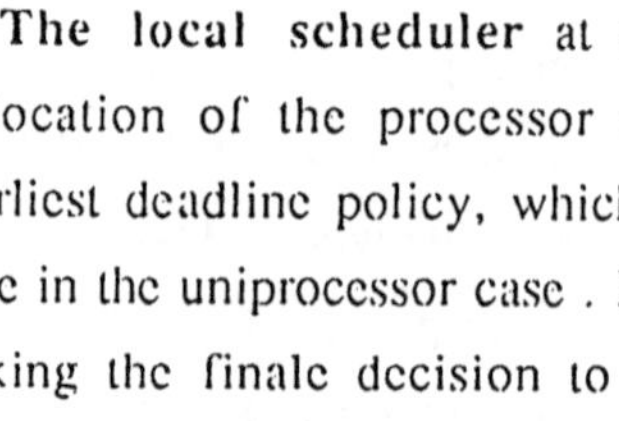

Figure 7: the MO2 distributed scheduling policy

The local scheduler at a site take charge of allocation of the processor (s) according to the earliest deadline policy, which is the most optimal one in the uniprocessor case . It is the responsible of taking the finale decision to accept or refuse the execution of an object locally.

The global scheduler manage the interface with the local scheduler, it's role is to choose the location (site) where objects must execute in case of overloading. It has four main functionality's [2]: The exchange policy of information between sites, the migration phase initiation policy, the choice policy of the object to transfer and the choice policy of the transfer site.

5: Description of the Scheduling Model

The model is composed of n sites, in a loosely coupled distributed system. Each site contain a set of distinctes resources, $R_1, R_2, \ldots, R_n$. A resource is an abstraction and can include CPU, I/O devices, files, etc. A resource is active if it has processing power, otherwise, it is passive. For example, a CPU or a physical device is active, but a file is passive. Thus, always, a passive resource must be used with some active resource [15]. An active class is a scheduling entity. The following characteristics of an active object, O, are assumed known when it arrives:

1. The worst case computation time, C(O);
2. The deadline, D(O), by which the object must complete;
3. the resources requirements of the object. An object will request at least one active resource and zero or more passive resources.

6: The local and distributed scheduling ofactive objects

The real-time scheduling algorithm which we present in this paper belong to the category of distributed, dynamic and cooperative algorithms. It is a flexible one which use a symetric heuristic that combine the two heuristics "The initiative for the transmitter site" and " the initiative for the receiver site " [2]. In the first one, the overloaded site attempt to look for help by interrogation of other sites. In the second one, the idea is to let the sites fewly loaded propose their helps to the overloaded sites by the sending messages [8],[9]. Each site in the distributed system has a component of the scheduler. Each component contains a local scheduler, a bidder (the global scheduler), a dispatcher, and a site surplus manager (surplus is defined as the amount of computation time on a site between the time of arrival of the new unguaranteed object and its deadline [12]). The local scheduler at a site is invoked when a new active object (an instance of an active class) arrives at that site. It decides if the new object can be guaranteed at this site. The guarantee is realised by a guarantee function (It determines if there is enough surplus processing power to execute a newly arriving active object before its deadline). If the new object cannot be guaranteed locally, then it is either rejected or is handed over to the bidder object. The bidder on a site is responsible for determining where an object that cannot be locally guaranteed should be sent. It does this through a combination of focused addressing and bidding (distributed scheduling) [11], [14]. In focused addressing, an object will be sent directly to another site based on its (partial) knowledge about the other sites in the system. In bidding, the site will send out a request for bid message to other sites; sites with sufficient surplus will respond with a bid reflecting this surplus. The site with the object will send it to the site which offers the best bid. In addition to sending its objects to other sites, the bidder object make bids in response to requests from other sites. The dispatcher is the system program that actually schedules the guaranteed objects. One of the assumptions underlying of this scheduling algorithm is that sites can estimate the surplus of other sites. This requires that sites keep each other informed about their surplus. This can be done by the node surplus manager in the following manner. The site surplus manager on each site periodically calculates the site surplus . The computed site surplus is sent to a selected subset of sites in the system. The selection is to be based on the proximity of the sites, on who sent objects to this site recently, and on whether the objects were guaranteed. The size of the subset is proportional to the amount of surplus .

7: Conclusion

MO2 is an attempt to integrate into the same approach, modelisation of static relationships between objects as in DBMS, and modelisation of dynamic interactions between objects as in a real-time system. The scheduling approach that we have used is exclusively designed for distributed systems. The algorithm has the following main features: It is a distributed scheduling technique where the sites are unmarked, the algorithm is designed to schedule on-line both periodic and non periodic objects. This version presents some delay communication problems due to a very important message exchanges. Our current work, is to improve this version in order to reduce considerably the delays communication and take into account the intrinsic characteristics of the MO2 model. An evaluation of performance of this version will be done in the QNAP II simulation langage.

References

[1] K. R. ABBOTT, H.GARCIA-MOLINA. "Scheduling Real-time Transactions: a Performance Evaluation", ACM Transactions on Database Systems, Vol 17, No. 3, September 1992, pages 513-560.

[2] M. ALABAU, T. DECHAIZE. "Ordonnancement Temps-Réel par échéance", Technique et Science Informatique. Vol 11 -No3/1992, pages 59 à 123.

[3] A. ATTOUI, M. SCHNEIDER. "An Object Oriented Model for Parallel and Reactive System", IEEE Real-Time Systems Symposium, San Antonio, Texas, Dec 1991.

[4] A. ATTOUI, M. SCHNEIDER. "SO2: A Flexible Object-Oriented Management System", 2nd Internationl Conference on Reliability and Robustness of Engineering Software (RRES-91), Milan, 22-24 April 1991.

[5] F. BRISSAUD. "Des Associations pour un Modèle à Objets", 4èmes Journées Pratiques et Outils Logiciels d'aide à la conception de systèmes d'information, Nantes, 25-27 September 1990.

[6] R. HULL, R. KING. "Semantic Database Modeling: Survey, Applications and Research Issues", ACM Computing Surveys, Vol. 10, n° 3, Sept. 1987.

[7] P. KRUEGER, M. LIVNY. "The Diverse Objectives of Distributed Scheduling Policies", Proc. IEEE Symposium on Distributed Computing Systems (1987), p. 242-249.

[8] B. MECIBAH, A. ATTOUI. "Techniques de Mises en Oeuvre d'un Ordonnanceur Temps-Réel pour le SGBD Orienté Objet et Temps-Réel MO2", in the Eleventh IASTED International Conference May 19-21, 1993 Annecy FRANCE

[9] B. MECIBAH, A. ATTOUI. " Dealing with the scheduling problem in the MO2 distributed object-oriented real-time DBMS", In the proceedings of the european simulation symposium 1993. October 25-28, 1993. DELFT, The NETHERLANDS.

[10] K. RAMAMRITHAM, J. A. STANKOVIC, W. ZHAO. "Distributed Scheduling of Tasks with Deadlines and Resource Requirements", IEEE Transactions On Computers, Vol. 38, No. 8, August 1989.

[11] R. G. SMITH. "The Contract Net Protocol: High-Level communication and control in a distributed problem solver," IEEE Transactions on computers, Vol. C-29, N°. 12, Dec 1980.

[12] J.A.STANKOVIC, "Evaluation of a Flexible Task Scheduling Algorithm for Distributed Hard Real-Time Systems", IEEE Transactions on Computers, Vol. c-34, No. 12, December 1985.

[13] P. KRUEGER, M. LIVNY. "The Diverse Objectives of Distributed Scheduling Policies", Proc. IEEE Symposium on Distributed Computing Systems (1987), p. 242-249.

[14] J.A.STANKOVIC "A Serious Problem for Next-Generation Systems", Computer, October 1988.

[15] W. ZHAO, K. RAMAMRITHAM, "Distributed Scheduling Using Bidding and Focused Addressing", in Proc.Symp.Real-Time Syst., Dec 1985.

Andreas H. Zins (Hrsg.)

Strategisches Management im Tourismus

Planungsinstrumente für Tourismusorganisationen
Geleitwort von Josef Mazanec

1993. 36 Abbildungen. XII, 164 Seiten.
Broschiert öS 420,–, DM 60,–. Hörerpreis: öS 336,–
ISBN 3-211-82475-8

(Springers Kurzlehrbücher der Wirtschaftswissenschaften)

Preisänderungen vorbehalten

Das Buch versucht, in fünf Einzelbeiträgen bewährte Konzepte aus dem strategischen Management der Konsum- und Investitionsgüterindustrie in das touristische Anwendungsumfeld mit dem Schwerpunkt Tourismus-Organisationen hineinzutragen. Fragen der Funktionen, der Nutzenstiftung und der Systematik von Strategieentwicklung werden einleitend behandelt. Überlegungen zur Leitbildentwicklung für ein touristisches Zielgebiet konkretisieren im Anschluß daran ein immer häufiger benutztes Instrument zur Strategiefindung. Die systematische Bewertung der Erfolgschancen eines Zielgebietes auf internationalen Absatzmärkten zeigt der folgende Beitrag auf, der ein neues Konzept einer hierarchischen Portfolio-Analyse vorstellt. Aus einem verhaltensorientierten Blickwinkel diskutiert der Beitrag „Lifestyles im Tourismus" die Verwertbarkeit von psychographischen Segmentierungskriterien. Einen stärker methodenorientierten Zugang zur touristischen Marktsegmentierung verschafft der letzte Beitrag, der den Einsatz und die Ergebnisverwertung des Automatischen Interaktionsdetektors in Kombination mit der Diskriminanzanalyse aufzeigt. Der einheitliche Aufbau aller Kapitel bestehend aus Inhaltsübersicht, Lernziel, theoretische Aufbereitung, Illustration durch ein aktuelles Fallbeispiel und Literaturempfehlung sollen dem fortgeschrittenen Studenten wie auch dem interessierten Praktiker einen effizienten Zugang zu den vorgestellten Instrumenten gewähren und insbesondere den kritischen Einsatz für eigene Anwendungssituationen fördern.

Springer-Verlag Wien New York

Sachsenplatz 4–6, P.O.Box 89, A-1201 Wien · 175 Fifth Avenue, New York, NY 10010, USA
Heidelberger Platz 3, D-14197 Berlin · 37-3, Hongo 3-chome, Bunkyo-ku, Tokyo 113, Japan

GPSR Compliance

The European Union's (EU) General Product Safety Regulation (GPSR) is a set of rules that requires consumer products to be safe and our obligations to ensure this.

If you have any concerns about our products, you can contact us on ProductSafety@springernature.com

In case Publisher is established outside the EU, the EU authorized representative is:

Springer Nature Customer Service Center GmbH
Europaplatz 3
69115 Heidelberg, Germany

Batch number: 10732720

Printed by Printforce, the Netherlands